For Harumi Yoshida
and Tokiyo Yoshida

TOWARDS (IM)MEASURABILITY of ART and LIFE

Published by
Archive Books

Written and edited by
Miya Yoshida

CONTENTS

Acknowledgements

This book results from the support provided by numerous individuals and institutions, with their suggestions collected, revised and given a final form. Here, I would like to thank the following individuals and institutions for their support for the project and realisation of this publication. The research project on art and measurement started as my postdoctoral research at the Center for Digital Culture at Leuphana University, Lüneburg, in 2013. My appreciation goes to Timmon Byers and Ulf Wuggenig, who understood the potentials of the project at an early stage in its development. I am also grateful to the colleagues at the Center for Digital Culture who supplied me with feedback and references about measurement, and to all the contributors in connection with the "Dialogues": Chihiro Minato, who travelled all the way to Lüneburg to participate in the event, Sophie Houdart, who generously shared her on-going research, Lucy Powell, with whom I share mutual interests and exchanged ideas and questions on measurement, Oxana Timofeeva, who emphasised the significant capacities of subjectivity in the formation of knowledge, Patricia T. Clough, who travelled to Lüneburg to shared her crystalised knowledge and views on measurement despite the heavy snow storm that was hitting New York City at the time, and Matt Mullican, who shared his dedicated work. I would also like to express my gratitude to Hannes Loichinger, Janik Leenen, and Oona Braaker for their practical assistance. "Dialogues between an Artist and a Scientist" was realised with the support of the European Union's European Regional Development Fund, the Institut Français, the Kunstraum at Leuphana University, and the GBFund Japan.

I would also like to express my thanks all the artists who shared not only their works, but also their own personal experiences, stories and anecdotes, and contacts with colleagues. I am grateful to Helmut Draxler who offered me the deep insights of his knowledge and his support, Johanna Schäfer for the many stimulating conversations, Clemens Krümmel for his readings of my text and the translation of the introduction, Ursula Walbroel and Alexander Roob for their generous support, Amy Klement and Brigitte Nicole Grice for their careful copywriting and proofreading, and Chiara Figone and Annika Turkowski of Archive Books for their fantastic assistance and support. My sincere thanks also go to the Reversible Destiny Foundation, the Eames Foundation, the 21st Century Museum of Contemporary Art in Kanazawa, the Museum für Naturkunde Berlin, the GAK in Bremen, the Mai 36 Galerie in Zurich, Johnen Galerie, Galerie Esther Schipper, and Galerie Capitain Petzel in Berlin, New Directions Publishing, which generously provided me with the images, texts, and reproduction rights for the works, and the Stiftung Kunstfonds and Stiftung Oehmen, which provided support for the publication. I extend my appreciation to all of those who helped me over the years, especially my family, including my father, who passed away right after the last "Dialogue" event, and my close friends in Germany, Korea, Japan, and other parts of the world, especially Kazuyo Nakamura for her continuous encouragement and support over the last twenty years, Martin Noergaard for his uplifting and warm support, and Hyejin Jung, Christian Piepenbrock, Karin Rebbert, Britta Lorch, Viola Rusche, and Hauke Harder for their advice and support.

*Towards
(Im)Measurability
of Art and Life*
Introduction by
Miya Yoshida

Noticed or unnoticed, measurement is occurring all the time in our everyday lives. Measurement forces every dimension of our life into quantifiable units and predefined categories: We not only measure time, distances, weight, combustion value, temperature, et cetera, but there is also – especially in recent times, in which we have witnessed an economising and monetising of all aspects of life – a discernible urge to quantify elusive things such as productivity, creativity, et cetera, in order to be able to submit everything and anything to endlessly repeated evaluation processes. Measurement is, among other things, a disciplinary mechanism created to assign ("absolute" and "relative") value by means of segmentation and comparison. In the field of science, measurement is, at least by today's epistemological standards, a reduction of complexity. It is based on the logic of mathematics, coercing both subjects and objects into standardised modules.

Contemporary measurement, however, embraces and includes diverse scales, temporalities, and conditions. Many of the predefined categories activated in this context cannot be grasped by human senses, and therefore also cannot be grasped directly without technological aids. The diversity of human perceptions, whether conceived as individual or super-individual, raises serious questions. Because when two individuals use a particular term of measurement, it is almost self-evident today that they do not mean the same "thing". Might one concept be adopted to measure things as varied as the weight of an orange, the severity of an economic crisis, or the effects of the Fukushima catastrophe, the quality of education, individual abilities, "likes" on Facebook, bodily reactions, or emotions? Would diversity of this kind affect the general concept of measurement and thus transform it into something else?

In the 1960s, the notion of paradigm shifts, which highlighted the "socialised" power of science and science as a cultural point of view, was introduced so as to question the social implications of science and its ideological constructs. In post-structuralism, the ideal relationship between words and things met its demise in measurement: as measurement error theory claims that measuring operations fail to link what we observe, how we describe it, and how we reduce it to the form of data, because of imprecise semiotic relations in language and inexact processes of data extraction (Lembert, 1982).

However, after fifty years of shifts of this kind, the social power of science has also come to include a neoliberal view of science-as-art, as management-*cum*-measurement, hence increasing tendencies towards quantifying every dimension of our life in numbers or categories for evaluation. Through strongly proiritising economic gain over "progress" in a modernist sense, current neoliberal capitalism modifies the norms of productivity to include those of the work of the so-called creative industries as a means to propagate art's productivity, and to modularise and thus quantify the arts and put the results into numbers (prices of artworks, number of viewings, popularity amongst viewers, number of locations, and so on). In order to make labour and consumption compatible in this neoliberal relationship, measurement takes on an essential role as a method of identification, management, and evaluation. By reflecting such realities, how can we think differently so as to develop a new framework and language for a more adequate way of understanding measurement?

A number of studies on measurement that have been carried out in recent years in sociology, cybernetics, media studies, and social science employ simulation in order to use computation in data processing. But questions still remain with respect to the adequacy of language, methods of knowing, and how to engage with a new terrain of objects, especially in the field of humanities and culture. In responding to shifts in science and technologies, current philosophies attempt to elaborate a new ontology and consequently broaden the worldview of science.

For example, Simondon's concept of transduction overcomes the idea of boundary in segmentation and comparison, and goes beyond the ontological dichotomy between machine and human as well as between humans (Simondon, 1980). In affect theory, Clough contemplates measurement as an ontological practice and emphasises that the act of measuring brings the experience of affect into consideration, entails measurement that centres on relationships rather than objects, and draws attention to process rather than to result (Clough, 2008). Parisi claims that algorithmic architectures should instead be considered as real objects (Parisi, 2013). From an epistemological perspective, the current, strong belief in data is analysed in detail in the biopolitical connection between vision and reformation of reason (Halpern, 2015).

These ontological and epistemological studies broaden a conceptual terrain of measurement, while more recently, in aesthetics, Hoel Sissel rethinks the boundaries between images, words, and numbers, and elaborates a process of objectification that varies according to neither the subject nor the object, but rather only according to the level of cognition. She brings attention back from affects to cognition and concludes that a dynamic correlation of the subjective and the objective produces different viewpoints of measurement (Sissel, 2014). This means that a new hypothesis is required to study a semiotic relation between the languages we use (instrument) and what we see in phenomena (observability).

When measurement is viewed as a practice, it is important to recall that data processing, especially visualisation, actually necessitates many aesthetic decisions. This makes contemporary practices of measurement appear to be no longer guided primarily by reason. Although, historically, measurement has always contained aspects of subjectivity, enlightenment in modernity aimed at excluding them based on ideological tenets of democracy and the necessities of administration (Porter, 1997). The intervention of computation indicates the importance of re-embracing, rather than excluding, subjectivity in the concept of measurement. By understanding measurement as comprising subjectivity and constructing reality, rather than merely reporting on it, the potential of artistic innovation has great relevance to a practice of participation in thinking and exercising the languages of measurement.

Can One Measure
the Sense of the Real?

"Images don't show matter; they show what matters."
—Vilém Flusser, *Into the Universe of Technical Images*

Modern technologies follow systematic processes of thinking in order to measure reality in quantitative terms; they represent the results in what they claim to be a numerical "clarification". The logic and directionality of thinking, from intention, through reasoning, to arriving at a result, has contributed much to the knowledge, understanding, and even predictability of various phenomena. In 1963, Hannah Arendt looked back at the dramatic trajectories of nuclear physics in the first half of the 20th century and tried to sum up the scientific outcomes represented in the new technologies developed at the time.[1] There, she quotes Heisenberg's conclusion: "A definite and final limit to the accuracy of all measurements obtainable by man-devised instruments for those 'mysterious messages from the real world'",[2] and addresses the fact that the development of science had reached a crucial point on its own path in terms of logics and aesthetics, She also recognises the difference between philosophic truth and scientific truth. Her insights in this text inspired me to question the constitution of a "politics of aesthetics in measurement": What does "accuracy" in measurement actually mean? Does it mean the same thing as what is commonly called "exactitude", or "precision", or "quality" of measurement?

When quantum ontology deconstructs classical ontologies and opens up a space where "as if" becomes "as if it *is*", the imaginary potential can be counted as a part of being and existence. American theorist and former physicist Karen Barad writes that, "measurements are discursive practices of mattering and world-making: matter and meaning do not pre-exist but rather are co-constituted via measurement intra actions."[3] She goes on to elucidate a "quantum ontology" with three characteristics – no determinate boundaries, properties of objects within phenomena,

---

[1] Hannah Arendt. "The Conquest of Space and the Stature of Man", in *The New Atlantis: A Journal of Technology and Society*, no.18 (Fall, 2007(1963)).

[2] Ibid., 44.

[3] Karen Barad, *What Is the Measure of Nothingness? Infinity, Virtuality, Justice: 100 Notes, 100 Thoughts*, Documenta Series 099 (Berlin, 2012).

and no determinate contingent meaning – and that these three factors affect each other, which means that the phenomena cannot be separated from any intra-acting agencies, including the agency of the perceiver (Barad, 2012). This theory directs contemporary thinking about measurement into an all-inclusive world. It expands the means and meaning of measurement and also changes the *location* of accuracy in measurement. Simultaneously, it also divides the possible meanings of "measurement" into two basic categories: one represented by *measuring reality*, another by *measuring the sense of the real*. The former is based on the scientific logic of "close reading", to "zoom in, look, and listen with ever increasing sensitivity, to move to finer and finer scales of details".[4] Such exploration navigates the acts and means of measurement in the direction of "more" – more data, details, and proofs. The latter transfers the exercise of measurement to the realm of the imaginary and transforms acts and meanings into other concepts of measurement – the sense of the real. How, if at all, is it possible to measure a sense of the real? Which sorts or which directionalities of thinking does this imply?

More urgently and pressingly – if ever these words mean anything – the Fukushima catastrophe of 2011 confronted us with the same problem of how to understand "accuracy", and also epitomises the deadlock of a modernist directionality of thinking. Jean-Luc Nancy, one of the first intellectuals in Europe to react to the catastrophe, contemplated the intricate, contemporary reality, both blessed and cursed with technologies, and postulated ways of imagining the future that are different from knowing "more" and doing "better": By this, he means that instead of orienting our imagination based on calculation and following a straight line of thinking so as to improve, control, conquer, or overcome Nature or "the unknown", we need to identify and propagate other ways of imagining (Nancy, 2012). In other words, the whole process of thinking about measurement is called into question.

With the goal of investigating the influence of alternative methods, languages, and formation of thinking on aesthetic understandings of measurement, this publication explores thinking in visuals and in dialogue with artists, social scientists, and a cultural theorist. It consists of three parts: an essay, *Exercises in Measurement*, in which a number of pertinent artistic concepts are presented and discussed; *Symbolic Engineering:*

---

[4] Ibid., 1.

Measurement, Aesthetics, and the Rules for Art – A Conversation with Helmut Draxler, which explores the potential role of art in the algorithmic society; and documentation of the event series *Dialogues between an Artist and a Scientist*, which took place from December 2013 to January 2014 at the Kunstraum at Leuphana University Lüneburg, in Germany.

Following the introduction, the first section begins with my essay, *Exercises in Measurement*. The text combines works of conceptual and post-conceptual art in an attempt to reinterpret them and consider their conceptual relevance within the context of measurement. Measurement is an abstract notion, it is quite inclusive, and the practices related to it are extremely diverse. This text does not intend to cover artworks comprehensively, historically, or objectively. Instead, it revisits art practices, literature, and poetry in order to question processes of measurement in visual thinking, to then think through visuals. It aims at employing concepts and languages of measurement to connect that notion to imaginary dimensions or institutions. For this reason, the text does not refer to the great numbers of practices based on existing conventionalities of measurement and its illustrative documentation – including data visualisation, computer graphics, automatic technical images, et cetera.

The text is certainly not directed against scientific measurement; it rather addresses a specifically contemporary emphasis on measurement while seeking out different possibilities of knowing. It begins with the paradoxical idea in Situationist thinking that, in acts of measuring, the unit depends on situations, and then looks at contemporary artists' "pataphysical" experiments connected with measurement and their creative expansion of the concepts of measurements in four sections: 1) de-institutionalising measurement, 2) from universality to ubiquity of measurement, 3) dancing with accuracies, and 4) im/measurability of life. Although the selection of artworks that follows may not seem to be directly related to conventional understandings of measurement at first glance, it does refer to the potentiality and questionability of concepts and processes of measuring, modifying structures, and producing its own mechanisms, instead of adhering to existing systematic patterns or taking over conventional structures in order to shift the *location* of accuracy. Closely examining these artworks enables us to find new criteria, keywords, links, and associations so as to afford more space to the use of measurement in everyday life.

Traditionally, aesthetic concepts have emerged from a hierarchical universalism, of which philosophy and art history have been proponents. However, I neither employ artworks to prove or illustrate a theory, nor aim to "apply" theories to artworks. Rather than examining existing artistic productions in the guise of pursuing a rationalist epistemology, my position takes art neither as an object nor as a subject of research – but as a method of thinking. Instead of sorting art practices back into existing historical contexts and categorisations, I understand art as an enigmatic constellation of things, images, words, and signs within a process of searching and thinking; I take a non-hierarchical approach to loosely (freely) subsuming these artworks within the more general framework of measurement. In this sense, this essay is about producing and inventing. In processes of making, the order in which thinking and questioning take place may not follow the same procedure as that of conventional research. This holds the challenge of trying to link interdisciplinary examples in discursive, but still "accurate" ways. In German, "zählen" means "counting", "*erzählen*" means "storytelling". Thinking along each practice and appreciating it not as (art) history but as "a story" (Deutscher, 2005), this essay assembles various stories about measurement that embrace paradox, contradiction, and humour. Mobilising the "language game" of measurement (Wittgenstein,1953), the essay tries to create and introduce incidents of ideas, conceptual methods, acts, and processes of measurement that dwell in a conceptual transition between science (technology) and everyday life.

The second section is *Symbolic Engineering: Measurement, Aesthetics, and the Rules for Art – A Conversation with Helmut Draxler*, an art theorist and curator (DE/AU). It is an exchange of thoughts and reflections on concepts of modernity in art history. In classic aesthetics, art always features an inseparable relationship between measurement and proportion. Plato says: "Thus, if measure exists, so do the arts; and conversely, if there are arts, then there is measurement. To deny either is to deny both" (Skemp, 1952). Starting from the idea of art as measurement, the dialogue reconsiders the avant-garde tradition of art and life with respect to algorithm-oriented society, and shifts its relevance based on the perspective of the vast range of methodologies involved in the different practices of artistic thinking in which its political importance is still relevant.

In the third section, *Dialogues between an Artist and a Scientist*, three conversations situated at the intersection of artistic and scientific approaches to the theme of politics, epistemology, and the aesthetics of measurement were conducted in pairs, each consisting of an artist and a social scientist. The first dialogue, which focuses on "Aesthetics of Measurement", is conducted by Matt Mullican (USA), an artist, and Patricia T. Clough (USA), a sociologist. Considering the self both as subject and object of research, Mullican and Clough discuss rethinking the aesthetics of measurement based on the translation of their personal experiences and psychiatric issues as objects in the socio-cultural space. Systems of measurement and quantitative and qualitative methods are applied and questioned broadly in the sphere of research as well as in everyday life. In his biographical lecture-performance *Who Feels the Most Pain?* Mullican addressed the question of perceiving and receiving reality, fiction, and the imaginary, and the possibilities of representing them. The presentation starts with a look back at the 1970s, when his interest lay in the human perception of colours under different light conditions. This extremely reductive perception gradually altered his view of the world toward seeing it as nothing but the phenomenon of light, which thus requires him to investigate the ontological boundaries between life and death. Setting up a sensory experience of pain as both an epistemological and ontological measurement of reality, his works develop through diverse artistic experiments: through inventing a fictional figure named Glen in the space of drawings in order to investigate the location of pain in the imaginary space, through encountering a cadaver in a laboratory so as to test its sensory experience, through collecting crime scenes in a cartoon to examine how death (pain) is illustrated, and through hypnotising himself in public so as to use himself as medium for observing sensory experiences of the self based on the states of other individuals. Extensively using all kinds of possibilities in visual media – painting, drawing, film, photography, computer graphics, installation, et cetera – Mullican has continued measuring the aesthetic boundary between life and death, the unconscious and the conscious, the real and the imaginary, and so on.

In her performative presentation titled *The Calculative Aesthetic, Objects and Unconscious Desire in the Age of Big Data*, Clough takes up both unconscious desire and her childhood memories to open up a space of an epistemological unconscious as an object of study in sociological research. In the age of big data, she claims that algorithms give a certain quality to quantity. The enormous speed of the processing of information changes our understanding of the conscious and the unconscious, and the calculative aesthetic makes us recognise our unconscious capacities, which affect different conceptualisations of numbers and quantity. A new inquiry is therefore necessary so as to reconsider the current distinction between quantitative and qualitative measurement as well as between objects and systems.

The second dialogue, "Epistemology of Measurement", was conducted by the artist Lucy Powell (UK) and Oxana Timofeeva (RU), a philosopher and cultural theorist. Powell is interested in forms of intelligence and knowledge not limited to human beings, but also comprising animals and plants, while Timofeeva has been exploring the unconscious tendency in philosophy with respect to how the use of animals has produced particular scientific, political, and artistic knowledge as a *metaphor*. Powell's presentation of four of her artworks is an experiment to test epistemological measuring capacities in her artworks, which deal with animals, insects, and plants in different media – photography, video, text, installation, et cetera. First, in *The Memory of Sheep*, she compares our epistemological capabilities to those of sheep, and shows fifty portraits of sheep in order to present and question their individuality. *A Place Where Things Are*, a five-minute video work, traces a fly moving around in a space in order to show a fly's spatial senses (see Cortázar, *The Witnesses*) The third example, *We Are Here*, plays a human voice manipulated to sound like a computer in order to examine the acoustic qualities of humanness and our capacity to perceive and recognise. The last example, a short Super 8 film, *Impossible Line*, documents the process and effect of hypnotising a chicken. Referring to *The Ecological Thought* by Timothy Morton, she introduces a quote from Darwin's *The Descent of Man*: the differences are "of degree and not of kind". Powell uses her artistic approach to seek out the differences of degrees between human and non-human, and measures them through situating her self in between human, animal, and machine. Through mentioning the scientifically proven genetic resemblance between humans and other species, she concludes that the division (between human, non-human, and animal) is a human construct based on human measurement, and that measurement thereby depends on point of view. The artist proposes stepping away from recourse to the binarity of the im/measurable.

Through analysing a metaphor of animals used in the development of the history of ancient Greece, Timofeeva develops a general approach in which this traditional pattern of ascending hierarchy is inscribed. The idea of a universal order of the world, positing that animals are "better" than plants, that humans are "better" than animals, men are "better" than women, free citizens are "better" than slaves, et cetera is first found in Aristotle. According to her reading, all these divisions and boundaries actually represent a particular tension between ontology and epistemology, politics and psychoanalysis, and humans and animals in ancient Greek society, rather than a universal and ideal form of thought. This suggests that philosophy is deeply embedded in the order of a specific cultural, historical, or even personal context – as any knowledge production then therefore also is. The order of the world – how we measure the world – as defined by philosophy gives rise to a new question for study. Temofeeva emphasises that one important role of the imaginary comprises creatively shaking up a system of measurement so as to make it more unstable, imaginative, and surrealistic.

She sees such potentials in the unstable field of "human animality", in re-producing order in a radical way, rather than in the stable division between human and animal, which can only develop as endless self-alternation.

The third dialogue, "Politics of Measurement", took place between Chihiro Minato (JP), a photographer, and Sophie Houdart (FR), an eth-nologist currently engaged in a research project on ways of measuring danger. Their dialogue developed around the measurement hype that was particularly present in relation to the catastrophe in Fukushima. Minato presented his and other artists' observations on measuring radiation in Japan after the explosion of the Fukushima-Daiichi nuclear plant and the se-vere earthquakes on 11 March 2011. He presents two maps of Japan show-ing the spread of levels of radioactivity after the Fukushima catastrophe. Both published the same day, 12 October 2011, one map was from *Tokyo Shimbun* (a popular newspaper in Japan), the other from *The Japan Times* (an English-language newspaper). Comparing the two maps, he explains tricks of visual presentation that were used to "format" facts for the national and international public. He points out that smooth, circular lines on the maps of the north-eastern part of Japan do not necessarily reflect the reality of radioactivity, because this measurement cannot be reduced to a simplified line. These lines indicate adjustment and manipulation by bureaucracy rather than reality. His presentation reveals the politics of measurement that are concealed in visual representations such as maps, charts, or diagrams. Through incorporating field research activities in Fukushima that were conducted by a group of artists and citizens, he presents alternative indicators of measurement for archaeological, historical, agricultural, and cultural re-sources in the region. Based on the powerful flow of data, he concludes that action based on a singular and fixated conceptual approach to measurement by authorities only occurs within its own logic – like measuring repeatedly based on false premises, with no way out.

Sophie Houdart, who is currently conducting her research at the Labo-ratory of Ethnology and Comparative Sociology at the Center for Scientific Research in Paris, is particularly interested in methodologies of producing knowledge about tiny and invisible "things". Her contribution refers to rich historical as well as contemporary examples of "know-how". The first part of her text, which focuses on an investigation of how air was measured in Europe and the instruments involved in doing so back in the 17th and 18th centuries, presents many interesting and peculiar experiments in science: Robert Boyle's air pump; the cyanometer, an instrument for measuring the blueness of the sky, created by Horace-Bénédict de Saussure and used by

Alexander von Humboldt on his expeditions in South America, and used by Joseph Priestley and others to measure the purity and virtue of types of air. It was, however, that research's poetic rather than scientific quality that made a big impact on social developments in previous centuries and was actually used by jurists and politicians to develop social models linked to those of the present. In the second part, Houdart reflects on those historical examples in connection with her current field work in Fukushima, which closely observes a process of learning about a new environmental situation after the catastrophe as well as ordinary people's – organic farmers, artists, activists, citizens, et cetera – invention of an alternative method of measurement for dealing with levels of radioactivity. A particularly interesting example is the use of trees and mushrooms in forests for absorbing radiation, thus doing away with a small amount of radioactivity over time. Beyond the accumulation of methodologies in the field of science, passionate individuals are thus also carrying out experiments; and this research shows qualities of experimental practices that resemble historical examples. She summarises two ways of considering measurements and numbers: one based on a system of knowledge accumulated by science, with one corresponding to one number, one spot, place, site, et cetera, in order to refer to the composition of the whole. The other relies on the spirit of DIY: observing and experimenting oneself based on daily experience. The two parts of her presentation suggest that the conceptual terrain of measurement is not limited to the fields of science alone, but is also more widely applicable.

Based on the idea of art as another form of measurement, three different formats – essay, conversation, and dialogue – are brought together in the book so as to further explore this notion. Each contribution offers insightful materials and suggestions for broadening concepts of measurement that are based in aesthetics and ethics, and proposes its own standpoint for presenting different combinations of an onto-epistemological proposition that implies its own process, time, and methods. As each contribution occurred over the course of two years, bringing them all together in the form of this publication contributes to synchronising and synergising the various contributions more intensively.

*Auf dem Weg zur
(Nicht-)Messbarkeit
von Kunst und Leben*
Einleitung von
Miya Yoshida

Ob wir es nun bemerken oder nicht: In unserem alltäglichen Leben finden eigentlich ständig Messungen statt. Das Regime der Messung zwängt jede Dimension unseres Lebens in ein Korsett quantifizierbarer Größen und vorbestimmter Kategorien: Wir messen nicht nur Zeit, Entfernung, Gewicht, Brennwert, Temperatur etc., es ist auch – vor allem in jüngster Zeit, da wir mit einer Ökonomisierung und Monetarisierung sämtlicher Lebensaspekte konfrontiert sind – ein Begehren festzustellen, naturgemäß schwer fassbare Dinge wie Produktivität oder Kreativität der Quantifizierbarkeit zuzuführen. Dies geschieht in der Absicht, ausnahmslos alles und jedes endlos wiederholten Evaluierungsprozessen zu unterwerfen. Messung ist unter anderem eben auch ein disziplinärer Mechanismus, der mit Hilfe von Segmentierung und Vergleich Werte („absolute" wie „relative") zuweisen soll. Im Bereich der Wissenschaft bedeutet Messung, zumindest nach heutigen erkenntnistheoretischen Erkenntnissen, stets auch eine Verringerung von Komplexität. Sie gründet sich auf die Logik des Mathematischen und ordnet Subjekte wie Objekte standardisierten Modulen unter. Doch umfassen und inkludieren *heute* gebräuchliche Messverfahren durchaus unterschiedliche Maßstäbe, Zeitvorstellungen und Bedingungen. Viele der in diesem Kontext aktivierten, schon vordefinierten Kategorien lassen sich mit der sinnlichen Wahrnehmung des Menschen nicht erfassen, was auch bedeutet, dass sie sich nicht ohne technologische Hilfsmittel erfassen lassen. Die Vielfältigkeit menschlicher Wahrnehmung, fasst man sie nun als individuelle oder über-individuelle, wirft ernsthafte Fragestellungen auf. Denn wenn zwei Individuen einen bestimmten Messbegriff anwenden, dann kann es heutzutage fast als selbstverständlich gelten, dass sie nicht dieselbe „Sache" meinen.

Lässt sich ein Konzept so übernehmen, dass es sich auf Dinge anwenden lässt, die sich so stark voneinander unterscheiden wie etwa das Gewicht einer Orange, die Qualität der Bildung, individuelle Kenntnisse und Fertigkeiten, „Likes" auf Facebook, körperliche Reaktionen auf bestimmte Reize, oder gar Gefühle? Deutet die gewaltige Diversität dieser möglichen Messungsanlässe auf notwendige Konsequenzen für unseren allgemein gebräuchlichen Begriff von Messung hin, muss er sich in eine andere Richtung entwickeln als bislang?

In den 1960er Jahren wurde der Begriff des „Paradigmenwechsels" eingeführt, mit dem die „sozialisierte" Macht von Wissenschaft wie auch Wissenschaft als kulturelle Perspektive in den Blick genommen wurde, in der Absicht, die gesellschaftlichen Folgen der Wissenschaften und deren ideologischen Grundlagen zum Gegenstand von Aushandlungen machen zu können. Im Poststrukturalismus erlebte die Idealbeziehung zwischen Worten und Dingen ihren Niedergang genau an der Stelle der Messbarkeit: denn Messfehlertheorien haben die Behauptung aufgestellt, dass es Messoperationen nicht in Einklang zu bringen gelingt, was wir beobachten, auf welche Weise wir es beschreiben, und wie wir es auf die Form von Daten reduzieren, und sie führen es auf die Unschärfe der in der Sprache gegebenen semiotischen Beziehungen und auf ungenaue Datengewinnungsprozesse zurück (Lembert, 1982). Nach fünfzig Jahren, in denen es immer wieder zu solchen Wechseln gekommen ist, hat sich dem gesellschaftlichen Machtkomplex der Wissenschaften eine neoliberal geprägte Auffassung von „Wissenschaft als Kunst", von Management-*cum*-Messung zugesellt, aus der sich in wachsendem Maße die bereits erwähnten Tendenzen zur Quantifizierung noch des letzten kleinen Aspekts unseres Lebens durch Zahlen in auswertungsorientierten Kategorien ableiten. Indem er ökonomischen Zugewinn über „Fortschritt" im überkommenen modernistischen Sinn stellt, verändert der gegenwärtige neoliberale Kapitalismus Produktivitätsnormen so, dass auch die Arbeit der so genannten Kreativindustrien – als Mittel zum Nachweis einer Produktivität von Kunst sowie zu deren Modularisierung und also auch Quantifizierung – dazu gehört. Ergebnisse auch solcher Arbeit lassen sich so in Zahlen fassen (Preise von Kunstwerken, die Anzahl von „views", Popularität bei bestimmten Betrachter/innengruppen, Anzahl von Orten etc.). Um Arbeit und Konsum in einem solchen neoliberalen Verhältnis kompatibel werden zu lassen, fällt der Messung eine entscheidende Rolle als Verfahren der Identifikation, des Managements und der Auswertung zu. Wie nun kann es uns angesichts solcher Realitäten gelingen, anders zu denken, mit dem Ziel, einen ganz neuen Bezugsrahmen, eine neue Sprache zu schaffen, durch die sich ein sinnvolleres Verständnis von Messung ergibt?

Bei einer Anzahl von Studien zur Messung, die in jüngerer Zeit in der Soziologie, der Kybernetik sowie den Medienwissenschaften durchgeführt wurden, kamen Simulationen zum Einsatz, um bei der Datenverarbeitung Computerprozesse einsetzen zu können. Doch bleiben hinsichtlich der Angemessenheit von Sprache, Wissensmethode und Methoden des Umgangs mit einem neuen Gegenstandsbereich durchaus Fragen offen, vor allem im Bereich der Geistes- und Kulturwissenschaften. Als Reaktion auf die neuerlichen Verschiebungen, zu denen es in Wissenschaft und Technologie gekommen ist, bemühen sich heute diskutierte Philosophien um die mögliche Herausarbeitung einer neuen Ontologieauffassung, die eine erweiterte Weltsicht der Wissenschaften einleiten könnte.

So lässt beispielsweise Gilbert Simondons Begriff der „Transduktion" die Vorstellung hinter sich, bei Segmentierung und Vergleich müssen von einer „Grenze" gesprochen werden. Sein Begriff richtet sich auf die Überwindung der ontologischen Dichotomie zwischen Mensch und Maschine bzw. auch derjenigen zwischen Menschen (Simondon, 1980). In der Affekttheorie betrachtet Patricia T. Clough Messung als ontologische Praxis und betont in diesem Zusammenhang, dass der Messakt die Affekterfahrung in Erwägung ziehen lässt, was zu einer Vorstellung von Messung führt, die sich anstelle einzelner Objekte auf Beziehungen konzentriert und sich eher dem Prozess als dem Ergebnis zuwendet (Clough, 2008). Luciana Parisi fordert, algorithmische Architekturen seien als reale Objekte aufzufassen (Parisi, 2013). Aus erkenntnistheoretischer Perspektive findet der derzeitig starke Glaube an Daten detaillierte Analyse im biopolitischen Nexus des Sehens und der Reformierung von Vernunftbegriffen (Halpern, 2015). Die genannten ontologisch und epistemologisch ausgerichteten Studien erweitern das Begriffsfeld der Messung erheblich, wohingegen vor kurzem im Bereich der Ästhetik eine Untersuchung von Aud Sissel Hoel zu einer Neufassung der Grenzziehungen zwischen Bildern, Worten und Zahlen geführt hat. Sie arbeitet einen Objektivierungsprozess heraus, der sich nicht nach Subjekt oder Objekt, sondern lediglich entsprechend der jeweiligen Kognitionsebene unterscheidet. Sie verschiebt das Augenmerk von den Affekten hin zur Kognition und kommt zu der Schlussfolgerung, dass eine dynamische Wechselbeziehung des Subjektiven und des Objektiven unterschiedliche Blickwinkel auf die Messung generiert (Sissel, 2014). Das bedeutet, dass es zur Erforschung der semiotischen Beziehung zwischen den von uns gebrauchten Sprachen und dem, was wir an Phänomenen beobachten können, einer neuen Hypothese bedarf.

Betrachtet man Messung als Praxis, dann erscheint wichtig, daran zu erinnern, dass Datenverarbeitung, insbesondere dann, wenn es um Visualisierung geht, tatsächlich eine Vielzahl ästhetischer Entscheidungen voraussetzt. Dies hat zur Folge, dass heutige Messpraktiken nicht mehr vorrangig vernunftgeleitet erscheinen. Zwar war Messung, historisch betrachtet, stets von subjektiven Aspekten begleitet, doch zielte die Moderne auf deren Ausschluss nach Maßgabe demokratischer Grundsätze und aufgrund administrativer Erfordernisse ab (Porter, 1997). Die Intervention der Computerrechnung verweist auf die Bedeutung der Wiederaufnahme, nicht des Ausschlusses der Subjektivität beim Verständnis der Messung. Indem Messung als Subjektivität einschließende und Wirklichkeit konstruierende und nicht nur verzeichnende Tätigkeit gefasst wird, erlangt das Potenzial künstlerischer Innovation gesteigerte Relevanz für eine partizipatorische Praxis beim Denken und bei der Umsetzung von Messungen.

Ist der Wirklichkeitssinn messbar?

„Bilder zeigen nicht Sachen, sie zeigen Sachverhalte."
—Vilém Flusser, *Ins Universum der technischen Bilder*

Moderne Technologien folgen also systematischen Denkprozessen, um die Wirklichkeit auf quantitativer Ebene zu vermessen; sie repräsentieren die Ergebnisse in einem Modus, den sie als numerische „Klarstellung" betrachten. Die Logik und Gerichtetheit des Denkens, von der Absicht über Argumentation bis zum Endergebnis, hat viel zur Kenntnis, zum Verstehen, ja sogar zur Vorhersagbarkeit verschiedener Phänomene beigetragen. 1963 blickte Hannah Arendt zurück auf die dramatischen Ereignisse, die die Kernphysik in der ersten Hälfte des 20. Jahrhunderts durchlief, und unternahm den Versuch, die durch die damals entwickelten Technologien gegebenen wissenschaftlichen Errungenschaften überblickshaft zusammenzufassen.[1] An dieser Stelle zitierte sie Heisenbergs Schlussfolgerung: „Eine definitive und endgültige Genauigkeitsgrenze aller mit Instrumenten von Menschenhand getätigter Messeung für jene ‚geheimnisvollen Botschaften aus der realen Welt',"[2]

---

[1] Hannah Arendt. „The Conquest of Space and the Stature of Man", in: The New Atlantis: A Journal of Technology and Society, Nr.18 (Herbst 2007(1963)).

[2] Ebd., S. 44.

und nahm auf die Tatsache Bezug, dass die Entwicklung der Wissenschaften einen entscheidenden Wendepunkt auf seinem eigenen auf Logik und Ästhetik bezogenen Weg erreicht hatte. Ebenso anerkannte sie die Differenz, die philosophische von wissenschaftlicher Wahrheit unterscheidet. Ihre Einsichten in diesem Text haben mich dazu veranlasst, die Konstitution der „Politik einer Ästhetik der Messung" in Frage zu stellen: was bedeutet „Genauigkeit" eigentlich im Zusammenhang der Messung? Bedeutet dieses Wort dasselbe wie die „Exaktheit", „Präzision" oder „Qualität" einer Messung?

Dekonstruiert Quantenontologie die klassischen Ontologien und eröffnet sie einen neuen Raum, in dem das „Als ob" zum „Als ob es *ist*" wird, dann kann das imaginäre Potenzial als Teil von Sein und Existenz betrachtet werden. Die US-amerikanische Theoretikerin und ehemalige Medizinerin Karen Barad schreibt: „Messungen materiell-diskursive Praktiken der Entstehung von Materie: Materie und Bedeutung sind intra-aktiven Messungen nicht vorgängig, sondern werden vielmehr durch sie mit gebildet."[3] Sie erläutert im folgenden eine „Quantenontologie" mit drei wesentlichen Merkmalen – keine festgelegten Grenzen, keine Eigenschaften von Objekten innerhalb von Phänomenen und keine Begriffe mit bestimmten Bedeutungen – und dass diese drei Faktoren sich wechselseitig affizieren, dass sich also die Phänomene nicht von irgendwelchen intra-agierenden Handlungsformen, einschließlich der Handlung der Wahrnehmenden, trennen lassen (Barad, 2012). Diese Theorie richtet das zeitgenössische Denken der Messung auf eine alles einschließende Welt aus. Sie erweitert Mittel und Bedeutungen der Messung und verändert zugleich den *locus* der Genauigkeit beim Messen. Zugleich unterscheidet sie zweierlei mögliche Kategorien des Begriffs „Messung": die eine wird durch die *Vermessung der Wirklichkeit* repräsentiert, die andere durch die *Vermessung des Wirklichkeitssinns*. Während sich erstere auf die Wissenschaftslogik des „close reading" gründet, „sich an das Nichts heranzuzoomen, sich mit immer größerer Sensitivität und Schärfe zu sehen und zu hören, sich auf immer genauere und feinere Maßeinteilungen der Einzelheiten von ... zuzubewegen (...)".[4] Eine solche Erkundung lenkt die Akte und Bedeutungen der Messung in Richtung eines „Mehr" – mehr Daten, mehr Einzelheiten, mehr Beweise.

---

[3] Karen Barad, Was ist das Maß des Nichts? Unendlichkeit, Virtualität, Gerechtigkeit: 100 Notizen, 100 Gedanken, Documenta-Reihe, Nr. 99, Berlin 2012.

[4] Ebd., a.a.O., S. 1.

Letztere dagegen überträgt die Ausübung der Messung in das Reich des Imaginären und verwandelt Akte und Bedeutungen in andere Messungsbegriffe – den Wirklichkeitssinn. Wie, wenn überhaupt, wäre ein solcher Wirklichkeitssinn denn überhaupt messbar? Welche Denkweisen, welche Denkrichtungen hätte dies wohl zur Folge?

Weitaus dringender und eindringlicher – falls diese Worte jemals eine Bedeutung hatten, dann hier – hat uns die Katastrophe von Fukushima im Jahr 2011 vor dasselbe Problem gestellt: Wie ist „Genauigkeit" zu verstehen? Sie hat zugleich die modernistischem Denken eigene Gerichtetheit des Denkens als Sackgasse erwiesen. Jean-Luc Nancy, einer der ersten europäischen Intellektuellen, die auf die Katastrophe reagierten, bezog sich auf die komplexe zeitgenössische Wirklichkeit, der die Technologien gleichermaßen Segen und Fluch sind, und forderte in Bezug auf die Zukunft Vorstellungsweisen, die an anderem orientiert sind als an quantitativer Wissenserweiterung und permanenter „Verbesserung": Damit meint er, dass wir, statt unsere Einbildungskraft auf Kalkulation zu vergeuden und einer geraden Denklinie zu folgen, um die Natur oder „das Unbekannte" zu verbessern, zu kontrollieren, zu erobern und zu überwinden, andere Arten von Einbildung finden und vertreten müssen (Nancy, 2012). Anders ausgedrückt bedeutet das, dass der gesamte auf Messung bezogene Denkprozess einer grundlegenden Fragestellung anheim steht.

Mit dem selbst gesetzten Ziel, dem Einfluss alternativer Methoden, Sprach und Denkformationen zu ästhetischen Auffassungen von der Messung auf den Grund zu gehen, erforscht die vorliegende Publikation das Denken in visuellen Kategorien und in Dialogen mit Künstler/innen, Sozialwissenschaftler/innen sowie mit einem Kulturtheoretiker. Sie besteht aus drei Teilen: Einem Essay, *Exercise in Measurement*, in dem ich eine Reihe themenrelevanter künstlerischer Konzepte präsentiere und diskutiere; *Symbolic Engineering: Measurement, Aesthetics, and the Rules for Art – A Conversation with Helmut Draxler* ist ein Dialog, in dem es um die mögliche Rolle der Kunst in der algorithmischen Gesellschaft geht; den dritten Teil bildet schließlich die Dokumentation der Veranstaltungsreihe *Dialogues between an Artist and a Scientist*, die im Zeitraum zwischen Dezember 2013 und Januar 2014 im Kunstraum der Leuphana Universität Lüneburg stattfand.

Der erste Teil, im Anschluss an diese Einleitung, beginnt mit meinem Essay *Exercises in Measurement*. Dieser Text führt Werke aus Conceptual art und Post-Conceptual art in dem Versuch zusammen, sie neu zu interpretieren und zu einer Einschätzung ihrer konzeptuellen Bedeutung im Kontext der

Messung zu kommen. Messung ist ein abstrakter Begriff, der jedoch recht inklusiv ist; die mit ihm zusammenhängenden Praktiken sind äußerst unterschiedliche. Dieser Text ist nicht in der Absicht verfasst, die genannten Kunstwerke umfassend, historisch perspektiviert oder gar objektiv zu behandeln. Er wendet sich vielmehr noch einmal künstlerischen Praktiken, Literaturen und Poetiken zu, um Verfahrensweisen der Messung im Zusammenhang visuellen Denkens befragen zu können, um sich dann dem Visuellen selbst zuzuwenden. Beabsichtigt ist die Anwendung von Begrifflichkeiten und Sprachen der Messung mit dem Ziel, diesen Begriff mit imaginären Dimensionen oder Institutionen zusammen zu denken. Aus diesem Grund bezieht sich der Text nicht auf die zahlreichen Praxisformen, die ihre Grundlage in existierenden Konventionen der Messung und in deren illustrierender Dokumentation haben – wozu ich in diesem Zusammenhang auch die Visualisierung von Daten, computergenerierte oder -prozessierte Grafik, automatisch geschaffene „technische Bilder" etc. zähle. Der Text bezieht sicherlich keine Stellung gegen wissenschaftliche Messverfahren; vielmehr geht er auf eine spezifisch zeitgenössische Hervorhebung der Messung ein und befindet sich dabei ständig auf der Suche nach anderen Möglichkeiten des Wissens. Er beginnt mit jener paradoxen Vorstellung, die sich im Denken der Situationistischen Bewegung findet, nach der die bei Messakten zugrunde gelegte Maßeinheit situationsabhängig sei, und wendet sich dann in vier Abteilungen den „pataphysischen" Experimenten einiger zeitgenössischer Künstler/innen zu, die mit Messung und der schöpferischen Erweiterung der Begrifflichkeiten um die Messung zu tun haben. Die Abteilungen heißen, ins Deutsche übersetzt: 1) De-Institutionalisierung der Messung, 2) Von der Universalität zur Ubiquität der Messung, 3) Tanz mit Genauigkeiten und 4) Nicht/Messbarkeit des Lebens. Obwohl die Auswahl der im folgenden behandelten Kunstwerke nicht immer in direktem Bezug zu konventionellen Auffassungen von Messung zu stehen scheint, bezieht sie sich doch zumindest auf die Potenzialität und Fragwürdigkeit von Begriffen und Prozessen des Messens, auf die Veränderung von Strukturen und die Herausbildung eigener Mechanismen, statt weiter bestehenden Systemmustern anzuhängen oder konventionelle Strukturen zu übernehmen, um den *Ort* der Genauigkeit zu verschieben. Eine genaue Auseinandersetzung mit diesen Werken erlaubt uns neue Kriterien, Stichwörter, Verbindungen und Assoziationen ausfindig zu machen, um dem Gebrauch der Messung einen größeren Platz im so genannten alltäglichen Leben einzuräumen.

Traditionell entspringen ästhetische Begriffe einem hierarchisch verfassten Universalismus, zu dessen Berfürworter/innen auch Philosophie und Kunstgeschichte schon gezählt haben. Doch werde ich hier Kunstwerke weder zum Nachweis oder zur Illustration einer bestimmten Theorie verwenden, noch beabsichtige ich, irgendwelche Theorien auf diese Kunstwerke „anzuwenden". Statt bestehende künstlerische Produktionen unter dem Deckmantel einer rationalistischen Erkenntnislehre zu untersuchen, sieht meine Position Kunst weder primär als Objekt noch als „Subjekt" der Forschung – sondern vielmehr als Erscheinungsform einer Denkmethode. Statt künstlerische Praktiken nur in bereits existierende historische Kontexte und Schubladen zurückzuordnen, verstehe ich Kunst als enigmatische Konstellation von Dingen, Bildern, Worten und Zeichen, die mir in einem Prozess des Suchens und des Denkens begegnen; ich habe mich für eine nicht-hierarchische Vorgehensweise entschieden, um diese Kunstwerke mit einiger Freizügigkeit dem allgemeineren Bezugsrahmen der Messung zu subsumieren. In diesem Sinne geht es in diesem Aufsatz um Produktion und Erfindung. Bei Prozessen des Machens entspricht die Reihenfolge, in der sich Denken und Befragen einstellen, nicht unbedingt derselben Verfahrensweise, die bei sonst üblichen Recherchen genutzt wird. Dies birgt die Herausforderung, interdisziplinäre Beispiele auf diskursive und dennoch „akkurate" Weise miteinander zu verknüpfen. Im Deutschen steht das Wort „zählen" in engem Zusammenhang mit dem Wort „erzählen". Indem er an jeder behandelten Praxis entlang denkt und diese jeweils nicht als (Kunst-) Geschichte, sondern als „eine Geschichte" (Deutscher, 2005) würdigt, versammelt der vorliegende Essay eine Reihe von Geschichten über Messung, die sich paradoxer, widersprüchlicher und humorvoller Formen bedienen. Er mobilisiert das „Sprachspiel" (Wittgenstein, 1953) der Messung und versucht so, Begegnungen von Ideen, konzeptuellen Methoden, Handlungsformen und Messvorgängen zu stiften, die im konzeptuellen Schwellenbereich zwischen Wissenschaft (Technologie) und Alltagsleben zu finden sind.

Der zweite Teil dokumentiert unter dem Titel *The Aesthetics of Measurement* ein Gespräch mit dem Kunsttheoretiker und Kurator Helmut Draxler – ein Austausch von Gedanken und Reflektionen über Modernebegriffe in der Kunstgeschichte. In der klassischen Ästhetik zeichnet sich Kunst immer durch ein untrennbares Verhältnis von Maß und Proportion aus. Platon sagt: „Wenn es also Messung gibt, dann gibt es auch Kunst; umgekehrt, wenn es Kunst gibt, so gibt es auch Messung.

Eines von beiden zu leugnen bedeutete beide zu leugnen." (Skemp, 1952) Ausgehend von der Idee einer Kunst als Messung beschäftigt sich der Dialog noch einmal mit der Avantgarde-Tradition des Verhältnisses von Kunst und Leben im Hinblick auf eine algorithmusorientierte Gesellschaft. Es verändert seine Relevanz ausgehend von der Perspektive der ungeheueren Menge unterschiedlicher Methodiken, die sich im Zusammenhang verschiedener Praktiken künstlerischen Denkens herausgebildet haben, in denen noch eine politische Bedeutsamkeit Relevanz besitzt.

Für den dritten Teil, der den Titel *Dialogues between an Artist and a Scientist* trägt, wurden drei auf der Schnittfläche zwischen künstlerischen und wissenschaftlichen Ansätzn zu den Themen Politik, Erkenntnistheorie und Ästhetik der Messung angesiedelte Gespräche jeweils in Paaren aus einem Künstler/einer Künstlerin und einem Sozialwissenschaftler/einer Sozialwissenschaftlerin geführt. Der erste Dialog, der sich um die „Ästhetik der Messung" dreht, entspannt sich zwischen dem Künstler Matt Mullican (USA) und der Soziologin Patricia T. Clough (USA). Ausgehend von der Vorstellung, nach der das Selbst sowohl als Subjekt als auch als Objekt der Forschung gelten kann, diskutieren Mullican and Clough eine gedankliche Neufassung der Ästhetik der Messung auf der Grundlage der Übertragung ihrer persönlichen Erfahrungen und psychischen Problemstellungen als Objekte im soziokulturellen Raum. Systeme der Messung sowie quantitative und qualitative Methoden werden angewandt und umfassend befragt, sowohl im Bereich der Forschung als auch im Alltagsleben. In seiner biografischen *lecture performance* „Who Feels the Most Pain?" hat sich Mullican mit der Wahrnehmung und Rezeption von Wirklichkeit, Fiktion und Imaginärem auseinandergesetzt – und mit den Möglichkeiten ihrer Repräsentation. Die Präsentation beginnt mit einem Rückblick auf die 1970er Jahre, als die menschliche Farbwahrnehmung unter verschiedenen Lichtverhältnissen um Zentrum seines Interesses stand. Diese äußert reduzierende Wahrnehmung verändert nach und nach seine Weltsicht, in sofern er sie in der Folge nur mehr als Lichterscheinung sah, was ihn darauf zur Erkundung der ontologischen Grenze zwischen Leben und Tod brachte. Mit der Setzung einer Sinneserfahrung von Schmerz als erkenntnistheoretischem und ontologischem Gradmesser der Wirklichkeit, durchlaufen seine Werke eine Entwicklung in unterschiedlichen künstlerischen Versuchsanordnungen: Mit der Erfindung einer fiktionalen Figur namens Glen, die sich im Raum von Zeichnungen bewegt, um den Sitz des Schmerzes in diesem imaginären Raum zu ermitteln, durch die Begegnung mit einer Leiche in einem Labor zur Erkundung sinnlicher Wahrnehmung, durch das Sammeln von

Tatorten in gezeichneter Form, bei denen die interessante Frage ist, wie der Tod (der Schmerz) illustriert wird, und durch Selbsthypnose in öffentlichen Situationen, mit dem Ziel, sich selbst als Medium der Beobachtung sinnlicher Erfahrungen des Selbst auf der Grundlage von Bewusstseinszuständen Anderer zu benutzen. Durch den umfassenden Gebrauch aller möglicher visueller Darstellungsmedien – Malerei, Zeichnung, Film, Fotografie, Computergrafik, Installation etc. – setzt sich Mullican seit langem mit der Vermessung der ästhetischen Grenze zwischen Leben und Tod, Unbewusstem und Bewusstem, Realem und Imaginärem auseinander.

In ihrer performativ angelegten Präsentation „The Calculative Aesthetic, Objects and Unconscious Desire in the Age of Big Data" nimmt Clough sowohl ihr unbewusstes Begehren als auch ihre Kindheitserinnerungen als Ausgangspunkte, um einen Raum für ein erkenntnistheoretisches Unbewusstes als Gegenstand ihrer soziologischen Forschung zu öffnen. Im Zeitalter von Big Data, so ihre Behauptung, verleihen Algorithmen der Quantität eine gewisse Qualität. Die enorme Geschwindigkeit, mit der Informationen verarbeitet werden, bewirkt eine Veränderung unserer Vorstellung davon, was bewusst und was unbewusst ist, die kalkulative Ästhetik lässt uns unsere unbewussten Kapazitäten erkennen, die unterschiedliche Auffassungen der Bedeutung von Zahl und Quantität hervorrufen. Darum ist eine neuerliche Untersuchung notwendig, mit der die gegenwärtige Unterscheidung sowohl zwischen quantitativer und qualitativer Messung wie auch zwischen Objekten und Systemen einer Neubewertung zu unterziehen ist.

Der zweite Dialog, „Epistemology of Measurement", fand zwischen der Künstlerin Lucy Powell (GB) und der Philosophin und Kulturtheoretikerin Oxana Timofeeva (RU) statt. Powells Interesse gilt Intelligenz- und Wissensformen, die nicht auf Menschen beschränkt sind, sondern auch Tiere und Pflanzen umfassen. Timofeeva dagegen hat sich mit einer unbewussten Tendenz in der Philosophie beschäftigt, die damit zu tun hat, in welchem Maße der Gebrauch von Tieren spezifische wissenschaftliche, politische und künstlerische Wissensformen als *Metapher* hervorgebracht hat. Powells Präsentation von vier ihrer Kunstwerke ist ein Experiment, das erkenntnistheoretische Messmöglichkeiten in ihren Werken erproben soll, die sich in unterschiedlichen Medien – Fotografie, Video, Text, Installation etc. – mit Tieren, Insekten und Pflanzen auseinandersetzen. Zunächst vergleicht sie in der Arbeit *The Memory of Sheep* unsere Erkenntnisfähigkeiten mit denjenigen von Schafen, und dazu zeigt sie fünfzig Porträts von Schafen, um deren Individualität zu zeigen und zugleich zu hinterfragen. *A Place Where Things Are*, eine fünfminütige Videoarbeit, folgt den Bewegungen einer

Fliege in einem Zimmer, um das räumliche Orientierungsvermögen der Fliege zu zeigen (vgl. hierzu auch die Erzählung „Die Zeugen" von Julio Cortázar). Beim dritten Beispiel mit dem Titel *We Are Here* wird eine menschliche Stimme abgespielt, die so manipuliert wurde, dass sie wie ein Computer klingt, um die akustischen Besonderheiten des Menschlichen und unsere Wahrnehmungs- und Erkenntnisfähigkeiten zu untersuchen. Das letzte Beispiel, der kurze Super8-Film *Impossible Line*, dokumentiert Vorgang und Auswirkungen des Hypnotisierens eines Huhns. Sie greift ein Zitat aus *The Ecological Thought* von Timothy Morton auf, in dem es um Darwins *Abstammung der Arten* geht. Darin wird gesagt, das Unterschiede „gradueller Natur und nicht aufgrund verschiedener Arten" bestünden. Powell nutzt ihren künstlerischen Ansatz, um die graduellen Unterschiede zwischen Menschlichem und Nichtmenschlichem herauszuarbeiten und misst diese, indem sie sich selbst zwischen Mensch, Tier und Maschine situiert. Wenn sie die wissenschaftlich bewiesene genetische Ähnlichkeit zwischen Menschen und anderen Spezies erwähnt, dann um zu dem Schluss zu kommen, dass die Trennung (zwischen Menschlichem, Nichtmenschlichem und Tierischem) ein von Menschen gemachtes, auf menschlicher Messung basierendes Konstrukt ist, und dass darum Messung eine Frage des Blickwinkels ist. Die Künstlerin schlägt in diesem Sinne vor, sich des Rückgriffs auf das binäre Modell des Nicht/Messbaren zu enthalten.

Mit ihrer Analyse der in der Entwicklung der Geschichte des antiken Griechenlands verwendeten Tiermetaphorik, erarbeitet Timofeeva einen allgemeinen Ansatz, in den dieses traditionelle Muster einer aufsteigenden Hierarchielinie eingeschrieben ist. Die Vorstellung einer universellen Weltordnung, im Zuge derer die Behauptung aufgestellt wird, Tiere seien „besser" als Pflanzen, Menschen „besser" als Tiere, Männer „besser" als Frauen, freie Bürger/innen „besser" als Sklav/innen, etc., findet sich zum ersten Mal bei Aristoteles ausformuliert. Timofeevas Interpretation zufolge bedeuten all diese Unterscheidungen und Grenzziehungen tatsächlich eine besondere Spannung zwischen ontologischer und epistemologischer Perspektive, zwischen Politik und Psychoanalyse und zwischen Menschen und Tieren in der griechischen Gesellschaft der Antike, und nicht etwa eine universelle und ideale Form des Denkens. Das verdeutlicht, dass die Philosophie zutiefst in der Ordnung eines spezifischen kulturellen, historischen oder gar persönlichen Kontexts verankert ist – und das trifft dann folgerichtig auch auf jedwede andere Art der Wissensproduktion zu. Die Ordnung der Welt – wie wir die Welt vermessen –, so, wie sie von der Philosophie bestimmt wird, wirft für die forschende Neugier eine neue Frage auf.

Temofeeva legt Wert auf die Feststellung, dass eine wichtige Funktion des Imaginären darin besteht, ein Messsystem schöpferisch in Erschütterung zu bringen, um dieses zu destabilisieren, es fantasievoller, surrealistischer zu machen. Sie erblickt solche Potenziale in dem instabilen Bereich „menschlicher Tierhaftigkeit", in der radikal aufgefassten Reproduktion von Ordnung, und nicht in der Aufrechterhaltung der stabilen Trennlinie zwischen Mensch und Tier, die sich nur als endlose Selbst-Alternierung entwickeln kann.

Der dritte Dialog, „Politics of Measurement", fand zwischen dem Fotografen Chihiro Minato (JP) und der zurzeit an einem Forschungsprojekt zu Möglichkeiten der Messung von Gefahr arbeitenden Ethnologin Sophie Houdart (FR): statt. Ihr Gespräch entfaltete sich um den Messungs-Hype, der sich besonders im Umfeld der Atomkatastrophe von Fukushima bemerkbar machte. Minato präsentierte seine eigenen Beobachtungen, aber auch diejenigen anderer Künstler/innen, zu Strahlungsmessungen nach der Explosion im Atomkraftwerk Fukushima-Daiichi und nach den verheerenden Erdbeben am 11. März 2011. Er zeigte zwei Karten Japans, auf denen die Ausbreitung von Radioaktivitätsniveaus im Anschluss an die Katastrophe gezeigt werden sollte. Beide Karten waren am selben Tag, dem 12. Oktober 2011, veröffentlicht worden, die eine stammte aus dem *Tokyo Shimbun* (einer auflagenstarken japanischen Tageszeitung), die andere aus der *Japan Times* (einer in Japan erscheinenden englischsprachigen Zeitung). Über den Vergleich der beiden Karten erläutert er die Tricks in der visuellen Darstellung, die zur „Formatierung" von Fakten für ein nationales und ein internationales Publikum benutzt wurden. Er wies darauf hin, dass sanft geschwungene, kreisförmige Linien auf den Karten des nordöstlichen Teils von Japan nicht unbedingt die Realität der radioaktiven Verseuchung wiedergeben, denn Messungen wie diese lassen sich nicht auf eine einfache, durchgezogene Linie reduzieren. Diese Linien weisen Spuren der Anpassung und Manipulation durch die nationale Bürokratie auf, nicht solche, die der Realität entspringen. Minatos Präsentation legt Politiken der Messung offen, die sich hinter visuellen Darstellungen wie Karten, Plänen oder Diagrammen verbergen. Da er auf Feldforschungsaktivitäten einer Gruppe von Künstler/innen und Bürger/innen zurückgreifen kann, ist er in der Lage, alternative Messindikatoren für archäologische, historische, landwirtschaftliche und kulturelle Ressourcen in der Region vorzuführen. Auf der Grundlage mächtiger Datenströme kommt er zu dem Schluss, dass ein Handeln, das in Bezug auf die Messung durch die Behörden auf einem einzelnen und festgelegten konzeptuellen Ansatz beruht, sich nur innerhalb seiner eigenen Logik ereignet – als würde man wieder und wieder auf der Grundlage falscher Prämissen Messungen anstellen, aus denen in dieser Konstellation kein Ausweg besteht.

Sophie Houdart, die derzeit mit ihrer Forschung am Labor für Ethnologie und Vergleichende Sozialwissenschaften am Pariser Centre de Recherche Scientifique befasst ist, interessiert sich ganz besonders für Methodiken der Wissenproduktion, und zwar vor allem das Wissen über winzige und kaum sichtbare „Dinge" betreffend. Ihr Beitrag bezieht sich auf zahlreiche historische wie auch zeitgenössische Beispiele für „Know-how". Der erste Teil ihres Texts, der sich auf eine Untersuchung zur Messung der Luft in Europa und die dafür im 17. und 18. Jahrhundert eingesetzten Instrumente konzentriert, stellt viele interessante und eigentümliche wissenschaftliche Experimente vor: Robert Boyles berühmte Luftpumpe, den Cyanometer, das von Horace-Bénédict de Saussure entwickelte und von Alexander von Humboldt auf seinen Südamerikaexpeditionen eingesetzte Instrument zur Ermittlung des Blauheitsgrades des Himmels, das von Joseph Priestley und anderen zur Überprüfung von Reinheit und Güte der Lüfte verwendet wurde. Doch war es eher die poetische als die wissenschaftliche Qualität dieser Forschungen, die in vergangenen Jahrhunderten großen Einfluss auf gesellschaftliche Entwicklungen ausübte und von Juristen und Politikern eingesetzt wurde, um Gesellschaftsmodelle zu entwickeln, die mit denen der Gegenwart in Beziehung standen. In einem zweiten Teil reflektiert Houdart über historische Beispiele zu ihrer derzeitigen Feldforschung in Fukushima, bei der ein Lernprozess über den Umgang mit einer neuen Umweltlage nach der Katastrophe aus großer Nähe beobachtet wird, ebenso wie die von gewöhnlichen Leuten – Biobauern und -bäuerinnen, Künstler/innen, Aktivist/innen, Bürger/innen – erfundenen alternativen Messmethoden, die das Leben mit wechselnden Strahlungsniveaus unterstützen. Ein besonders interessantes Beispiel ist der Einsatz bestimmter Baum- und Pilzarten in den Wäldern zur Absorption von Strahlung, durch den im Laufe der Zeit ein kleiner Teil der Radioaktivität abgebaut werden kann. Jenseits der Methodenschwemme im Bereich der Wissenschaften führen also auch leidenschaftliche Einzelne Experimente durch; und diese Forschung weist Qualitäten einer experimentellen Praxis auf, die an historische Beispiele erinnern. Houdart spricht zusammenfassend von zwei Verfahrenswegen bei der Beschäftigung mit Messungen und Zahlen: der eine basiert auf einem von der Wissenschaft akkumulierten Wissenssystem, bei dem eine Messung einer Zahl, einem Punkt, einem Ort, einer Stelle etc. entspricht, um die Komposition des Ganzen wiederzugeben. Das andere verlässt sich auf den Geist des Do-it-yourself: selbst beobachten, selbst experimentieren, Tag für Tag eigene Erfahrungen machen. Beide Teile ihrer Präsentation deuten darauf hin, dass der begriffliche Bereich der Messung nicht auf den Bereich der Wissenschaft begrenzt, sondern weitaus allgemeiner anwendbar ist.

Mit der gemeinsamen Grundidee der Kunst als einer anderen Form der Messung kommen drei verschiedene Formate – Essay, Gespräch und dialogische Präsentation – in diesem Buch zusammen, um den Begriff der Messung zu erweitern. Jeder der Beiträge bietet aufschlussreiche Materialien und Anregungen für ein erweitertes Verständnis von Messung, die ihre Grundlagen in Ästhetik und Ethik haben und ihren eigenen Standort zur Präsentation unterschiedlicher Kombinationen onto-epistemologischer Thesen aufweisen, die einen eigenständigen Prozess, eine eigene Zeit und eigene Methoden voraussetzen. Da alle Beiträge im Lauf der vergangenen zwei Jahre zustande kamen, vermag ihre gesammelte Präsentation in Form dieser Veröffentlichung vielleicht zur Synchronisierung und wechselseitigen synergetischen Intensivierung der Texte und Werke beitragen.

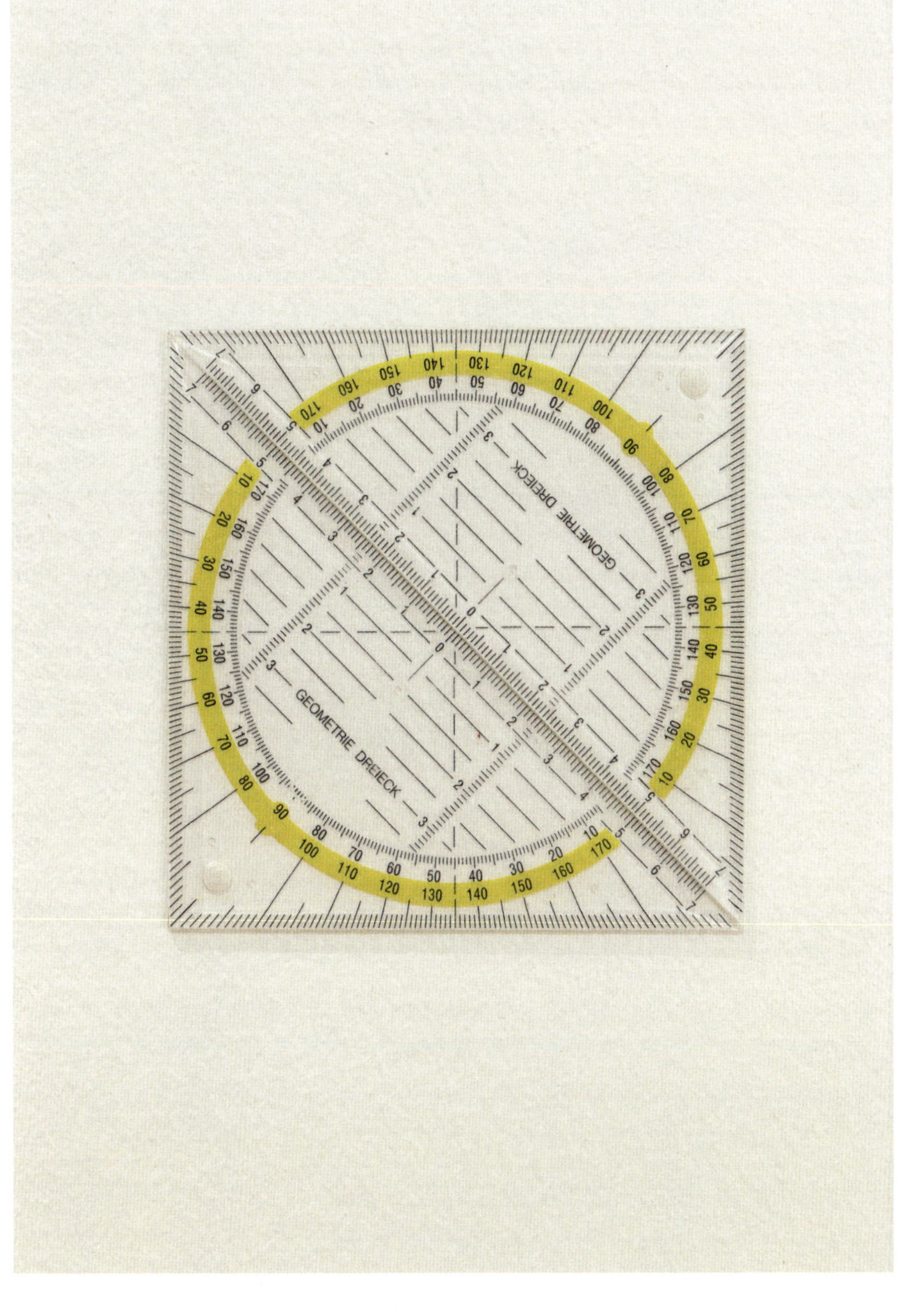

Ceal Floyer, *Circle*, 2015, two set squares, 11.4 x 11.4 cm, (CF242), courtesy the artist and Galerie Esther Schipper, Berlin, photo © Andrea Rossetti

As she does quite frequently in her work, Floyer here turns everyday objects against themselves by taking them literally. Very innocently confronting the two different "precisions" used in the industrial production of plastic set squares and the measurement print on their surfaces, the "Circle" in this elegantly casual work remains one that is broken.

Exercises in Measurement

Lemon:

lemon
past lemon
after lemon
cut-out of a lemon
animal's lemon
painting of a lemon
sliced lemon
before or pre- lemon
image of a lemon
memory of a lemon
illusion of a lemon
subject: lemon
hidden lemon
area of a lemon
dream of a lemon
last lemon??
reflection of a lemon
photo of a lemon
almost lemon
moving transitional lemon
impression of a lemon
actual lemon
this is a lemon
model of a lemon
drawing of a lemon
misapprehension of a lemon
still lemon (if possible)
another translation of a lemon
and you, you just thought they were sour

Shusaku Arakawa & Madeline H. Gins, "Chart of Lemon",
from *The Mechanism of Meaning*, Chapter 3. Presentation of
Ambiguous Zones, exhibition catalogue, the National Museum
of Art, Osaka, 1979, 17.

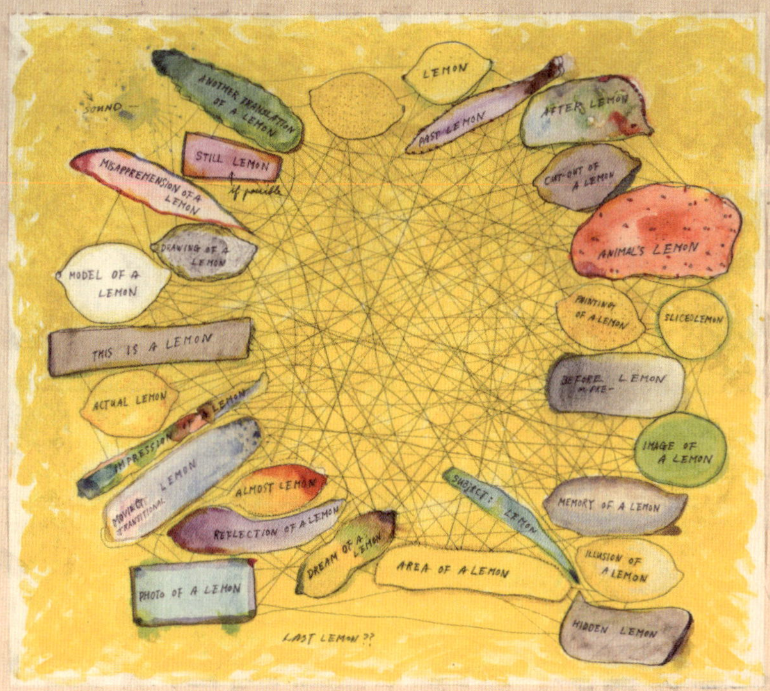

Shusaku Arakawa, *Ambiguous Zones of a Lemon,*
Sketch no. 2, 1970, watercolour, graphite, art
marker, collage on paper, 90.8 x 73.7 cm
© 2015 Estate of Madeline Gins. Reproduced
with permission of the Estate of Madeline Gins and
Reversible Destiny Foundation. Photo: n/k

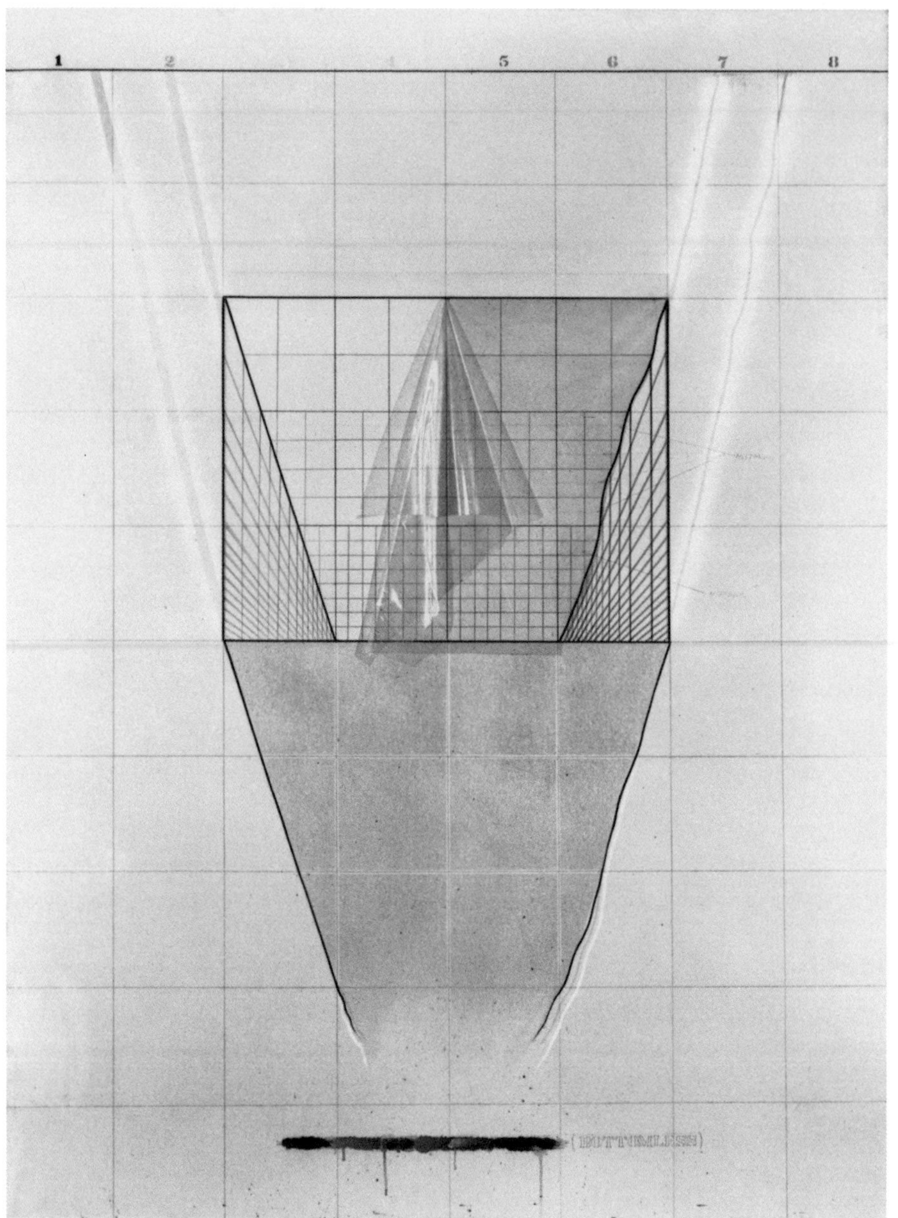

Shusaku Arakawa, *Bottomless*, 1963–64, mixed
media, acrylic and pencil on canvas, 182 x 121.9 cm
© 2017 Estate of Madeline Gins. Reproduced
with permission of the Estate of Madeline Gins
and Reversible Destiny Foundation. Photo: n/k

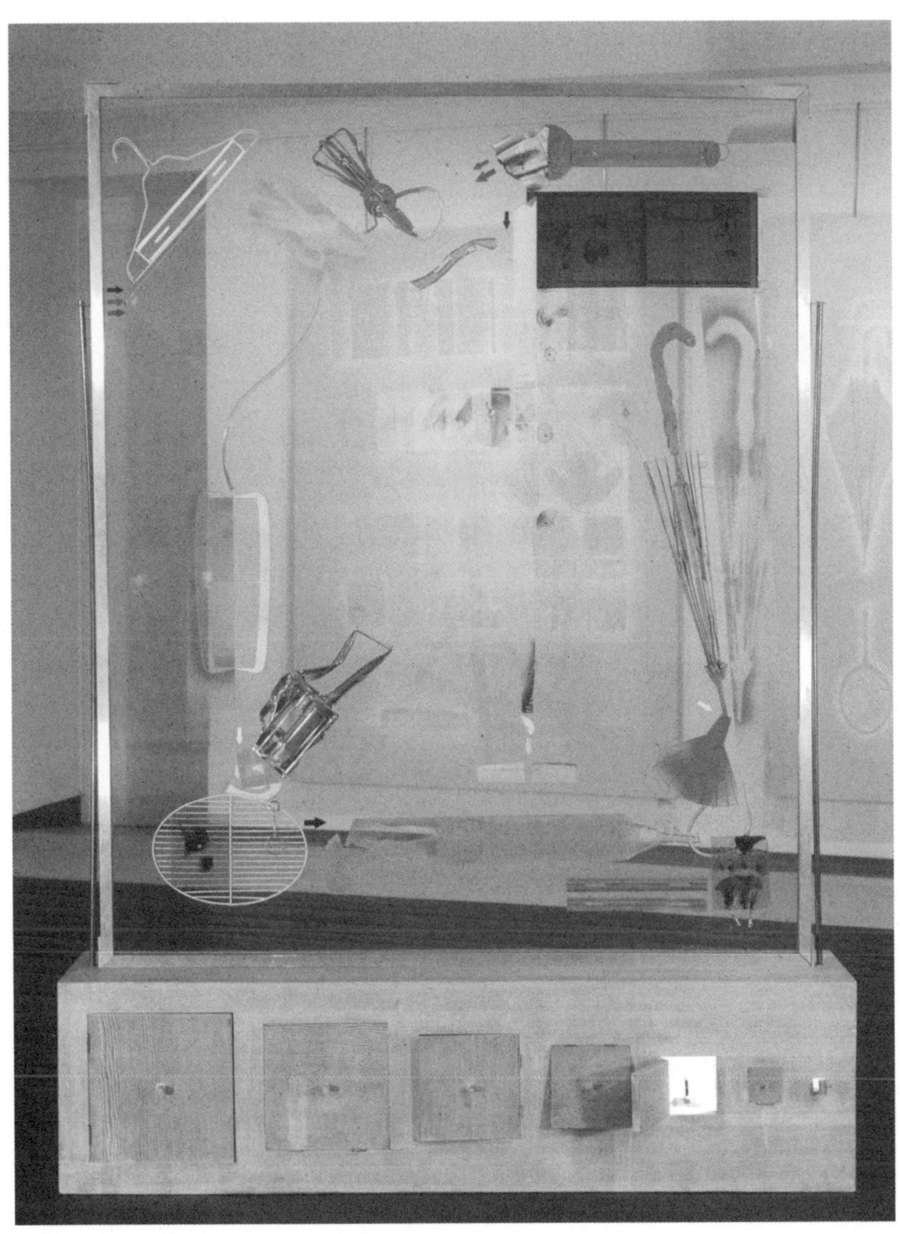

Shusaku Arakawa, *Diagram with Duchamp's Glass as a Minor Detail*, 1964, (installation view of Arakawa: *Diagrams*, Dwan Gallery, Los Angeles 1964), mixed media sculpture, 228.6 x 167.7 x 55.9 cm © 2017 Estate of Madeline Gins. Reproduced with permission of the Estate of Madeline Gins and Reversible Destiny Foundation. Photo: n/k

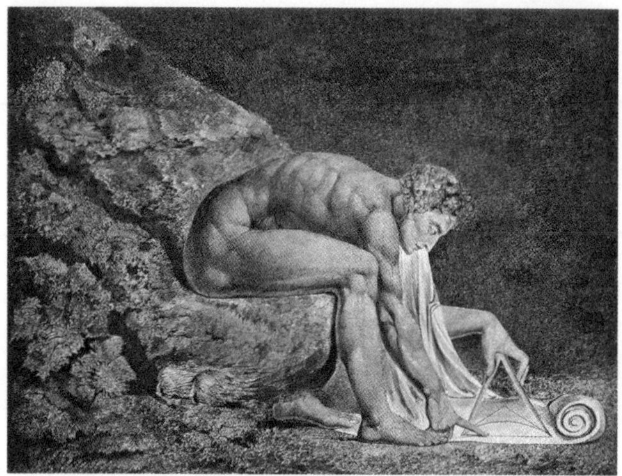

William Blake
Newton, 1795–1805
460 x 600 mm
Tate Britain, London

William Blake's pictorial comment was intended as a critique of the scientific thinking that Sir Isaac Newton's theories represented. Blake also questioned his single, fixed point of view in measurement in writing the famous text "Urizon" (your-reason). In contrast to Newton (and the vast majority of today's thinkers), for Blake, mythology was a methodology that he deemed sufficiently sound analytically that it could be entrusted with measuring the world. Based on this thinking, he set out to develop what he called a "visionary physics".

Exercises in Measurement
Miya Yoshida

"A new foundation for all measures."[1]

Over the last century, metrologists have achieved great progress in their search for precision in the standardisation of units of measurement, and most have long since been updated based on more appropriate definitions. For decades, the International Prototype Metre Bar was a historical unit for measuring length. It was first replaced by the wavelength of radiation, and then by the speed of light. Today a metre is defined as "the length of the path travelled by light in vacuum during a time interval of 1/299 792 458 of a second".[2] And, this fraction of a second can be derived from the energy structure of a caesium atom, since atomic clocks have set the benchmark for precision for almost fifty years. Following the modern definition of the metre, other units of measurement were replaced as well. Metrologists have striven to apply the same principle of measuring with light to all the other base units, especially to the kilogram, the mole, and others so as to create a common foundation for all kinds of measures. "A new foundation for all measures" – this is a slogan used by The National Metrology Institutes (NMIs) in homologising the units for all kinds of measurements. According to the NMIs, the new light-based definitions of these units will soon be completed and are likely to be legislated by 2018.[3]

---

[1] This was the headline of the news section on the website of The National Metrology Institute of Germany on 26 March 2015.

[2] http://www.bipm.org/en/publications/si-brochure/metre.html.

[3] https://goo.gl/83zR3Z.

While creating such perfect precision for measurement units is a considerable achievement, the question of *who* is actually able (or in a position) to measure such accuracy becomes inevitable. Does it still allow an individual to question the correctness of a given measurement with reasonable doubt? The quest for accuracy in measurements is connected to the modernist ideologies of "progress" and requires more complex technological facilities and higher knowledge in order for it to succeed. In 1889, when the metre unit was introduced based on the idea of the globe, that unit was not only divorced from its formerly close connection with the human body and everyday life; it became institutionalised in parallel to the emergence of professionalism and the establishment of bureaucracy. Such exploration has caused the agency and knowledge of measurement to move away from any one person and into the hands of experts – "a body of paid experts, who (a)re licensed, or otherwise recognised as being the guardians of an officially approved and restricted body of knowledge"[4]. Measurement can no longer be autonomous, and is clearly compartmentalised into symbolic and practical levels. What to measure, how to measure, and who measures – these questions have always been influenced by the culture of capitalism, bureaucracies and institutional politics, which require the standardisation and the precision of measurement (Weise, 1997). Thereby, "a new foundation for all measures" actually reflects the achievement not only of science, but also of neoliberal capitalism and bureaucratisation of society, and today these questions are more deeply entangled with them than ever before.

How, then, might it be possible to search for different ways of knowing and to exercise different concepts of measurement? How might one actually obtain a different idea of what a unit is, another way of thinking and knowing, instead of accepting everything as immutable, as things that have no fluctuation in mass, or unexplained drifts? Would it be possible to say that "a new foundation for all measures" is only the starting point for a re-thinking of measurement? Some experts answer questions about the need to replace units by saying that such an action is insignificant, that practically nothing will look different on the level of everyday life, et cetera.

---

[4] Starhawk. *Dreaming the Dark: Magic, Sex, and Politics* (Boston: Beacon Press, 1997), 199. The quote originally comes from the context of the exclusion of female labour from the economy in the establishment of capitalism in the 16th and the 17th centuries. It refers to the elevation of professionalism, as a result of which witchcraft in particular came to be regarded as unsubstantiated knowledge in society and something evil.

However, such a split is inherently problematic, as it wrongly considers an issue that is actually only the tip of the iceberg. Real changes happen invisibly; their influence may be hard to recognise in everyday life. And this may also accelerate the contemporary tendency towards basing one's beliefs solely on data, on its "process of processing" – a result provided by independently functioning institutions. This is not a superficial question that can be regarded as distanced from reality; where this shift directs us and how it reshapes our epistemologies and ontologies is a valid question. When aesthetics come into play, the "game" of measurement changes from science to art. This might suggest other ways of knowing and understanding, and guide us towards different notions and acts of measurement.

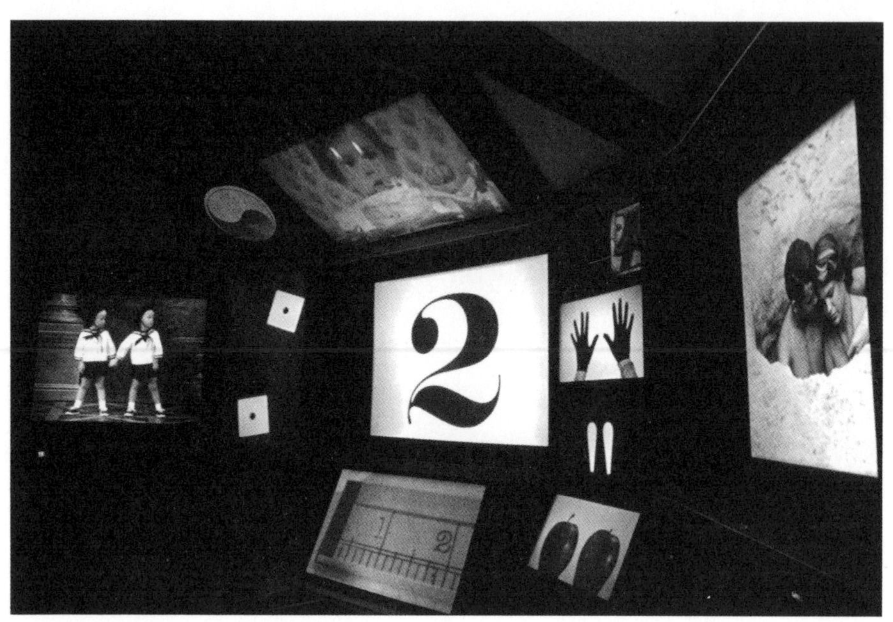

Eames used many different images at once to communicate the idea of "two" in the IBM presentation called *Think*.

Charles and Ray Eames, *Think*, 1964, multi-screen installation © 2017 Eames Office, LLC (eamesoffice.com)

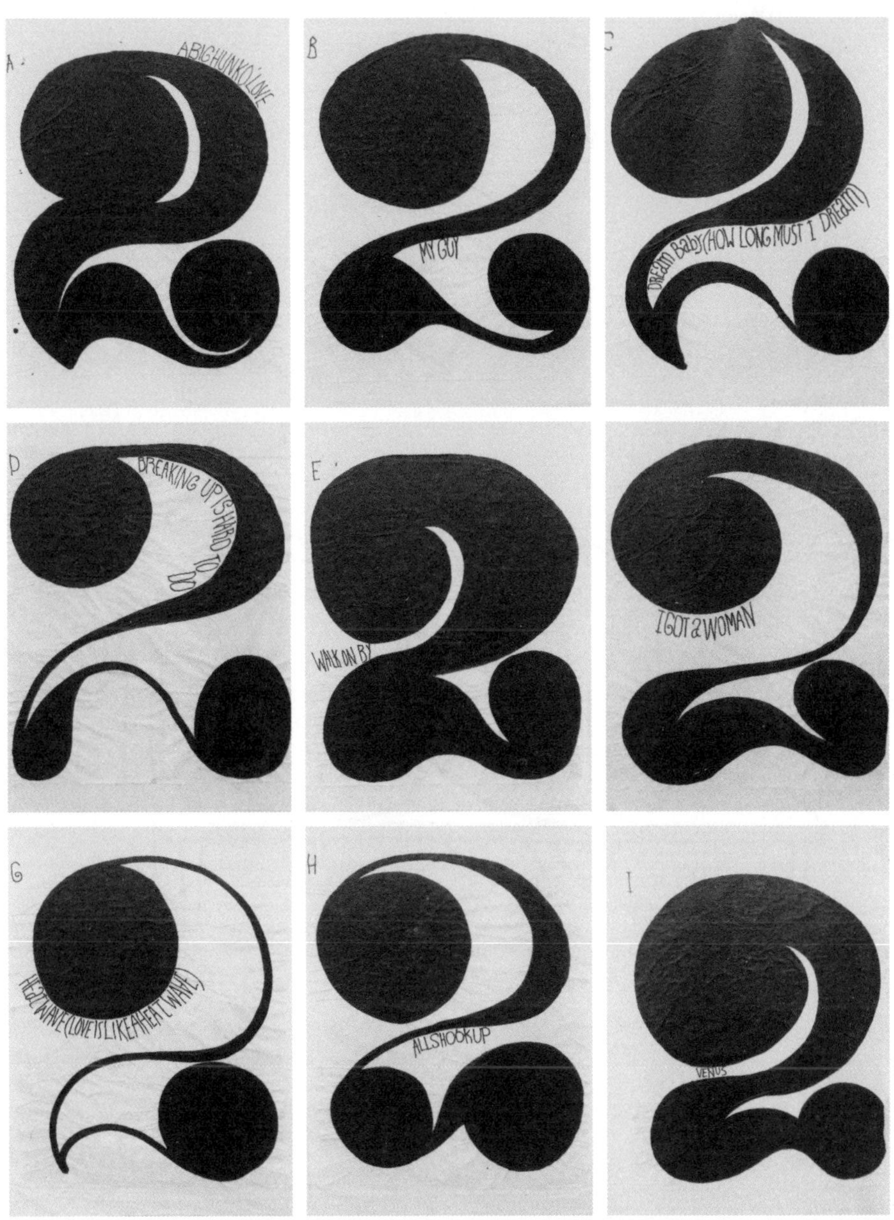

Matt Mullican, *Untitled (Learning from That Person's Work)*
(details), 2005, ink and paper collage on bedsheet,
243.8 x 167.6 cm each, courtesy the artist and
Mai 36 Galerie, Zurich

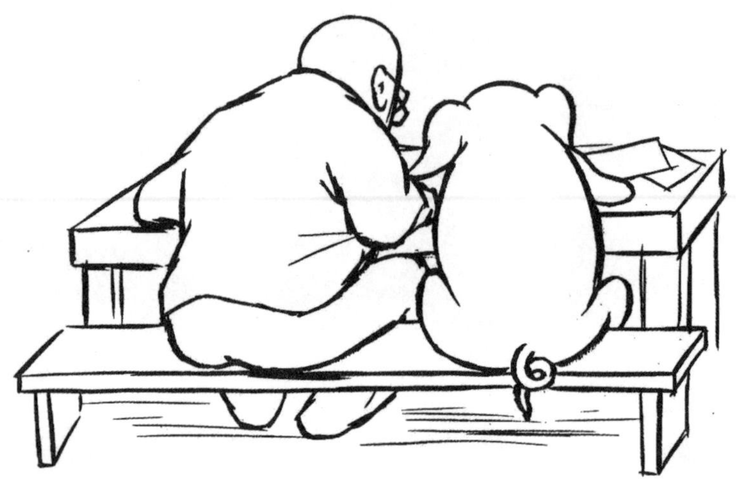

COCHON SAVANT AIDANT UN CHARCUTIER A FAIRE SES COMPTES

Chaval (Yvan Le Louarn, 1915–1968)
Cochon savant... From *Dessins parus dans
Paris Match,* 1951–1967, Paris, 2009

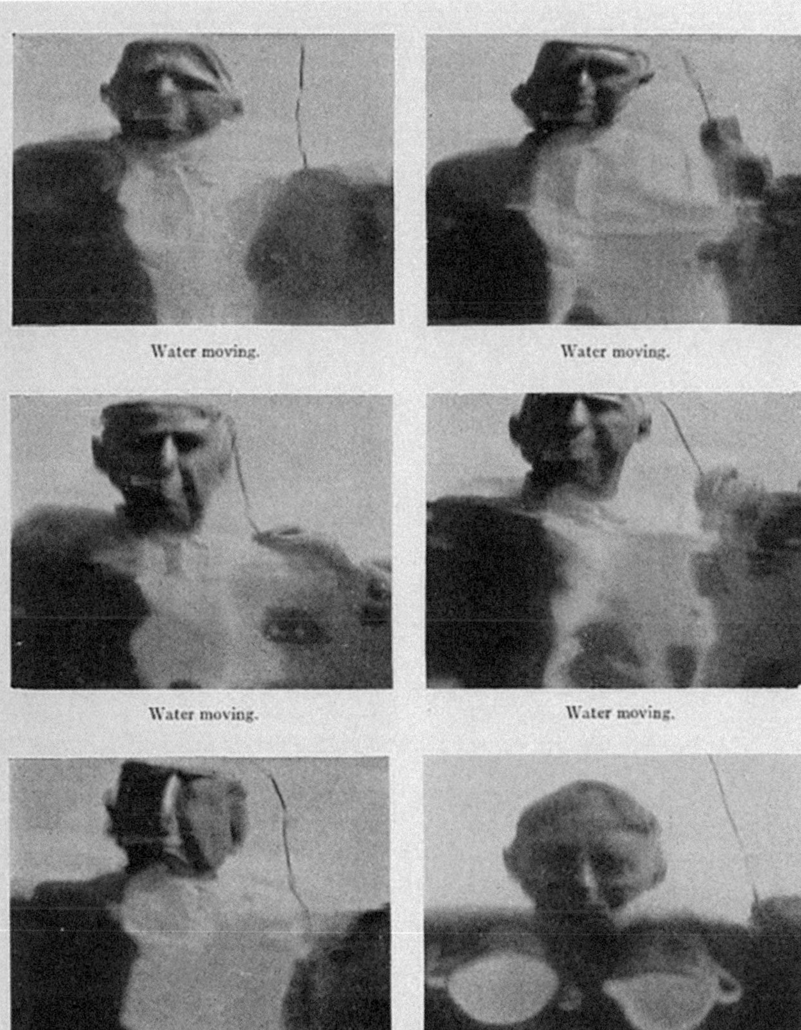

FIG. 30. AS THE FISH SEES THE ANGLER. AUTHOR AT END OF TANK
PHOTOGRAPHED FROM THE POSITION OF THE FISH UNDER
THE WATER

Edward Ringwood Hewitt, from *Secrets of
the Salmon*, New York, 1922

Unit Situational: De-Institutionalising Measurement

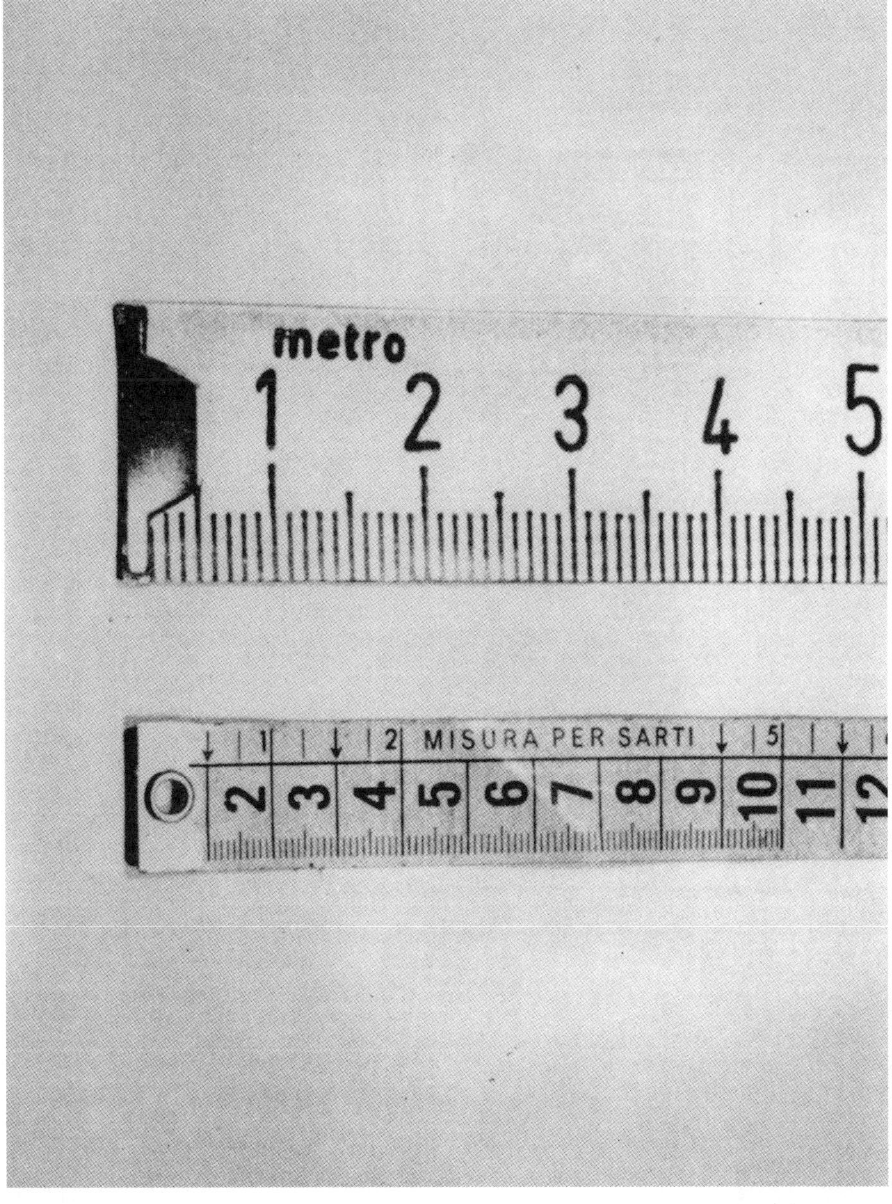

Giulia Niccolai, *Facsimile*, 1975, from *Tau/ma 5*, Achille Maramotti Editore, Reggio Emilia, 1976

The images of measuring tapes are copied and reproduced following data transmission via facsimile. The process obviously distorts the scale of the measuring devices. By juxtaposing the results of different distortions, the image shows that the absoluteness and universality of measurement is being replaced by a more situational and contextual paradigm.

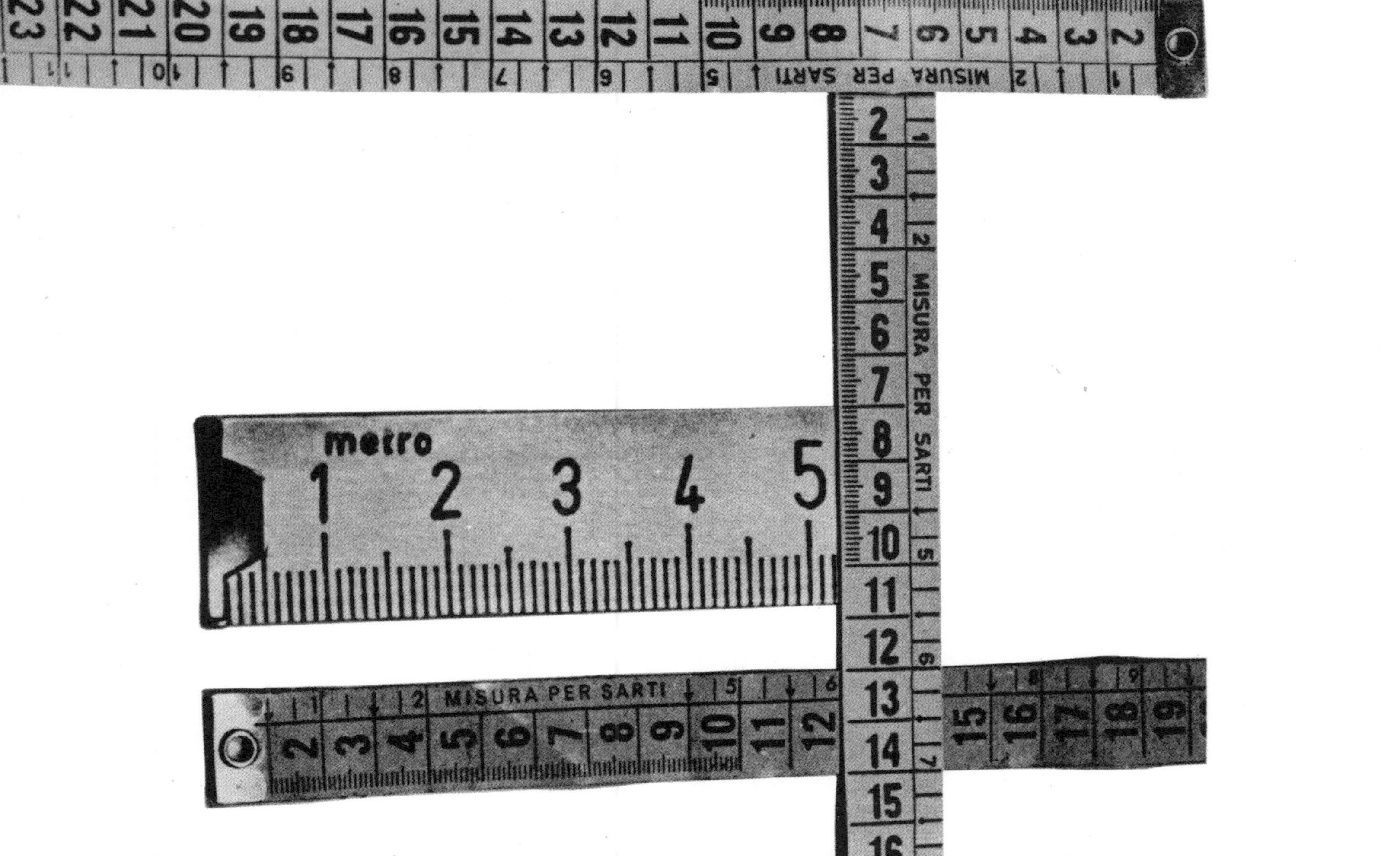

metro
MISURA PER SARTI
MISURA PER SARTI
MISURA PER SARTI

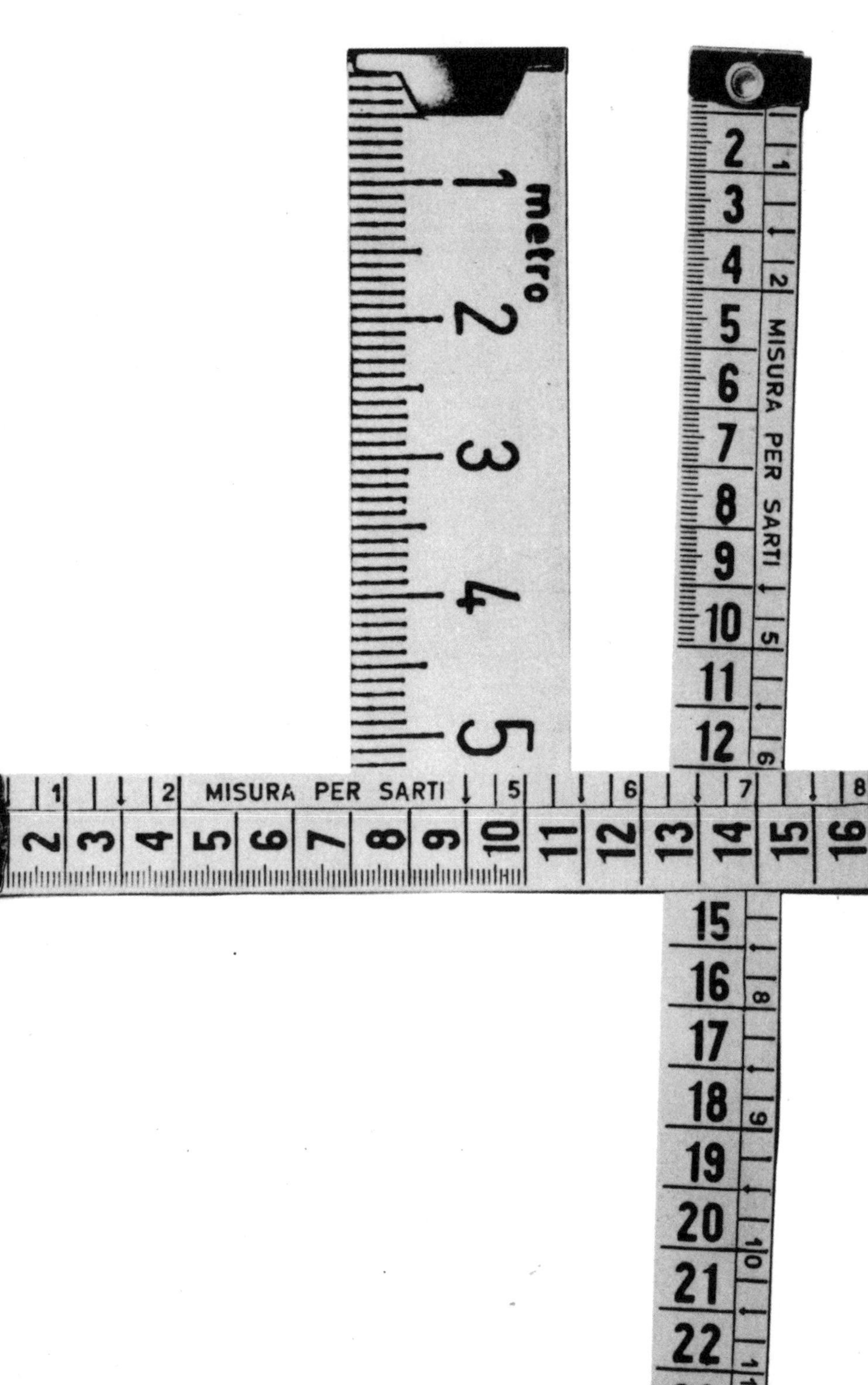

metro
1
2
3
4
5
MISURA PER SARTI
2
3
4
5
6
7
8
9
10
11
12
MISURA PER SARTI
15
16
17
18
19
20
21
22
23

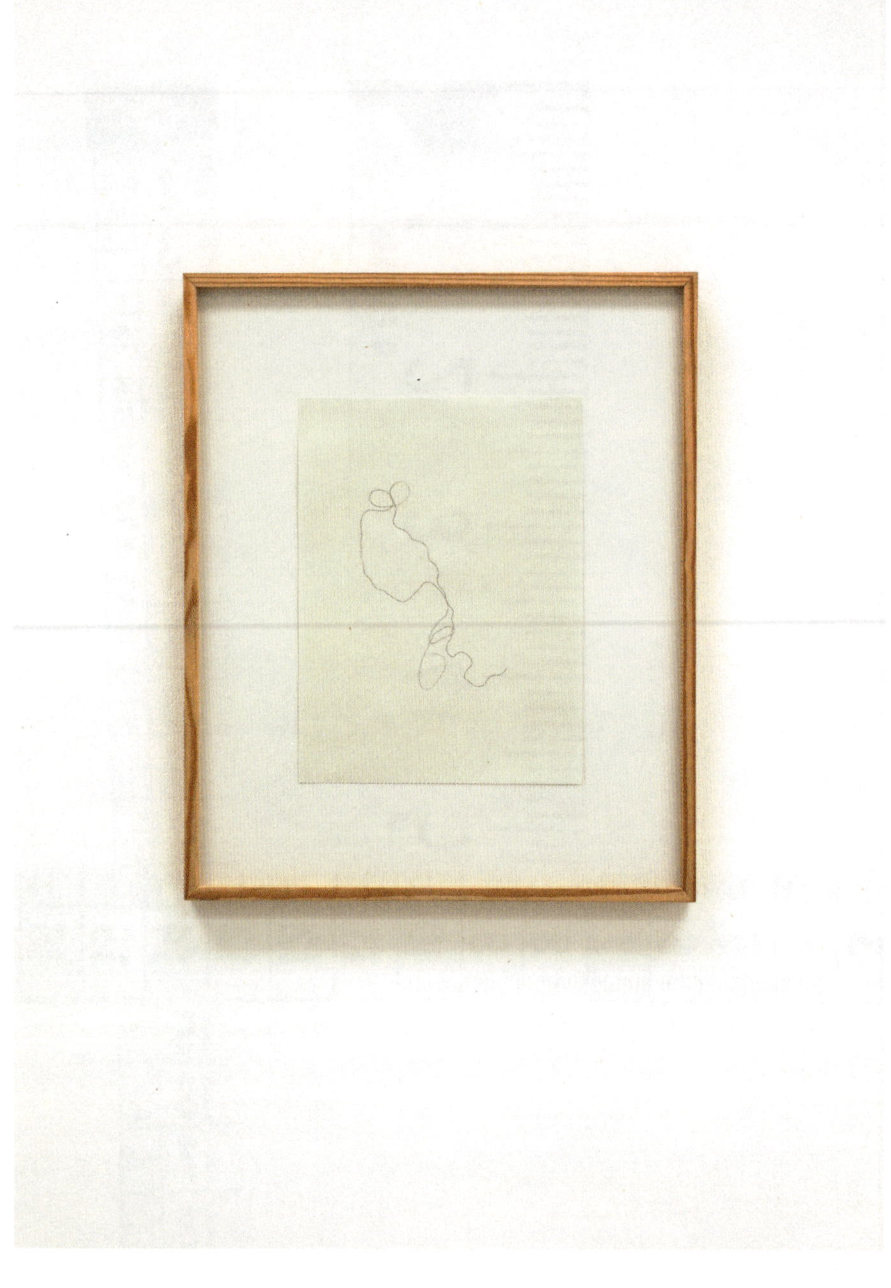

Karin Sander, *Hair Drawings*, 1998, 970 hairs
from 122 people, each pulled out and dropped
onto and fixed on a sheet of paper, 970 sheets of
paper, each 27.9 x 21.6 cm, framed each 45.3 x
38.7 cm, photos © Andrea Rosetti, 2012

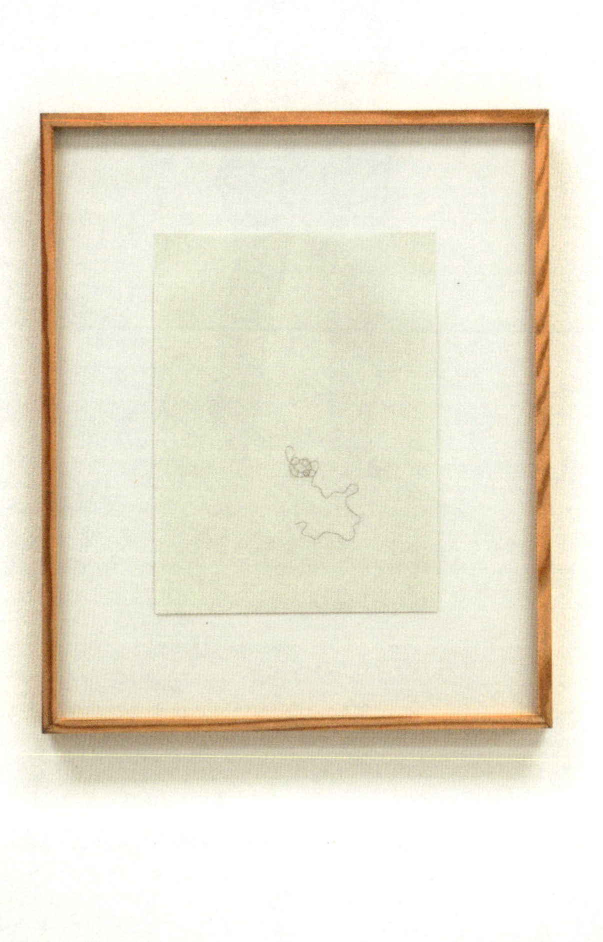

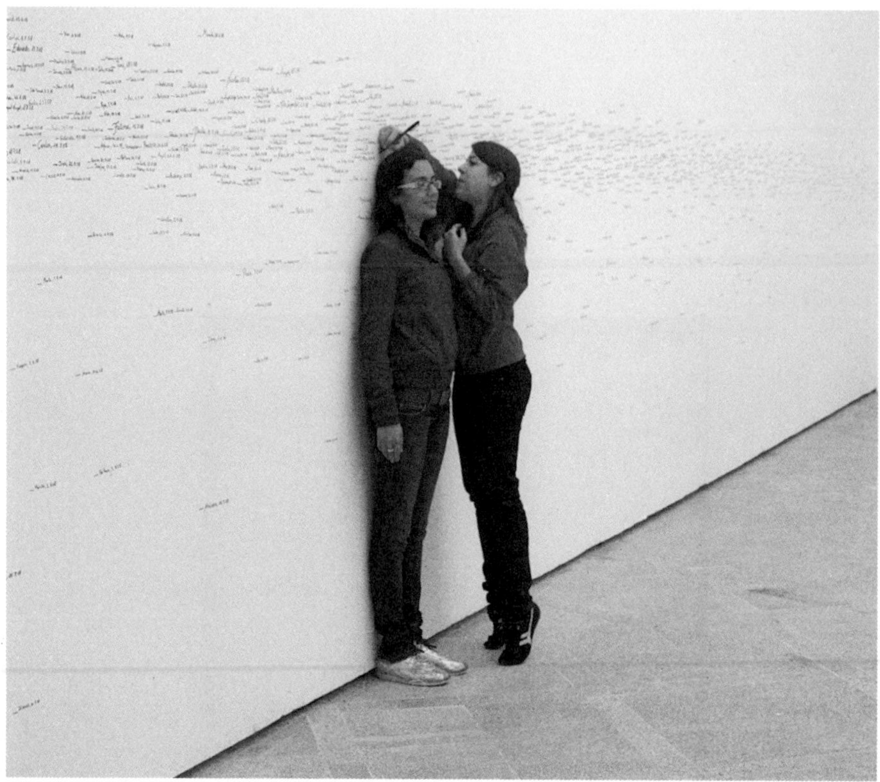

Roman Ondák, *Measuring the Universe*, 2007, performance, dimensions variable, photo: © Roman Ondak, courtesy the artist, Galerie Martin Janda, Vienna, Johnen Galerie, Berlin, and Galerie Esther Schipper, Berlin

In his work, Ondák considers every person to be a unit, and claims that measurement is about relationality, not accuracy. In one sense, it is the visualisation of a statistical inquiry regarding museum visitors. In normal statistics, each person is abstracted in such a way that he or she is readable as "one". Here, each "one" is given a physicality of its own. This highlights an unexpected combination of data: counting visitors and combining the results with information about their height, date of birth, name, et cetera. Ondák thus turns the current evaluation system of museums, which is based solely on sociological methods of statistics, on its head.

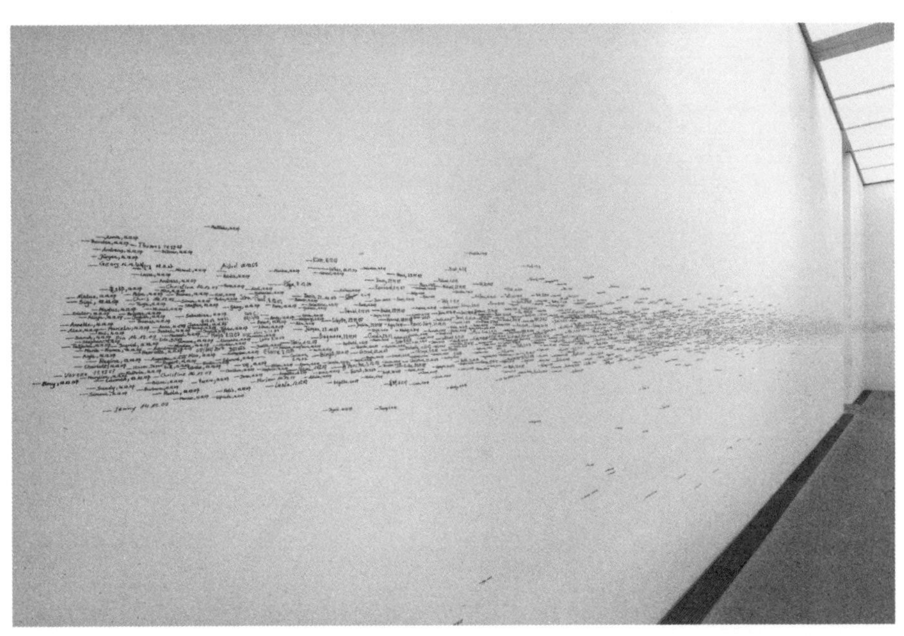

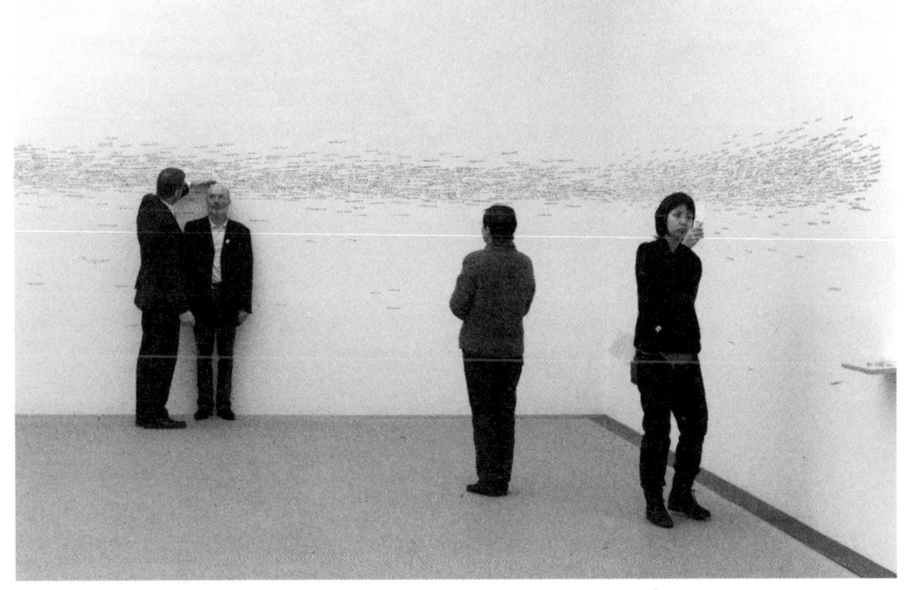

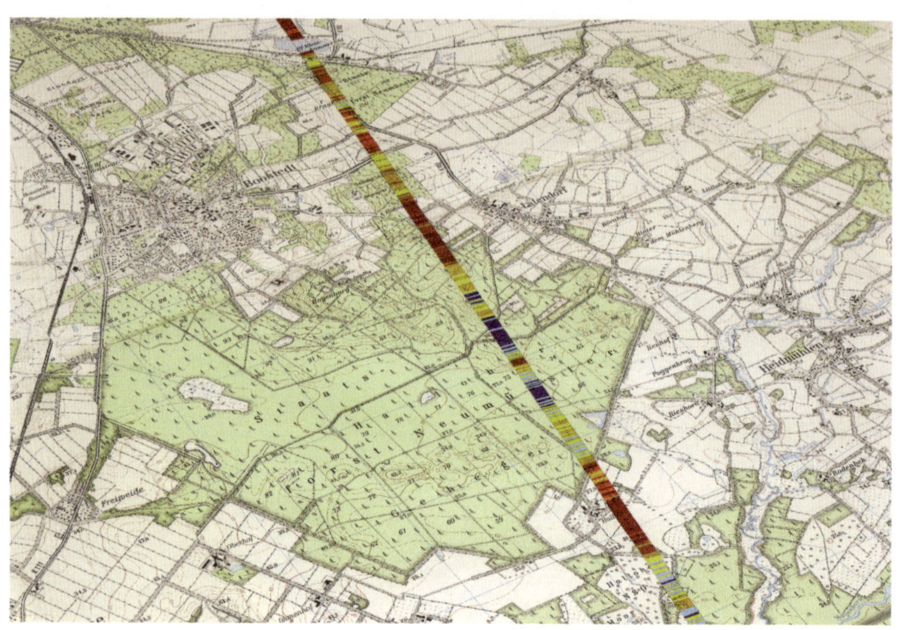

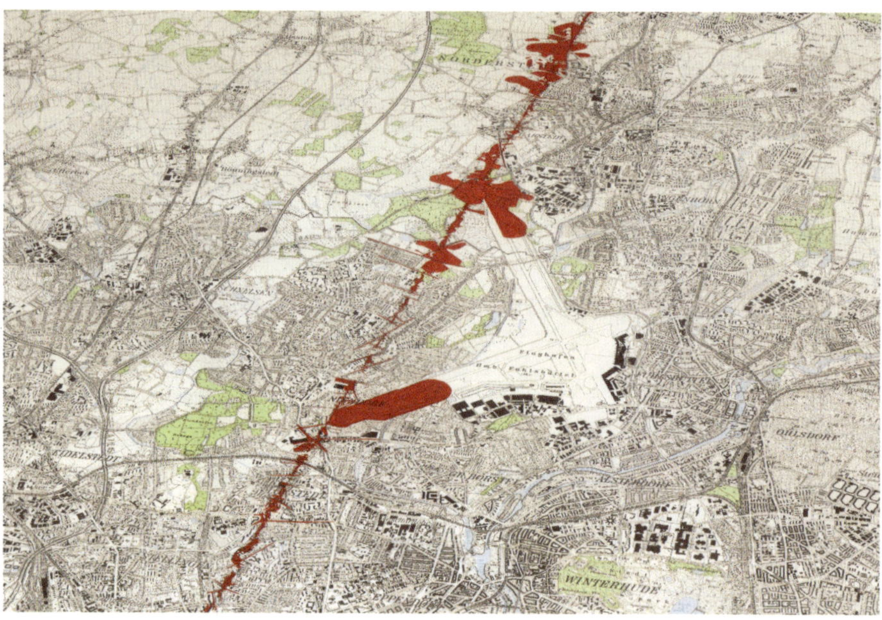

Till Krause, top: *Handykarte / Mobile Phone Map* (detail),
bottom: *Blickfeldkarte / Field of View Map* (detail), 2001,
acrylic paint on offset print / eighteen topographic maps,
1:25000, mounted on map canvas, 408 x 91.5 cm, photos
© Tobias Hübel

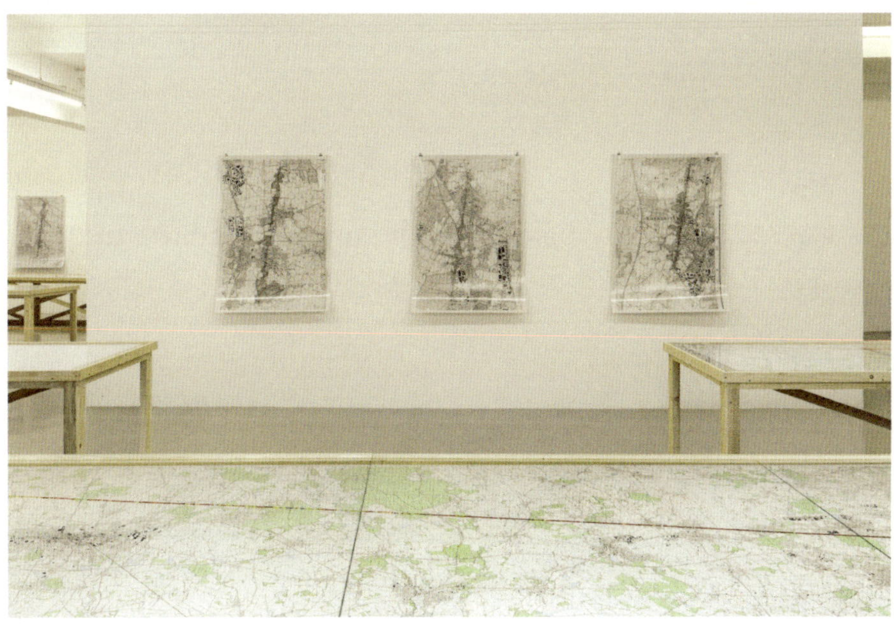

Till Krause, front: *Handykarte / Mobile Phone Map*, 2001, acrylic paint on topographic maps, 1:25000, mounted on map canvas, 408 x 91.5 cm, back: *Blickfeldkarten / Field of View Maps*, 1:25000, light jet print on baryta paper, 128 x 93 cm, 2001 / 2016, photo © GAK Gesellschaft für Aktuelle Kunst, Tobias Hübel

Maps are intricate interfaces, where politics, economy, and technology encounter each other in their respective uses of measurement. Special signs, particular fonts, specific ways of depicting, and other detailed rules for mapping provide a good representation of the great accumulation of knowledge regarding measuring lands and territories over the course of history. Till Krause reflects such condensed histories in his map of Schleswig-Holstein, a federal state in Northern Germany – but what sets his work apart from standard mapping practices is that he specifically adds measurement practices perceived by his body to his further development of established mapping systems. The artist walked from his home in Hamburg to Kiel – a distance of approximately 100 kilometres – with the map in his hand, and then compared what he saw around him with what the map depicted. He counted components of the landscapes and urbanscapes he passed –

tall buildings, houses, theatres, stations, football fields, bakeries, gardens, car dealers, cows and horses, streets, small paths, the mobile phone coverage, et cetera – and listed them on a sheet of paper appended to the map, but also made marks on the map itself. To name only one distinguishing aspect of his practice, it makes sense to consider the intermittent red lines drawn into the map, where each new beginning and end denotes the distance that the artist was able to see without his view being blocked by buildings, hills, or other disturbances. While his measurement follows the rules of cartography – that "a map should be different from the reality" – or "the map is not the territory" (Foucault), it simultaneously becomes his personal and temporal trajectory. Corresponding to this, in a certain sense, Krause's works overlay the order of the universal with the parameters of contemporary society and realities from a personal point of view in order to create a visualisation of the limited validity of measurement in time-space. His works collect historical, sociological, and economic measurements in the format of a map; it thus ceases being a map and instead becomes a medium that, in a mode of artistic practice akin to early examples of land art and/or conceptual art, creates marginal and layered annotations and comments on measured reality.

Time:
a wind that blows both inside and outside the tree.

Moss:
when time rolls out the green carpet.

Simon Lewis, *Observances*, 2007,
high-resolution giclée prints,
60 x 20 cm, courtesy the artist
and Galerie Ursula Walbroel.

Dust:
when time dresses objects in its passing.

Sleep:
an undisclosed number of rehearsals for the end.

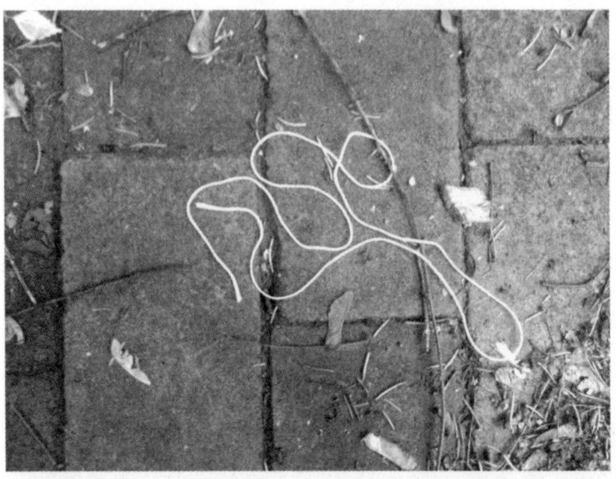

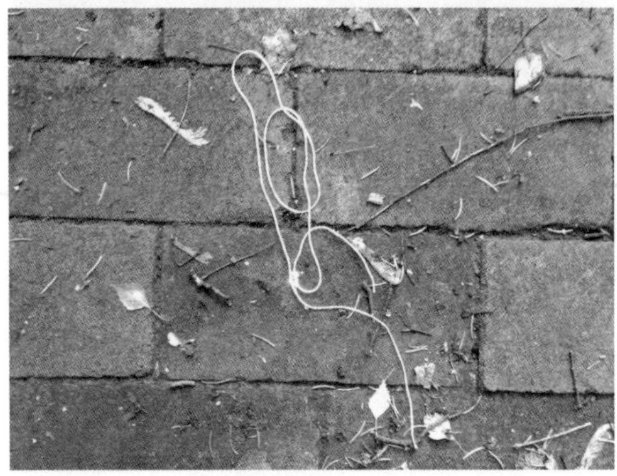

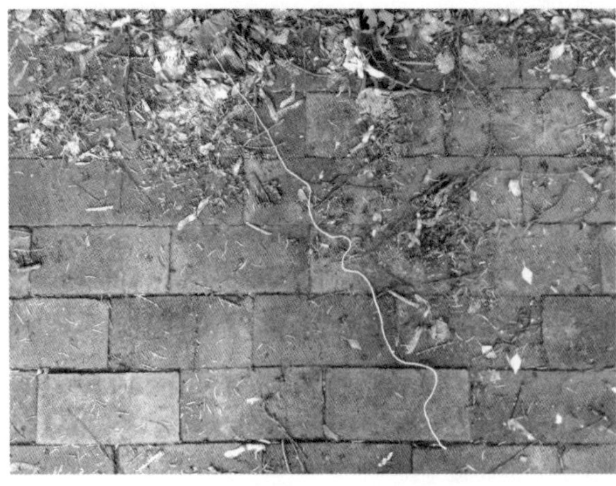

Hwayeon Nam, *Ant Time*, 2015,
27.5 x 34 cm © Hwayeon Nam

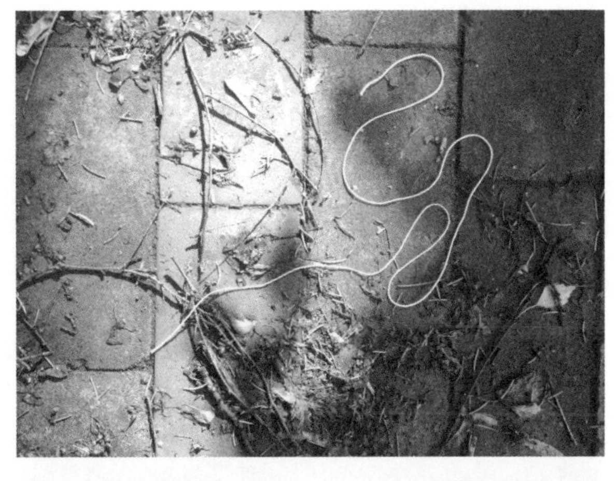

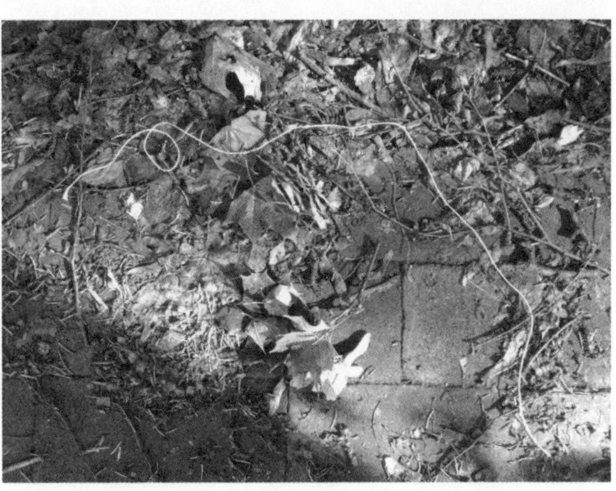

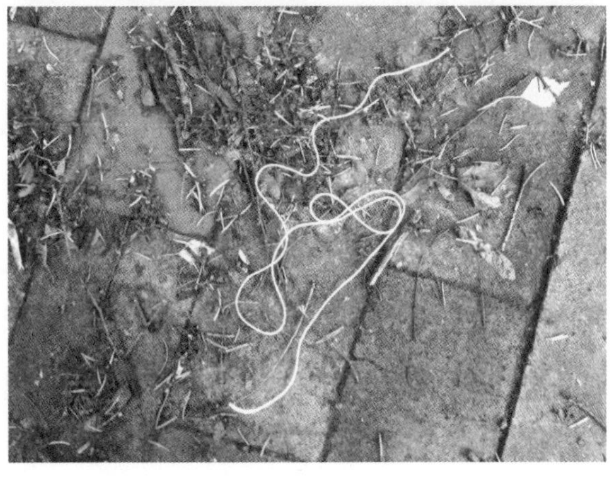

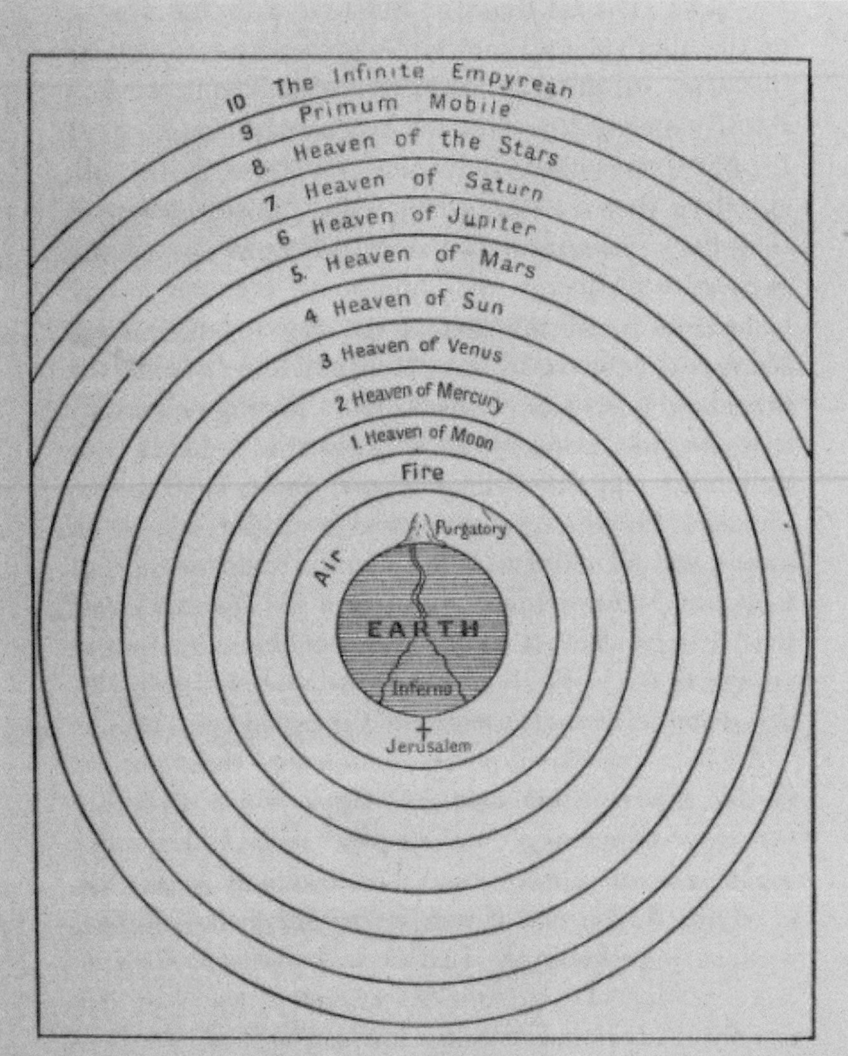

Fig. 45. The Universe of Dante.

The Universe of Dante, from *M. A. Orr, Dante and the Early Astronomers,* London and Edinburgh, 1914.

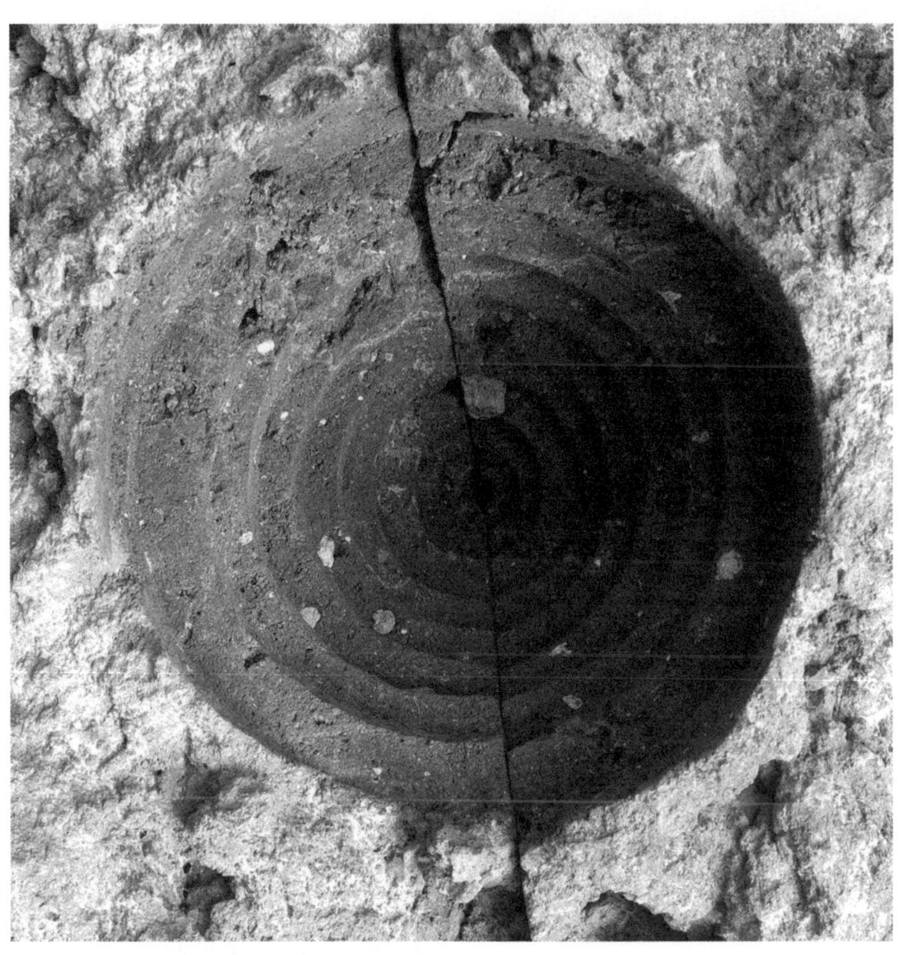

Romana Schmalisch, *Hölle im Durchschnitt
(Hell in cut-away view)*, 2008, lava rock,
32 × 32 × 32 cm

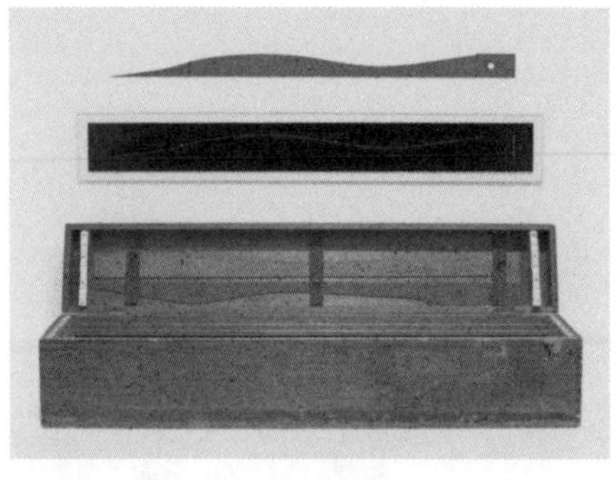

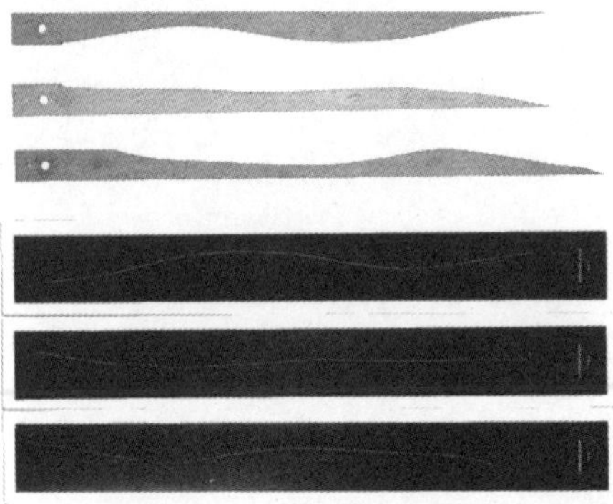

Marcel Duchamp, *3 Standard Stoppages*, 1913–14, wood box 28.2 x 129.2 x 22.9 cm, with three threads each 100 cm in length, glued to three painted canvas strips (13.3 x 120 cm), each mounted on a glass panel (18.4 x 125.4 x 0.6 cm), three wood slats (6.2 x 109.2 x 0.2 cm), shaped along one edge to match the curves of the threads

In *3 Standard Stoppages* (1913, Paris), from a height of one metre, Duchamp dropped three one-metre-long strings onto pieces of canvas, where they were subsequently fixed; he modified them to become his own "unit" in a seemingly paradoxical, chance-based practice of measuring. Later, this unit served as a conceptual basis in the development of one of his most renowned works, *The Large Glass*. Instead of adhering to traditional ideas of perspective, the work, which is based on a module he produced, presented an alternative understanding of measuring space. In this pseudo-scientific experiment, he used chance operations not only as a creative method, but also as a conceptual space that was meant to liberate technical as well as visual vocabularies of measurement. "Though he glibly referred to *3 Standard Stoppages* as 'a joke about the meter', his description of its outcome reads like a mathematical theorem: 'If a straight horizontal thread one meter long falls from a height of one meter onto a horizontal plane twisting as it pleases [it] creates a new image of the unit of length.'" (Website MoMA)

Unit Situational:
De-Institutionalising Measurement

In response to the new invisible realities that were identified based on previous discoveries such as X-rays, electrons, radioactivity, wireless telegraphy, et cetera, in the early 20th century, it is well known in art history that, at that time, Marcel Duchamp was an individual who prominently engaged with the concept of "units" and liberated the concept of accuracy in measurement to respond to notions derived from theories regarding a non-Euclidian space. With his ideas of a "playful physics", from a discipline of chance, he established a mechanically and symbolically "fixed" unit (*3 Standard Stoppages*) for measuring quasi-realities.[5] Based on his awareness of different existing ideas and systems of measurement, he joked that the single-minded French used metrology in bureaucratisation, thus undermining the legitimacy of "accuracy" and "succession" without any manipulations or contracts. His works visually presented how the notion of measurement expands and shifts the location of accuracy, from a rigorous structure and system of measurement to the imaginary and its inherent physicality, which includes flexible, and indeterminable and unpredictable factors – with the pleasure of measurement. Although his idea of unit is known for its connection with the non-Euclidean science that was emerging at the time, it is also relevant in that it is linked back to older systems of measurement that are based on "life", the pursuit of living, where units are not fixed, are more or less accurate, and include a systemic place for the *blank* inside the unit.

One such example is the traditional Japanese system of weights and measures, called 'shakkan' (尺貫).[6] For measuring volume, it employs a multitude of units that is confusing for those who are not familiar with them. They are called 'koku'(石), 'sho'(升), and 'go'(合), and are not based on abstract units; instead, the units are determined by the amount of rice needed each day for one person to survive (no matter how hungry s/he is).

---

[5] He proposed establishing an alternative Bureau of Standards: a Ministry of Coincidence in a "Regime of Coincidence". In his seminal work *3 Standard Stoppages* (1913) he dropped three one-metre-long strings onto canvases, letting them twist and they pleased, and thus created a new shape for the unit of length ("the metre diminished") based on gravity and a discipline of chance. The unit, which does not fit any system exactly, but instead exists as accurately "fixed chance", is later used for the series of major works that he created on his search for an alternative understanding of measuring space.

[6] In history, there are many similar examples of units based on human labour: the "yoke" in Kent, the "Jungeram" in Ancient Rome, the "acre/ac" in England, the "Morgen" in Germany, and many others. A "yoke", for example, was a unit of land measurement used for tax purposes at the time of the Domesday Book. It was equal to a quarter of a sulung. A sulung was the amount of land that could be ploughed by four ox-pairs (or approximately two hides), a yoke was therefore a pair of oxen, representing the amount of land that could be cultivated by a pair.

One 'go' equals the amount of rice required for a meal for one person, and one 'koku' is the amount of rice needed for one person to survive for one year (according to traditional calendars, one year is counted as 360 days). Furthermore, based on the idea of the yield of rice per 'koku', there are also units that were and partly still are used for the size of arable land / space – 'tan' (反), 'tsubo' (坪), 'jyo' (畳). One 'tan' equals the size of land on which one 'koku' (the amount of rice needed for one person each year) can be harvested. One 'tsubo' equals the size of land in which three 'go' (the amount of rice needed for one person each day) can be harvested. What interests me are the historical flexibility and adjustability that can be observed in the concept of the units employed, and this, correspondingly, is obviously also true for the system as a whole. Depending on the quality of land and the increased efficiency that it has been possible to achieve as a result of technological and agricultural developments, as well as accidental circumstances such as climate, over the last 500 years, the system has frequently been adjusted. Simultaneously, the space of flexibility and adjustability retained its connection with life on a micro-level. Under the conditions of modernity, systems like the 'shakkan' have, however, been disparagingly understood as imprecise, or inarticulate, especially after the metric system, along with other ideas of modernity, were introduced in Japan. It can be said that the system embraces phenomena and processes that are connected with measuring and holds on to ideas such as subjectivity, indeterminacy, and flexibility in its conceptualisations of units; thereby, the unit is rendered situational.

In the 1950s, the Situationist International flaunted the power of individual imaginaries to reflect on the city, the spectacle, and everyday life. Their approach, which includes concepts such as the temporalisation of space by means of an anti-objectifying stance, produced *psychogeography*, *dérive* (the "art of drifting"), and a harsh critique of advancing capitalism, which, for the Situationists as well as for other materialistic "anti" ideologies, was mediated by objects. Today, social relationships are mediated and produced not by objects, but by algorithms with an ever-increasing speed of circulation. Neoliberal economics, commodification, and social alienation have expanded from the level of culture and life to become a *necropolitics* of life and death. On the search for a notion of accuracy that reflects such contemporary realities, emotions, conditions, chances, surroundings, processes, et cetera need to be embraced in the concept of unit as well. Current theories of measurement, including quantum physics or quantum field theory, emphasise the inseparability of acts of measurement from each given, or hypothetical situation. The incorporation of Situationist thinking in the sphere of acts of measurement can also be seen in more recent avant-garde art and post-conceptual art, for example, in the personalisation of the universal unit (Stanley Brouwn), performative acts of adding an unexpected register, and the indexing and creation of parameters of measurement driven by its own purpose (Roman Ondák).

The previous pages take a look at various other examples of different accuracies of measurement in pataphysical experiments based on the Situationist notion of the unit. The *unit situational* visually presents how the notion of measurement can be expanded – and how it can shift the *location* of accuracy. It proposes re-imagining measurement, and represents a counter-approach to the rigidity previously asserted; it gives more space to the concept of unit as well as to that of numbers in order to show the various possible dimensions of measurement. Situation makes the concept!

Ant Time by Hwayeon Nam (2015) is a series of documentary photographs, each measuring 27.5 x 34 cm, that represent her attempt to capture how ants perceive time. This is done without imposing the structure of man-constructed time on them. Closely following the movements of the ants, the work traces their trajectories with a ninety-centimetre-long thread, and merges them with measurements of the duration of their unrecognisably subtle movements. In *Ant Time*, the thread marks the beginning and the end of each process of capturing ant time. This not only makes the ant, as the subject, perform its own time, it also includes the action as a central element for determining a unit of time. Accordingly, the duration performed by ants varies and also appears in a visually unique way in each photo document. This simultaneously also points to a different conceptual idea of time units. Standard space measurement is augmented so as to also be a measurement of time.

Ant Time is a combination of photographic realism, (pseudo-)scientific observation, and linguistic subversion that was made with the aim of problematising the generic abstraction of time and space. It is rather exceptional for ants to be recognised as "individuals", as Nam does. Normally, exemplified by the form of the ant farm, ants are symbolised as a mass. In the field of science, they are observed within the context of studies on colonies and how they behave in relation to their collective, and usually categorised into certain role patterns with regard to their role in social organisation. Understanding ants by means of such an approach puts the focus on measuring and evaluating ants predominantly according to their social value. Nam is, however, interested in the individuality of the single ant as a measurer of time, which seems similar to the approach adopted by Dr. Naruse – who elaborates the individuality of Medaka fish in the chapter "Dance with Accuracies". Individuality, namely, is still of importance for alternative measurements.

The method of tracing in measurement has already been used in a number of experiments within the context of art. David Hockney, for instance, apprehended how lines are drawn through following lines in drawings with his eyes. He imagined re-enacting the breath and the movement of the artist, and that, to him, was the act of measuring. For Andy Warhol, the act of tracing was a method of measurement that he used in order to understand the subject/object and its structure as well as its connection with the line traced in space.

Ant Time traces the breath, the viewing scope of the creatures as well as the spatial relationships they form with their bodies and the human body, connected by acts of measuring. The units in *Ant Time* are based on the ants' actions, which therefore means that every unit is presented in visually different ways, and the unit also varies as a result of different durations; 42 seconds, 47 seconds, 56 seconds, 1 minute and 3 seconds, et cetera. The variations are infinite. This resembles how time is perceived when fishing. It is the fish-to-come who decides about the consequences of your actions.[7] In a way, the subject of time can be transposed onto anything. Contemporary life governed by split-second timing increases the speed of its creation of precision, of approaching an idealised dot in the measurement of time.[8] *Ant Time* is opposed to the acceleration of exactitudes of time to the dot and re-centres the bodies of the ants and their movements, shifting from the gaze of human beings to that of ants. This is an animistic perspective on measuring time; it indicates the possibility of time re-centring any other life or objects – *anima* – so as to know and understand the biodiversity of the world from a multiplicity of perspectives in measurement. However, it should not be forgotten that it is the artist herself who establishes all the set-ups – observing, tracing, measuring and documenting – and, thereby, *Ant Time* shows the temporary result of negotiating between two different times: one Nam's, the other the ants'. The work is an attempt to find a way for the two species to co-existence. "Time is out of joint." Referring to the famous quote from *Hamlet*, *Ant Time* reveals different dimensions of time and visualises the fusion of two times, which is another way of perceiving accuracy in time – an accuracy that is based on others and on humans' lives and actions.

With their playful take on everyday physics, Karin Sander's *Hair Drawings* (1998) effectively demonstrate (but do not simply illustrate) measurement in a way that approaches pataphysical thinking. Without prior warning, the artist pulled one or two hairs from the heads of 80 individuals she encountered, dropped the hair, specifically and individually curled as it was, on a sheet of paper, based on gravity and chance, and fixed it on that support. Each *Hair Drawing* was then framed in a format of 28 x 21 cm – always with sufficient blank space around it. Every single hair is a thin individual line representing the respective person's own (hair) identity and (hair) individuality. None of them are the same.

---

[7] http://actionbiodiversity.org/2016/09/how-does-a-fish-measure-distance/

[8] For example, if we look at the measuring of time in a sports competition: setting a record time for a 100-m track race comprises competition for a difference of 0.02 – 0.1 seconds. https://en.wikipedia.org/wiki/100_metres

The artist observes the sensible difference of each single human hair in a range of 17 to 181 μm (millionths of a metre), and comments: "(The hairs) differ not only in length, colour, and thickness but also in the form, in an infinite variety of lines."

The *Hair Drawings* expand the investigation that is traced here to the language game of numbers. As part of the IBM-sponsored exhibit called *Think!*, American designers Charles and Ray Eames used many different images representing numbers, among which they examined the numeral "two" in order to communicate the idea of "two-ness". The images cover a wide range: twins, a young couple, two dots, two hands, two apples, two eyes, a Yin-Yang circle, the Arabic character for two, two centimetres on a ruler, et cetera. All these images are juxtaposed with each other so as to visualise the variety of "two". Using a similar approach, but in a more abstract and subtle way, the *Hair Drawings* expose a line consisting of hair to gravity and visualise the limitless diversification with eighty different versions of "one". A hair can have any kind or shape of line in order to show all the formal potential it includes – from "as it is", to "as if", and "as if it is". According to websites such as BioNumbers, the average number of hairs on the head of each person is approx. 90,000 to 150,000.[9] Just imagine, in the case of a couple, 180,000–300,000 possibilities of "one"! More speculatively, in a crowded train station, billions of billions of possibilities of "one" are constantly in motion. The *Hair Drawings* therefore point to the conceptual possibility of an infinite "one", which even includes time-space. This is, paradoxically, almost "all", the biggest possible opposite to "one". By disrupting the grammar of the reductive, operative, and mediative features that numbers have, the series of drawings thus transforms the concept of "one". Simultaneously, the *Hair Drawings* represent a possibility to "think number as a verb, not as a noun". Social scientist David Bloor has stated that, corresponding to the historical development of technologies, "numbers came to perform a new function by indicating the properties of the moving and active process of change", and he emphasises the necessity of the imagination that is needed to reinterpret the concept of numbers. His words reference Ancient Greek mathematics as well as contemporary computation theories; the *Hair Drawings* present how numbers perform in a space in contemporary daily encounters, and demonstrate a method that helps understand numbers as flexible and imaginative entities. Instead of using vocabulary such as "probability", "variability", or even references to an "untranslatability of numbers", the works mentioned here relocate the site of "number" outside of mathematical terrain, and give imaginary space to number – by being playful and maniacal at the same time.

---

[9] http://bionumbers.hms.harvard.edu/bionumber.aspx?id=101509

While surrealist aesthetics intentionally employed irrationality, calculations often imply a mathematical obsession and create numerical irrationality. *Hölle im Durchschnitt (Hell in cut-away view)* by Romana Schmalisch (2008) is a sculptural work that the artist made from a carved piece of lava rock as a part of her exhibition *Il braccio di Lucifero si pone 645 1⁄3 braccia*. The Italian title refers to a 16th-century study that set out to measure the length of Lucifer's arm, taking the detailed descriptions of hell and purgatory that Dante Alighieri presents in his *Divine Comedy* as its point of departure. With his obsession for mathematically precise measurements, he gives an almost visual quality to his text and attests to his belief in precision, despite the text's clearly metaphysical character. The strong fascination with Dante's ekphrastic text has given rise to numerous attempts at pictorial renderings – Botticelli's illustration being one eminent example. As the title quotation suggests, subsequent research was undertaken not only from an artistic, but especially from scientific points of view.

The biography of Galileo includes a fictitious scene, in which he, speaking in front of his audience at the Accademia Fiorentina, speculates about the size of Lucifer based on the classic aesthetics of proportion and measurement. "If the face of the giant is the size of Saint Peter's cone (the massive sculpture of a pinecone standing in the courtyard behind the Belvedere in Vatican City)", Galileo proclaims triumphantly, "it will be five arm-lengths and a half. Since men are usually eight heads tall, the giant's face will be eight times as large. Therefore, he will be forty-four arm-lengths tall." From this, he develops a formula: "Dante, the man, is to the giant as three is to forty-four. The relation of a giant to the arm of Lucifer is the same as the man is to the giant. The formula then must be three is to forty-four, as forty-four is to X. Therefore the arm of Lucifer is 645 meters. Since the length of an arm is generally one-third of the entire height, we can say that Lucifer's height will be 1.935 arm-lengths."[10]

When events that seem unfathomable are supposed to be expressed, historical cases such as this reveal the uncanny rhetorical power that is exerted by seemingly accurate numbers. Not only is this due to the habitual pull felt around all common conventionalities – numbers appear to have had a specific psychological potential to convince based merely on their presence. In ancient Greece, the numeral "1000" was also the word for "infinity". The Argentinian novelist and essayist César Aira recently provided his readers with contemporary descriptions of similar rhetorical effects as well as of the uncanny role that numbers have come to play in global economies. He is in a very playful, yet melancholic mood, when, in his short novel *Duchamp in Mexico*, he lets a reluctant traveller in the

---

[10] Quoted from James Reston, Jr., *Galileo: A Life* (New York and London: Harper Collins, 1994), 26–27.

new era of global economic inequality experience the conventional power of numbers as he scrounges through used bookstores in boomtown Mexico City. Every time the protagonist takes a walk, he somehow encounters one and the same large-format book on Marcel Duchamp for sale – at ridiculous prices. That, in itself, is not so very surprising; what really starts to get to him is not only that this book popularising the European avant-garde appears wherever he goes, but also that the prices rise and fall with no recognisable pattern. The price changes randomly along with the arbitrary walk, but once the value is expressed in a continuous sequence of written-out numbers, it creates the impression that there is an invisible structure, or at least a hidden script. If that is so, something that did not previously exist as a structure starts to take shape and appears as a structuralised phenomenon. Framing the recurring encounters with the Duchamp book as a repetitive event by means of numbers affects the situation and fabricates values and structures where there had been none.

By referring back to the endless historical debates concerning the length of Lucifer's arm over centuries and up to the present, Schmalisch's model of Dante's *Inferno* mockingly applies ancient calculations and depicts the circles of hell carved into a piece of lava. The sculpture, which is made from one solid block of lava, allows viewers to develop a clearer sense of the surreal aspects of rationality, or of something one could call the *surrational* absurdity that lies in the dysfunctionality in the "precision" of measurement.

As seen in the examples above, units are reconceptualised by specific situational encounters. By adding an animistic perspective to a mixed perspective, Nam adds an unexpected register that indexes and creates parameters of measurement in order to renegotiate time between humans and ants. Sander questions the abstractions encountered in the numerical quality of symbolic objects and speculates that the nature of numerical abstraction is infinite, thus counter to the understanding of number as precision; while Schmalisch demonstrates the precision that can be lost when measurement becomes a speculative mathematical obsession and pursuit in numbers. These three art practices can be understood as bringing methods of measurements back closer to our bodies and as expanding the horizon of acts of measuring within the banality of everyday life in order to shift the location of accuracy in measurement.

From Universality to Ubiquity of Measurement

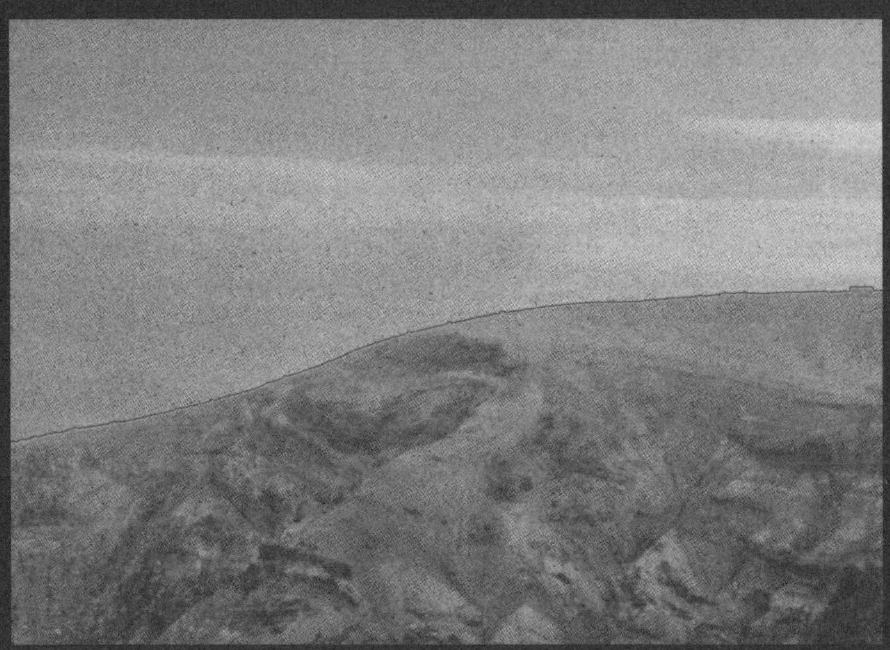

Shiho Yoshida, *Survey/Mountain*, 2016,
Lambda print, 50.8 x 61 cm © Shiho
Yoshida, courtesy Yumiko Chiba Associates.

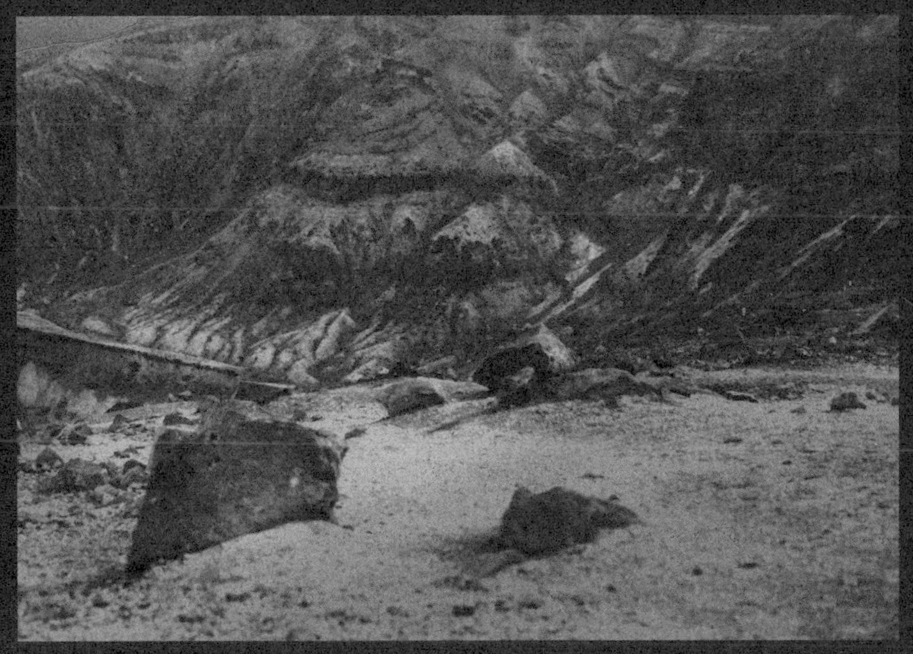

Shiho Yoshida, *Survey/Mountain*, 2016,
Lambda print, 100 x 69 cm © Shiho Yoshida,
courtesy Yumiko Chiba Associates.

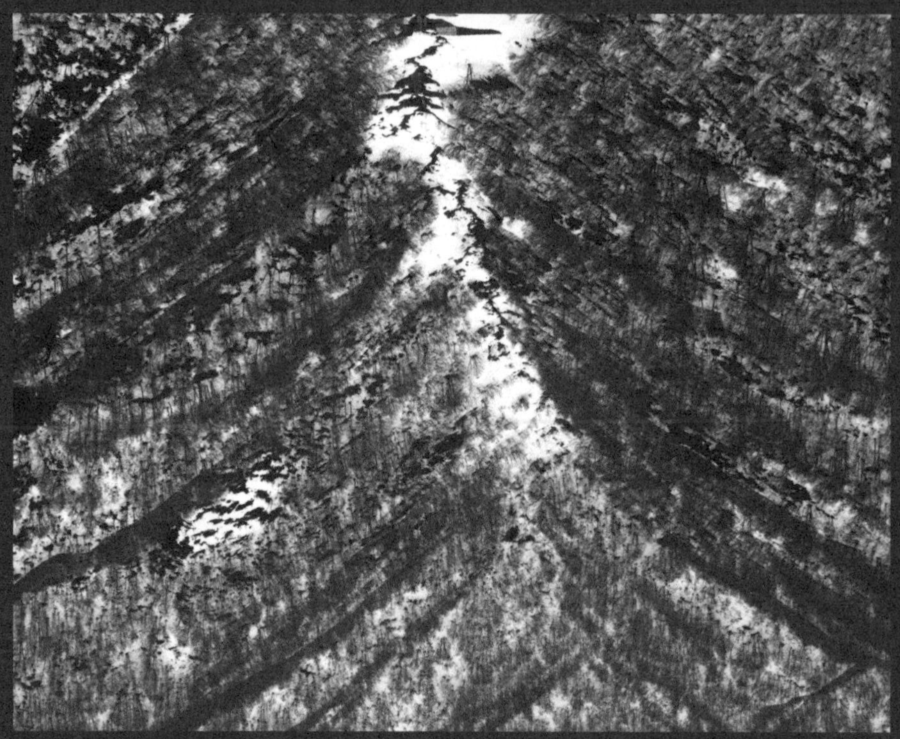

Shiho Yoshida, *Survey/Mountain*, 2016,
Lambda print mounted on acrylic panel
(wooden panel on the bottom), 27.9. x 35.6 x
2.8 cm © Shiho Yoshida, courtesy Yumiko
Chiba Associates

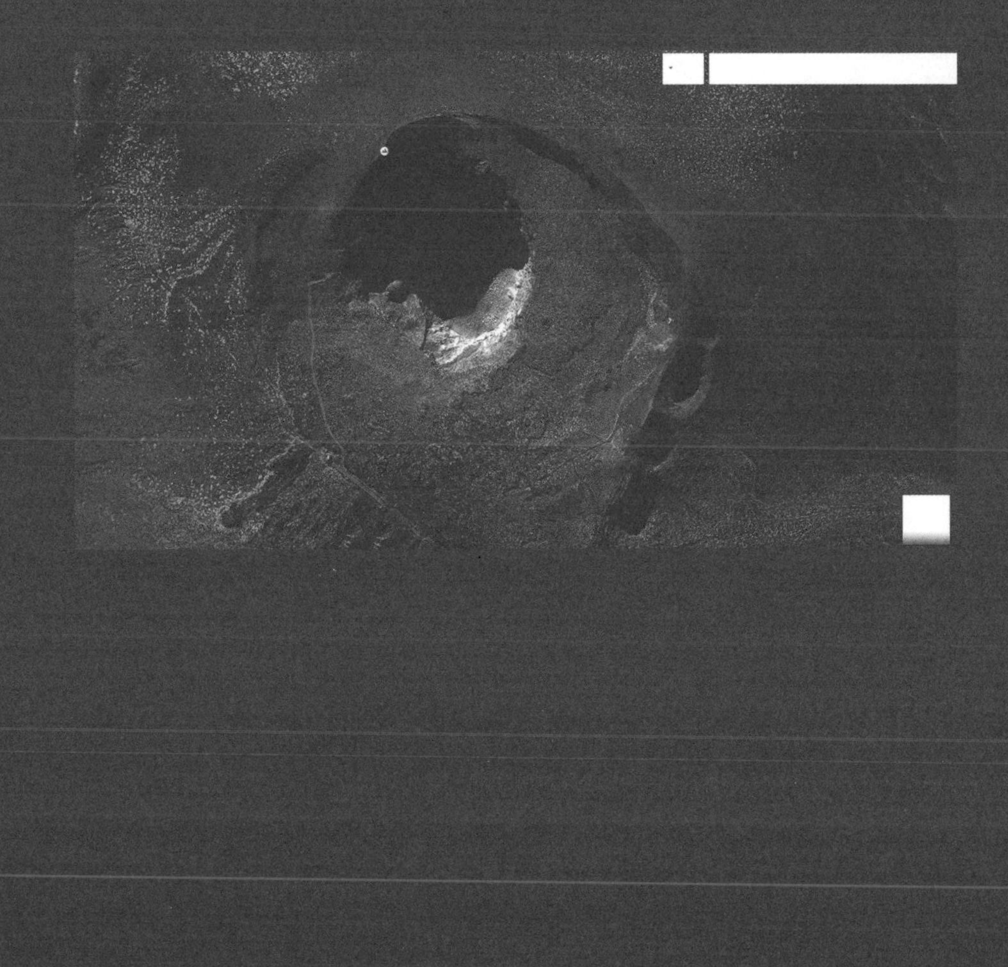

Shiho Yoshida, *Survey/Mountain*, 2016, gelatin silver print, 50.8 x 61 cm © Shiho Yoshida, courtesy Yumiko Chiba Associates

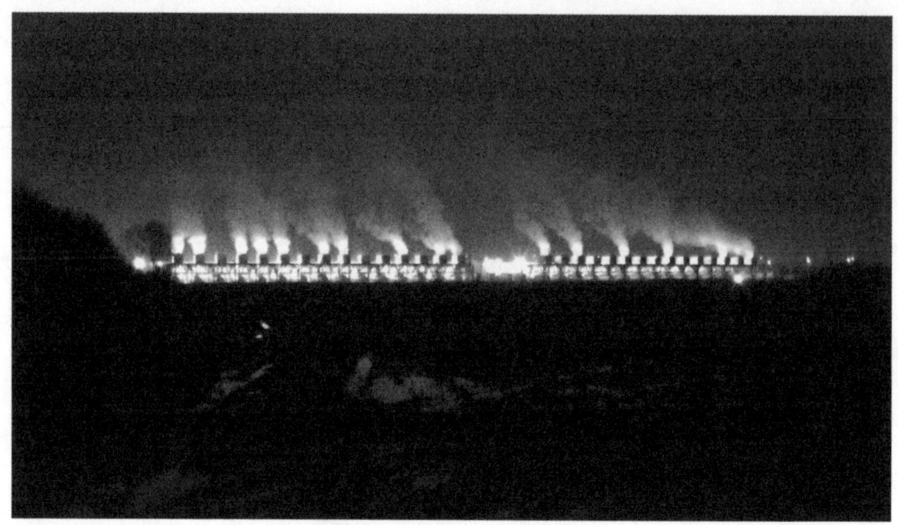

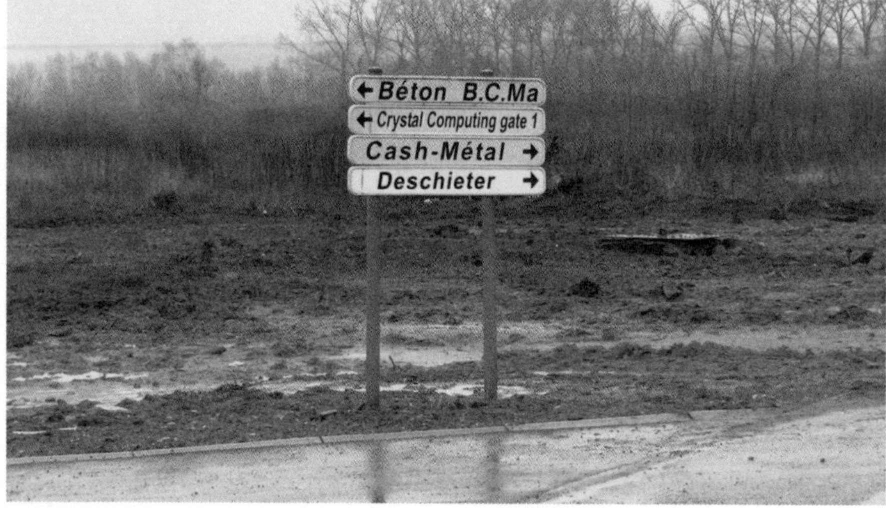

Ivar Veermäe, *Crystal Computing (Google Inc., St. Ghislain)*, 2014, full HD video, 9:19 min.
© Ivar Veermäe

Crystal Computing is a video work that uses stylistic elements of documentary, bordering on surveillance footage, and is aimed at investigating Google's identically named data centre in Saint-Ghislain, Belgium, which is the largest Google data centre in Europe and the second largest in the world. According to recent information provided by Google Inc., around the time the film material was shot, this centre housed 296,960 servers, with

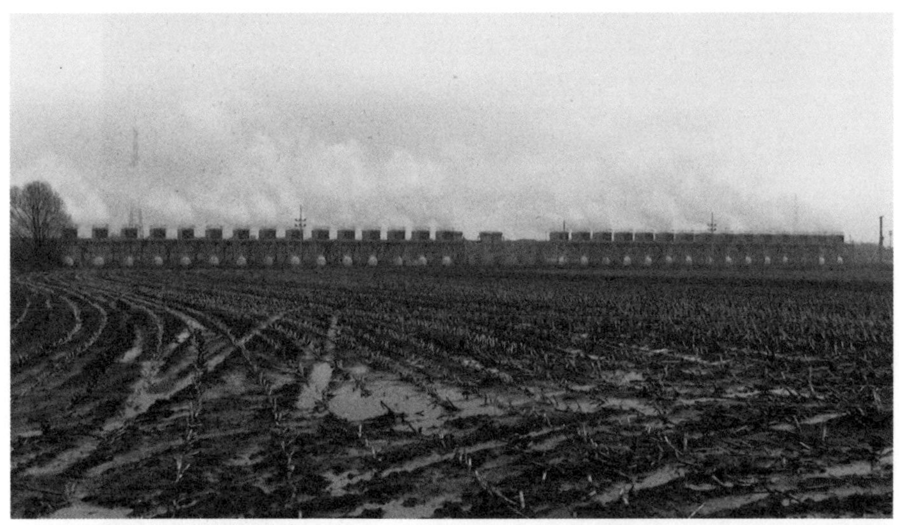

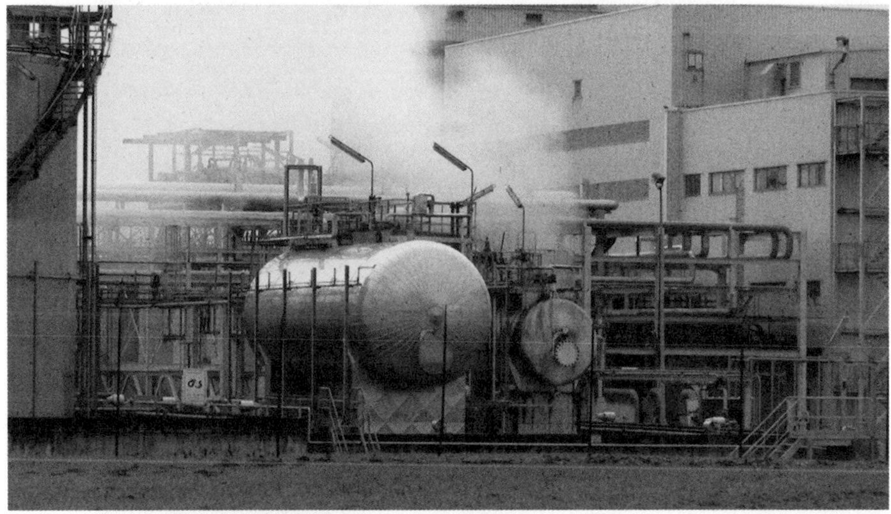

prospects of rapid expansion. After the data centre officially refused him admittance to the plant as a regular visitor, Veermäe made a secret research trip to Belgium. "Crystal computing" refers to the importance of materiality and locality in the infrastructures of big network companies, an importance that is often concealed under immaterial, "cloudy" advertising rhetoric. Ironically, this company's name represents the hidden agendas of the corporation as addressed in the video; it also singles out the routine practice of establishing subsidiaries as a tax avoidance scheme, which is popular among multinational corporations. The artist visually "out-measures" the corporation by documenting its unsightly material reality on video. The work creates its subversive position by countering Google's activities of collecting, observing, and analysing user data by returning the gaze and starting an analysis of its own.

Franz John, *Sky Nude*, 1992, 24-hour
performance for the exhibition *Trivial
Machines*, Karl Ernst Osthaus-Museum,
Hagen, flatbed scanner, computer, light
from the sky © Franz John

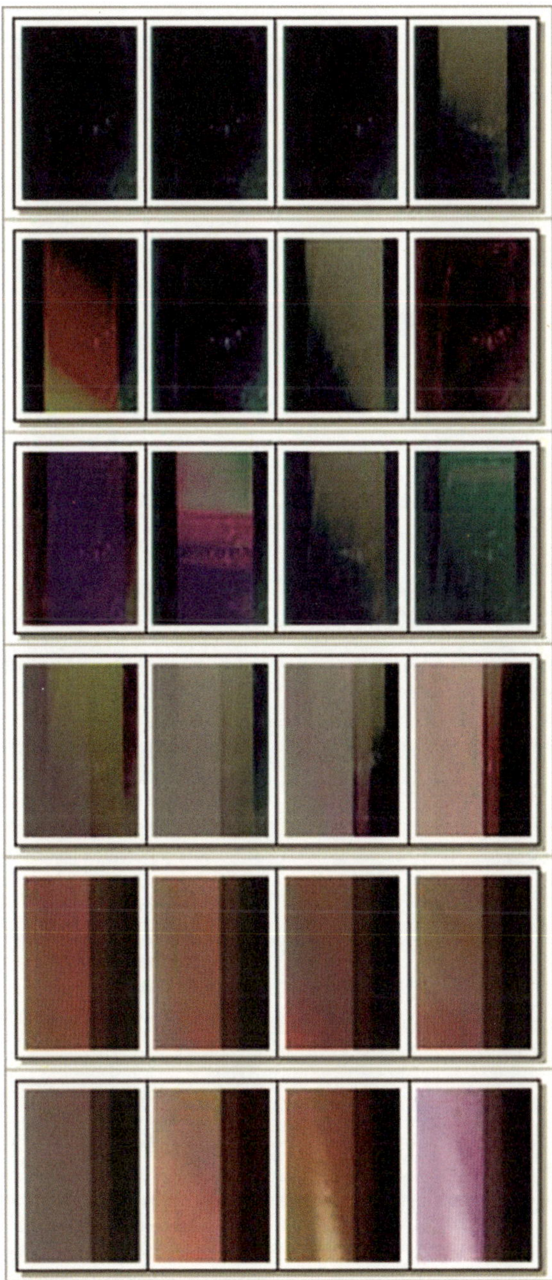

This project presents the "creative ab/use" of a scanner – one of the first models available to and affordable for a broader public. Instead of directing the scanning light of measurement to a two-dimensional, closed space in order to scan it, as is the usual practice, the artist directs it towards the sky, towards the open space above the glass surface of the scanner. This simple procedure disorients the logic and mechanism of the scanner and reveals the blind spots of this technology. It creates a contrast between different notions of measurement that shows that popular notions of measurement may be much more diverse than actual technological measurement, which always comes with a set of assumptions and strict presuppositions from which one is really not supposed to deviate – although these deviations have time and again proven to be the paths that lead into the actual technological future.

Karin Sander, *Museum Visitors 1:8,* installation view at Labor K20, 2010, 3D body scans of living persons (scale 1:8), in the colour of their choice, monochrome 3D printing, plaster material, height ca. 10–22 cm each

This is a series of miniature, figurative sculpture prints based on 3D body scans. The figures were originally conceived as "three-dimensional photographs" – though they are actually condensed technical portraits of (living) people who have literally been scanned from the top of their head to their toes, translated into digital data, and then exported to take on the shape of miniature sculptures. The first were already created some twenty years ago, and they visually present a process, technique, mechanism, and language of measurement, although the finish of this material, which, in the meantime, has become wildly popular and easily accessible, is still rather rough and casual. The artist has developed her concept in a playful openness – a range of methods between the scientific accuracy that is applied in the precise depiction, as well as the opposite: through replacing the interpretational "lifelike" effect that comes with traditional, for example painterly, depiction of details with technological, merely mechanical precision, and through giving it a variety of colours or printed-on photo-sourced textures. The subject of datafication and the patient sitter in a portrait session are merged and folded into one artistic object. As a result of Sander's artistic intervention, through which she completely appropriated the methods and processes of scanning measurement and reconstruction and transferred them to correspond to her concept of what an artwork is, these figures reveal the gap between the sensibilities of recognition and those of perception.

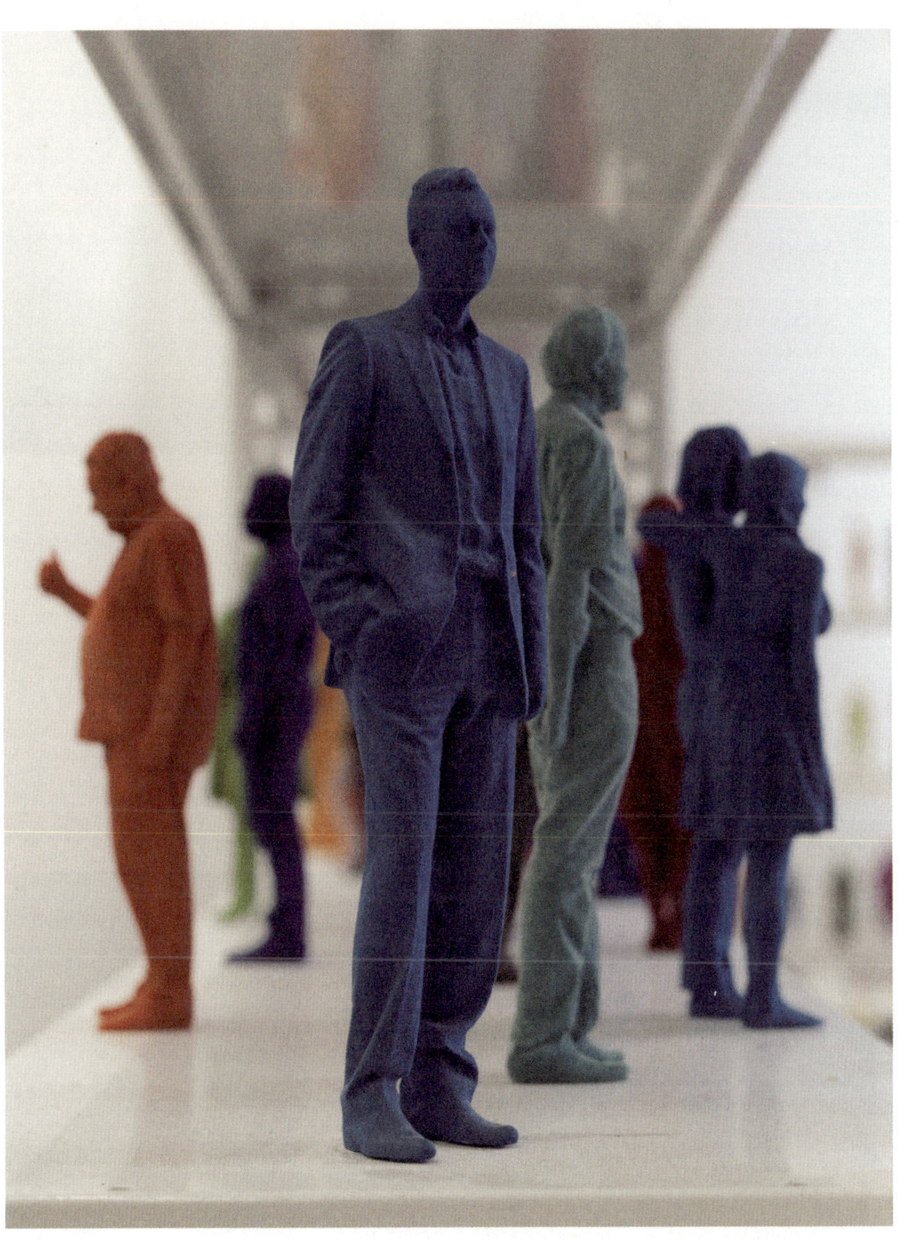

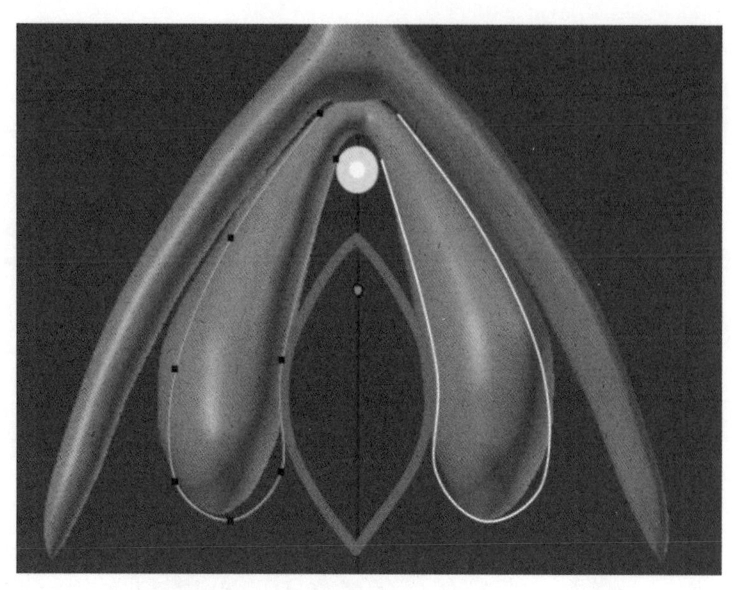

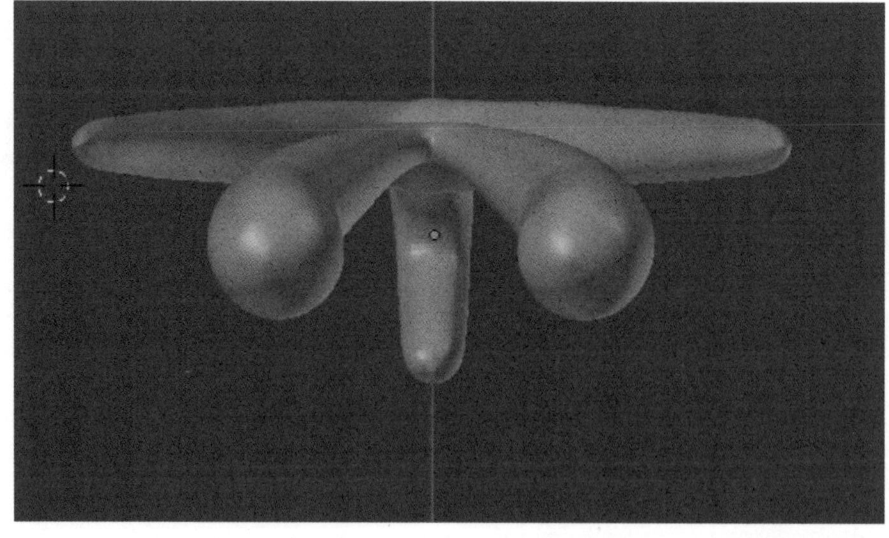

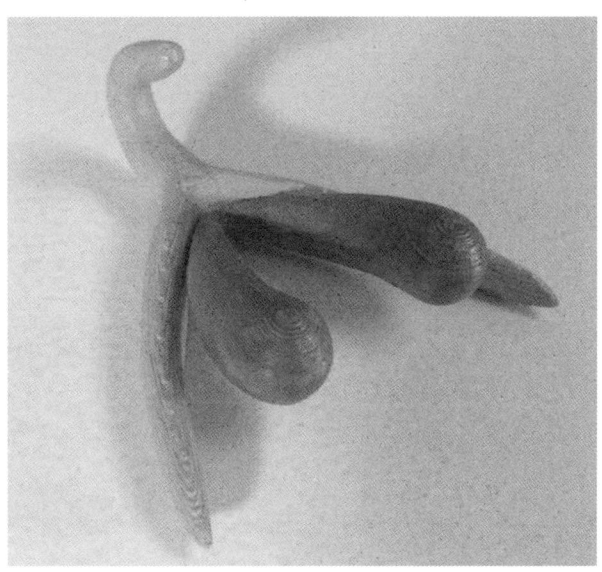

Marie Docher in collaboration with
Odile Fillod, *Les Imprimantes 3D/3D Scan
of a Clitoris*, 2016, 3D printing, digital images
© Odile Fillod, photo © Marie Docher

The *3D Scan of a Clitoris* is the first anatomically correct model of a clitoris used for educational purposes in French primary and secondary schools, from September 2016. Its source code, which allows for 3D printing of a clitoris model, is available "open source". This code was developed by Odile Fillod, a socio-medical researcher and creator of an anti-sexist web TV series at the Fab Lab, at the Cité des Sciences et de l'Industrie in Paris, and realised in collaboration with the visual artist Marie Docher. For the first time, this 3D scan of a clitoris allows for a more spatially accurate image of its shape, scale, and dimensions. It is 20 centimetres long in total! Resembling an orchid flower, it, surprisingly, seems to approximate the shape of a male sexual organ. Measurement in this case reveals that "gender" is a design relative to cultural modes of imagination and representation.

Rokudenashiko, *3D MK Boat Project*, 2014–,
fibre plastic © Rokudenashiko

Rokudenashiko literally means "good-for-nothing"
in Japanese; Megumi Igarashi uses it affirmatively,
even with pride, as her artist name. She has become
famous through initiating the *3D MK Boat Project*,
in which she scanned her vagina, enlarged the
scanned shape to the size of a kayak, and had the
small boat made of plastic fibre. The project has
succeeded in challenging social norms and ideologies
as represented in existing imaginaries about the
female body. Even though she used hi-tech measuring tools to ensure social recognition, the project has
actually provoked a number of both very emotional
political and legal reactions from society. Ironically,
what precision measurement also achieved is a precisely measured image of governmental and social
"tolerance" – but also of the current readiness to
cope with what contemporary technology makes
possible – as opposed to their antiquated views
of what sexuality "looks like". Along with this
provocative measurement, the project carefully
chose the mode and format of its representation so
as to refer to the particular aesthetics of the girls'
comics developed in 1970s popular culture in Japan.
This particular aesthetic double-questions social
and historical constructions of the aesthetics of
the female body, and places further emphasis on a
feminist critique of social measurement.

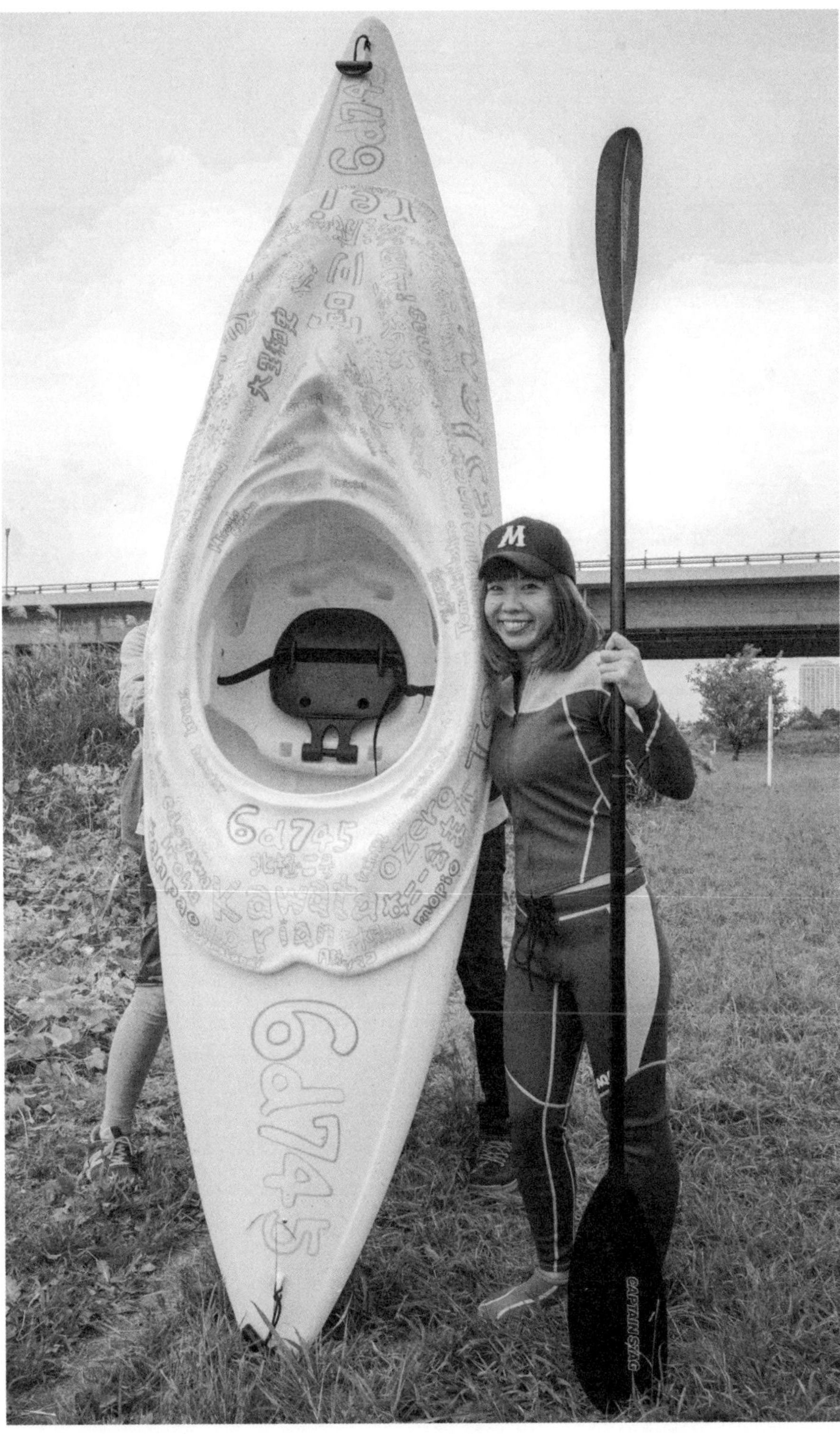

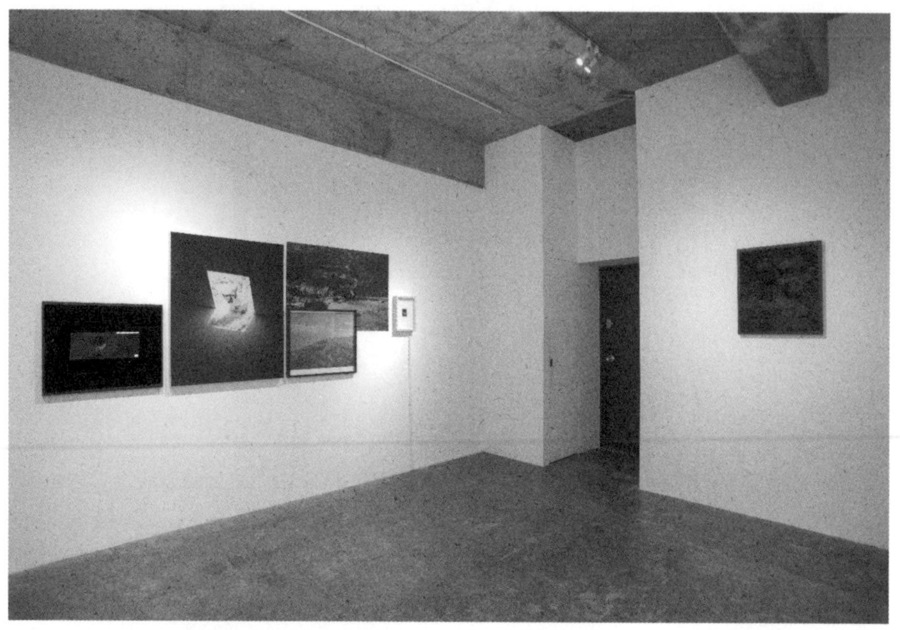

Shiho Yoshida, *Survey/Mountain*, 2016, installation view at Yumiko Chiba Associates, 2016 © Shiho Yoshida, courtesy Yumiko Chiba Associates

From Universality to Ubiquity of Measurement

"When images supplant texts, we experience, perceive, and value the world and ourselves differently, no longer in a one-dimensional, linear, process-oriented, historical way but rather in a two-dimensional way, as surface, context, scene. And our behaviour changes: it is no longer dramatic but embedded in fields of relationships. What is currently happening is a mutation of our experiences, perceptions, values, and modes of behaviour, a mutation of our being-in-the-world."
—Vilém Flusser, *Into the Universe of Technical Images,* 1986

"The memory on my hard disk has reached the limit as I had kept so many data related to mountains. I perceived the weight of the mountains themselves, a weight that could not exist, in the disk space full of images of mountains and other information I collected on them. (…) The virtual mountains had neither form nor location; I wanted to create a way to perceive them."[11]
—Shiho Yoshida, *Survey/Mountain*, 2016

Survey/Mountain (2016) is the title of an exhibition; it is also synonymous with a series of monochrome mountain photographs by Shiho Yoshida. The mountain ridges are pictured from various points of view, and the angles assembled to form the installation are formatted in different ways. One of the installations contains four photographs of one mountain, one of which is a framed Google Maps satellite image of the mountain surrounded by a wide black space. This image is processed to erase any pre-existing locative information. The second image, projected onto the corner of the wall, shows the ground level around the mountain turned 90 degrees counter-clockwise. The strong artificial light of the projector sets a point of focus in the centre of the image; the projected image nonetheless still remains rather unclear. It becomes apparent that the light in the image does not shine on it vertically from the sky outside; rather it comes from the inside, as if in a monitor. The third image is much more difficult to identify. It consists of two photographs – one pasted directly onto the wall, without a frame, another held directly in-

---

[11] From the artist statement for Shiho Yoshida's solo exhibition *Survey/Mountain*.

side a thin black frame, in order to create uneven blank spaces above and below the image. The framed photo is smaller and arranged to overlap the bottom left corner of the unframed photo, creating a visual effect that calls to mind two differently sized monitors standing in perspective. Both images are surely images of fragments of the unidentified mountainscape: It remains uncertain whether they belong to one and the same mountain. The larger image is layered, with the ground in front, a water expanse in the middle, and the crest of the mountain in the background, while the smaller one is a view of the mountain range from a distance, which also shows the sky above it. Curiously, thin lines outline the mountain range in both images. The fourth is the smallest image and is enclosed in a wooden frame, with a generously spaced passe-partout around it. Closer observation reveals that the image is actually presented on a very small monitor, almost hidden in its cave-like framing. All the photos visualise a particular presence of the mountain, but they convey a mixed impression, between proximity and distance; they appear familiar, but become perturbing upon closer scrutiny. Viewers are suspended between at least two states: They are somehow fascinated by the images, but cannot grasp exactly what they are.

As mentioned in the artist's statement, the photographic works of *Survey/ Mountain* resemble a geographic portrait of a mountain somewhere, but they visualise a "mountain of data" that exists nowhere in the world. The outline rendering the surface of the mountain is the visual language Yoshida chose so as to "give a form to the non-existing surface" of a mountain – a mountain is not a specific mountain, as an individual shape, but a mountain of data. This explains the peculiar feeling to which the images give rise to some degree, but it becomes clearer to those who obtain additional information about the specific photographic process, which compresses a series of actions. The artist more or less intuitively searches for and researches sites she finds interesting to visit, not because of their names or identities, but due to their shape and texture, and then starts collecting images on the net, eventually travels to that place, takes photographs of the landscape, compares her own images with those found on the net, enlarges, juxtaposes, and projects them on walls. She then proceeds to re-photograph and print them out as negatives, or sometimes uses them as data for another photographic work, in which she repeats the sequence of actions described. The artist characterises her process as a set of operations based on rules that she has established in order to come to an understanding of each landscape. The seemingly tedious procedure is diligently repeated in order to give the landscapes their "own" image; eventually they are "personalised" through being given *her* outlines (her own measurement):

For me, the process can be understood as her attempt, based on a broad variety of images of mountains, to sense the materiality of data – its volume, its texture, its shape, et cetera – through seeing, touching, smelling, drawing, turning around, inverting, and folding it, as if dealing with the surface of existing matter, with the "real thing". What she does in practice is hybridise different technical images and the structures behind them, and change the format and the interface to present them as her own images. Her set of operations is similar to the optical collection of data on the mountain, but with different sets of parameters in the external filters of measurement. Her repetitive process gradually *in-forms*, materialises the invisible pile of data, and shapes the data to make it visible. For the artist, specificity does not depend on a specific site, but rather on specific processes and formats – in this case, the formats of technical images such as photography, projection, geomapping, et cetera. Accordingly, the format assumes a key role when it comes to understanding measurement.

Yoshida's set of operations in her production process also indicates how sensory attention is distributed and organised under particular technological conditions. The artist's intimate relationship with the mobile phone as a means of accessing digital networks may be a typically contemporary position. Her condensed technical images present visuals in which acceleration and the specific forms of attention that are enacted in searching, recording, and displaying information "produce new forms of observation and rationality". Orit Halpern points out that: "Our forms of attention, observation, and truth are historically influenced and trained and shaped in a certain way by the structure and the framework of technology."[12] Reflecting on this point while thinking in and through *Survey/Mountain*, we certainly need to closely observe her particular form of attention or observation, her truth, which is organised around her choice of format, rather than around the interpretation of any real physical space. This actually indicates a new imagination, a novel way of understanding hybrid space, and it also considerably changes the meaning of scale, perspective, and line.

In 1977, Charles and Ray Eames produced the short film *Powers of Ten* as a commissioned work for the then-emerging data giant IBM so as to visually demonstrate "the relative size of things in the universe", in increasing and decreasing magnitudes, over the duration of roughly nine minutes. The film begins by observing a couple of picnickers on a lawn by the side of a lake in

---

[12] Orit Halpern, *Beautiful Data: A History of Vision and Reason since 1945* (Durham and London: Duke University Press, 2014), 7.

Chicago, to then transport the viewer in two opposite directions: zooming out to the edge of universe in a rapid progression through powers of ten, and then, zooming in onto and into the hand of one the picnickers – until it reaches the horizon of experimentally verifiable knowledge at the level of a proton inside a carbon atom, shown in a schematic rendering within a DNA molecule in a white blood vessel. Thirty-five years later, in 2012, Google produced *New Powers of Ten*, rhetorically framed by a mobile phone display, apparently to evocatively refer to the present of digital images and aesthetics. Both films visualise the relativity of things like scale – and the ontological facts of a world in which the human is still the inert centre – as a quick adventure.

According to a popular online dictionary, scale is used – *mathematically* – to represent the relationship (the ratio) between measurement on a model and the corresponding measurement on an object, such as 1:1, or 1:200. *Theoretically*, scale is understood as an ontological fact, as in the simplified example of a *matryoshka*, a Russian nesting doll. Although the new version of *Powers of Ten* was made based on more recent research results and using more contemporary technologies (moving satellite images) instead of an animation of still images, both films are principally the same, as they are based on an understanding of scale as relative. The notion of scale in *Survey/Mountain*, however, does not fit these definitions. The photographs are neither the method of measurement – calculated and produced in a specific ratio – nor do they render the data for display according to an automatic process, nor are they an ontological fact. They are opposed to such relativity. They are more like a presentation of the space that floats around and appears everywhere and anywhere: no matter at what point or at what height, structure, or parameter. As Yoshida hybridises different types, structures, and formats of images in order to quantify data and to re-process them into one image, the adoption of scale in her images is similar to the section of a candy bar: no matter where you cut or how you cut, the same layered pattern appears. This is, by definition, a completely different understanding of scale, which I would then call a scale of ubiquity. Yoshida's hybrid structure behind the image corresponds to the concept of perspective in a different way. In the context of art history, Cubism perceived and gathered a number of different perspectives of one object in one image plane, while *Survey/Mountain* merges them within the image by utilising the processing power of contemporary image technology. This also seems to be the way that the installation as a whole – as well as the layout of the two photographs situated on top of each other, which looks like a depiction of plural monitors – is constructed. Perspectives of space are replaced, both perception-wise and organisationally, by this layout of monitors, instead of being integrated into a linear perspective. Her photo-centric work, in other words, marks a shift in existing perspectives of measurement, in that it has moved on – from the universal to the ubiquitous.

Yoshida aims at a portrait of a mountainscape of data. Her attempt eventually leads her to seek new visual languages in order to grasp ubiquitous space, and to invent different concepts of "scale" and "spatial organisation" through these acts and in the process of measurement. In this case, measurement is a quantification not in the sense of an exact prediction of the future, but as a method of in-forming "ubiquity" anywhere and at any time. It employs methods and acts of measuring that are different from those historically established in the natural sciences.

For the artist, who grew up with images on her mobile phone and got used to complementing her perception of the world with image searches, it is particularly important that, to her, all types of images are equivalent. There are no significant differences between images she takes herself and those she finds on the net, since she is the person who chooses them. For her, images are *signs*: they comprise maps, Google Earth data, existing jpegs, even ideogrammatic characters, et cetera. Since the images are considered equal, the crucial role of her conceptual use of *format*, which functions as a way to frame images both conceptually and practically, becomes evident in her work. Here, format does not only mean size, proportion, and the blank space around it, it also refers to the mechanisms that are applied to the images such as media interfaces, interactive applications[13], and programming, all of which are essential on all levels of visual appearance. This visual appearance includes both the visible and the invisible, both the tangible and the intangible. Vilém Flusser once proposed that technical images are not representations, but projections, and this is why, in his view, they should be understood not through decoding a specific meaning, but through grasping their general structure and the purpose behind them (Flusser, 1986). The juxtaposition of different formats of mountain images reveals different kinds of becoming-matter of the "mountain as sign" (image) – a distinction that is necessary to see why her work also represents a new approach to an artistic understanding of measurement. This also reflects aspects of Joseph Kosuth's classical work of conceptual art, *One and Three Chairs* (1965) – the way in which he juxtaposed a material, an objective chair with its image and the lexicographic definition of "chair" as equivalents. His approach was based on a reading of semiotics in search of a new notion of "concept". *Survey/Mountain* shifts this to the formation of the technical image, "the

---

¹³ Ibid., 36.

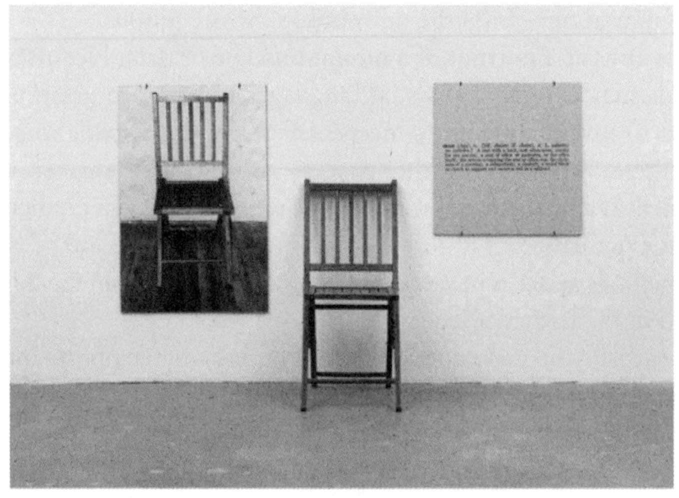

Joseph Kosuth, *One and Three Chairs*, 1965, wooden folding chair, mounted photograph of a chair, and mounted photographic enlargement of the dictionary definition for "chair": chair 82 x 37.8 x 53 cm, photographic panel 91.5 x 61.1 cm, text panel 61 x 76.2 cm, the Museum of Modern Art, New York

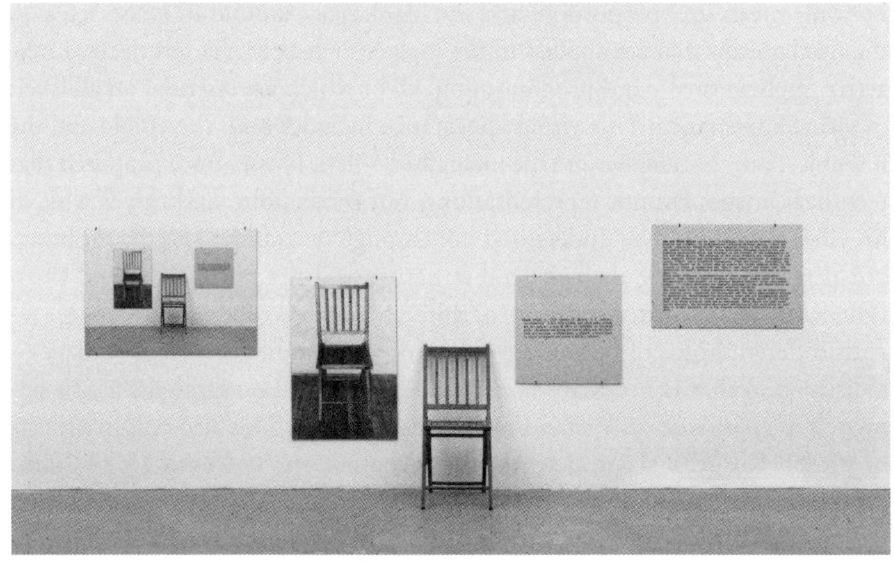

Antonio Guiotto, *One and Three, One and Three Chairs with Expansion Possibility*, 2012, installation project, reproduction of Joseph Kosuth's *One and Three Chairs*, photograph and enlarged art work statement, dimensions variable

logics of archiving, memory capacity, and interface". It corresponds to the formation of semiotics in the data society. *Survey/Mountain* is a conceptual artwork in that it indicates different grammars of understanding and knowing (measuring), of experiencing a sense of the real in a dimensionless world that is conditioned by a technological dataspace. It is the notion of "format" that seems to correspond to Flusser's historical quest for any new developments that the technical image now might bring: Format, both the given and the created, offers a new category in those language games that are now defining the measurement of contemporary reality.

The Affective Component of Technological Images in the Process of Knowing and Understanding

If one considers the daily use of navigation technologies, it becomes noticeable how the sense of the real in everyday life is framed and structured by the *format* of the technologies. Whether, Google Earth, car navigation, or other systems for identifying location – navigation directs us from one point to another in an urban space based on the logic of geometry. It correlates anticipated and actual movements by changing the length of a graphic line ending with an arrow. We look at the navigation map, compare it with the view in front of us, and continuously compare the two images, physically following the directions of the orientation device. The constant comparison between the geometry of the map and the realistic, "direct" view from the biological body has created a visual culture that relies on a set of actions to project geometry onto real landscapes. Geometry is internalised in the perception of the user, who projects it onto a real landscape and (re-)shapes the world to correspond to his/her sense of the real. The use of geo-location systems dissolves the Cartesian division of subject and object. Navigated persons have become integral parts of the lifeworld of the technical image. They become extended objects of invisible GPS geometry and simultaneously, as subjects, actively project their worldview. In this sense, any programme for identifying location *formats* a sensorial perception (a sense of the real) to become geometrical thinking, and functions as an invisible framing of time-space. With such an understanding of reality, the self is perceived as a dot – as a unit of attention – and experience as a line as the culmination of attention – and the body becomes the medium for collecting and processing attention. This symbolises how the sense of the real operates in everyday life, and indicates the tipping point in the development of affect for the technological image within processes of knowing

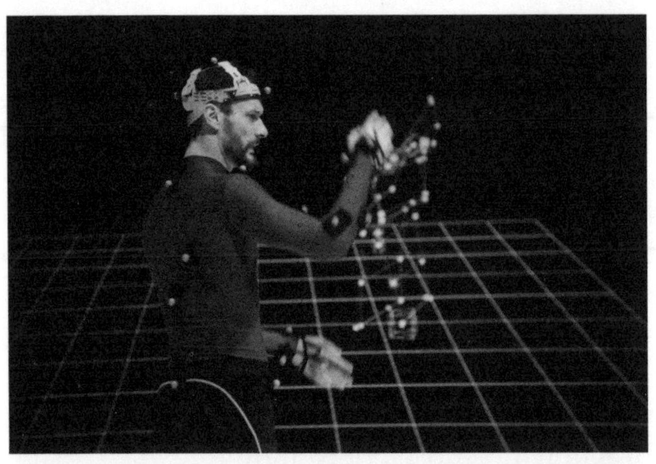

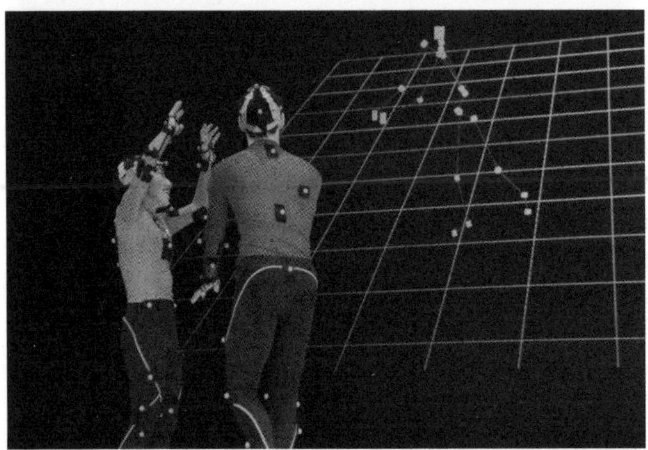

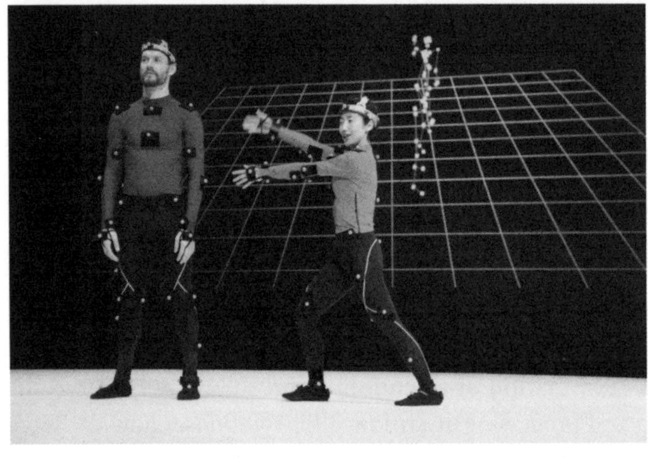

Yoko Ando and The Forsythe Company, *Research for Awareness in Motion (RAM) Project*, 2011– YCAM InterLab + Yoko Ando Joint Research and Development Project, courtesy the Yamaguchi Centre for Arts and Media (YCAM)

and understanding. The geometry that is internalised in the cultural use of technological images prompts us to produce other approaches to space, and even transforms sensorial perception of space into the ubiquitous in the sense elaborated here.

In the early 1990s, Deleuze described the kind of abstraction that was emerging in the transition from societies of discipline to societies of control. He foresaw the insignificance of the individual in the operative mode of society, spoke of a desubjectification of individuals, and said that individuals have been transformed into "dividuals and masses". The internalised geometry described in the previous paragraph plays a part in such desubjectification. A set of operations in *Survey/Mountain* is dedicated to the desubjectification of the mountain image in order to make it become a "ubiquitous mountain", and simultaneously to the artist's experience as it is traced along the outlines of the mountain – effectively rendering herself dividual while on the other hand personalising the landscape. What interests me here is not that geo-location technology functions as a device of desubjectification in a dimensionless space – it is actually the double process of dividualisation and personalisation – seemingly opposites – in a set of operations of knowing, understanding, and creating. This double process of *dividualising* (quantification of self) and *personalising* (using quantification for the subject's own purpose of creation) can be encountered in applied form not only in geo-location systems, but also in other surface technologies – such as 3D scanning, motion capture, and their respective visualisations/materialisations. For example, the Research for Awareness in Motion (RAM) project provides[14] us with an interesting case study on the affective effect that the use of motion capture technology already has on the "intuitive" movements of dancers. Two dancers wear a suit with eighteen motion-tracking sensors, whose measurement-based results can be experienced both visually in a large monitor projection as well as on the dancers' own bodies while they dance live. The dancers see the images previously recorded by the sensors as well as the live images of their own body movements. The two dancers make decisions about their body movements, about the forms and positions, based on the shared geometrical information that, in turn and simultaneously, is generated by their

---

[14] RAM is an experiment research project to develop a new vision of the embodiment of technology in dance performance. It started in 2011 at the Yamaguchi Centre for Arts and Media (YCAM) as a collaboration between a Japanese dancer, Yoko Ando, a dancer from The Forsythe Company, and programmers, and aims at innovating a new tool for understanding and creating movement for dancers, as well as applying the same technology for educational purposes.

bodies. The processing of motion data so as to give real-time feedback overlaps with something else: with a process of dividualisation; the actual body movement is simultaneously a process of personalisation and/or subjectification.

In a close study of the contemporary use of data in daily environments, Halpern introduced the term "communicative objectivity", which depicts the attitude shifted by recording and displaying information by means of technologies, new forms of observations, rationality, and the subsequent sets of actions based on economic management and analysis.[15] The term emerges from the contemplation of the Smart City, Halpern's model case of high-tech urban planning in Korea and its biopolitical governance, but here "communicative objectivity" is applied to a process of *aesthetic* production. "Communicative objectivity", she writes, is based on assumptions about the value of data and our habitual obsession with "visualisation" as well as our belief in the intensification of media devices. When technological images are involved in processes of knowing and understanding, they give rise to a considerable extra amount of information that has already been processed and filtered. When one sees extensive amounts of visual information on displays in front of one's body, it is noticeable in RAM that these images are information from identical sources, which circulate on the same level and in the same format. The situation is similar to observing oneself surrounded by (digital) mirrors, a reality relation that is in sharp contrast to those of *One and Three Chairs* by Joseph Kosuth and *Survey/Mountain* by Shiho Yoshida. In this sense, the choice of information may look broader in the different renderings; whether it is "richer" is far from clear.

Instead, constantly exposing the body to data in a state of "connectedness" may equalise the orientation and coordination of thinking between the dancers and the algorithms at work – to the point of neutralisation. However, in order to have an "external" filter, the dividual subject needs an "internal" one as well, since such a filter is an essential part of the site and instrument of measurement that the body is. The process of dividualisation *requires* a body – as opposed to processes of personalisation, and, to a certain degree, also of subjectification. Yoko Ando, one of the dancers and the initiator of the project, regards this movement as neither expressing any specific emotion nor based on any ideology; to her, it is "not inorganic" and comes with a "certain temperature".[16] This "temperature", which is characteristic of a specific emotion that is generated between the organic and the inorganic, is something that is produced in particular as the

---

[15] Halpern, *Beautiful Data*, 2014, 7.

[16] Yoko Ando interviewed by Takayuki Ito. The interview with Yoko Ando was conducted by Takayuki Ito (YCAM InterLab) and Richi Owaki (YCAM InterLab) on 21 March 2013.

result of the removal of all possible disturbances and incidental elements in each given situation. This "affective temperature" (or temperament) is also found in *Survey/Mountain*. In both cases it could be rephrased as an absence of a high, "passionate" temperature, and is rather more like the steady, but relatively low temperature that comes into existence when accuracy is pursued in a rather obsessive manner. The temperature is the reflection of the obsession of the dividual subject as well as its inner desire for data when uncertain; consequently, it fantasises participation in the intensified as well as "intensifictional" (i.e. pseudo-interactive) process of feedback. Accordingly, such an aesthetic develops towards a psychological process, opposed to the outward appearance of interactivity between the artificial opposites of (rational) reason and(irrational) emotion.

The body is the agential site of inter- and intra-actions that forms and unfolds space-time and actively projects one's own measurement onto the world, instead of being exposed to measurements solely from the outside. Measurement is inside the body. This does not only concern subjective imaginaries, but also the body returning as an integral component that is indispensable to any understanding of measurement today. Ultimately, this double processing always directs the accuracy of measurement in perception and action from a bird's-eye view. The image can never be experienced as a whole, but always becomes a section, a fragment, or a part of a larger picture in the distance. In *Survey/Mountain*, the image is a non-specific expressive gesture; it tends toward the realm of "meta" images; instead of being a monolithic entity in itself, it retains being in repetitious self-alignment with an outer framework (not the "outside"). When image becomes *meta-image*, movement becomes *meta-motion* (gesture). It is produced in a singular praxis without having to be processed. This means that the type of measurement involved in surface technologies is unavoidably linked to a sense of the ubiquitous, rather than to ideas of the universal.

In the realm of measuring, a sense of the real, a sense of the "grid" is, however, transformed into something metaphorical, and merely indicates an exterior devised to gain access to a larger conceptual space. Here, that blank space appears to hold more significance than millions of dots at the intersections of horizontal and vertical lines. The blank indicates potential energies and imaginaries where the sense of the real emerges and grows. *Survey/Mountain*, 3D body scans, and the motion-tracking technologies used in the RAM project practice a sense of the real that actively dismisses the boundaries between image and matter. Such an approach to reality implies a notion of measurement that arises from the inside instead of the outside, and has a neither dichotomous nor paradoxical relationship to the real and the virtual, the digital and the analogue, the human and technologically sensory, the self-made or the existing, or even the self and

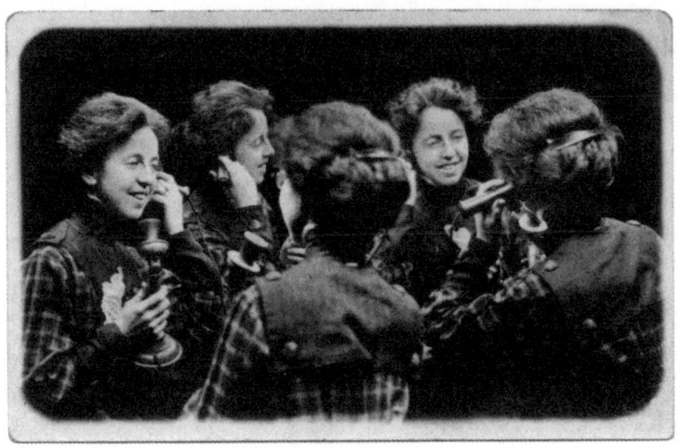

Unanimous Conference Call, made by Chatelain – 117 S. Burdick,
Kalamazoo, postcard, Collection Heinz-Werner Lawo, Berlin,
Uneinsamkeiten/Unsolitudes Blog © Irwin Reichstein

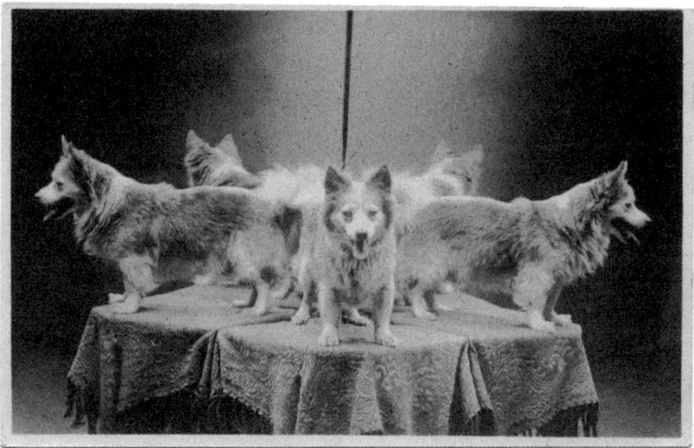

Unknown Dog, Myers-Cope Co., 1521 & 1635 Boardwalk,
Atlantic City, N.J., postcard, courtesy Collection Irwin
Reichstein, Ottawa. Uneinsamkeiten/Unsolitudes Blogs
© Irwin Reichstein

the other. Instead, the equivalence of these poles emerges under conditions that are bi-directionally permeable. There is nothing paradoxical here, since everything becomes equivalent. This creates a peculiar sense of the real that combines intimacy and distance; familiarity and strangeness are integrated to eventually merge into one, which Gins and Arakawa attempt to generate by means of architecture, as I explore in the following section, "Talking back to the Light: Nameless Architecture and Its Critique of Epistemology".

To borrow an expression from Yoko Ando, measuring the sense of the real presupposes a "certain temperature". At the same time, it also presupposes one thing "not tuning with the other". This represents a sense of borderlessness within the meta-image; ultimately, there is only one relevant difference between codes: *dividuals*. The artworks mentioned here visualise and address the "measurement of ubiquity" that is brought about by the light-based measurement paradigm, and thus indirectly refers to our dependency on and penetratedness by communication through the "shallow" surfaces of media in order to understand the world. These works grasp other notions of surface that might correspond with new concepts of a "lightscape" (or "post-landscape") of measurement, and create a novel language that aligns with a changed sense of reality.

Talking Back to the Light: Nameless Architecture and Its Critique of Epistemology

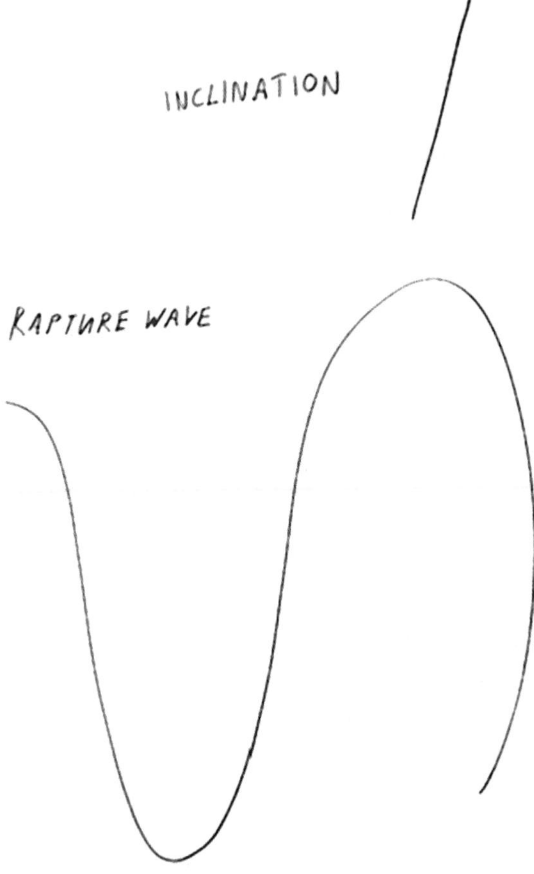

Robert Estermann, *Rapture Wave, Inclination,*
2016, marker on flipchart paper, 140 x 110 cm
© Robert Estermann

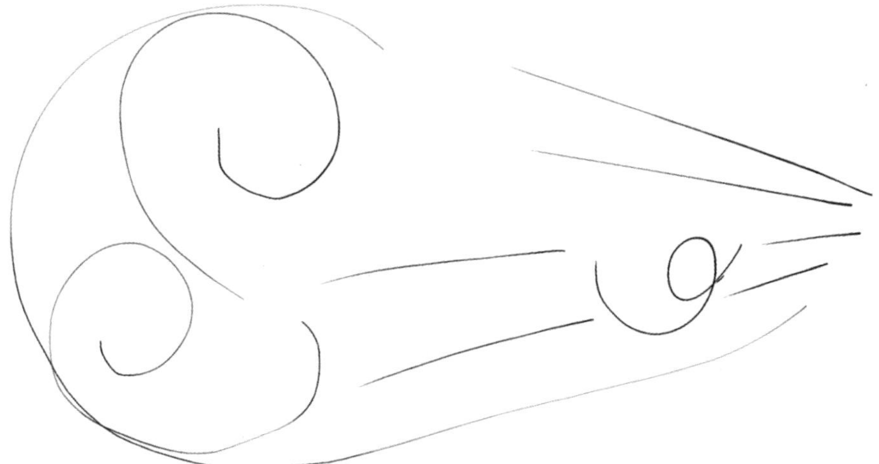

Robert Estermann, *The New EYE*, 2016, whiteboard, marker, 120 x 220 cm © Robert Estermann

Estermann's drawing shows lines which supposedly depict how light moves inside the eye – thus questioning the existing popular belief and accepted scientific fact that light can only move in a straight line, as long as it is not de- or reflected. Light here assumes a kind of life of its own, or develops its own "will" – as it curls itself up into spiral forms that resemble the ideal of the dynamic lines that was so crucial in the aesthetics of progress in European and international modernities around the beginning of the 20th century. Here, invisible entities and their dynamic movements are measured not by ultra-waves, electrical signals, or X-rays, but by what the artist calls his "bio-imagination". This introspective method that the artist has invented for himself reflects, senses, and speculates about things that appear and take shape in the form of lines.

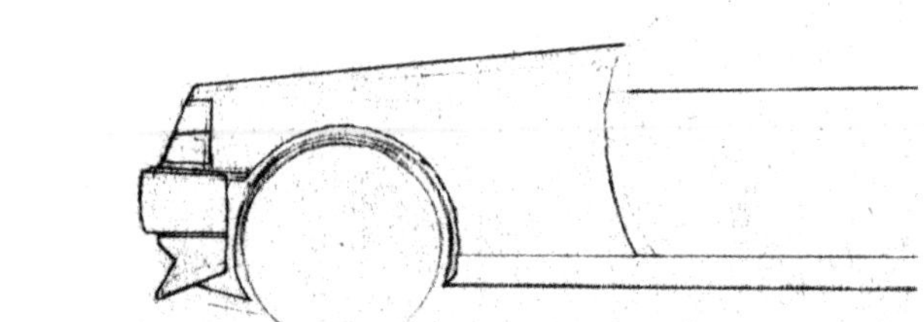

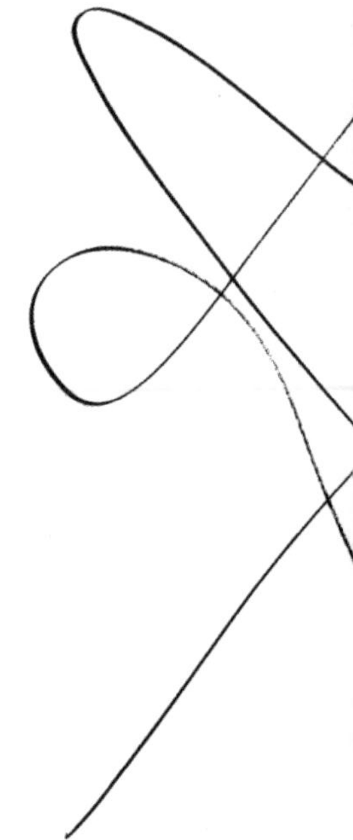

Robert Estermann, *Spectacular Interferometry III*,
(1982–)2017, digital collage, 446 x 906 cm
© Robert Estermann

Spectacular Interferometry is a combination of two
drawings – one is a series of collages made from car de-
signs that the artist did as a teenage back in 1982, the
other is a drawing from the more recent series *Modern
Beach Design* – abstract line drawings on the theme
of beach landscapes from 2008. In the early 1980s,
Estermann was obsessed with the measurements of cars.

He measured and wrote down even the time it took
to draw the (unfinished) car drawings. The drawings
are meant to be enlarged to their full scale – as "real
life-size cars" – with a size of ca. 4-metres-high and ca.
9-metres-wide – which is actually bigger than a regular car. The work experiments with scales – combining scale in everyday life and the "(non-)scale of a
modernist dream" into one picture plane. The artist's
method of "bio-imagination" successfully captures the
social imagination of the 1980s as well as the affect it
has on measurement today – and makes both perceivable as one entity in the form of a collage drawing.

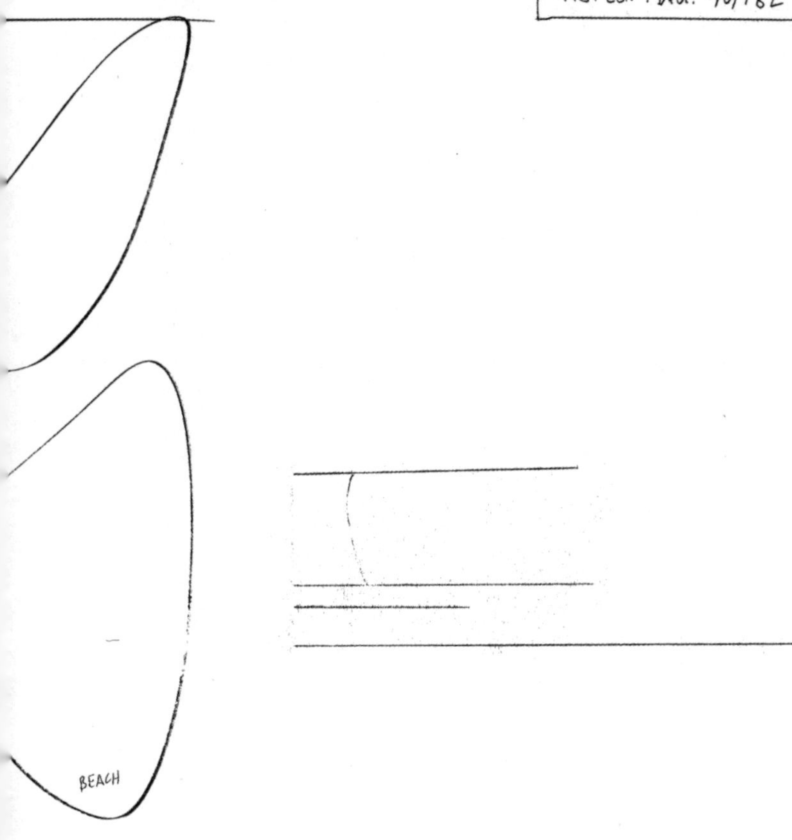

SKY
BEACH
Ms. im Design. Schwester von S.1 Z.1
Ab. ca. 1 Std. 16,782
Ms: 1:20

alphabet (orig. 1981) by Inger Christensen,
trans. Susanne Nied, New Directions
Publishing, New York, 2001

According to the translator's note, the length
of each section of Inger Christensen's alphabet
is based on the Fibonacci sequence, a mathematical sequence beginning 0, 1, 1, 2, 3, 5,
8, 13, 21..., in which each number is the sum
of the two previous numbers. Christensen has
worked a lot on a "systematic poetry" that
keeps the structure and opens up different
dimensions/spaces of numbers – by using
sound, letters and words/non-words/words
as they emerge.

alphabet

by Inger Christensen

1   apricot trees exist, apricot trees exist

2   bracken exists; and blackberries, blackberries;
       bromine exists; and hydrogen, hydrogen

3   cicadas exist; chicory, chromium,
       citrus trees: cicadas exist;
       cicadas, cedars, cypresses, the cerebellum

4   doves exist, dreamers, and dolls;
       killers exist, and doves, and doves;
       haze, dioxin, and days; days
       exist, days and death; and poems
       exist; poems, days, death

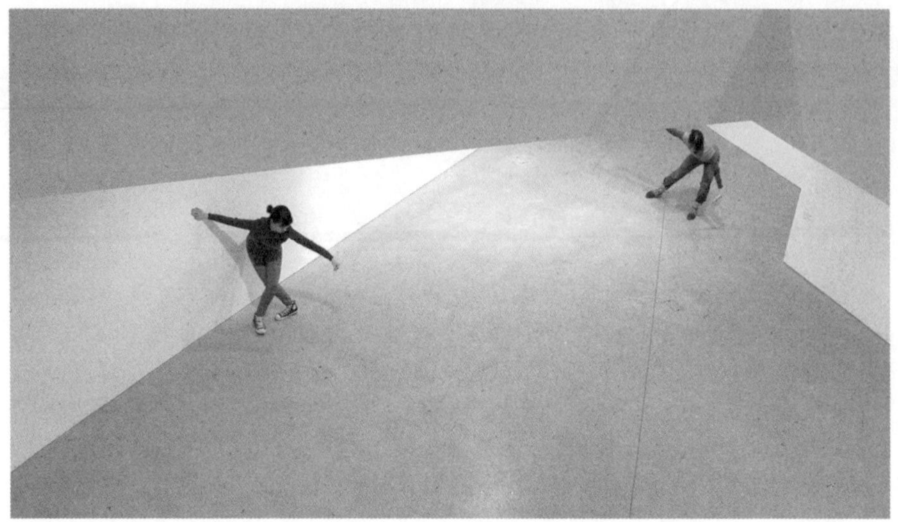

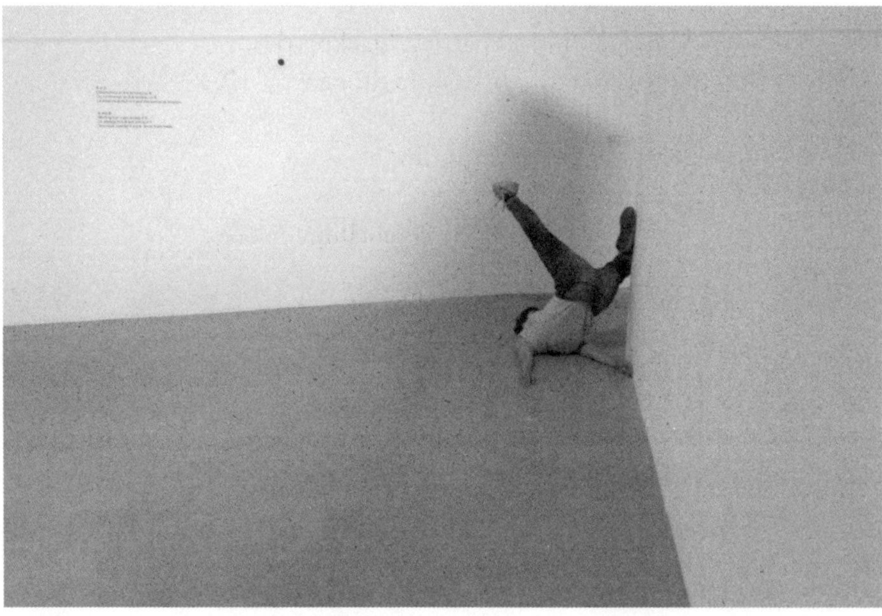

Hwayeon Nam, *Dimensions Variable*,
2013–14, performance at Songwon Art
Center, Seoul, and Palais de Tokyo, Paris,
photo Hwayeon Nam, courtesy the artist

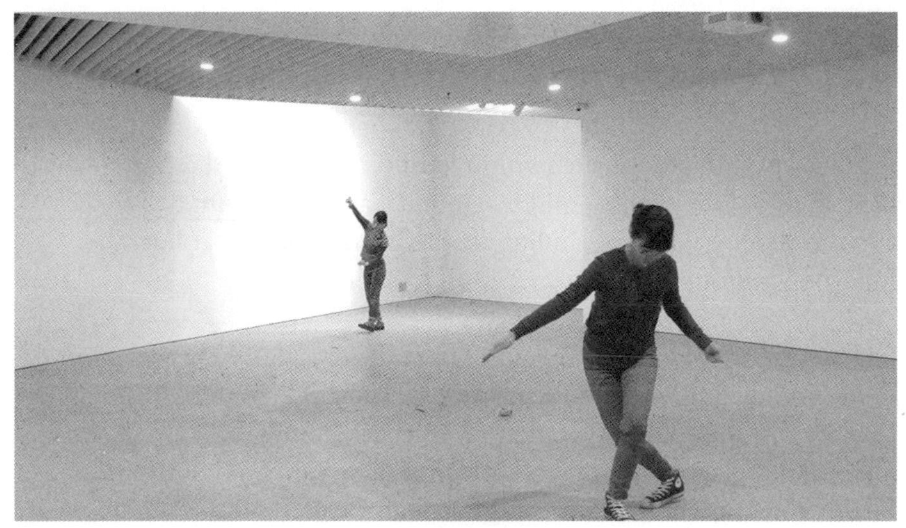

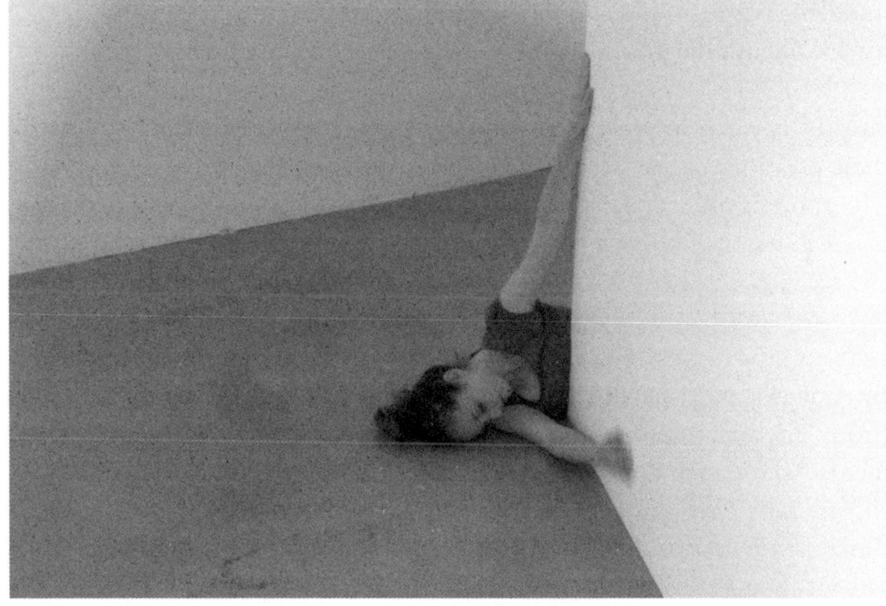

Event-maps

Event-maps, ubiquitous site (within locally circumscribed areas),
have distinct foregrounds, middle grounds, and backgrounds. Briefly
coordinated engagings of landing site define (sculpt out) at least the
following positions:

forebackground, foremiddleground, foreforeground, middlebackground,
middlemiddleground, middleforeground, backbackground,
backmiddleground, backforeground, forebackground,
forebackmiddleground, forebackforeground, foreforemiddleground,
foreforeforeground, backforebackground, backforemiddleground,
backforeforeground, middleforebackground, middleforemiddleground,
middleforeforeground, middlebackground, middlebackmiddleground,
middlebackforeground, foremiddlebackground,
foremiddlemiddleground, foremiddleforeground, foreforebackground.

Surprisingly, the logical geographies of most philosophers make no use of
these positionings for describing events of the world.
The above is only a partial list of critical positionings in the event-map.

By Arakawa and Madeline Gins
(from "Architecture: Sites of Reversible Destiny – Architectural Experiments After Auschwitz-Hiroshima". In Arakawa and Madeline Gins,
*Architecture: Sites of Reversible Destiny – Architectural Experiments After
Auschwitz-Hiroshima* (London: Academy Editions, 1994), 21.

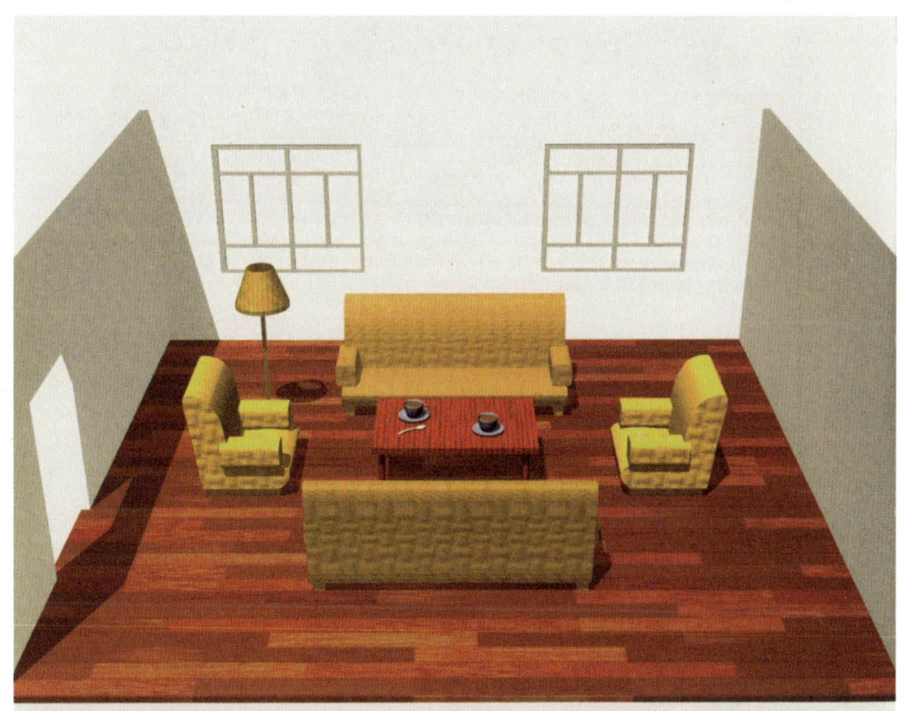

Shusaku Arakawa and Madeline Gins. Illustrations from *NOTEBOOK*: "Constructing the Perceiving of an Ordinary Room / Generating a Site of Reversible Destiny", 1994, digital rendering; dimensions: n/a © 1994 Estate of Madeline Gins. Reproduced with permission of the Estate of Madeline Gins and Reversible Destiny Foundation. Photo: n/k

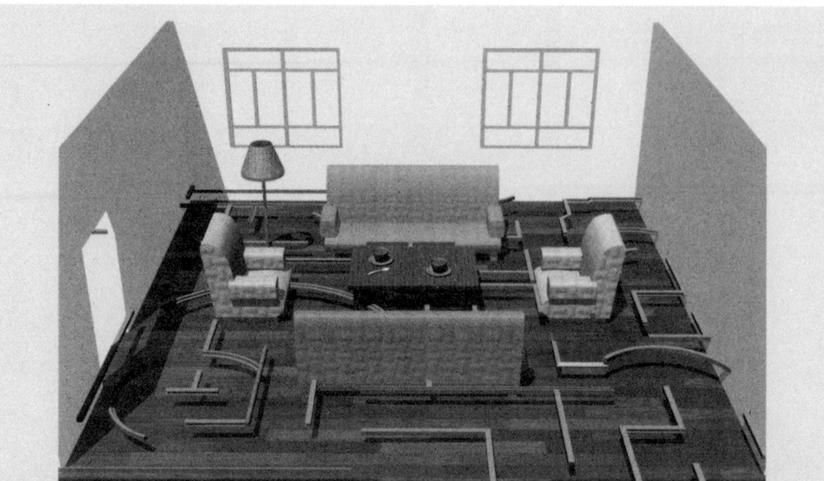

A labyrinth layer imposes directions on the body as narrowly and as pinpointedly as does a regularly-constructed labyrinth; it impedes the body's passage to nearly the same degree; but, unlike an actual labyrinth, it does this out in the open for all to see.

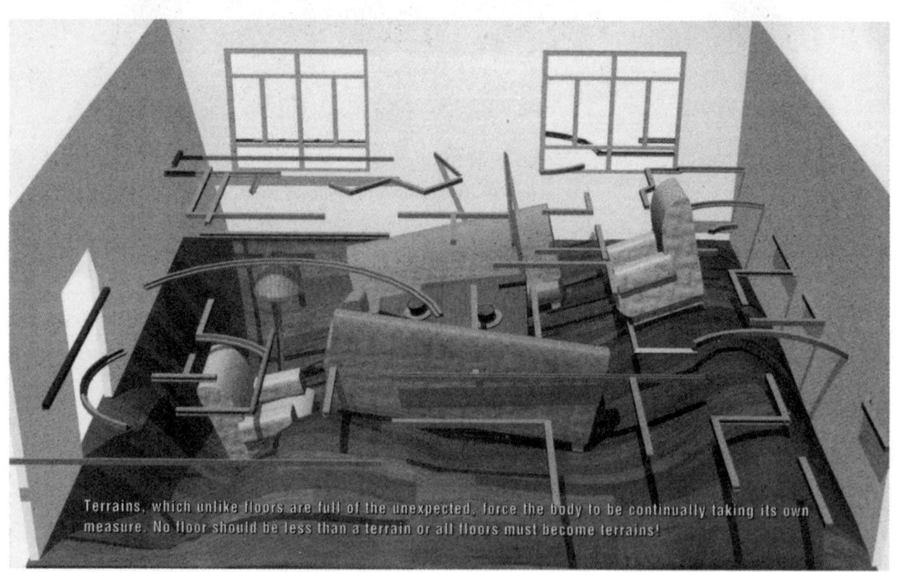

Terrains, which unlike floors are full of the unexpected, force the body to be continually taking its own measure. No floor should be less than a terrain or all floors must become terrains!

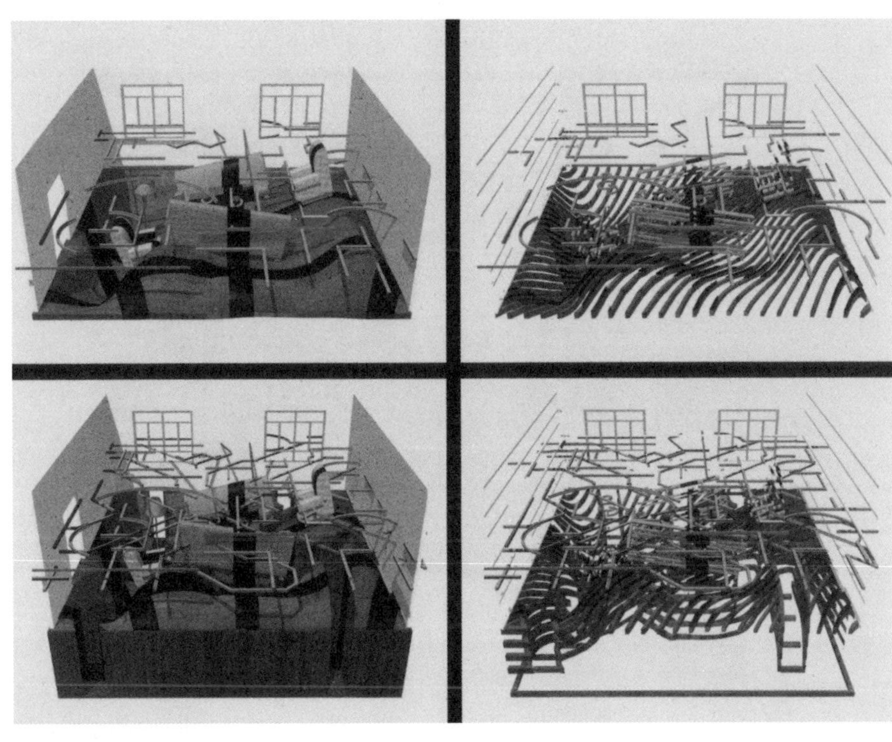

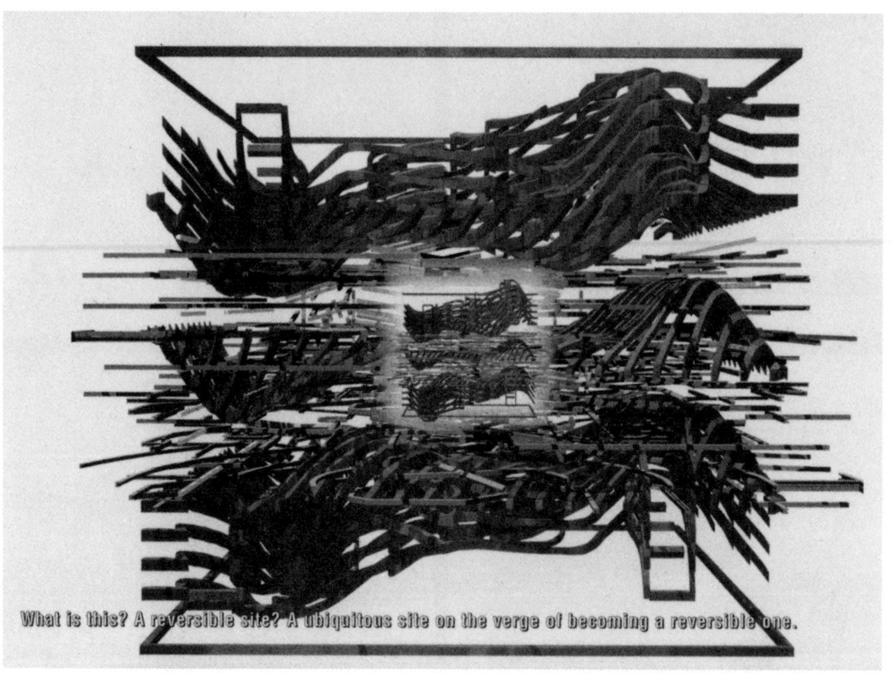What is this? A reversible site? A ubiquitous site on the verge of becoming a reversible one.

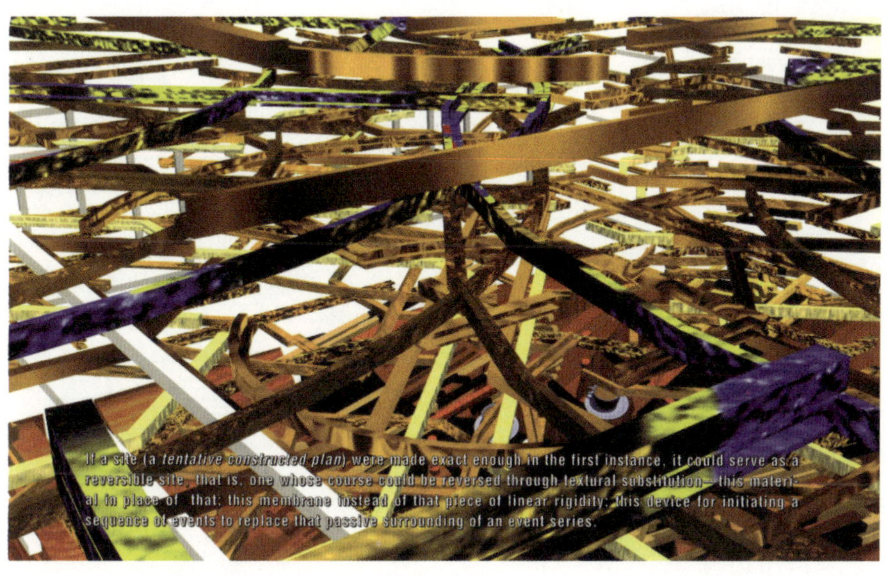

If a site (a *tentative constructed plan*) were made exact enough in the first instance, it could serve as a reversible site, that is, one whose course could be reversed through textural substitution—this material in place of that; this membrane instead of that piece of linear rigidity; this device for initiating a sequence of events to replace that passive surrounding of an event series.

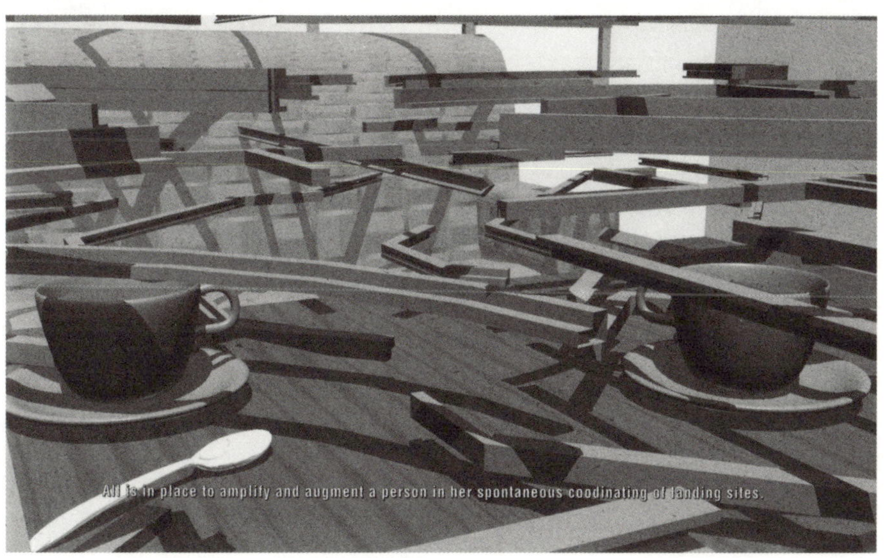

All is in place to amplify and augment a person in her spontaneous coodinating of landing sites.

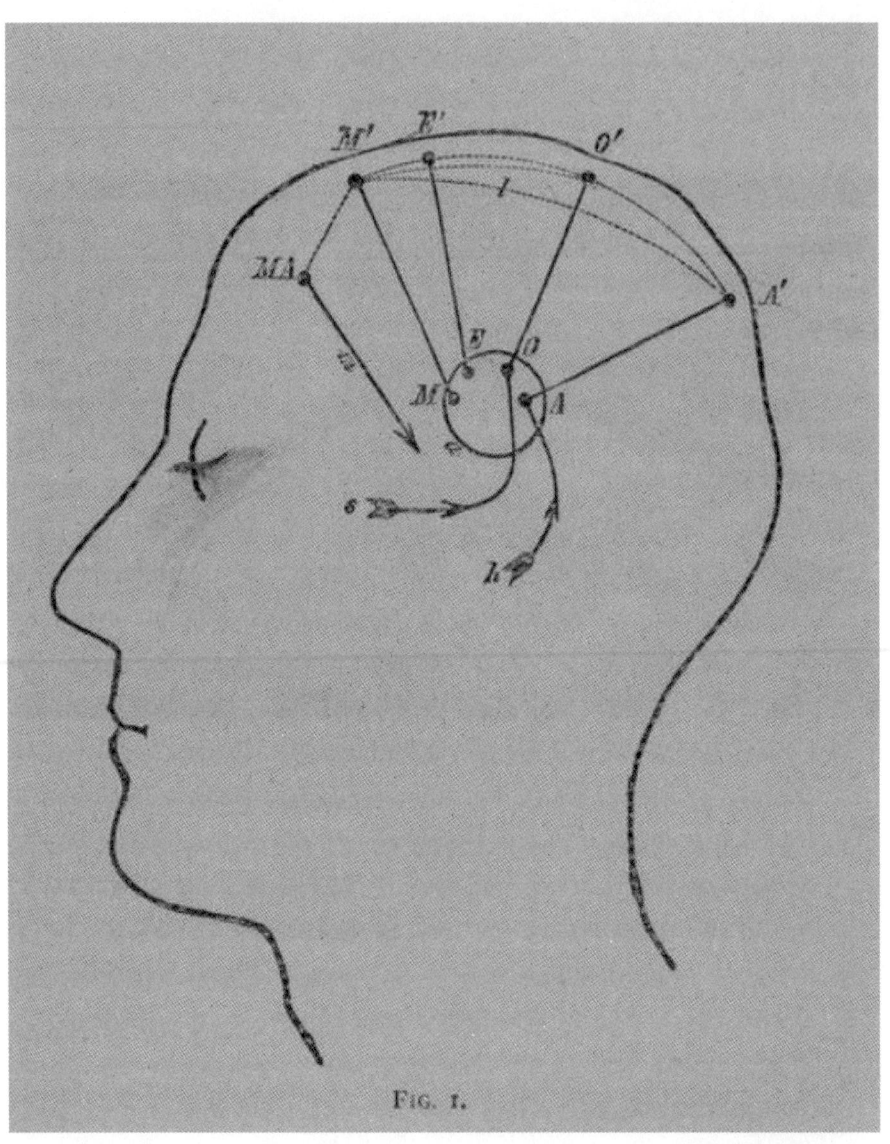

"How to Acquire and Strengthen
Will-Power", Richard J. Ebbard,
Modern Psycho-Therapy, London, 1903

Talking Back to the Light:
Nameless Architecture and
Its Critique of Epistemology

"12. The feeling of meaning:
Toward a demonstration of the affective role in cognition through an investigation of affective value as a measuring device; exercise for the movement of emotions in an attempt to set parameters for feeling through contortion, overlay, reversal and other disruptive systems: Assuming the validity of James Lange theory, if there is an internal sensory basis for feeling, what is the meaning of perception?"
—Arakawa & Gins[17]

Shusaku Arakawa, who spent most of his working life in New York City, created a series of abstract paintings early in his career. His paintings, from the late 1950s, but mostly from the 1960s, employed a recognisable style that was emerging in New York at the time – minimalist large formats that felt like premonitions of conceptual art. As one of the preeminent foundations of his work, Arakawa quite early on examined semiotics and grammar, while remaining dedicated to painting on canvas. He amalgamated everyday objects, texts, spaces, events, et cetera so as to make them into signs. He took apples, tea cups, a living room, himself, his friends' birthdays, a short entry in the Webster's Dictionary, et cetera, reduced all of them to lines, dots, or arrows in his paintings, and presented them along with geometric shapes such as cylinders, squares, circles, and grids. He occasionally combined words such as "mistake", "blank", or "line", or paradoxical aphorisms in the style of Samuel Beckett.

In his paintings, everything becomes a sign and is intended to become equivalent with everything else. It is laid out in an orderly manner on the blank space of the canvas. The paintings and other images often recall diagrams in scientific textbooks or exercises in mathematics, or adopt the format of a city map or part of an architectural plan. His conceptual aim was to have format accepted as paintings. In contrast to his geometric abstractions in two dimensions, the paintings hold their own with a strong sense of physical space – one may feel

---

[17] Arakawa & Gins, from *The Mechanism of Meaning: Work in Progress* (1963–71, 1978) based on Arakawa's method (New York: H. N. Abram, 1979), Chapter 12.

visually entrapped by them as if in a labyrinth. That labyrinth is dimensionless, beyond scale, and depthless and/or bottomless, like the world of the early 20th-century philosophical novel *Flatland*, or of *Gulliver's Travels* or *Alice in Wonderland*. Once a person is drawn into the space of the paintings, s/he has to navigate the self on his/her own using all of his/her bodily senses. They remind us that apples on a table "are" simply a line. As the title of one of his paintings shouts, *'No'! Says the Signified* (1971–72), Arakawa painted a world where all the signs are literally and conceptually framed, divided, twisted, and even erased, and words and texts are mirrored and arranged in a paradoxical way. The Japanese architect Arata Isozaki refers to the significance of arrows in Arakawa's painting. He understands that, for Arakawa, the arrow is "de-signified", devoid of function and meaning, with no capacity to direct or point anymore. The "arrow" as signifier becomes the "arrow as it is" (= nothing), and becomes a stimulator that actively produces simulacra. Thereby, Isozaki understands Arakawa's paintings as models – as models of simulacra that, to him, seemed strongly reflective of New York City. It is a legendary contemporary space – from today's globalising point of view, rather a small space – where all semiotics are dysfunctional and tend to dissolve. The beholder is a protagonist inside his labyrinth, there to explore the world's imaginative possibilities.

Parallel to these on-going explorations in painting, Arakawa met Madeline Gins, a poet with a physics degree, who would become his partner as of 1962. They collaborated on a long-term artistic investigation elaborating their own syntax of science, poetics, and discursive thinking about life and death. The first outcome of their collaboration is *Mechanism of Meaning* (1963–88), published in the form of a sketchbook in three instalments (in 1971, 1979, 1988); it was also presented in the format of exhibitions. Later on, *Sites of Reversible Destiny* would mark their in-depth engagement with architecture. Both projects were pursued with a high level of intensity; they can be said to teem with inspiring thoughts and practices in and on the periphery of architecture, a transitional field that they simultaneously associated with a wide range of interdisciplinary references from literature, philosophy, physics, biology, to linguistics, et cetera. The hyper-density and complexity of their works produced the gravitas and sometimes also the bulky feeling of a rather hard-to-digest avant-gardism. As quickly becomes clear, this happened for a reason: there is no *digestif* to help ameliorate difficulties in understanding many of their works. While his early paintings are understood as models of simulacra, here I would like to link one of Arakawa and Gins' later projects, *Sites of Reversible Destiny*, to another, but different model of a generator of a ubiquity of measurement from *Survey/Mountain*. While Yoshida sees images as sign, Arakawa perceives not only the image but also everything as sign. With Madeline Gins, his life-long partner, they aim at creating a new format of life/death by devising architecture as an incubator of praxis, where measurement in the body can emerge and actively perform.

The *NOTEBOOK*, one of their early works and part of the second project, *Sites of Reversible Destiny*, is highlighted here, as it shows the complex of Arakawa and Gins' experimental praxis in a set of visuals with step-by-step instructions. From today's perspective, choosing an "ordinary room" as their formal starting point (as they do) might seem affirmative and indicative of a facile, surface-value critique of a post-Benjaminian, bourgeois interior space, but here the historical distance to a work that originated in the early 1990s needs to be taken into consideration. The sequence of digital architectural images of a "generic" American-style living room was produced with a then-current CAD software; Arakawa and Gins are actually treading new ground here aesthetically – although these aesthetics certainly already look very dated to us today. They are quite advanced artistically as well, since they apparently take up the language of architectural planning and analysis with very little aesthetic distance – in the consequentiality of their visual strategy, this was probably also seen as a bold move – from the "humanising" self-referentiality of 1980s computer art, which is still tangible in the earliest parts of this series – garish colours and cheap-looking textures included. But the aesthetic strategy soon begins to move on from this provocative outset: With increasing degrees of complexity, a great diversity of analytical layers and cuts is applied to the "ordinary room" – this does not stop with it being dissected and dissolved; it rather increasingly resembles an explosion that seems to propose a kind of "explosive architecture" or space. This is, by all appearances, not far removed from the deconstructive aesthetics being discussed around that time, but it does not stop there. The ordinary room explodes and becomes limitless, labyrinthine, immaterial. Marcel Duchamp once said: "If a shadow is a two-dimensional projection of the three-dimensional world, then the three-dimensional world as we know it is the projection of a four-dimensional universe." Partly sharing the understanding of space that becomes apparent in this quote, Arakawa and Gins further elaborate their notion of space from one to n-dimensions, by relating it to an architectural thinking that is based on a manifestation of events created by active engagement.

The *NOTEBOOK* now describes their original ideas regarding how to measure and materialise such a space based on the body. Like various other artists who were working in performance art, dance, and early conceptual art at the time, but unlike the vast majority of then-existing contexts of "fine arts" and architecture, their praxis re-centres the human being as an organism (instead of likening it to an algorithm), and presents a systematic artistic approach to producing a new grammar of measuring time-space, one that understands itself as a stance that opposes the logic of efficiency and as countering forces of a double process of dividualisation and personalisation, combined with an internalised intensification of geometry.

NOTEBOOK
In *Architecture – Sites of Reversible Destiny*[18]
SUBJECT: Landing Sites
TITLE: Constructing the Perceiving *(sic!)* of an Ordinary Room!
                  Generating a Site of Reversible Destiny
AUTHOR: The Perceiver

NOTEBOOK presents a set of exercises with the intention of having readers/viewers fill the inevitable blank spaces with a series of imaginative, perceptual, and sensual praxes. As mentioned, the book begins with an image of an ordinary living room. It is furnished with two sofas, two chairs, a table on which there are two cups of coffee, a standing lamp, and two stylised windows. Over forty graphic renderings of this room, accompanied by short instructions at the bottom, provide navigational directions for following the adventure. Every image visualises how to abstract an ordinary room into a space consisting exclusively of geometrical signs. It also demonstrates how perceptions are formed and transform a blank space from three-dimensionality to n-dimensionality, and thus make it possible to provide a provisional construction plan, something the artists call "perceptual landing sites".

In a first step, all of the objects are reduced to dots and lines of different lengths. The living room is turned into a skeleton-like assemblage. The lines are multiplied, superimposed on top of each other, shifted, and twisted. They gradually define the path for an imaginary walking movement, change views and shift prevalent modes of perception, for example into an X-ray depiction, and can be said to imag(in)e and collect the perceptions of others. With the full impact of an unexpected force, the body loses its balance, its secure standing on the floor. The artists write, "No floor should be less than a terrain. All floors must become terrains." Interestingly, some images also show what we usually do not desire to construct – namely: mistakes, or failures. It is clear that these

---

[18] Madeline Gins and Shusaku Arakawa, *Architecture – Sites of Reversible Destiny* (New York: Academy Editions, 1994).

steps do not occur in the name of harmony or perfection. Instead, they are about making things work based on the power of the will and the "real" encounter as part of an *event*. Here, it is noticeable how many conceptual elements in the *NOTEBOOK* are still similar to features of the early painting works from the 1960s, which intensively investigated the life-world using geometrical means and were part of Arakawa's invention of his own aesthetic interpretation of symbols and signs. For example, the concept of *blank space* (as the *arrow* in other works) serves as a keyword that is crucial for understanding his painting. The blank becomes the pivotal motif, a compositional device, and an abstraction of the living room that very much resembles early specimens of his paintings, such as *Alphabet Skin* (1965–66), where the reduction of the object and the architectural components to mere lines and the representation of shadow as dots encounters the use of paradoxical aphorisms and "mistakes" as important components in the overall process. All this can be seen in the earlier works and was consistently applied in his work for nearly forty years.

The artistic practice behind the *NOTEBOOK* is a shared artistic attempt to simulate the world of Arakawa's paintings and Arakawa and Gins' experimentation as seen in the *Mechanism of Meaning*, but transposed to a different medium. In the world of lines and dots, the *blank space* becomes a site of "energy-matter" (Arakawa) and "a structural parameter" (Isozaki) for constructing a tentative site. Arakawa regards architecture as a potential container and as a mental tool used to produce ubiquity of measurement beyond dimensionism, so that the prototype of the *blank* would become an experimental site of time-space. As their motto, "questioning in a 360-degree way", elucidates, their exercise continues to explore multiple viewing directions as well: towards the north, south, west, and east. Distances begin to disintegrate and evaporate into *ubiquitous space*. The views from different distances – a close-up of coffee cups and sofas, and simultaneously the downtown cityscape and natural landscapes – are integrated into the spaces in between the lines, or compressed as colourful, thick lines to be inserted in the process of constructing a site. The spatial boundaries also lose their function, ultimately rendering the inside equivalent to the outside. Arakawa and Gins state that, for them personally, perceiving, believing to (have) perceive(d), and experiencing themselves as individuals (in the ubiquitous space of n-dimensions) are crucial aspects when it comes to being able to actively and simultaneously tentatively construct "perceptual landing sites".

"A single step leads one either directly into or indirectly out of the complete world picture or total event-map," they write. As they proceed further, the intensity of their images increases; they become covered with colourful lines and shapes that overlap each other. Short texts written in white letters are integrated in the image, which makes them hard to read, because stronger layers and elements almost cancel them out – a strategy that is actually applied to all kinds of signs. Even the space of the living room starts to look like an organism – like a monstrous caterpillar! After the excess of lines in the totally deformed living room, Arakawa and Gins all of a sudden insert a miniature image of the "perceptual landing site" located at its centre, and ask: "What is this? A reversible site?" The question contains their feeling of surprise, or their emotion of being stunned by the perception of the image with the miniature inside, as if they had unexpectedly discovered something – nothing less than the possibility of reversible time (of life and death). They then continue with this statement on their conceptual space: "A ubiquitous site on the verge of becoming a reversible one." This particular page may lead us closer to what the important point of the *NOTEBOOK* is within our context of measurement.

The page suggests that the exercise conducted in the *NOTEBOOK* is not meant to be any sort of systematically or otherwise established training programme, as in a generic textbook. It is closer to the zigzag process and trajectory of conceptual exploration that Arakawa and Gins follow – the road to their own simulacra. Importantly, their confusions, mistakes, failures, excitements, and surprises are integrated and make their appearance there in order to affectively address the reader. It should also not be forgotten that the speculative experiment is not designed to augment space, but to augment a "person" in his/her "spontaneous coordinating of landing sites", a process of "being switched over to act". The protagonist in the labyrinth is the beholder. The fundamental core of the reversible site is located within the body – in the *organism of that person* –; their architecture is a device for allowing the miniature to be present in the body of the beholder. Thereby, the exercise in the *NOTEBOOK* sketches out the skeleton, a plan for beginning our praxis of constructing a reversible site in a ubiquitous space of n-dimensions. Significantly, Arakawa and Gins generate the idea of measurement based on what they see as the collective organism, instead of on single subject(ivities), data collection, structures, and space emerging from algorithms.

Arakawa and Gins do not present work that offers concrete examples of measuring the world "from within". Rather, the *NOTEBOOK* can be seen as a book of nameless architectures (structures of situations) devised for actively measuring the world, which, paradoxically, merges three states of being – single work, meta-work, and generative work – into one. It thus unites two divergent statuses: It is a concrete work, but simultaneously also a model. The French philosopher Jean-Jacques Lecercle writes that the consistent paradox in their works is the pathway used to decentralise time and to take up a position that reckons with a materialism of space. He continues by stating that their systematic defamiliarisation of sense should actually be read as "the story of self-creation of the human species in space" and as creating "the fourth dimension of proposition, which takes us out of *doxa*, i.e., out of meaning, good sense, and common sense, into a paradox as the site of truth".[19] To seek accuracy in measurement, Lecercle's words suggest that Arakawa and Gins' aim of seeking and constructing landing sites in ubiquitous space is not just measurement, but rather the "Truth" of measurement, which "cannot be absorbed by automated repetition, or a set of operations", but has to be conducted in a performative way, and in events.

The appearance of "Truth", as it is encountered here (with a capital T), inevitably raises the question of what this is really all about. In devising their concept of "landing sites", Arakawa and Gins redefine ("nameless") architecture as the structure of a situation, as their reversible site within the process of a reconfiguration of self – the very self that initiates a space, rather than being controlled and governed by it or in it. Here, I understand the concept of "landing site" essentially as a critique of epistemology – epistemology that has been (mis)guided by the ideologies, norms, and common sense of each era, in a continuation of the progress and acceleration that has been brought about by more recent light-based technologies of perception and measurement. The *NOTEBOOK* comprises a valuable approach that facilitates an encounter with epistemology in "immanence, instead of progress",[20] and makes it possible to re-direct thinking and doing in a plurality of world dimensions.

While Arakawa and Gins's *Sites of Reversible Destiny* project adopts architecture as a conceptual device of active measurement for elucidating the structure of situations in ubiquitous space, *Dimensions Variable* by Hwayeon Nam accepts the centrality of time and employs architecture as a medium for reconfiguring time-based parameters on the human body. Both projects are a departure from systematic structural understandings of a situation and from a praxis that generates *events* as essential parts of their respective works. In contrast to the powerful language game proposed and played by Arakawa and Gins, Nam's approach situates the void of language and fills up space (including linguistic space) only with ephemeral movements that tentatively appear and then disappear again.

---

[19] Jean-Jacques Lecercle, "Gins and Arakawa, or The passage to Materialism", in *Architecture and Philosophy: New Perspective on the Work of Arakawa & Madeline Gins*, eds. Jean-Jacques Lecercle and Françoise Kral (Amsterdam and New York: Rodop, 2010), 18.
Art historian Carlo Ginzburg studies a traditional technique of de-familiarisation (ostranienie) that leads to scrutinising the self and the devices of art in general. In *Wooden Eyes: Nine Reflection on Distance*, trans. Martin Ryle and Kate Soper (New York: Columbia University Press, 2001).
[20] Ibid., p. 24.

Dimensions Variable is a series of performances based on a score written by the artist Hwayeon Nam that measures the time dimension inside a specific space. The score is composed of ten modules and consists of ten commands for actions, such as steps, vertices, planes, circles, and orbits, et cetera, with accompanying instructions. For example, one instruction in Module 2/Step says: "From one wall to another. Measure the distance between two walls by walking. Count the number of steps, and write down the number each time you arrive at different walls. Try to walk in as even strides as possible. Every wall can be used." Five modules are selected in a specific arrangement and structured as what Nam calls "Phrases". A set of "Phrases" is called a "Formulation" in the structure as a whole. Through creating every instruction as a "set", Nam provides a platform for openness, where all possible movements (measurements of time) can potentially emerge. The instructions are written down in order to direct performers, with the choice of vocabulary seeming to be a mix of architectural and military terminologies. This aspect also has to do with the fact that it is partly an extension of a part of her previous performance, *Operational Play*, which she developed based on commands used in the United States military.

In each performance, the artist selects and arranges modules in a specific order, which are then activated by the performers based on the free interpretations they develop in relation to their individual bodies. Her score is quite simple with the minimal signs in a fullness of blank space. *Dimensions Variable* attempts to replace unit-structured time as a rigid mechanism with subjective perceptions of the situated body. With reference to the idealism of time, Lecercle elucidates three levels of the concept of time as follows: "The centrality of time holds at both the collective, cultural, and individual level. At the collective level, this involves the traditions of our community, our roots, our collective destiny as a nation, a class, a species: from the *lendemains qui chantent* to the manifest destiny of the chosen people, a destiny we must deserve and towards which we strive in teleological tensions, because time, or history, is on our side. At the individual level, this involves the construction of identity through memory, from Locke to Proust."[21]

Dimensions Variable temporally borrows the "module" structure and concept as a unit in order to measure time as a hybrid all three levels – to actively explore and perform time by following the actions of the performers' bodies. It is a radical act to influence the function of time from a humble, but certain position of "individual". The artist understands the body as "a three-dimensional tool for mea-

---

[21] Ibid., 20.

suring the invisible", and lets the body in space intra-act and eventuate as the structures of the module, of architecture. The openness of the work actually allows the body to be the medium for the three levels of time and allows the social to merge into one so as to improvise (create) an alternative measurement of time. This decentralises time at a collective level and at present, and recentralises it on an individual level in duration, instead of adopting the idealism of time. Each performer's body produces a measurement of time through reflecting memories in the body instead of the mind. Attention should be given to the fact that multiple performers (two or three depending on the project budget) are coordinated at times to enact the same score with different timings, though they occasionally enact different scores individually. This transforms the concept of the unit not only from a fixed (still) to a flexible state, but also from the idealism of a single construction to a materialism by means of plural inventions. Nam's work concerns time both as a social construct and as something that is embedded in all kinds of forms and lives. Through renouncing any kind of "movement modules", *Dimensions Variable* generates the event of re-writing the "social contract" (Badiou, 1998/2006) of time with society.

Dimensions Variable includes a lot of blank space, especially in the score for the performance. It comprises minimal linguistic expression, or, more precisely, only signs that Nam has defined. The space around the score is simply white – no words, no signs, no drawings. – Despite the intensive thinking and determination by the artist that is behind the work, at first glance, there might seem to be a lack of intensity. However, the penetration of wordlessness and speechlessness in the work prioritises the bodies of the dancers and the moments of their actions of measuring out of their bodies – measurement in the body. While the blank portions of the score represent indeterminacy and inseparability from the body in space, accuracy of measuring time is actualised solely in the space, and the unit structure of time disappears when the action is completed. And, transcripts of time, which are probably able to remain on the level of the collective for a longer period of time, can only be fabricated out the moment when tentative constructing is happening at the site. In this way, Nam's work is quite opposite to that of Arakawa and Gins. Both Nam and Gins and Arakawa pursue how measurement in the body can take charge of our ways of knowing, understanding and creating our lives. Through initiating a radical praxis of re-writing time and emancipating it from institutional and bureaucratic governance, *Dimensions Variable* gives rise to a modernistic structural view of time. That is, the work accepts the ephemeral nature of the organism (the subject) that measures time.

*Dance of
Accuracies*

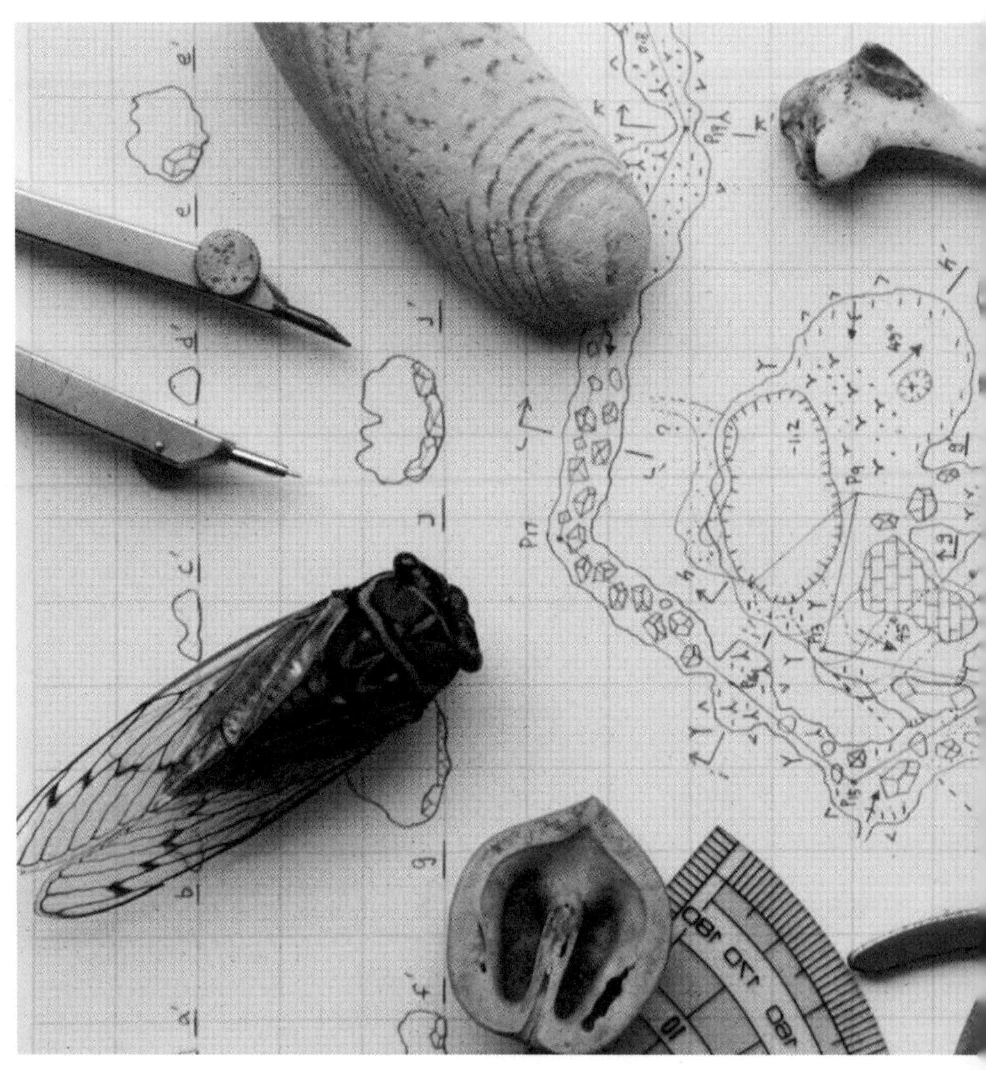

Com-Pass Cave Unit, *The Act of Looking/Survey Map* (detail) 2008, pencil drawing on graph paper, 30 x 30 cm, photo: Katsuhiro Ichikawa © Toru Koyamada

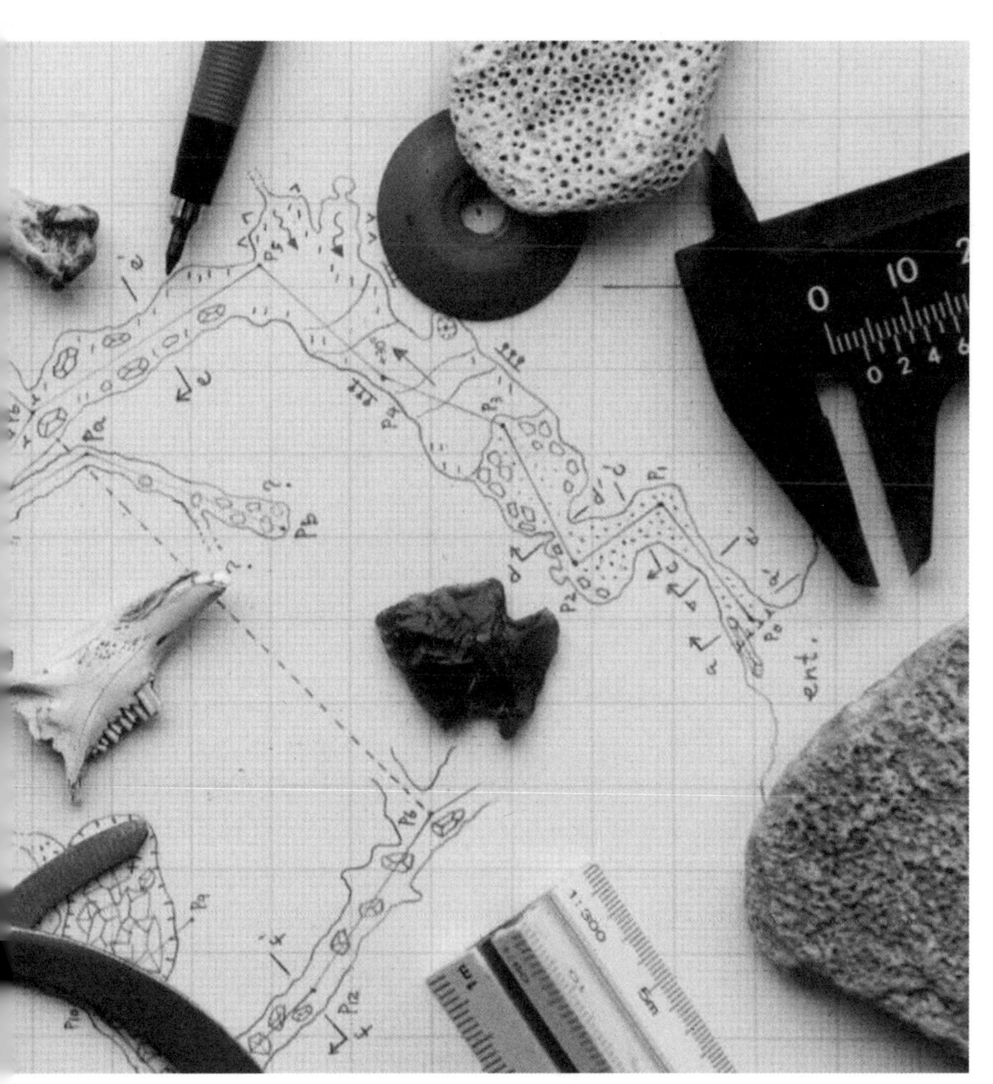

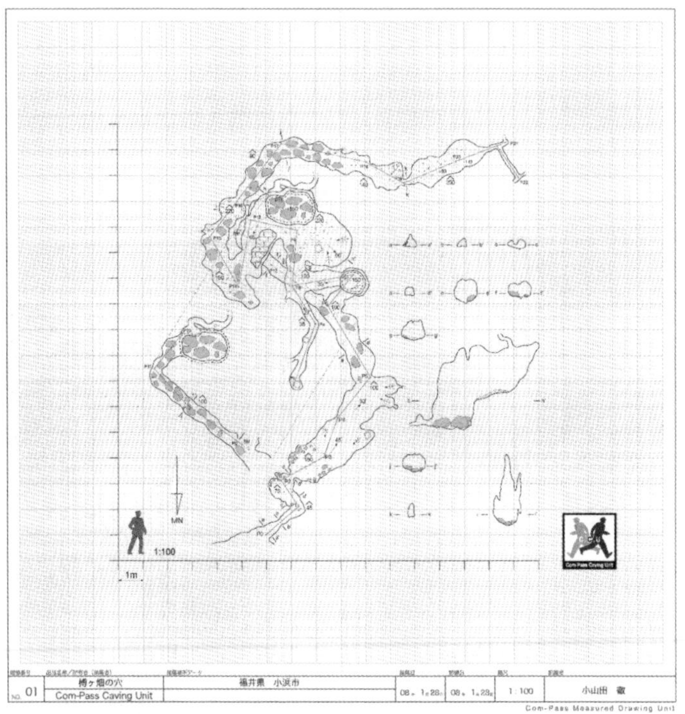

Com-Pass Cave Unit,
*The Act of Looking/
Survey Map*, 2006,
pencil drawing on
graph paper, 30 x 30 cm
© Toru Koyamada

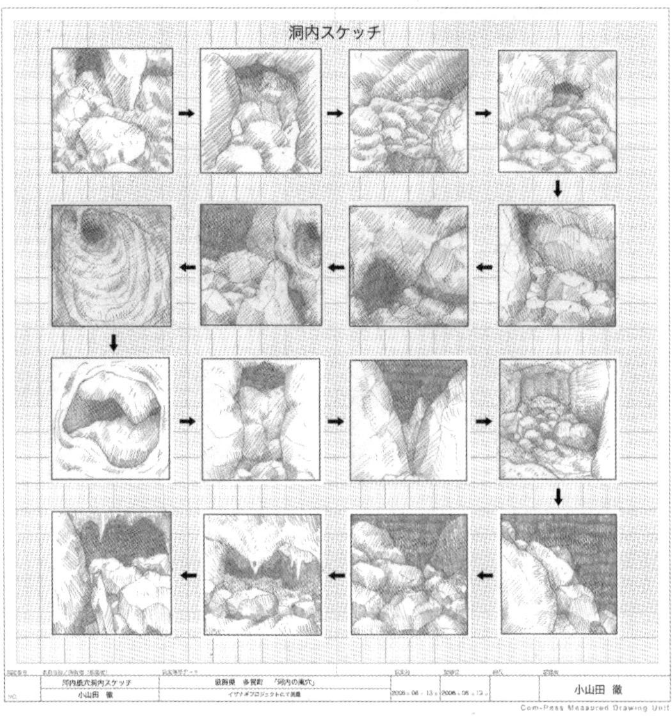

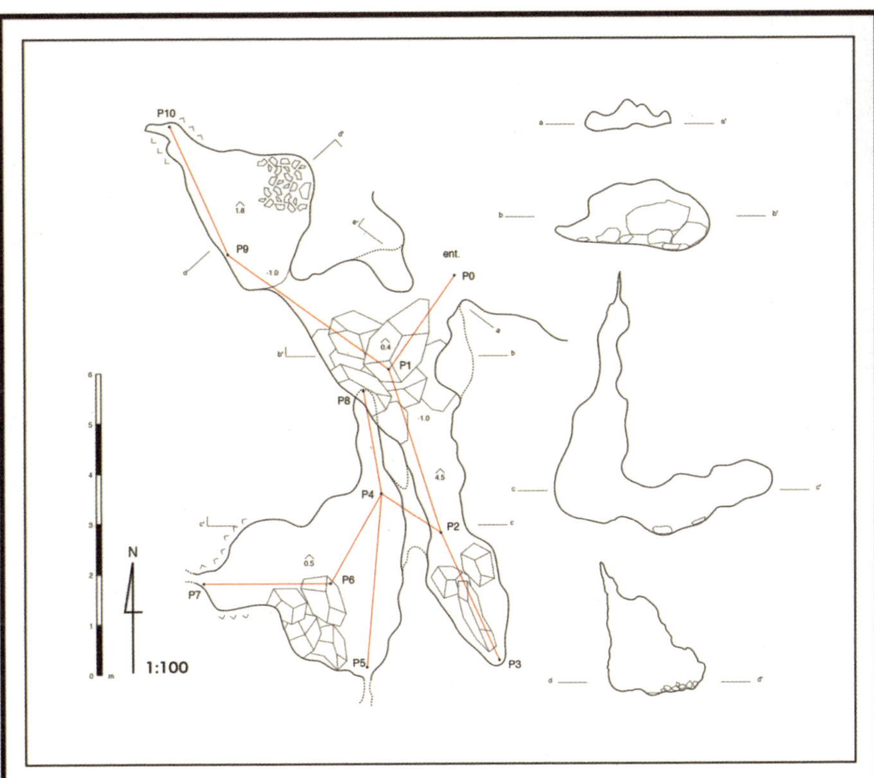

ドヤ洞

2012年

5月13日（日）10:11

測量／中野

スケッチ／小山田

point	斜距離	方位	斜角	P高	P天	P右	P左
P0				0	0.5	1.2	1.4
P0 - P1	2.0	216	7	1.0	0.3	2.9	2.0
P1 - P2	4.0	162	-31	0.3	4.5	2.1	1.0
P2 - P3	3.2	155	29	0.3	0.4	0.4	0.2
P2 - P4	1.5	303	-15	0,4	0	2.2	4.0
P4 - P5	3.6	185	15	0.1	0.2	0.3	0.3
P4 - P6	2.2	210	20	0.4	0.1	1.0	1.2
P6 - P7	3.0	270	37	0.1	0.1	0.4	0.1
P4 - P8	2.1	350	-10	0.1	0.1	0.2	0.2
P1 - P9	4.4	305	-25	1.1	0.7	2,5	0
P9 - P10	3.0	335	-20	0.7	1.2	0.1	0.3

Com-Pass Cave Unit, *Doya Do*,
The Act of Looking: Survey Map,
2012, pencil drawing on graph paper
30 x 30 cm © Toru Koyamada

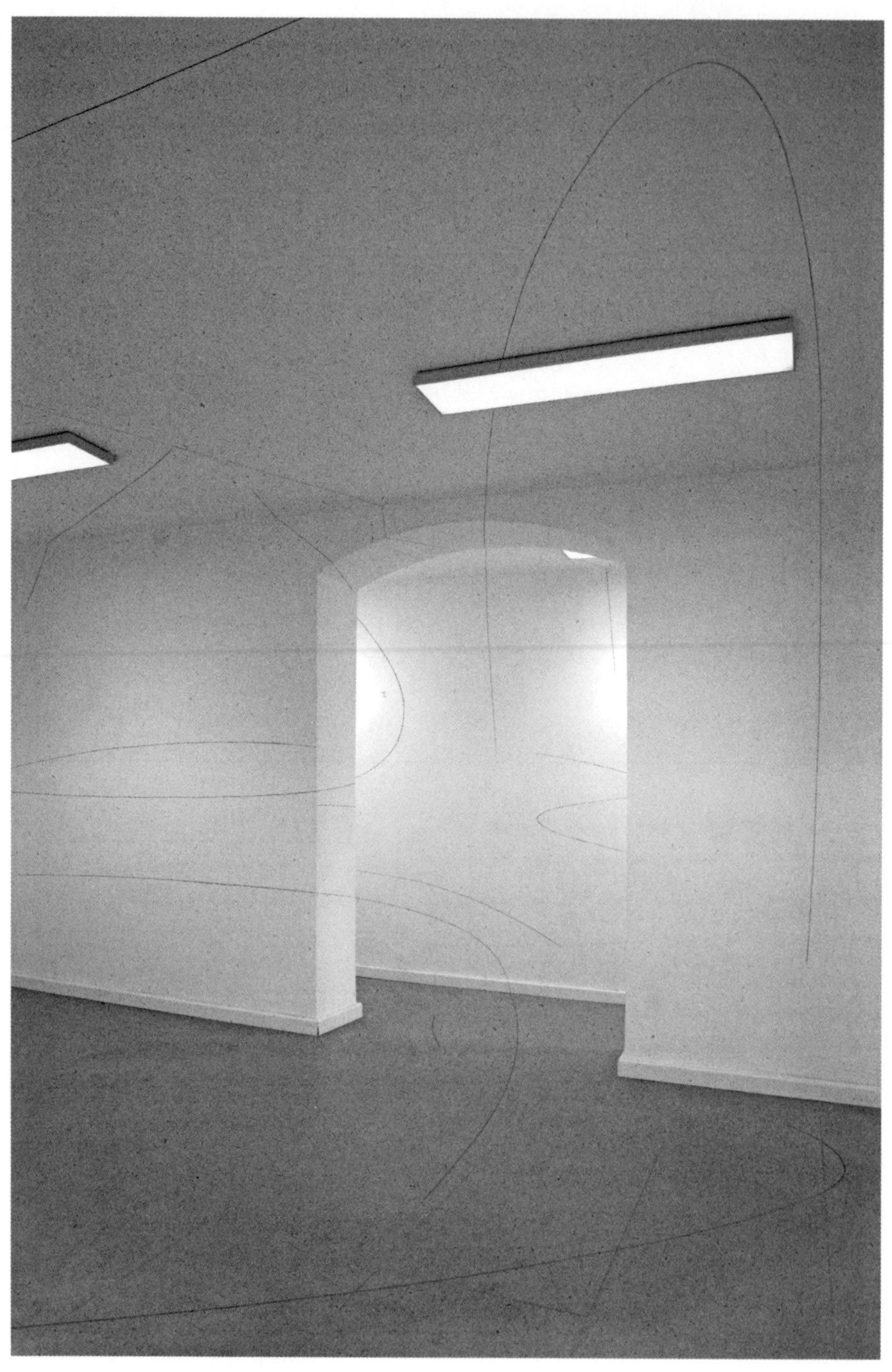

Asako Tokitsu, *Incidence Inside*, 2016,
Fourteen lines, fourteen viewpoints, 2016,
site-specific installation, O&O DEPOT,
Berlin, charcoal, crayon directly on wall,
photo © Dmitri Lavrow

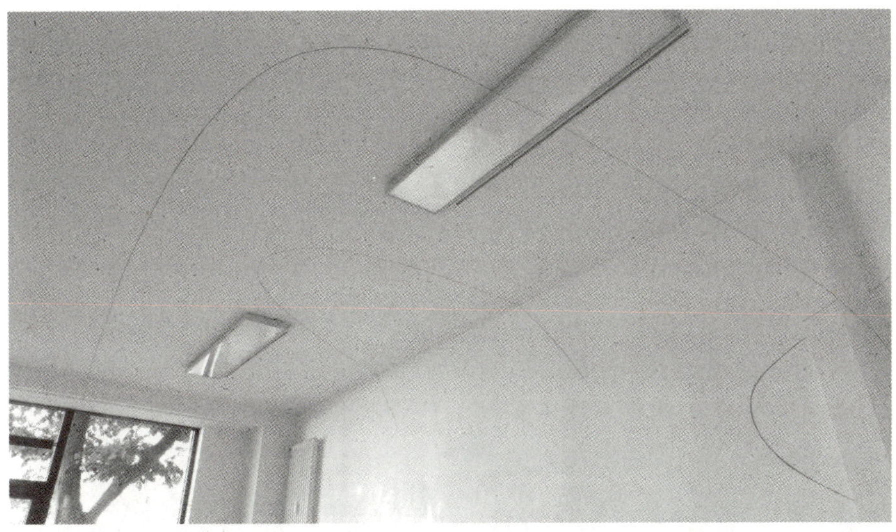

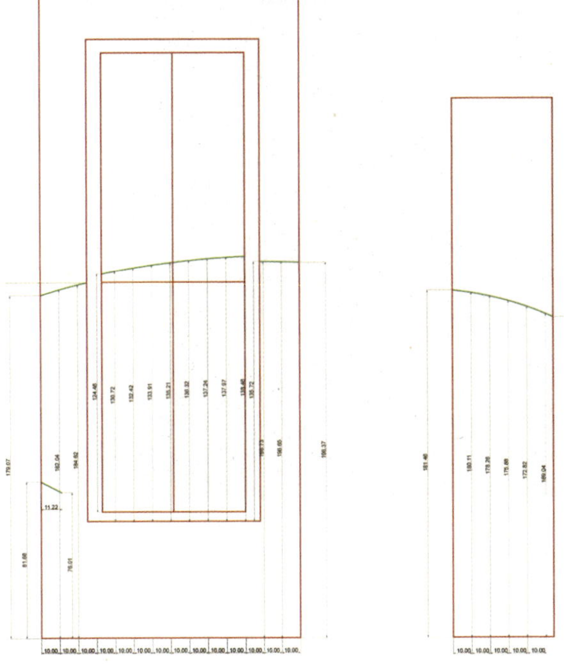

Asako Tokitsu, *Incidence Inside*, 2016,
details of measuring and drawing a line
that cannot be calculated by computation,
photo © Dmitri Lavrow

Digital modelling & rendering by Steve
Gödickmeier, René Kobel ©Asako Tokitsu

Over the last thirty years, Asako Tokitsu
has been working site-specifically on spatial relationships of lines. The artist realises
that some lines are not calculable, which is
why she combines both calculable and in-
calculable lines in her installations. As
part of the group exhibition *Listening to
Lines* (Ginza Maison Hermès, Tokyo, 24
April – 5 May 2015), she reflects on her
experience working with assistants, which
led to unexpected results in her installation. Her assistants were commissioned to
draw a line high up on one wall of the exhibition space, while the artist supervised
them while sitting on the floor, in order to
be able to have a view the entire wall. After
working together for a while, the assistants' hands and the artist's brain started to
synchronise, as Tokitsu recalls. This synchronisation filtered out all unnecessary
factors and created a line that is very so-
phisticated; these are "better" lines than
the ones she herself or a computer could
have calculated. They are "better" in that
they appear to be more complex in their
morphology, while seeming to be more
spontaneous and "natural" at the same
time. In other words, the synchronisation of
two (or more) subjectivities opens up a
shared platform of measurement and precision. (From a conversation with Tokitsu, 30
July 2016, at O&O Depo Gallery, Berlin)

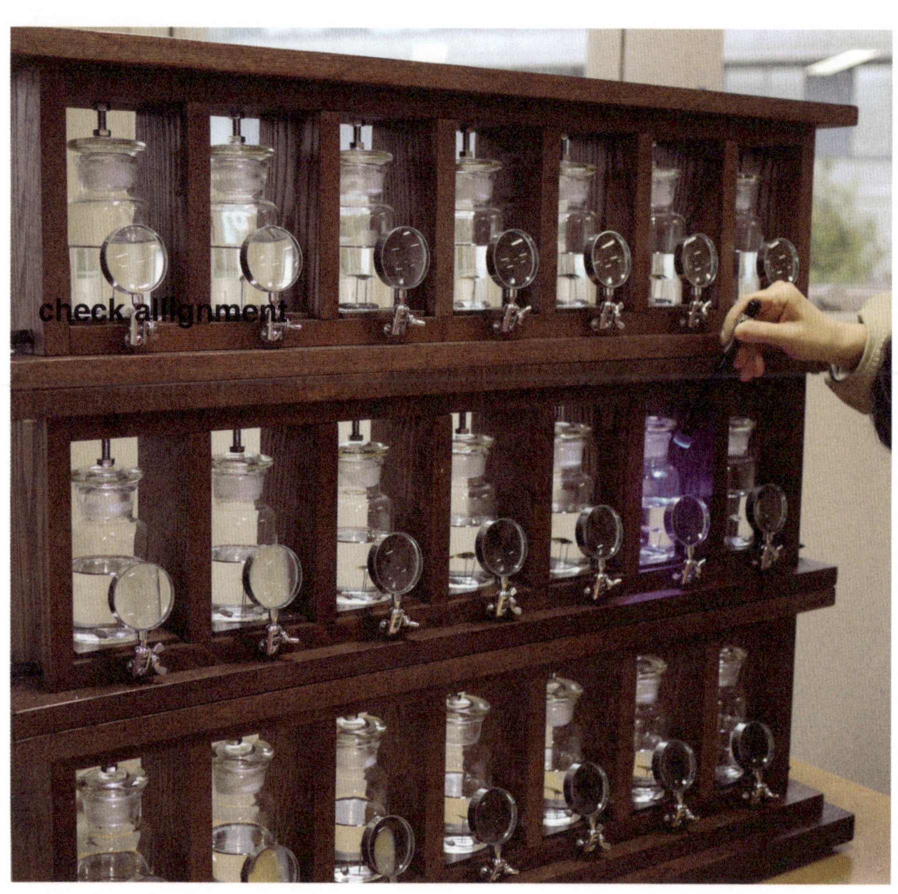

Toru Koyamada (in collaboration with
Dr. Kiyoshi Naruse), *Diversity Maniacs*,
2011, mixed-media installation,
80 x 60 x 17 cm © Toru Koyamada

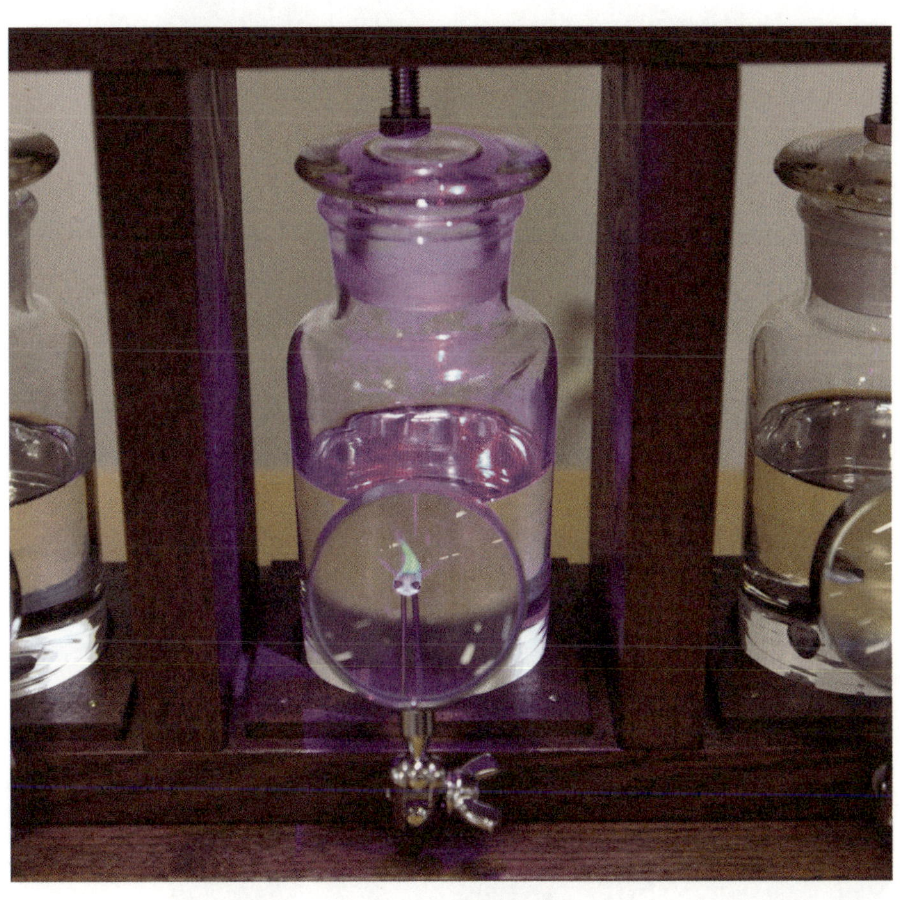

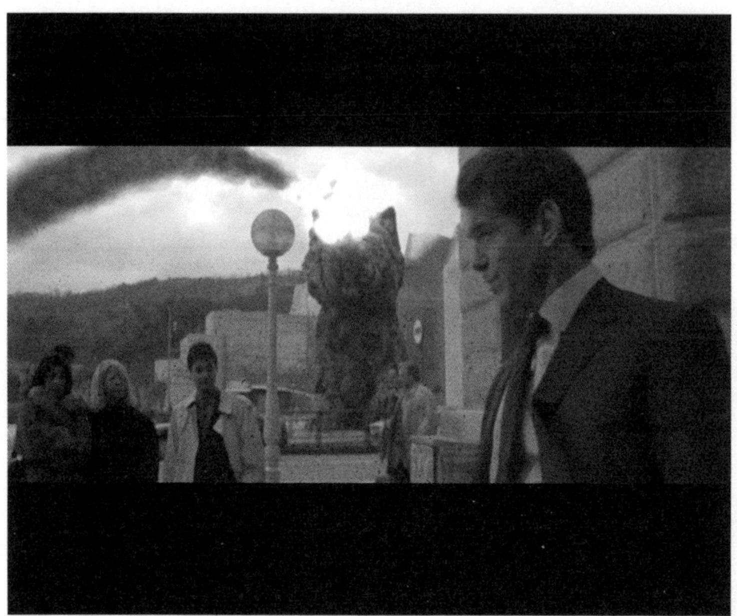

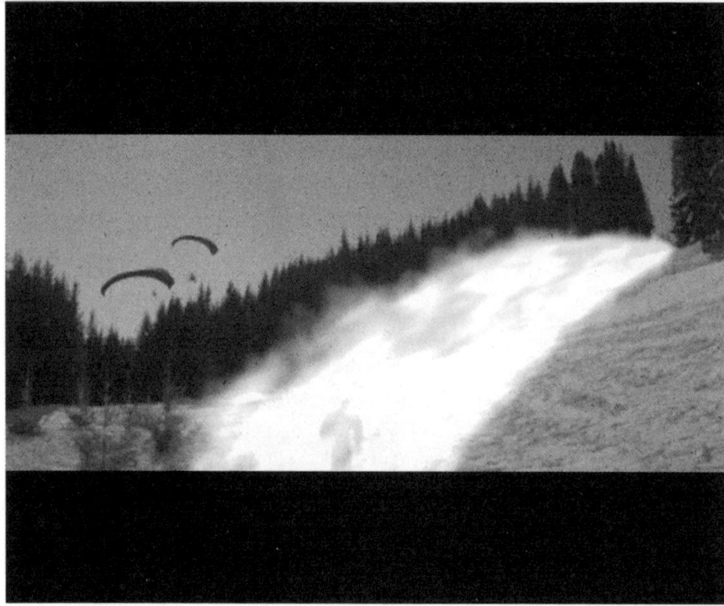

Julien Prévieux, *Post-post-production*, 2014,
SD video, 120 min.

Julien Prévieux completely rebuilds the eponymous episode of the James Bond series: Each plan is embellished with additional special effects, including explosions, fires, avalanches, or smoke.

Smoke and fire are added in an exaggerated way and pop up here and there. The spectacularising of the visual effects transcends narration and transforms the film into a generator of instant pleasures. Corresponding to the logic of "technological progress" and "improvement of quality", Prévieux extends the production chain by means of a mimetic posture. This consequently changes the means and the meaning of accuracy in measuring.

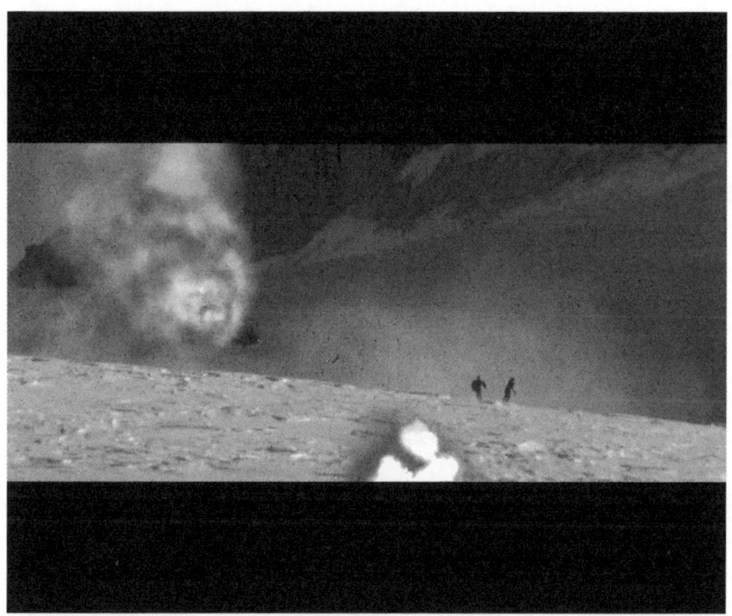

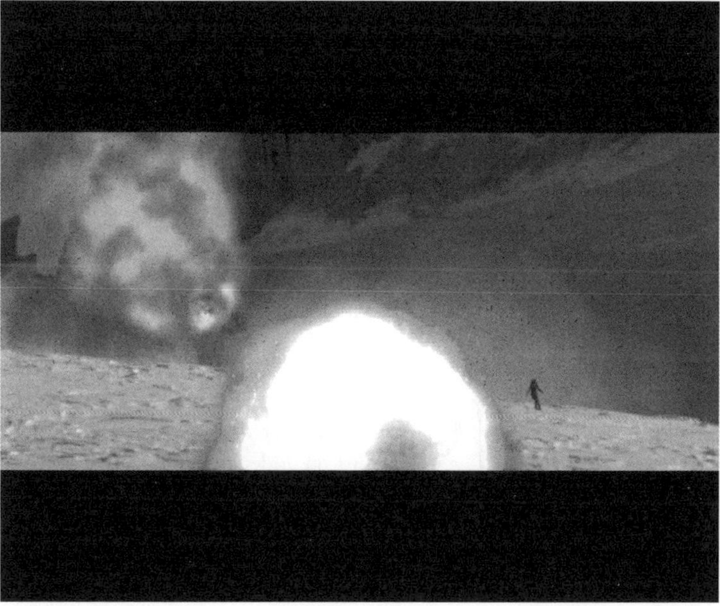

Here, accuracy is no longer the result of calculation or a precise rendering of reality. The construction of measurement is organised around sensory perception, and exactitude is actively constructed by the aesthetics of (Hollywood) image industries, which cross the border between reality and "realities" (of over-production). The speed of calculation is continuously increasing, and so is the power to alter images – as is visible in high frame-rate photography and pixel clouds, the frequent practice of manipulating images or the use of modelling techniques. *Post-post production* indicates a point at which measurement in the production of images implodes.

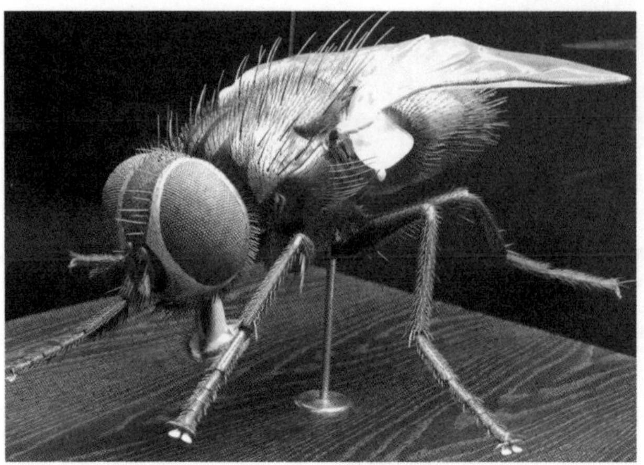

"At first, it didn't seem so strange to me that a fly would
fly around upside down if he felt like it, because although
I had never seen such behavior, science teaches us, that
that is no reason to reject out-of-hand what our own senses
tell us no matter how out of the ordinary. (…) Later, (…)
I realized that there were some practical difficulties. If flies
were to take flight with their mouths down or on their
backs, they could escape from anywhere due to their well-
proven agility, but when imprisoned, a pitcher or even a
glass box could disturb this natural behavior or could even
hasten their death. Of the 10-15 days of his life, I wondered
how many remained for this poor little creature – which
was right now floating legs up in a state of pure bliss just
two inches from my face? I knew that if I notified the
Museum of Natural History, they would send some
Galician armed with a net which might cause a horrible
splat of my incredible discovery. (…) In less than an hour
(It must be understood that the life of a fly passes with
incredible speed if compared to my human life). I decided
that the only solution was to reduce little by little the
dimensions of my room until the fly and I would be
confined to the smallest possible space."

Julio Cortázar (1914–1984), *The Witness*, 1965, translated by Thomas
Christensen, San Francisco, 1998

Alfred Keller, *Fly*, 1932
© Hwa Ja Götz, Museum für
Naturkunde Berlin

Dance of Accuracies

"Through structure comes an apparent chance."
—Channa Horwitz

Acts of Looking: Survey Map is a series of documentations resulting from a survey study of caves on the periphery of Kyoto – conducted by a group of cultural workers who call themselves the Com-Pass Cave Unit. The study starts by having cave divers make precise measurements; this eventually results in a report in the form of a map that is a pictorial rendering of the caves they have examined, but also details scientific regulations and rules applied in speleological measurement. Closer scrutiny of the drawings of caves enables viewers to trace the different movements and actions of the cave divers – walking, crawling, measuring, and recording in darkness at over twenty locations, using various tools and working in a team.[22] Finding their direction by means of a compass, they use a clinometer to calculate the angle of incline and distance between two spots. In addition, they also use a laser or normal measuring tape for distance, height extremes, relative distance to the surrounding walls above, below, left, and right; to draw a map on site, they use a generic pencil with a protractor (a graduator) and a triangle. They also take note of shapes, specific conditions, and topographical details, and of whatever else they might find in the course of their passage through the caves. The draftsperson, a member of the survey team, analyses the data collected and converts them into two-dimensions through applying geometrical calculus. Weeks sometimes elapse between the date of the survey and the date of the drawing.

In *Survey Map*, a plan with cross-sections is given the most space. It shows the shapes of passages and constructs a side view (long–profile or projection) in order to give viewers an idea of the different levels of the cave and how they are connected. The hand-drawn images show that the appearance of the sections continually changes. The overview of the cave is shaped like an unidentifiable organism. The pencil lines are sensitive and look fragile, it immediately becomes

---

[22] The measuring process is always conducted by a team of cave divers. The final drawing of a cave provides essential information including the number and name of each cave, the area name, grade, credits (team members' full name and jobs during the session), survey date(s), draftsperson and date, scale bar, direction (of True North and Magnetic North) of instrument calibration. Ken Grimes, *Cave Mapping – Sketching details – A guide to producing a useful cave map*, ASF Cave Survey and Mapping Standards Commission (2000).

evident that their level of detail – the measured numbers, the short notes attached, et cetera – requires a high level of concentration. By means of common symbols and signs, the map gives more concrete information about surface features, navigational data, rigging, and special features such as stairs, additional paths, excavations, et cetera. All the amazing details of the cave are expressed by a synthesis of dots, outlines, numbers, signs, and symbols. The complexity of the space shaped over thousands of years is compressed onto the scale of a sheet of graph paper.

Surveying caves requires great effort, but still it is not easy to prove the accuracy of survey maps, at least not in any tangible way. This may sometimes depend on the equipment and conditions,[23] and sometimes on how the teamwork of the cave divers and the draftsperson functions. After long struggles in the darkness underground, mis-measurement and mis-recordings can occur without anyone being aware of them, but it is not easy to find or detect such errors. According to the BCRA (British Cave Research Association), accuracy is evaluated based on a combination of six grades (for a cave line) and four classes (for a passage). A grade is roughly divided by the facts of measurement, the quality of the equipment, and the realisation of geometric precision in the real conditions of the cave, while class is about the site of the recording – how precisely the divers can locate the recording point.[24] A grade for the position where the measurement takes place is described +,- (more or less) within a limited range. Computer technology, portable devices, and software have recently been developed to meet these challenges. For example, a lightweight 3D laser scanner is available to measure spaces more efficiently and to generate a high-resolution 3D map consisting of billions of points. Here, the accuracy is based on the idea of a centre (dot) defined by geometry, even though the additional notes regarding grade, amusingly, speak of the necessity of "trained experience" in using the device as well as of "follow(ing) the spirit of the definition and not just go(ing) by the letter". Geometrical thinking identifies the location as an intersection within the grid, which also grasps spatial relations through linking and correlating other dots. This thinking is oriented towards the dot as an absolute unit. In this sense, the dot represents accuracy in this type of measurement work.

---

[23] It is interesting that the basic actions that comprise cave surveys have fundamentally not changed over the course of the last 250 years. According to the British Cave Research Association, the use of magnetic survey methods is registered as "high grade", meaning it employs a high degree of accuracy. On-going development of topographic measuring devices and software is taking place, but is still incomplete or flawed by systematic or random errors, et cetera – at least when compared to other technologies.

[24] http://bcra.org.uk/surveying/

Meanwhile, if we take another look at *Survey Map*, despite the aim of being as "objective" as possible through following the set of speleological rules mentioned, the character, personal interests, and degrees of enthusiasm of the draftspeople can still be distinguished in and in between the subtle lines. While *Survey Map* satisfies the criterion of accuracy in a scientific sense, it also embraces various personal modes of accuracy. Here, the question is not about being more or less accurate. It is rather a different type of accuracy – accuracy in the sense of whether something really exists, or not, which is similar to the mode of the digital; accuracy is also not gradually developed in a process of drawing. Accuracy includes the imaginary spaces of "as if" and "as if it is". It is bound to the subjectivity of the speleologists and the draftsperson as enacted in the physical action of cave diving and drawing, and per se also has to include their respective reflections and intuitions. Here, we find an intuitive understanding of the environment without an analysis of the details. Such accuracy does not adhere to any centres, or follow intersections of lines. Accuracy is not confined to the ultimately immeasurable mental image of a dot; it lies, if at all, in an all-encompassing darkness. Cave surveys are part of a tradition of scientific drawings, which are apprehended and drawn by a special draftsperson, or sometimes by scientists themselves in order to documents the object of research. However, in the conditions in caves, the only centre available to the measuring mind is subjectivity, a subjectivity that moves, intra-acts, transforms, and mutates. In this sense, accuracy in the sense of measuring what is real does not have to respect the boundaries between the objective and the subjective, the real and the imaginary; it therefore expands the understanding of (in)accuracy.

The accuracies of the sense of the real combined with the accumulation of scientific units of measurement can form a strong magnet that opens up very different perceptions. It may be even more striking to observe this within the context of science, rather than within the context of art, perhaps because of the double pleasure of scientific and artistic accuracies. Accuracy in the sense of the real needs a frame so as to limit the field of view – so as to allow it to emerge in the first place. It can be a matter (a frame, an image, a box), a substance, a body, a perception, or, more conceptually speaking, a system, an institution, et cetera. In *Survey Map*, the setting as a whole – the system on which the survey is based, including the rules and medium of cartography (grids on graph paper, size of the paper, pencil, et cetera) – functions as framework and actually as a sort of frame: framework, because it is a structure and system of drawing, and a sort of frame since it brings particular limitations such as the rules, timeframe, and space of drawings. But it is not a frame that needs to be resisted or that might primarily represent limitations. It is obvious that the draftsperson/artist enjoys the progress of going from "free" actions to drawing based on a set of scientific rules. Two approaches to pursuing the two accuracies are there from the beginning, always juxtaposed with each other, coexisting in parallel. As results, both accuracies appear in the same image: one is the accuracy in measuring reality through adhering to the grammar of geometry and the rules of speleology; the other is the accuracy in measuring the sense of the real that emerges from something very personal – the mind, body, and history of the draftsperson/artist him/herself. The former leads to a dot, the latter remains in a ubiquitous space.

A different, but still comparable attitude towards the use value of scientific "hard data" is turned into an observable event in the collaboration of an artist and a scientist: There is a similar sense of humour and a relish for playing with the logic of measurement in *Diversity Maniacs* (2011) by Toru Koyamada (in collaboration with Kiyoshi Naruse, biologist). It invites the audience to closely contemplate the faces of tiny fish and the differences between them in small details – using magnifying glasses installed in front of glass laboratory vessels sitting on an historical Edo-period wooden shelf. "Just as no two human faces are the same, this is also true for the *medaka*!" says Dr. Kiyoshi Naruse, an ichthyologist – who is also Koyamada's collaborator in this project and is researching the genome of *medaka* (Oryzia), a tiny, only 3.5-centimetre-long species of fish that lives in sweet water habitats in Japan. The intimate knowledge that the scientist collects by observing the *medaka* makes it very clear that he has great admiration for the details of the diversity of individuals. In spite of their apparent uniformity and commonness, his approach makes it possible to measure the individual "being", to not only trace and report it, but to also perceive and construct it with the eyes of an aficionado. After intensively observing the fish again and again, it is, frankly speaking, not that easy to recognise the individuality that Dr. Naruse talks about so passionately. Is his heightened sensory perception real, or is it surreal? One may assume that, over the many hours and days of observing and accompanying the fish, he must gain an understanding of each fish that is based not only on appearance but also on their movement, behaviour, character, et cetera. This is what the eyes of a "maniac" (as Koyamada says) are able to perceive. His huge amount of knowledge may ultimately also make it possible for us to one day see and measure the differences between the fishes' faces. The extremely subjective measurement practiced by the scientist opens up another terrain of measurement, which differs from mechanical and automatic modes of measurement and draws an ambivalent borderline between the real and the imaginary. This is the fascination of *Diversity Maniacs*, whose accuracy is located beyond measurability.

Koyamada met Dr. Naruse as his assigned scientific partner in an "art-meets-science" type of exhibition project, and initially had a hard time figuring out what the point of his contribution – the fish observatory – actually was. After recognising the epistemological logic of this configuration, he became enthusiastic about its potentially "maniacal" quality and deepened the dialogue, up to the point at which he decided that it would make sense to present his findings in another – art-related – context, so as to introduce the notion of complexity in acts of observation as well as explicitly position it against certain abusive forms of abstracting life by means of standardisations of measuring. In other words, with *Diversity Maniacs*, Koyamada and Naruse present the praxis of a "defamiliarisation of the familiar". Naruse "defamiliarises" the generalised species classification *medaka* – the most familiar fish in Japanese culture – by confronting species with the individual, and, certainly not least, by projecting an animistic perspective on specific, individualising traits of their faces. To Koyamada, this state of not-knowing seems to hold great potential for any kind of new discovery. For him, it is accompanied by open-mindedness, which is not only an "extra", but also an absolute requirement for any imaginable advancement of knowledge – and, in a number of ways, it is also a parameter for the description of "measurement from the inside". He gives a context to Naruse's alternative understanding of measurement to thus highlight its conceptual precision. Here again, two different praxes of measurements meet and open up an opportunity to present themselves. Another example of double accuracies that indicates the ubiquity of measurement in a more directly perceivable way in comparison to art works that I introduced in the previous sections. The slight patina of the chosen format of display for this recontextualisation suggests that the artist is interested in the history of genetic research and has considered the "timeless" quality of this situation after experiencing the limits of measurement that can only be apprehended from the outside. Accordingly, the precision of measurement can be made apparent by the context; in the end, both need to be cultivated: the ubiquitous inner space as well as the space outside the body.

*Im/Measurability
of Life*

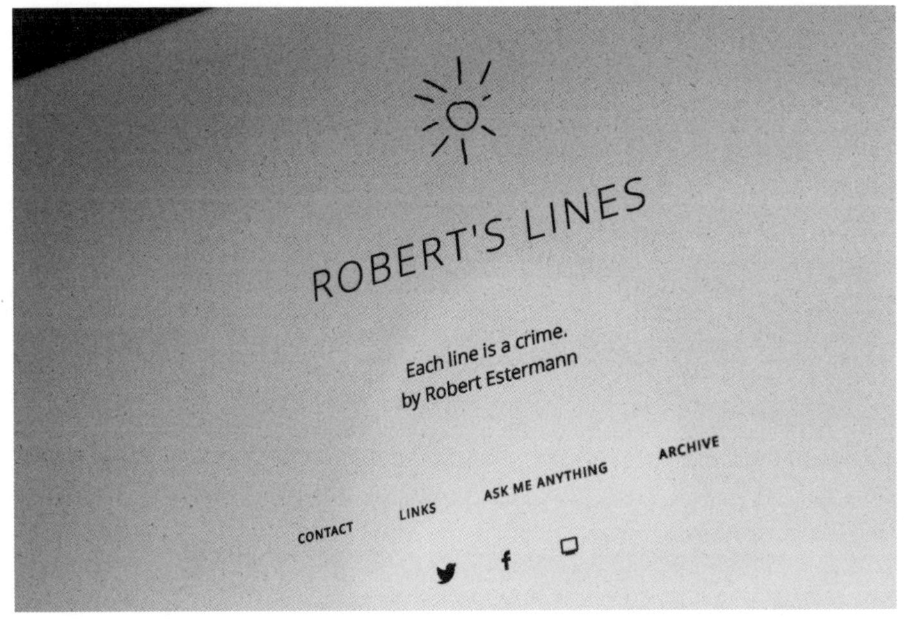

Robert Estermann, photograph of a
screen shot of his Tumblr page, 2017
© Robert Estermann

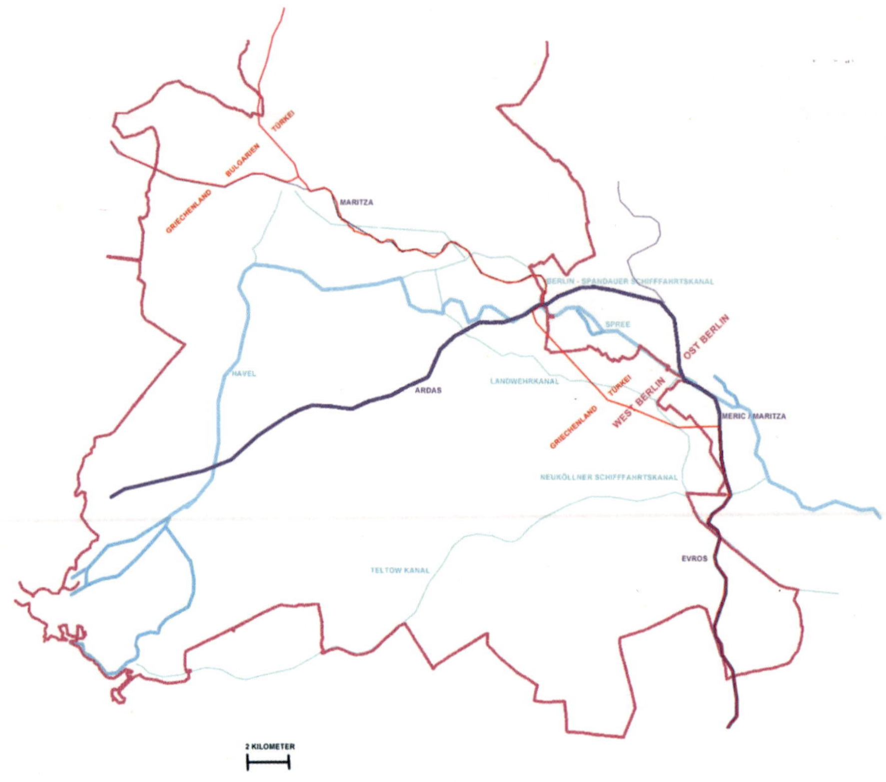

Birgit Auf der Lauer & Caspar Pauli, *Research for Grenzfährservice, Grenzfährservice III*, 2014, digital collage map © Caspar Pauli

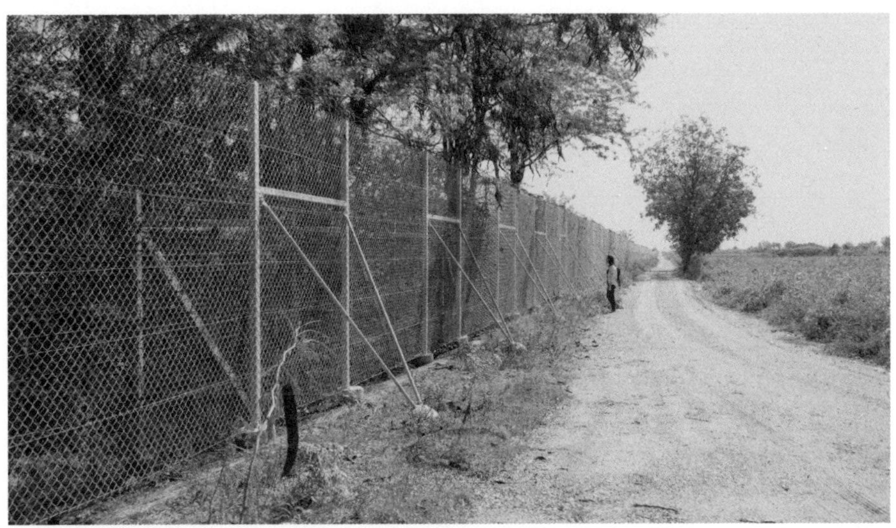

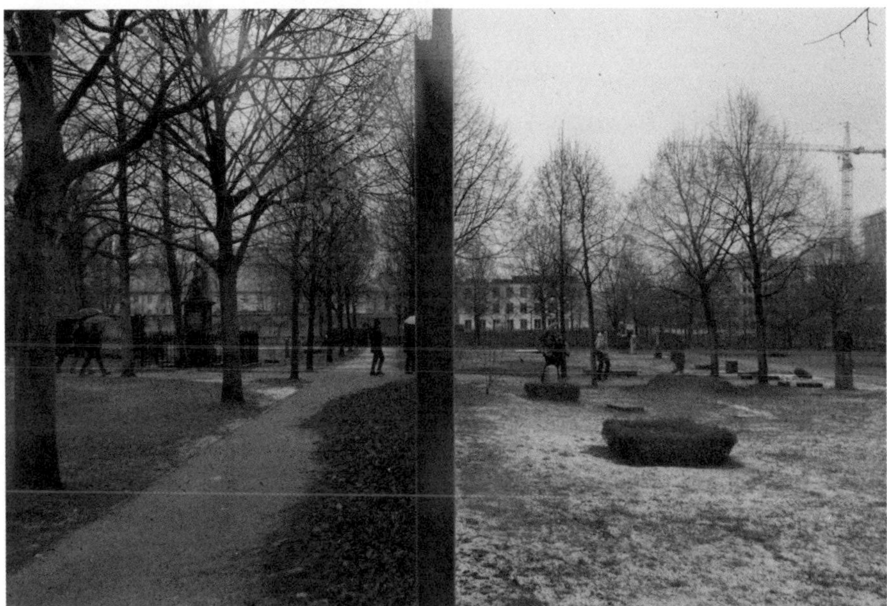

Upper image from Greece, Birgit Auf der Lauer
& Caspar Pauli, *Research for Grenzfährservice,
Grenzfährservice III*, 2014–15 © Caspar Pauli

Lower image from the Berlin performance walk
Birgit Auf der Lauer & Caspar Pauli, *Research for
Grenzfährservice, Grenzfährservice III*, 2014–15,
performance, duration: 2.5 h © Paul Holdsworth
& Daniela del Pomar

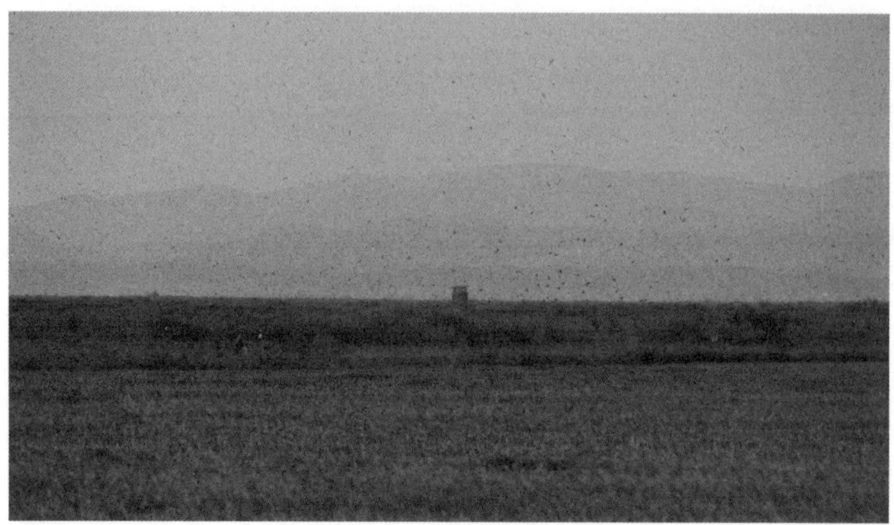

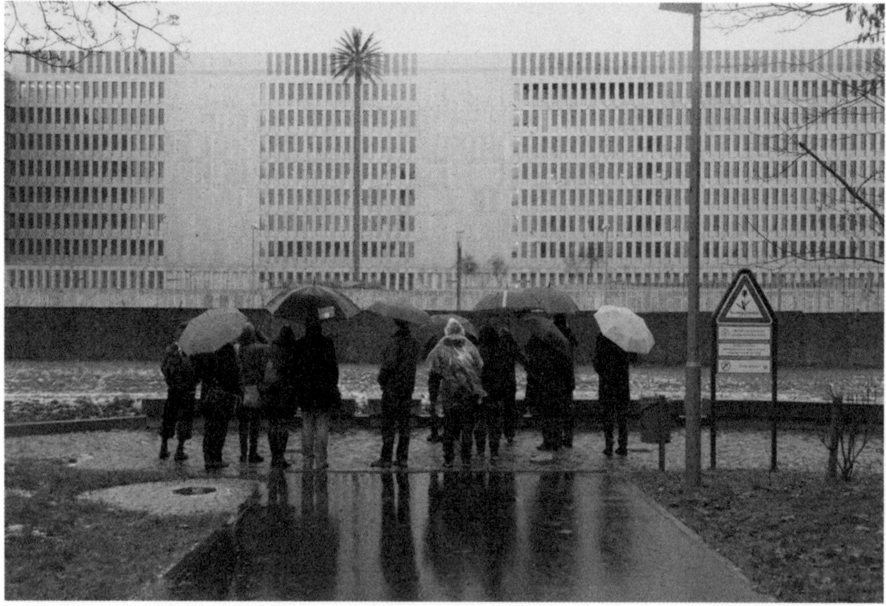

Upper images from Greece, Birgit Auf der Lauer
& Caspar Pauli, *Research for Grenzfährservice,
Grenzfähreservice III*, 2014–15 © Caspar Pauli

Lower images from the Berlin performance walk,
Birgit Auf der Lauer & Caspar Pauli, *Research for
Grenzfährservice, Grenzfährservice III*, 2014–15,
performance, duration: 2.5 h © Paul Holdsworth
& Daniela del Pomar

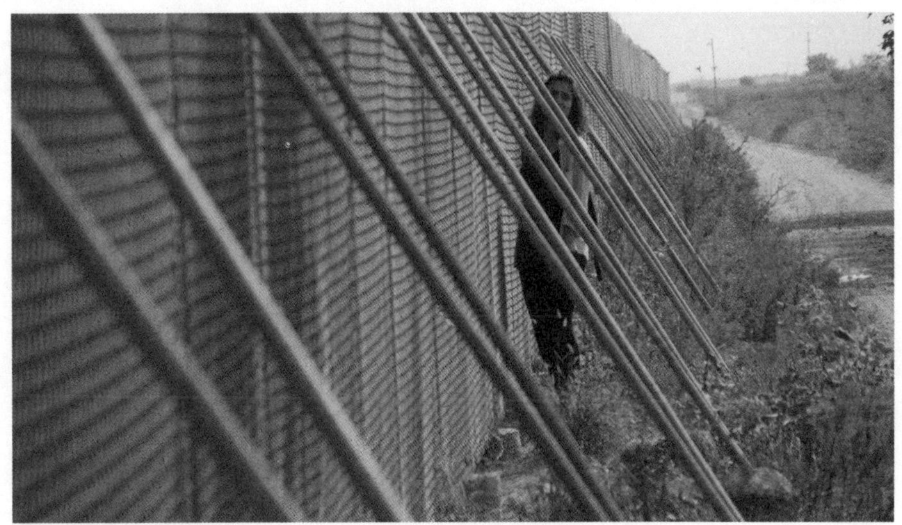

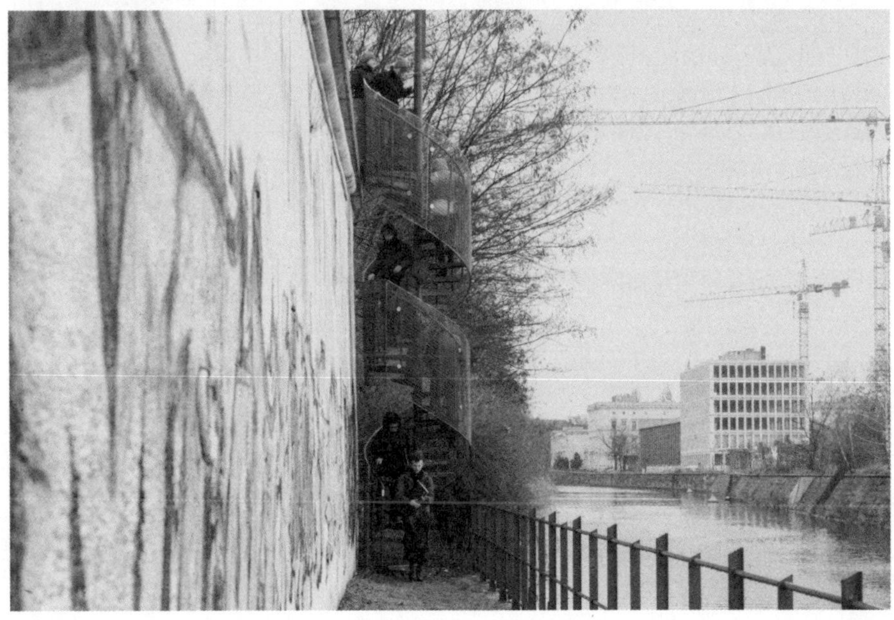

alphabet/
10 (j) June nights atom bombs

by Inger Christensen

atomic bombs exist
Hiroshima, Nagasaki
Hiroshima, August
6th, 1945
Nagasaki, August
9th, 1945

140,000 dead and
wounded in Hiroshima
some 60,000 dead and
wounded in Nagasaki

number standing still
somewhere in a distant
ordinary summer

since then the wounded
have died, first many, most, then fewer, but
all; finally
the children of the wounded

stillborn, dying

many, forever a
few, at last the
last; I stand in

my kitchen peeling
potatoes; the tap
runs, almost
drowning out the children in the yard;

the children shout,
almost drowning out
the birds in the
trees; the birds
sings, almost

drowning out the whisper
of leaves in the wind;
the leaves whisper,
almost drowning
the sky with silence,

the sky with its light
and the light that almost
since then has recalled
atomic fire
a bit

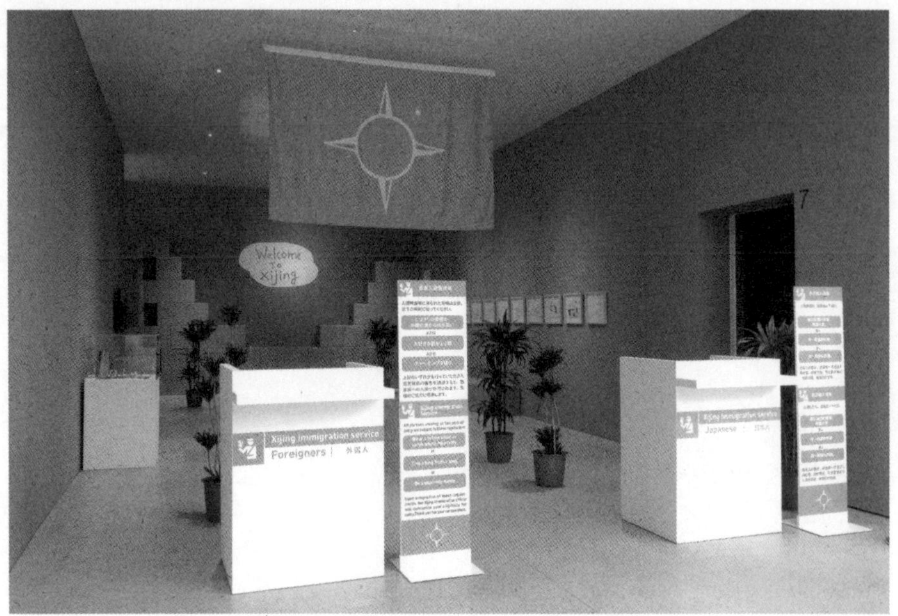

Installation view of the Xijing Men exhibition *Xijing Is Not Xijing, Therefore Xijing Is Xijing*, 29 April 2016 – 28 August 2016, 21st Century Museum of Contemporary Art, Kanazawa, photo Keizo Kioku, courtesy 21st Century Museum of Contemporary Art, Kanazawa; artworks depicted © the artists

Xijing Men, *Chapter 3: Welcome to Xijing – Xijing Immigration Service* (installation view), 2012, mixed media, dimensions variable, courtesy the artists

The Xijing Men is an artists' collective consisting of three members: Chen Shaoxiong (China), Gimhong-sok (Korea), and Tsuyoshi Ozawa (Japan). The Xijing Men are from the fictitious city of Xijing, an imagined political entity in East Asia, meaning "western capital". The wordplay has its roots in the names of real cities: Beijing (northern capital), Nanjing (southern capital), and Tokyo (eastern capital). The Xijing Men constantly face communication barriers amongst themselves, but nonetheless develop various practices in fields including performance, drawing, photography, et cetera. Their sceptical attitude towards the kinds of measurement enacted in drawing national, political, and other social borders is accompanied by pointed satire on existing norms, experiences, and perceptions.

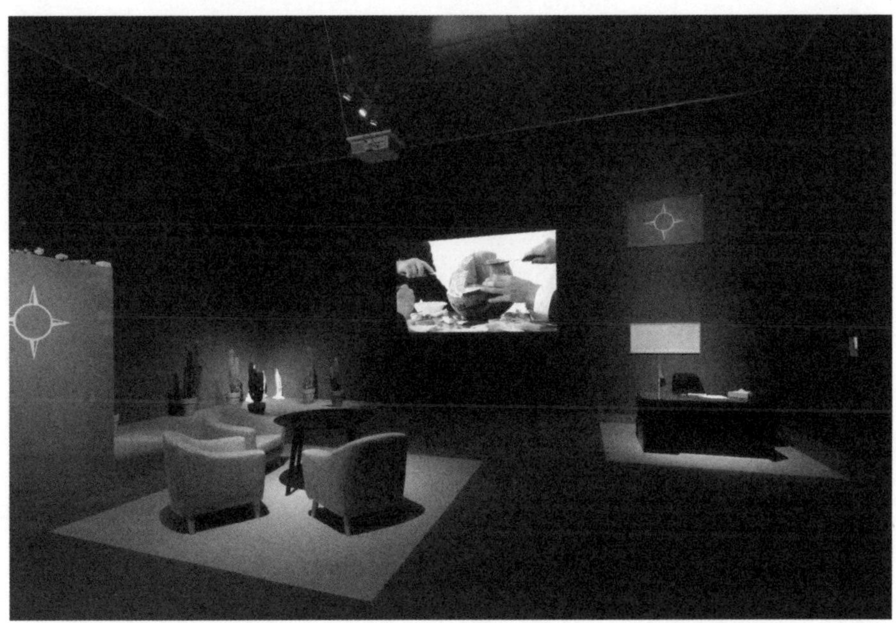

Xijing Men, *Chapter 4: I Love Xijing –
The Daily Life of Xijing Presidents*
(installation view), 2009, mixed media,
dimensions variable, video: 17 min.,
courtesy the artists

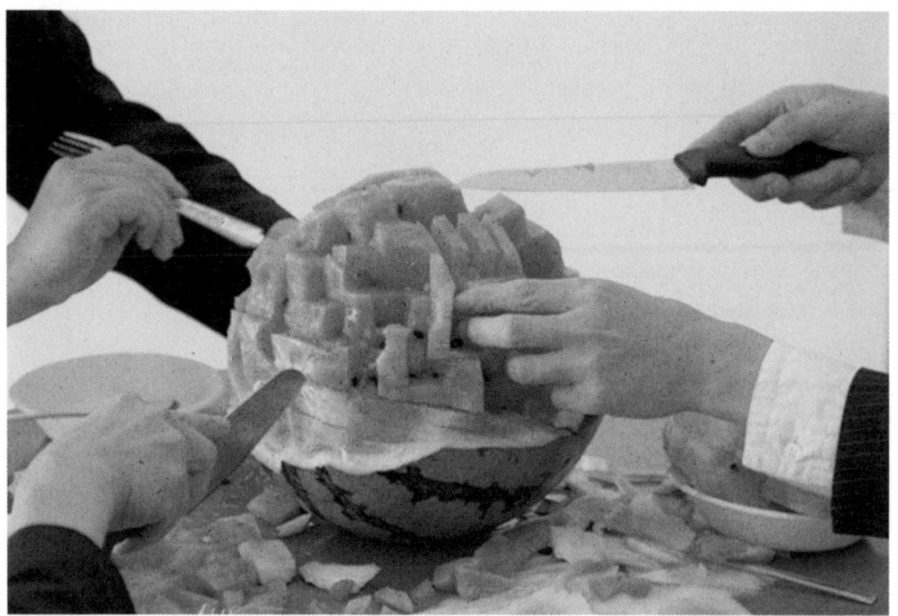

Xijing Men, *Chapter 4: I Love Xijing – The Daily Life of Xijing Presidents: The Urban Planning of Xijing*, 2009, video, courtesy the artists

Imprecision as precision:
The first image with the watermelon is a still image from the video *I Love Xijing – The Daily Life of Xijing Presidents* (Chapter 4: "Urban Planning"). This video depicts each of the Xijing Men handling national policies as a president, for fourteen days each. To make Xijing a prosperous, fun nation, they employ unique methods of visualising and solving problems related to education, urban planning, economics, territory, defense, and food. The video concludes with the Xijing Men producing Xijing currency (XIP) printed on sheets of Kleenex.

The Xijing Men, Opening Performance
at the Gwangju Biennale 9, 2012, photo
© Miya Yoshida

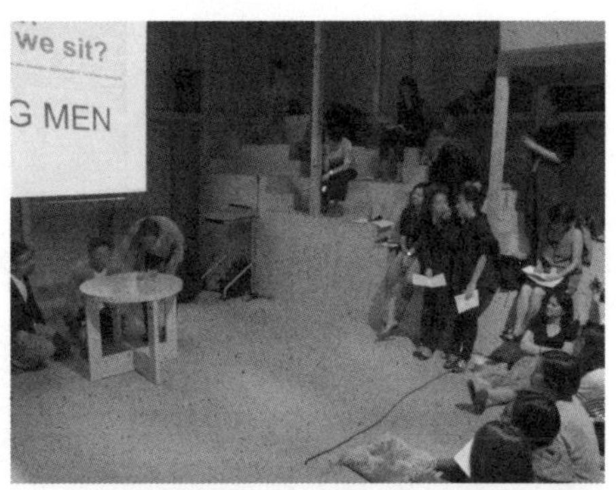

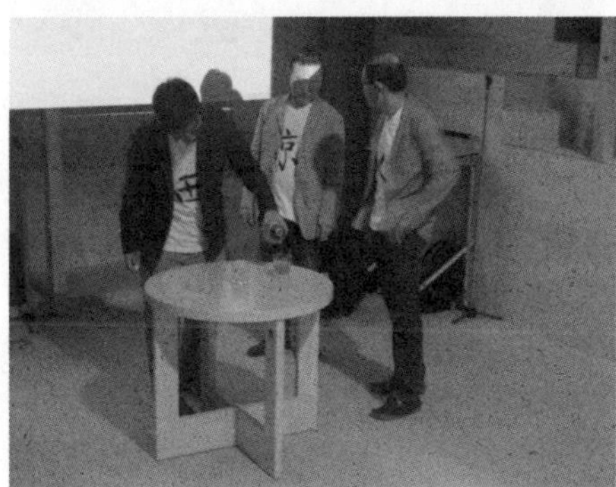

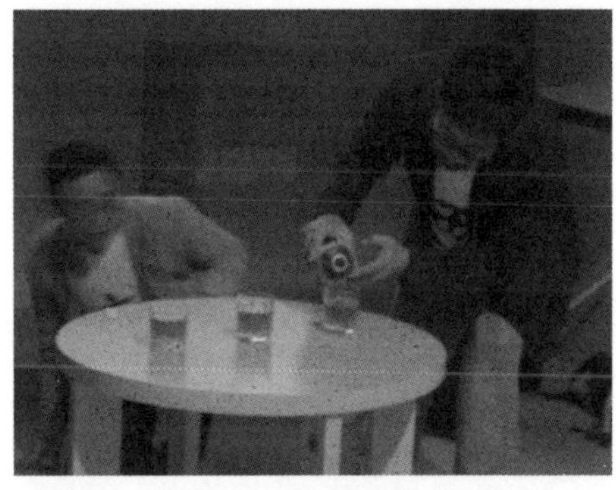

Another set of images shows a short performance offering a re-enactment of the Equality of Encouragement Act found in the video performance *Constitution of Xijing*. The members of the Xijing Men take turns pouring tea into three glasses. They measure the exact quantity of tea in one glass, check and add more to the two other glasses, make comparisons, and then continue adding more or less until they achieve an equal distribution of tea. After several trials, the three of them agree on an outcome and make a toast to drink up the tea in each glass. Using direct observation as a measuring device and keeping tabs on the levels of tea, the outcome is bound to centre on their relationship. Both works present processes of measurement produced in different relations; they demonstrate that the apparent imprecision of sensory measurement can eventually prove to produce a mutually agreed, negotiated precision.

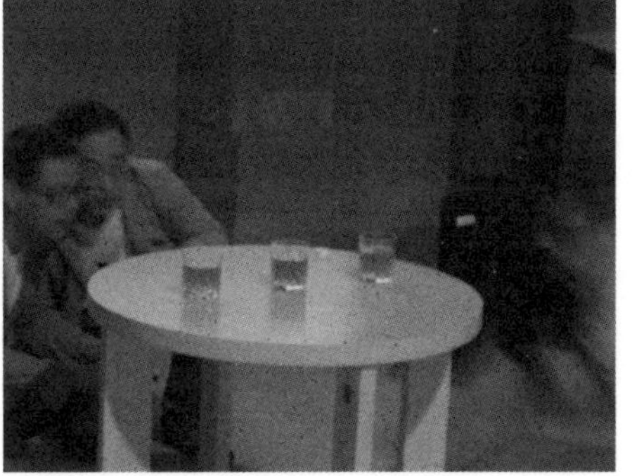

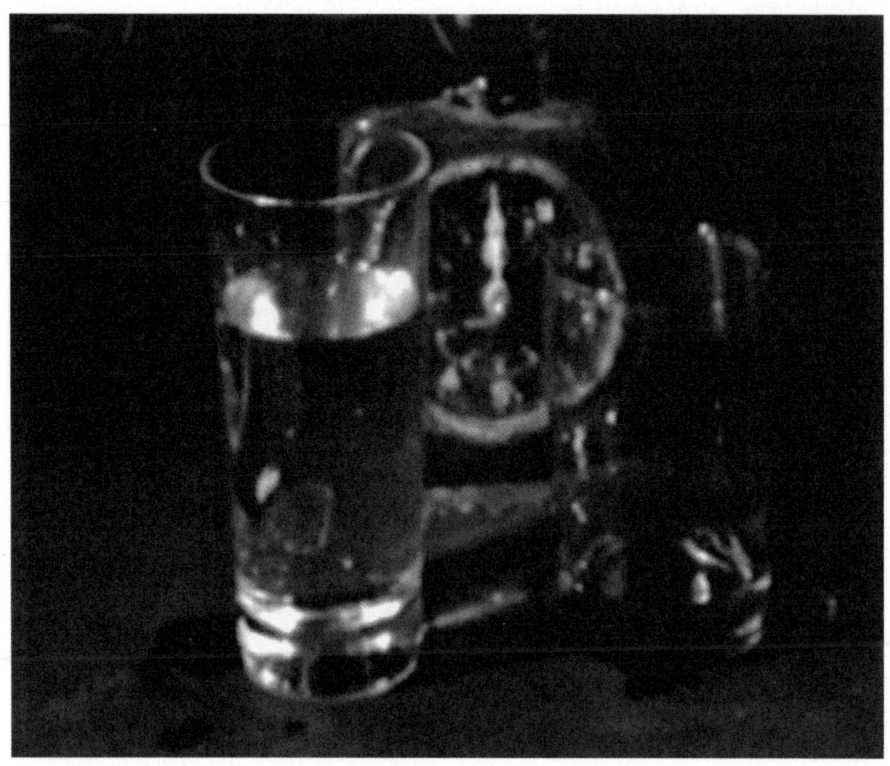

John Baldessari, *Four Minutes of Trying to Tune Two Glasses (For the Phil Glass Sextet)*, 1976, PAL video, black-and-white, sound, 4:09 min., courtesy John Baldessari

Using nothing but his own senses, American conceptual artist John Baldessari tunes two glasses (in other words, a unit of measurement for the volume of water) by touching the glasses with a thin stick, while also performing a random action, as can be seen in this short video. His action shows the significance of a subjective understanding of measurement, and places the focus on using our own bodies as a means of experiencing and measuring the world around us.

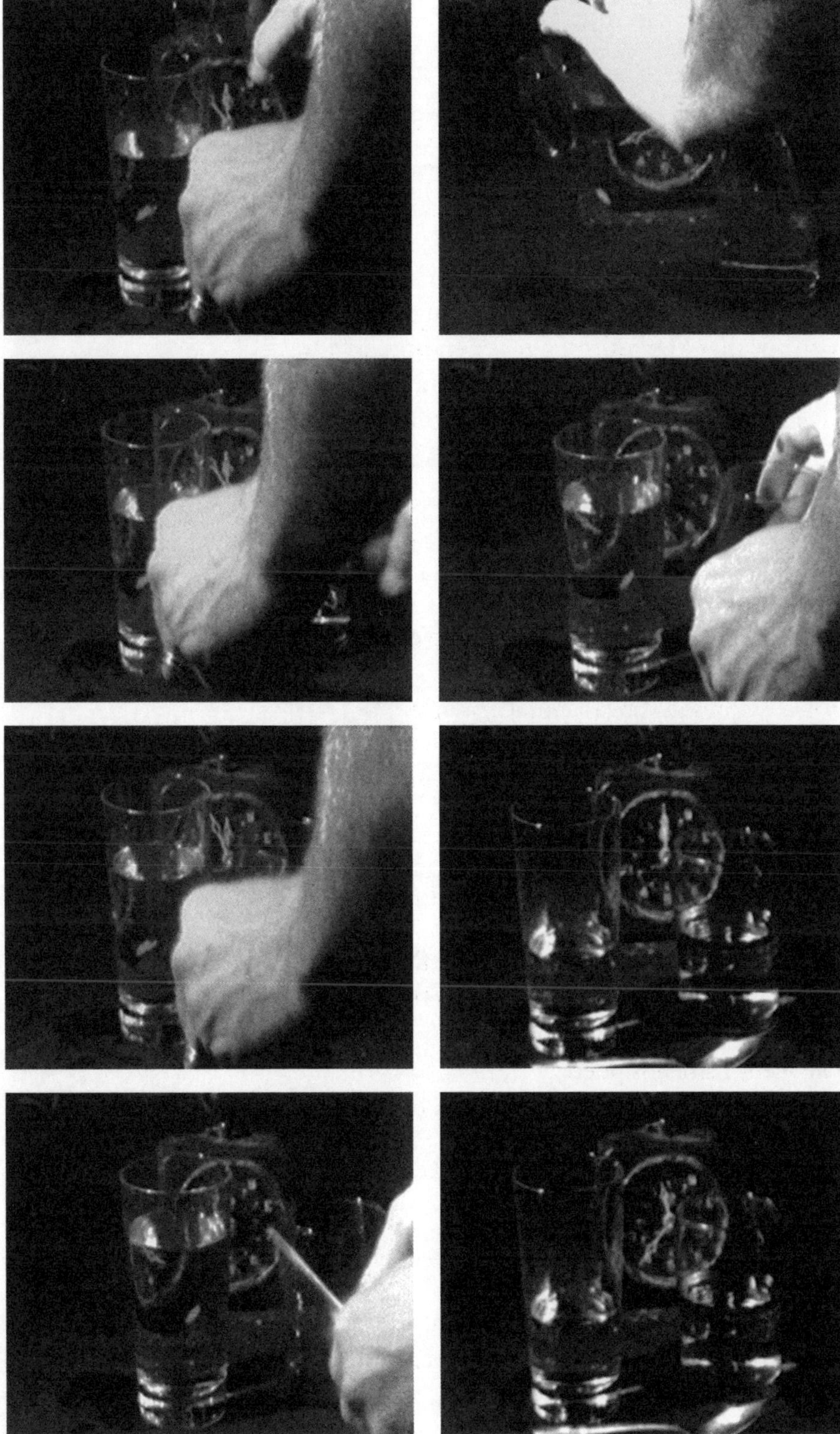

Numbers

By Sion Sono

First I needed to have something counted – precisely.
So I might as well make it the number of weeds.
Count everything!
Blossoms.
Why not blossoms.
Count the number of cherry blossom petals!
Actually, that kind of thing never ends up as a waste.
First, you set the range, like, 1 centimeter.
Then, you need to thoroughly count inside that range.

Let's say, a primary school
In a playing field in that school
How many cherry blossoms
How many cherry blossom petals
We checked the range, and we checked their numbers,
to come closer to the scent
When we find the precise numbers there,
we can align ourselves with that scent
Probably our sense of smell already knows the numbers
Scents always have numbers inside.

The town population, the number of pupils there in elementary school, …
On that day, at that time …
How many insects, how many butterflies, how many ants,
how many green caterpillars were there.
We need to count them – precisely.
The scent I smell is poetry.
The Government must use poetry in order to create precise numbers.

How many teardrops fell.
Count that number.
The school poster said we will return some day.
When is that day.
Need to count the days from now on.
Count precisely when that day will be.
I mean, somebody has to live to tell.

Count.
At least, as in old stories that used to get passed on,
With just the right amount of truthfulness,
It might be just once, one time, one day, one second
– or anytime.
In that place, at that position, that latitude,
whatever comes up will do.
Whatever you count, count it in that very instant.
The numbers need be told.
The numbers need be taught.
Or, you count yourself.
Or, count your lined up hungry teeth.
Count yourself.
You are the number one you need to start with.

Or, you have to tell about the redness of your gums.
Or, you have to tell the sadness of it.
Don't let politicians claim they can't explain in numbers.
You need to force them to express these things numerically.
Go on, tell them – they need to count everything.
Demand of them to express everything in numbers.
What is "literature" good for
If it cannot express the deaths, the teardrops, all the suffering
they half express as "an enormous number"
– with a precise number.
If politicians complain they cannot count something so ephemeral,
fading with the seasons.
Art should do that.
Try to precisely count at least the "one",
even if only once.

In Sion Sono, *Land of Hope*, Tokyo: Little More, 2012.
Translation by Miya Yoshida.

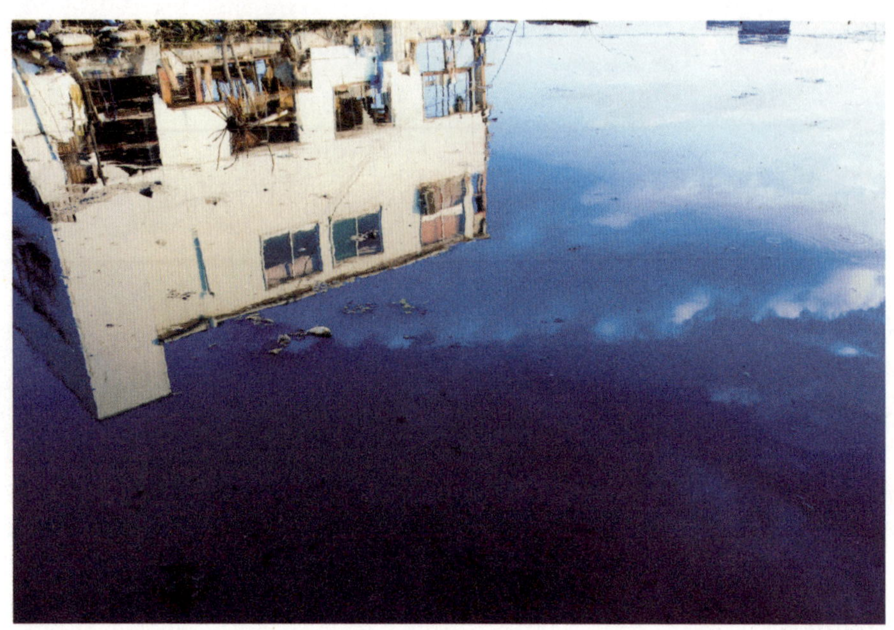

Toshie Kusamoto, *Untitled*, 2011,
photograph ©Toshie Kusamoto

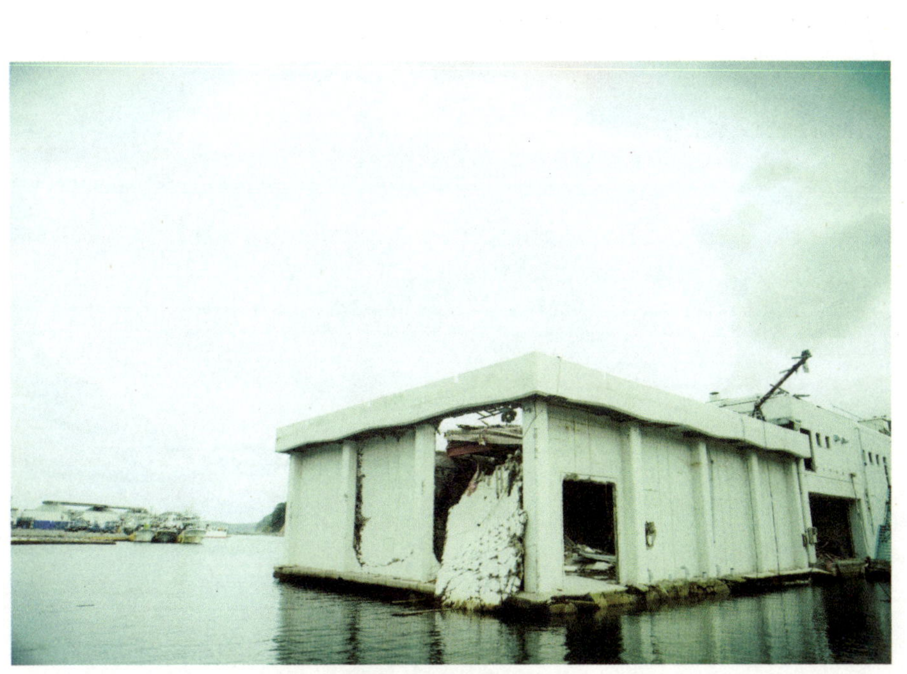

Tap-Tap
Nobuaki Date

Those who want to get things done – can't deal with a tap-tap attitude
It'd just make them look half-assed.

Those who like to get others to do things – can't deal with a tap-tap attitude either.
It makes them appear as sluggish do-nothings.

Those who won't do without their merry banter – they can't deal with tap-tap.
It just disturbs their natural back-and-forth

Those seeking out the secret of youth – tap-tap just isn't their way
How could they accept their bodies' limit like that?

Between a past unresolved and a future not grasped
There's the image of a present only sketchable in dots
The sound of those who try to draw it: tap-tap.

Translation by Miya Yoshida

Tap-tap
Nobuaki Date

Wer weiterkommen will, kann sich mit tap-tap nicht begnügen,
Allzu leicht wirkt das unfertig!

Wer was geschafft kriegen will, der sollte tap-tap vermeiden,
Da sieht man schnell wie eine lahme Schnecke aus.

Wer ungern auf sein Geplänkel verzichtet, lässt die Finger vom tap-tap,
Das stört nur den gewohnten Atemrhythmus.

Auch wer das Geheimnis ewiger Jugend sucht, kann mit tap-tap nichts anfangen,
Das hieße ja, die eigenen Grenzen hinzunehmen.

Zwischen unbewältigter Vergangenheit und nur vage ertastbarer Zukunft
Liegt das Bild einer Gegenwart, der man sich nur punktweise annähern kann.
Wer so zeichnen will, macht: Tap-tap.

Translation by Clemens Krümmel

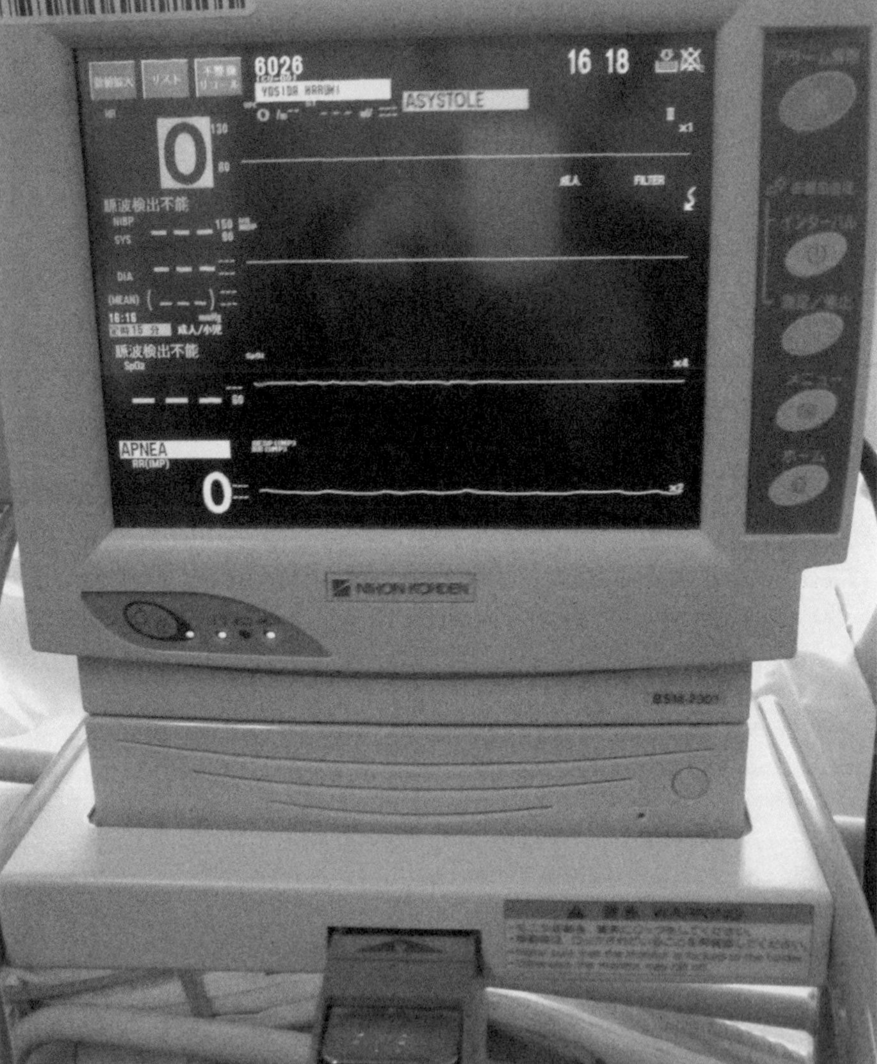
CH 6026
MO-NK063
6026
YOSIDA HARUMI
ASYSTOLE
16 18
HR
130
80
脈波検出不能
NIBP
SYS
150
80
DIA
(MEAN)
16:16
収時15分　成人/小児
脈波検出不能
SpO2
80
APNEA
RR(IMP)
NIHON KOHDEN
x1
FILTER
x4
x1
WARNING

Im/Measurability of Life

"Mind is a living measure which achieves its own capacity by measuring other things."
—Nicholas de Cusa, *The Layman on Wisdom and the Mind*, 1450

For more than a year, the artist duo of Birgit Auf der Lauer and Casper Pauli engaged in a research project on human trafficking and produced a performative work titled *Grenzfährservice* (Border Ferry Service) *II + III* (2016), which was conducted in the form of a walk in the city of Berlin.[25] Pointing out the river Spree as a representational line of reference that demarcates borders both in nature and in politics, their walk takes participants through the centre of Berlin for a period of approximately two hours. In this walking performance in and around the Gorki Theater, two geographic situations are addressed: One refers to the border between Turkey and Greece, the relatively short voyage to cross the ocean from Turkey to Lesvos Samos, Chios, and other Greek islands, as it is considered by migrants today, the other to the former border between West and East German in the 1970s and 80s. The stories told during the walk gradually present the results of their examination of cases of people being smuggled from one country to the other. The schedule for the walk instructs participants to stop at several points in Berlin-Mitte such as the Bundeswehrkrankenhaus (Federal Army Hospital), where both German soldiers as well as soldiers and civilians from other countries are sent for medical treatment, the park at Invalidenfriedhof (Invaliden Cemetery) along the river Spree, the Bundesnachrichtendienst (Federal Intelligence Service), the main building of Humboldt University, et cetera. The walk gives the people who participate a narrative about the experiences of people who succeeded in crossing the border as well as of those who engage in smuggling professionally.

---

[25] The walk was hosted by the Berliner Herbstsalon and the Gorki Theater on 14/15, 21/22, 28/29 November 2015.

Each part of the narrative is closely connected to the site, but also to the economy of the particular time. Participants stand at the exact place where the smuggling of people from the East to the West began, and where secret information was exchanged. The narrative goes like this:

A BStU (The Stasi Record Agency / Die Behörde des Bundesbeauftragten für die Stasi-Unterlagen) file on the "Westberliner Schleuser-Löwin" from the late 70s gives us some information on how prices were calculated. In the file, it says that the KMHB boss, the "Lioness" as she was called, was also connected with two diplomats (coloured gentlemen), who performed diplomatic service in the German Democratic Republic. They would demand a sum of fifteen to twenty thousand Deutschmarks for smuggling to take place.

Elsewhere in the BStU documents, there is evidence that makes it seem probable that there was a negotiation between her and a customer. A down payment of DM 12,500 was made. Since this was a "special price for friends amounting to 25,000 DM, the deposit was only half of the total sum."

The river flowing right in front of the participants is where people actually swam across, where they drowned, and in some cases were shot. How did the soldiers measure the moment at which to fire? How do migrants measure the risk of stopping or actually crossing the border? Familiarity with the geographic situation and physical involvement with the site allows the power of the narrative to unfold even though a considerable amount of time has passed.

With the historical case of Berlin and current anecdotes about the border between Turkey and Greece taking turns in the narrative, there is a juxtaposition of two seemingly unrelated situations on one and the same platform. This reveals the shared, pivotal point of politics and life in both cases, but also shows the differences in geographic distance and scale. Approximately 1.8 million migrants crossed the borders to Europe by sea and on the land route via Turkey and Albania in 2015. The narrative gradually reveals economic details about the land route, the system of calculation that is used for those who want to cross the river – a river that is a political border between two worlds, and the measurement of life and death. While narrating the imagined situation of being smuggled in a truck while riding a subway train, details like the size of the truck are added associatively.

"This is the price list: The cost for hiring a truck is 100,000 Turkish Lira. When you rent it, you want to put as many people as possible inside the truck. 200 people can fit into a big one. One daytrip from Istanbul to Athens, or to the islands, costs 5,000 Euros per person, and it is a guaranteed journey. If the first attempt fails, you can try to travel again at another time."

"The competition is tough, and people immediately know who offers good service and who does not. The 5,000 Euros are distributed amongst all the individuals who participate in the work: the boss, driver, boatman, guide, organisers, informers, and officials. We cannot do this for less than 5,000 Euros."

These numbers share an important specificity, instead of the generalisations that one commonly hears about acts of fleeing. Concrete details about costs add a personal quality to the numbers and provide another kind of access to intersections that make it possible to learn about the realities of crossing borders in greater detail. The numbers are minuscule, at least compared to those published in official statistics concerning the effect that migration supposedly has on the economy. The regular, constantly updated survey asks: How many refuges have arrived this month? Which countries do most migrants come from? Where are they going? How do the migrants get to Europe? How dangerous is their journey? Which European countries are the most "affected"? Et cetera. The statistical numbers may allow us to obtain a general overview of refugee issues, however, these numbers are usually based on the interests of those who are on the other side of the fence. Auf der Lauer and Pauli say, " At the border control, as soon as a person is registered, she or he becomes data. If not, she or he becomes noise. No documentation means that a category of "no data" is created, which does not refer to any existence, or that the category itself does not exists."[26] This needs to be remembered as a basic principle with respect to the numbers in those statistics. In other words, format decides what (dis)appears, thereby, the series of numbers are the reflection of the structure and the system of formatting shaped by political, economical, bureaucratic, and ethical consequences.

The Fukushima catastrophe and its aftermath have provided us with a bitter object lesson on the specificity and usability of numbers. In his poem *Numbers,* the film director and writer Sion Sono addresses the shared experience after the catastrophic events in Fukushima, which are also represented and expressed in numbers. A great deal of measurement has been done in order to learn about the probable effects of the invisible doses of radioactivity.

---

[26] Conversation with the artists at their studio on 15 February 2016.

Responding to these numbers, the poem playfully works with the logics of counting. It voices the poetic postulation of counting every last detail in this "new world", with the intention of expressing the numerical aspect of the events hyperbolically, in the sense of an exaggerated or even ironic counter-action. This reveals the absurdity of the idea of reducing the immeasurability of realities, including life and death, to numbers. At the same time, it also re-directs the facts from passive measurement to an active kind of measurement. Counting does not remain a mere depiction; it is the condition for remembering. By in-sisting on acts of counting in every imaginable instance, the self is ultimately saved from being measured (from being passive), since it takes charge of acts of measurement (of being active) itself. Active counting produces a situation in which one is able to regain control, since it is a tool that does not permit any imprecise decisions to be made. The poem makes *imagination* start to count, but not in the sense in which oppressive power systems do so.

The fact that Auf der Lauer and Pauli utilise numbers in a similar way is one aspect; it also becomes evident that the invisibility of the protagonist in the format of the "walk" is very meaningful for them. Quite a number of art-works deal with similar, contemporary political and ethical issues using some kind of visual representation. However, the walk in *Grenzfährservice* makes its protagonists completely invisibility – these protagonists include the individuals that the artists interviewed as well as those who are referred to in their field re-search. Only the artists and the participants in the walk are visible. The absence of protagonists is the most characteristic trait of this work. It maintains a certain distance to the topic and directs the focus of the project to an attitude towards the political and ethical issues at stake that is not primarily informative, but rather imaginary and self-reflective. The artistic intention behind the walk is to add each person's own opinion on the questions that arise during it, just as active counting works. The walk attempts to link the measurement of life un/registered and death un/documented to the lives of the participants.

In her poem *alphabet*, the Danish poet Inger Christensen asks if the meaning of death could remain unchanged after Auschwitz, Hiroshima, and Nagasaki, and after the countless bombings and endless wars that continue to occur until today. The poet sees the present issues as essentially being part of a continuum that originates from all these past tragedies, and asks the reader to reconsider the vulnerability of life in relation to his/her life. The American art historian Rosalyn Deutsche links the artistic depiction of the invasion of Iraq by the United States (around the time she wrote the text in 2009) with that of the historical tragedies created by the atomic bombing of Hiroshima and Nagasaki and other nuclear experiments. She observes common attitudes – impatience and melancholy – in the politics around the time of the Iraq invasion as well as back in the 1940s, and incorporates psychoanalysis to highlight two attitudes: human beings' "special capacity for regression" and a heroic masculinism that she understands as "an orientation towards ideals of wholeness that disavows vulnerability"[27]. Her insightful critique of political landscapes is quite relevant in contemplating the current situations in and around Europe, such as the on-going conflicts and bombings in Syria, the rise of and violent acts by ISIL (Islamic State of Iraq and the Levant), the series of acts of terrorism in Paris, Brussels, Istanbul, and Berlin, on-going conflicts in Rwanda, Somalia, Angola, Sudan, Liberia, and Burundi, the situation in the Ukraine, et cetera. On all levels, politics are questioned regarding their capacity for patience and reflection, both in tracing the self and the other. Thereby, the ability to develop questions during the *Grenzfährservice* walk can be regarded as a strategy for measuring the level of regression within ourselves: How much are we able to confront, and to what extent can we regard both the self and others as vulnerable lives in a long-term perspective? This means that asking questions is not only the way to know the other, but also to understand the self – the ubiquitous regressions, aggressivity, and egoism that accumulate in us in society today.

Life and death are measured and institutionalised and become marketable at every decisive point in politics, the economy, ethics, and technology. Such contemporary realities constantly necessitate initiations of various ways of re-imagining numbers and their affects in order for them to retain their gravity even after an abstraction of realities into signs has occurred. Every act of crossing borders, facing catastrophes, being dragged into tragedies, and many other unconventional events, demands finding diverse approaches to and different modes of measurement, instead of fixing measurement to one singular approach. Acts of knowing, understanding, and thinking should not be limited to the operational level of signs. Acts of active measurements should instead circulate in all directions and on all levels so as to retain the "gravity" and "temperature" of diverse realities.

Grenzfährservice is an ephemeral work. It focuses on the importance of the particular, of specificity and individuals, rather than of groups or collectives. It is a fragile practice, but that is why it is strong – strong not like an energy explosion, but like the extended continuity of vibration and oscillation through time-space.

---

[27] Rosalyn Deutsche, *Hiroshima after Iraq: Three Studies in Art and War* (New York: Columbia University Press, 2010), 3.

Concluding Remarks

This essay brings aesthetics into the "game" of measurement. It exemplifies different artistic practices as concrete intersections of concepts of "unlearning" existing concepts and norms of measurement – and of learning types of measurement that are located and enacted inside the body. While, in neoliberal capitalism, quantification is constructed and utilised as a "communicative objectivity" needed to perpetuate systems of speculation and excessive bureaucratisation, this text aims at positing the power of the imaginary as a practice that is of the essence today, and at highlighting an "active" kind of measuring in order to speculatively develop a different notion or interpretation of what is considered quantification. Shifting the notion of "measurement" from measurement to "measurements", it sets out to diversify the means and meanings of measurement.

Active measurement is neither humble, nor is it particularly naïve. It produces a situation in which one enables oneself to regain control. It creates new relationalities between images, objects, signs, and "the world". Wishing to present and to emphasise such a diversity of "measurements", I have included additional images of artworks – in addition to those art practices elaborated in the text: unexpected taxonomies used for indexing new parameters (Nam, Ondák); numbers capable of evoking a concrete gravity behind the abstraction and, used not as nouns but as verbs, to *imagine* in a new way (Eames, Sander, Sono); the rhetorical power of numbers and the absurdity of the expansion of mathematical thinking that is now still noticeable when it is encountered outside its "own" terrain (Schmalisch, César); format as a method for re-establishing a personal relation with the structured world of data (Yoshida, John, Arakawa); observance as measurement inside the body (Naruse and Koyamada, Krause, Lewis); and the reconfiguration of life as a conceptual challenge to all notions of measurement (Gins and Arakawa) – to name just these. Some practices can be regarded as conceptual devices, some are generators of "active" measurement, some show shifts in the nature of measuring, and some introduce new methodologies and new associations.

My thinking has developed along with and out of these practices. This is why this text cannot just be harmonious and unifying; its contradictions have instead been constitutive. In my understanding, it is important to retain some degree of discursiveness. The idea of a "unit situational", for instance, contradicts contemporary tendencies toward "ubiquitous" measuring, and this contradiction also penetrates equivalences anywhere, anytime. This, however, also refers to the urgent demand for plural concepts, processes, methodologies, and vocabularies when it comes to stimulating associative imaginaries of measurement. Like in the *NOTEBOOK* developed by Gins and Arakawa, this essay addresses ways of knowing, understanding, and (re)searching measurement – moving in a zigzag line. This is about active measuring and about being measured back. Active measurement itself, to be sure, will of course not suffice to redirect the apparent tendencies of neoliberal capitalism and the bureaucratisation of society. We need to invent new ways of understanding and using language – instead of abusing language in neo-Orwellian memes such as "alternative facts", "post-factual society," et cetera. In this regard, poetry as well as poetics is very important in conducting measurement. They show us potentials and essential perspectives of understanding through language, such as a "precise number in measurement to find the smell" (Sono, cf. p. 20). We need measurements that can "tell the smell". Together with active measurement and the invention of languages, what appeared as the "hype" of measurement can now be transformed from oppressive control to a "renaissance" of quantification that is based on measurement inside the body. Let the imaginary take more and better care of measurement!

Bibliography

Agamben, G. (1999). Aby Warburg and the Nameless Science. In *Potentialities: Collected Essays in Philosophy*. Trans. Roazen, D.H. Stanford: Stanford University Press, 89–103.

Aira, C. (1997/2016). *Duchamp im Mexiko*. Trans. Laabs, K. Berlin: Matthes & Seitz Berlin.

Albrecht, D. (1997). *The Work of Charles and Ray Eames: A Legacy of Invention*. New York: Harry N. Abraham.

Arakawa, S. and Gins, M. (1979). *The Mechanism of Meaning: Work in Progress (1963–71, 1978)*. New York: H. N. Abram.

Arendt, H. (1963). The Conquest of Space and the Stature of Man. *The New Atlantis: A Journal of Technology and Society*, no. 18, Fall 2007, 43–55.

Badiou, A. (2008/1990). *Number and Numbers*. Trans. Mackay, R. Cambridge: Polity.

Badiou, A. (2006/1998). *Being and Event*. Trans. Feltham, O. London: continuum.

Barad, K. (2012). What Is the Measure of Nothingness? Infinity, Virtuality, Justice. *100 Notes. 100 Thoughts*. Documenta Series 099. Berlin.

Bolaño, R. (2009/2004). *2666*. Trans. Wimmer. New York: Picador.

Bök, C. (2002). *'Pataphysics': The Poetics of an Imaginary Science*. Evanston, Illinois: Northwestern University Press.

Bloor, D. (1991) *Knowledge and Social Imagery*. Chicago: University of Chicago Press.

Buchloh, H.D. B. (1990). Conceptual Art 1962–1969: From the Aesthetic of Administration to the Critique of Institutions. *October*, 55, Winter, 105–43. Boston: The MIT Press.

Christensen, I. (2001/1981). *alphabet*. Trans. Nied, S. New York: A New Directions Book.

Clough, P. T. (2000). *Autoaffection – Unconscious Thought in the Age of Technology*. Minneapolis and London: University of Minnesota Press.

Clough, P. T. (2008). The Affective Turn: Political Economy, Biomedia and Bodies. *Theory, Culture & Society*, 25 (1), 1–22. London.

Combes, M. (2012). *Gilbert Simondon and the Philosophy of the Transindividual*. Trans. LaMarre, T. Cambridge, Massachusetts and London: The MIT Press.

Crosby, A. W. (1977). *The Measure of Reality – Quantification and Western Society, 1250–1600*. Cambridge: Cambridge University Press.

De Cusa, N. (1450/1989). *The Layman on Wisdom and the Mind*. Trans. Fuhrer, M.L. Ottawa: Dovehouse Editions.

Deutscher, G. (2005). *The Unfolding of Language – The Evolution of Mankind's Greatest Invention*. London: Arrow Books.

Deutsche, R. (2010). *Hiroshima After Iraq: Three Studies on Art and War*. New York: Columbia University Press.

Deleuze, G. (1990). Postscript on the Societies of Control. *October*, 59 (Winter 1992), 3–7.

Deleuze, G. (1988). *Foucault*. Trans. Hand, S. Minneapolis: University of Minnesota Press.

Deleuze, G. (1990/2003). *The Logic of Sense*. Trans. Lester, M. London and New York: continuum.

Flusser, V. (1986/2011). *Into the Universe of Technical Images*. Trans. Roth, N.A. Minneapolis and London: University of Minnesota Press.

Foucault, M. et al. (2010). *The Birth of Biopolitics: Lectures at the Collége de France, 1978–1979*. New York: Macmillan Palgrave.

Freud, S. (1915). Thought for the Times on War and Death. *The Standard Edition of the Complete Psychological Works of Sigmund Freud*. Strachey, J. (ed. and trans.). London: Hogarth. Available at: https://www.panarchy.org/freud/war.1915.html

Gins, M. and Arakawa, S. (1994). *Architecture – Sites of Reversible Destiny*. New York: Academy Editions.

Gins, M. and Arakawa, S. (2002). *Architectural Body*. Alabama: University of Alabama Press.

Gins, M. and Arakawa, S. (2006). *Making Dying Illegal – Architecture Against Death: Original to the 21st Century*. New York: Roof Books.

Ginzburg, C. (2001). *Wooden Eyes: Nine Reflections on Distance*. Trans. Ryle, M. and Soper, K. New York: Columbia University Press.

Grimes, K. (2000). *Cave Mapping – Sketching details – A guide to producing a useful cave map*. ASF Cave Survey and Mapping Standards Commission.

Halpern, O. (2014). *Beautiful Data: A History of Vision and Reason since 1945*. Durham and London: Duke University Press.

Henderson, L. D. (1999). *Duchamp in Context: Science and Technology in Large Glass and Related Works*. Princeton: Princeton University Press.

Hiroko, A. (ed.) (1995). Arakawa, S. and Gins, M., *Site of Reversible Destiny – Yoro Park Gifu*. Gifu.

Hoel, A. S. (2012). Images And Measurements Across Arts And Sciences. *Cassirer Studies*, V/VI (2012/2013), 157–85.

Ishikawa, H. (2003). *Nippon no Size – Shintai de hakaru Shakkanhō*. Kyoto: Tankousha.

Isozaki, A. (1996). Yajirushi Sakka no Arakawa wa Naze New York de/to Fugū nanoka. *Revue de la pensée d'aujourd'hui*, 24 (10), 388–93.

Lecercle, J-J. and Kral, F. (2010). *Architecture and Philosophy – New Perspectives on the Work of Arakawa & Madeline Gins*. Amsterdam and New York: Rodopi.

Lembert, C. (1982). Structures, instruments, and reading in social and cultural research. *Structuralism and Sociology*, Chapter 12. New York: Columbia University Press.

Nancy, J-L. (2012/2015). *After Fukushima – The Equivalence of Catastrophes*. Trans. Mandell, C. New York: Fordham University Press. Originally published in French as *L'Équivalence des catastrophes (Après Fukushima)* © Èditions Galilée in 2012.

Noyez, E. (2012). *Measuring up – Measurement pieces and the redefinition of scale in conceptual art. Scale: Imagination, Perception and Practice in Architecture*. New York: Routledge.

Starhawk. (1997). *Dreaming the Dark: Magic, Sex, and Politics*. Boston: Beacon Press.

Situationist International. (1972/2003). *The Real Spirit in The International: Theses on the Situationist International and Its Time, 1972*. Trans. McHale, J. London and Sterling: Pluto Press.

Simondon, G. (1980/2012) *On the Mode of the Existence of Technical Objects*. Trans. Mellamphy, N. University of Western Ontario.

Simondon, G. (1992). The Genesis of the Individual. *Incorporations*. Crary, J. & Kwinter, S. (eds.). New York: Zone Books, 297–319.

Simondon, G. (1959/2010). The Limits of Human Progress: A Critical Study. *Cultural Politics*, 6(2), 229–36.

Skemp, J.B. (1952/1987). *Plato's Statesman – A Translation of The Politicus of Plato*. Bristol: Bristol Classical Press.

ORR, M.A. (Mrs. John Evershed), (1913). *Dante and the Early Astronomers*. London: Gall and Inglis.

Queneau, R. (1947/1981). *Exercises in Style*. Trans. Wright, B. New York: New Directions Books.

Perec, G. (1985/2009). *Thoughts of Sorts*. Trans. Bellos, D. Boston: David R. Godine.

Porter, T. M. (1997). *Trust in Numbers: The Pursuit of Objectivity in Science and Public Life*. Princeton: Princeton University Press.

Parisi, L. (2013). *Contagious Architecture: Computation, Aesthetics, Space*. Cambridge: MIT Press.

Renan, S. (1967). *An Introduction to American Underground Film*. New York: E.P. Dutton & Co.

Reston, Jr., J. (1994). *Galileo: A Life*. New York and London: Harper Collins.

Vaneigem, R. (1967/1994). *The Revolution of Everyday Life*. Trans. Nicholson-Smith, D. London: Left Bank Books.

Wise, M. N. (1995). *The Values of Precision*. Princeton: Princeton University Press.

Wittgenstein, L. (1953/1973). *Philosophical Investigations*. 3rd edition. London: Pearsons.

Artist and Exhibition Catalogues:

Stanley Brouwn: my steps 12.12.2005 – 1.1.2006. (2014). Galleria Massimo Mini. Milan: A+Mbookstore Edizioni et al.

A Distance of 336 Steps, A Distance of 2444601 Feet, A Distance of 2232 Ells. (2000). Brouwn, S. Amsterdam: Netherlands Foundation for Visual Arts.

Stanley Brouwn, "steps". (1971). Stedelijk Museum Amsterdam, (18 March – 18 April 1971).

COMMOTION – Julien Prévieux. (2004). Paris: Jousse en Entreprise.

Constructing the Perceiver – ARAKAWA: Experimental Works. (1991). Edited and published by The National Museum of Modern Art, Tokyo. Produced by the Bijutsu Shuppan Design Center. The exhibition of the same name was held at The National Museum of Modern Art, Tokyo (1 November – 10 December 1991), The National Museum of Modern Art, Kyoto (2 January – 5 February 1992), and Matsuzakaya Art Museum, Nagoya (28 June – 19 July 1992).

Invisible – Art about the Unseen 1975–2012. (2012). London: Hayward Publishing. The exhibition of the same name was held at the Hayward Gallery, London (12 June – 5 August 2012).

Karin Sander. (2012). *n.b.k. Exhibition. Brand 10*. Babias, M. (ed.) Neuer Berliner Kunstverein.

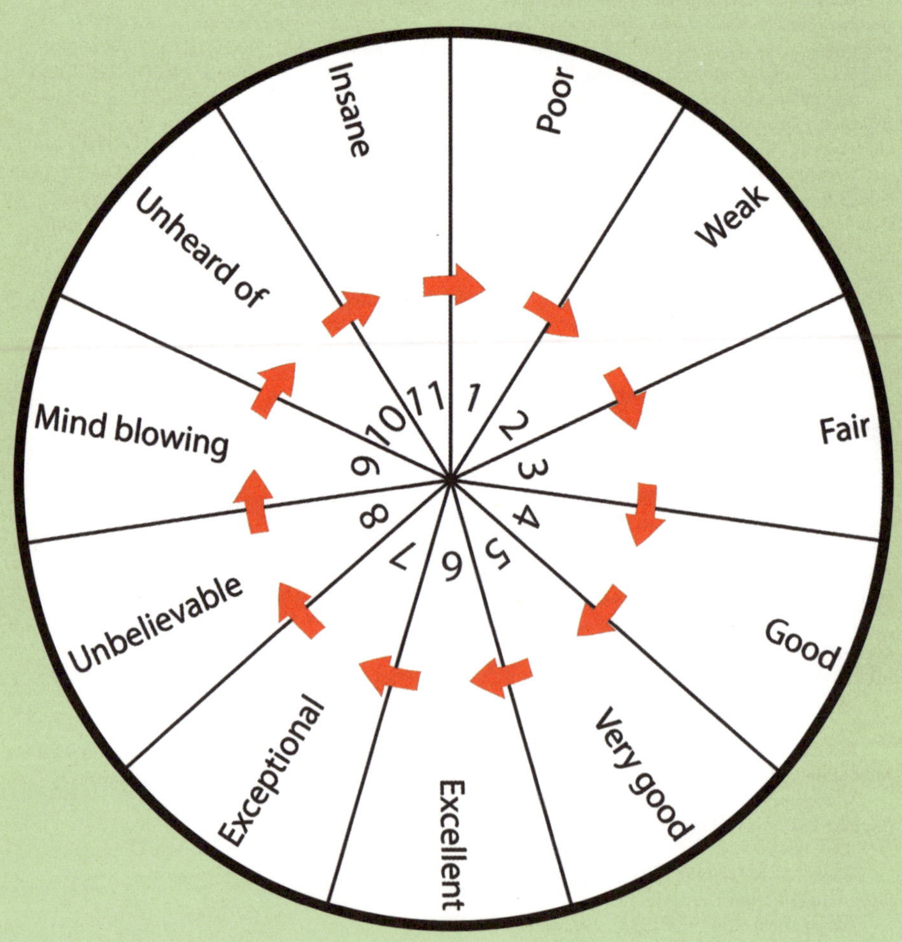

"Modified grading scale for the evaluation
of research proposal", from the conversation
with Helmut Draxler on 14 July 2015

Symbolic Engineering: Measurement, Aesthetics, and the Rules for Art
A Conversation with
Helmut Draxler

Helmut Draxler: For a long time, art has been regarded as being beyond measurement, through defining precisely what cannot be measured. But, obviously, a lot in art is based on measurement: proportion, harmony, composition. Traditionally, aesthetics were even understood as a set of rules. And, within modernism, there have been plenty of attempts to regain ground against the hegemony of subjective aesthetics. How would you situate contemporary art within these coordinates?

Miya Yoshida: What I find interesting in contemporary art is the embracing of a paradox of subjective aesthetics. Many conceptual artists attempt to rid their artworks of subjective aesthetics. To develop their ideas, they adopt diverse artistic strategies: chance, discipline, readymades, mathematic axioms, numbers, acts of counting, short written instructions or texts, or simply the displacement of objects, even disappearing artworks, et cetera in the process as well as in the production of art. At the same time, such works, on the other hand, become very personal and result in extremely subjective aesthetics. A paradox is thus inherent in artistic abstraction. When it comes into play in measurement, the scientific logic of measurement therefore does not necessarily function anymore. Such aesthetics succeed in presenting different levels of accuracy in the concrete forms of artworks, which I find fascinating. In the past two centuries, quantitative accuracy was recognised as central issue in science. The accuracy that is sought by means of mathematical measurement is one thing, but measurement also depends on criteria and norms. The sociologist Theodor Porter says: "More than one solution is possible, because more than one measurement regime is possible, and that means that there is a range of potentially valid measures."

According to his view of the validity of multiple potential measurements, it can be said that, in modernism, art problematizes classical aesthetics, norms, or the geometrically imaginary in mathematics. Referring to works by representative conceptual and post-conceptual artists such as Mel Bochner, Stanley Brouwn, Roman Ondák, the art historian, Elise Noyez has come up with the analysis that measurement is also employed as an artistic strategy to replace objects of spatial and perceptual experience. Following the line of thought of modernist art, I see that contemporary artists, including those mentioned above, attempt to explore the concept of accuracy in measurement by shifting the location from mathematical perspectives to specific situations, movements, and relationships, or by thinking around the topic of measurement through including the process and the act of measuring. How would you situate contemporary art, when you propound that art is all about measurement?

HD: For me the interesting point is to see how paradox works. Purely subjective and purely objective arguments are typical attempts in modernism to solve a problem through quite radically honing the argument in one direction. The problem seems to be solved, but it obviously quickly reappears. That's why it seems time to consider the problem more thoroughly, in the sense that there is definitely a tendency toward increasing accuracy in technical, economic, and administrative terms based on numeric methodologies, but also a tendency towards the opposite, toward the subjective, affective, or situative within different sorts of cultures. For me it seems quite obvious that there is a split within the symbolic, thus arranging two kinds of "culture" in a complementary way. The severity of this split even affects the tendencies toward overcoming it. Instead of trying to overcome this split again and again, it seems more fruitful to attempt to understand its logics and historical dynamics, and contemporary practices seem more interesting when they try to explore the subjective within the objective, and the objective within the subjective, without pretending to be able to overcome that polarity. Compared to pre-modern forms of measurement, contemporary forms can, therefore, only be discussed through recognising that split, as well as the tension it implies for any cultural, artistic, or political self-conception.

But maybe we can ground the problem in an even more general way. Because the romantic stance against measurement was essentially based on understanding life as something that largely transcends any confinement.

Life in the age of genetic engineering, however, seems to be based on measurement in many ways. How would you then reconsider the avant-garde tradition with respect to this problem, since its basic aspiration has been to reconcile art and life?

MY: The challenge for artists is how to deal with the invisibly calculated aesthetics produced by algorithms in approaching art and life. The algorithmic society increasingly calculates and observes reality from the viewpoint of the virtual, rather than the real. At the end of "Aesthetics of Measurement in Dialogue between an Artist and a Scientist", Patricia T. Clough emphasises the speed of digital technology, which "allows us to experience things that we could never experience ourselves directly, and never will". She also refers to her vision of a machine that realises non-conscious capacities of human beings in a networked entity. Such an algorithmic mode of thinking affects the understanding of the banal experience of everyday life. Everything becomes virtual, and what we think is "discursive" might only be a result of algorithmic calculations. In this sense, artists confront the situation in order to carefully rethink notions such as banality, the real and the virtual, the experience of everyday life, or even life itself. When notions of life, of experience change, artistic strategies for *art and life* must also undergo a transformation. How do artists tackle a new interpretation of art and life? Artists are always sensitive to the transformation of the social sphere. They actively respond it by crossing existing boundaries in norms, social structures, professional categorisations, et cetera. For example, phrases such as artist as writers in the 1960s, then, with the emergence of art in context, ethnographers in the 1980s and 90s, media architects around the new millenium, curators in the age of global mobility and networks, or researchers based on the new vision of artistic research in higher education. At the same time, artists are actually none of these either. They borrow vocabularies as well as actions from other fields, but artists are not socialists, political scientists, media theorists, neuroscientists, or physicists. Artistic strategies for art and life therefore continue to be crucial. However, in what way will standpoints in art and life still be relevant if how these notions are conceptualised changes? I don't know...

HD: I think it would again be helpful to distinguish the symbolic layers of art, technology, and life. What becomes intersected in "reality" still remains separated symbolically in many ways, and it might therefore be important to reckon with the insistence of symbolic layers. Technological utilitarianism and avant-garde emphasis correspond with each other in that both try to overcome the symbolic, although it is obvious that all they can achieve is a certain performance of the symbolic. The really interesting challenge would be to work on possible connections between "material" technological change and the symbolic arrangement of categories, or on what sediments from the symbolic into the layers of the material. Hence, what still seems interesting to me with respect to the avant-garde is not its ideology, but its vast array of methodologies, which might be read not as an achievement of a reconciliation of some sort, but as an exploration of on-going interactions between three of the most important symbolic registers of modernity: art, life, and politics. The political becomes visible here not just as a certain means towards a good end, but also as something that produces its own symbolic possibilities and obstacles, as well as its own materialities, meaning measurements working inside politics. This seems to be important precisely because, within political philosophy, measurements of time and space in particular have become objects of substantial critique, thus indicating a utility of the categorical dimensions of being for the capitalist alienation and exploitation of life. Does spontaneity still help counter measurement?

MY: Do you mean whether intervention or rapture causes friction against an endless flow of neoliberal capitalism? Instead of spontaneity, some people refer to slowness as a way to counter the accelerated speed. Might art therefore be a way to do so?

Worship of quantification as a social technology and the pursuit of efficiency have changed priorities, the order of things, in society. I am not sure if spontaneity is capable of being powerful enough to change the norm or the order of things. I see strategic potentials rather in countering segmentation, in employing different norms and orders of things to criticise measurement. From a quantitative viewpoint, mathematical aesthetics with big data, algorithms, computer calculations, and so on produce a shift from viewing a single piece of data as an object to the relational object. What might, therefore, help is creating and practicing a different relationship to measurements, without segmenting them. According to the logic of French Oulipianism (Oulipo), which criticises the rational not by means of the irrational – as the Surrealists attempted – but by means of the super-rational, i.e. measurement against measurement as a means to critique measurement. Do you see any potential in spontaneity? Does it help mitigate the power of validity in quantification through measurement?

This is where I see an overlap with the issue of artistic research. Would you take a position to change the rigour of art and research from inside the form of artistic research, or would you deny the form and be against critique and change from the outside…?

HD: First of all, I would say that I like the term super-rational, if we understand it less as a science fiction phantasy of a superior intelligence, and more as one of many layers of rationality, while including irrationality, or myth, or ideology, or symptom as different sorts of rationality. A purely rational rationality is probably not very rational, just as supercomputers are not necessarily really smart. That means that the rational and the spontaneous are not strict antagonists. Spontaneity depends on certain structural givens or it could not appear as such; and, vice versa, every planned rational structure needs subjective, even spontaneous elements to be able to gain momentum. This relationality cannot be suspended, but it can be addressed, and perhaps can be worked through from a psychoanalytical perspective. This could also include a tip for artistic research. It can only be taken seriously if it avoids rotten compromises. There is no reconciliation of art and research, except in bad art or bad research, and a triumph of bureaucracy. Artistic research therefore has to strive for the impossible, to be good art and good research. But how might we measure its achievements and failures?

MY: I agree that the two cannot be reconciled. Do you remember that we once joked around about the grading scale for the evaluation of my (failed) research proposal? We transformed the five hierarchical categories (1: Weak, 2: Fair, 3: Good, 4: Very Good, 5: Excellent) by adding more categories to expand them into a circle (6: Exceptional, 7: Unbelievable, 8: Mind-blowing, 9: Never heard of, and 10: Do not know what to do!, which lies next to 1: Weak)

Inventing diverse methodologies in art practices can open up not only different forms and processes, but also different orders of thinking in research, as well as different attitudes towards research itself. I once heard an artist say, "All I know is how to start the project. So, please do not ask me how to proceed with it!" – a question that is always asked in the research proposal in connection with getting the project started.

HD: The main allegations against measurement, even on the part of bourgeois critics, concern the rationalisation and bureaucratisation of life.

Do you see anything to defend in rationalisation and bureaucratisation, or could you envision a perspective on measurement that does not necessarily encompass rationalisation and bureaucratisation?

MY: The standardisation of measurement was born with the aspiration of universalism and developed alongside the ideology of equality in democracy in 19th-century France. Regarded as a type of standardisation, bureaucratisation is the birth of professionalism. Bureaucracy requires legitimation in numbers. It is thereby possible to see the nature of bureaucratisation as serving to expand the category of applied fields and studies – applied mathematics, applied physics, and although it may not be exactly the same, but nonetheless, to a certain degree, applied forms of art and art history such as curatorial and mediation studies, business and administration studies, et cetera. (It might be said that artistic research is mistakenly framed as an applied form of research.) It's not about either good or bad. Applied mathematics is different than standard mathematics. I see the current hype and proliferation of various applied fields as a particular development along the lines of rationalisation and bureaucratisation. The rationalisation and bureaucratisation of education reflects and corresponds to the development of putting more emphasis on applied studies.

What exactly do you find lacking in such a rationalisation and bureaucratisation of life?

HD: I think you're right. Everything today seems to have become "applied", and therefore generates specifically bureaucratic forms of performance, between politics, administration, education, science, and art. There is a lack of responsibility that might be addressed by means of such procedures – in vain, however. And seemingly measurable means inherently become increasingly independent, thus fostering auxiliary sciences, encyclopaedic forms of knowledge, and controllable standards in thinking, politics, and art. I would not discredit these tendencies altogether: Although they are meaningful as a reaction to purely subjective, competitive claims and corruption, they simultaneously dominate any kind of expression much too strongly through establishing themselves as a new and completely unmediated form of mediation. That's why I think it becomes really important to reflect on practices of measurement from an historical perspective. Measurement today seems to be a fundamental principle in production and control. Do digital cultures in this respect just continue the logics of mechanisation and industrial capitalism, or do you see a different logic at play here?

MY: What exactly do you mean with "digital culture"?

HD: Well, in the early 2000s, "digital cultures" became a buzzword to replace something like "new media". But because everything has become digital in the meantime, the term seems to have lost its meaning …

MY: Yes, I see it as a very ambiguous notion and almost empty signifier today. As you point out, it's important to contemplate measurement as a problem of politics, rather than of science. At the same time, digital technologies also require us to reconsider measurement more politically than culturally. The birth and development of new technologies have never been neutral. In considering its origin and subsequent development, the Japanese social economist Hikotaro Tonoue contemplates that technology never directs itself against the logic of capitalism. That is the fundamental nature of technology. Digital technologies are more than ever so, from infrastructures – energy supplies, network connections, platforms, systems – to interfaces, both software and hardware. My observation, however, is that digital technologies do not refer to their infrastructures on a content level; they instead generate an aesthetics of *symbolicism*: a symbolising attitude, appearance, emotion, preference, attention, et cetera – as an action of clicking "friend", "like", "link", "go", and then counting them as a *"symbolic"* number. *Symbolic* quantity plays an a priori role in determining relationships. Such a symbolic mode of thinking fabricates symbolic desire and takes away and directs attention to a narrow and limited focus, and I assume that it contributes greatly to the current tendency toward populism in politics. *Symbolicism* goes together with the mechanism of measurement quite well. But things that are not symbolised are outside the frame of society, as if they don't exist. Does that make sense to you?

HD: Oh yes. Symbolic quantities seem to pose a real challenge to reflection. In a certain way, I think they've always existed as an imaginary element within every form of cultural articulation that is addressed to an audience. But, nowadays, in consumer profiles, online dating, and the like, symbolic quantity has become independent of any producer. It seems to signal the triumph of the "death of the author", the death of purely "readerly" texts. There are, however, limits to these procedures, not only internally; there's still a need for some sort of production or valued information, but essentially from the outside. Annoyance creates subcultures outside of symbolic quantities …

MY: I would like to refer to two examples pertaining to the absurdity of measurement based on *symbolicism*. The first is current historical studies revealing why the Japanese military never managed to develop any supply network for its own troops outside the country during World War II. One striking reasons is that the planning and execution of supply chains were never considered to be factors that might result in promotion in the military, which means that hardly any generals took the issue seriously enough, despite the fact that it was a crucial factor in the war. The other example is a current article in the Danish newspaper *Politiken* about the system for evaluating the police in Denmark. The article reports that most policemen in the country, also those with other duties such as detectives, were temporarily deployed on highways towards the end of year to check traffic speed limits, so as to reach the goal of evaluation points. The latter is a banal example, but does do a good job of capturing and reflecting how measurement-based systems operate in detail in society. These examples tell us that *symbolicism* directs attentions away from things that are central to a process, produces symbolic numbers, and makes us think and behave irrationally for the sake of a rationality of measurement. Similar examples can readily be found everywhere in contemporary society, and are recognised as being absurd. However, once *symbolicism* gets rolling, it seems unstoppable. If it this is the case, how can it be redirected in another way?

HD: I agree. Irrationality is an intrinsic element in every sort of rationality. Adorno and Horkheimer made this point in what they called "instrumental reason". They were, however, maybe all too consistent in their argument, thus only leaving space for some kind of weird art that was not considered spoiled by that sort of reason. Wouldn't it be more interesting not to see measurement as pure limitation, but also as a means of enabling cultural production and critique?

MY: I think it was John Cage who said that there are a hundred types of genders in mushrooms. I found this statement an amusing approach to introducing a playful mind-set for deconstructing the politics of gender from the inside. It situates gender politics in a completely different realm of imagination. To give another example: There is an idea in ancient Japanese mythology that there are eight million god/desses. Eight million does not refer to the actual number, but is instead a metaphorical way of expressing the countless number of god/desses in animism. God/desses can exist anywhere, in any form. However, one can also regard this number as a playful way of saying: "If one god hates you, there are still 7,999,999 god/desses left, one of whom may possibly like you!" This imaginative understanding of numbers, rather than being rigid, indicates the possibility to shift their power of validity in another direction. Juxtaposing plural measurements may, therefore, work in a way similar to shifting measurement from the terrain of mathematics to that of poetry. This has the potential to critique the articulation of accuracy through playing with the meaning and unmeaning of measurement. But we need a diversity of measurements here; otherwise it becomes nothing but a horror! Just like having eight million god/desses hating you!

HD: Is diversity essential for the aesthetics of measurement, or could you imagine other ways or strategies of using measurement within the rationalisation of production and control?

MY: To continue my previous response: Aesthetics of measurement may be able to shift a focus of attention that has already come to be steered by a symbolic mode of thinking, and diversify it with a logic of "pataphysics". Artistic practices comprise different directions or modes of thinking and a different process of abstraction from those employed in disciplinary fields in the sciences, including the humanities. They might sometimes be misunderstood as being irrelevant, minor, subjective, or self-centred. At the same time, subjective and illogical thinking is not necessarily always unscientific; it has long been discussed as a liminal space that allows for a critique of the all-inclusive character of scientific systems. Processing information in the world opens up different modes and constellations of knowledge, while simultaneously processing words/numbers back opens different paths and nodal points of information that are not predesigned according to criteria, structures, or systems. In this sense, the suspended nature of artistic practices, or the curatorial ability to capacitate has the strategic potential to contribute to reflecting and rearticulating the notion of measurements in the rationalisation of control. Or, is my belief in art too optimistic?

HD: Never ever. But art is surely not the solution; it only signifies one symbolic register within which modern "regimes" of measurement can be reflected. Like the humanities, art is not a neutral player in the field; it profits enormously from scientific, technological, administrative, economic, and political measurements. Its very prestige is perhaps based on the thoroughly measured space within modern societies. As such, it first of all requires internal forms of critique that refer to the delegating of symbolic terrains and the transfers of reason and affect that they involve.

MY: In the discussion of sociology and media studies, considering the endless process and feedback system involved in measurement calls attention to affects. In these fields of studies, it is affect that matters, and no longer epistemology. Do you see a limitation of epistemology in the regime of so-called "digital cultures"?

HD: Not in general, "digital cultures", if we continue to call them that, are still highly unstable symbolically. So, it will definitely take a bit of time to understand their specific rationalities. I'm just a bit sceptical of worldviews that claim that everything is getting more and more affective, except for the speaking position raising this claim. It's not possible to be exempted from affect. That's the essential lesson of psychoanalysis. The more you try to focus on the rational, the more affective the attempt will become. Let's simply relax for the moment.

MY: An increasing tendency towards a segmentation of life is another crucial issue in contemporary life within the neoliberal capitalist system, while "practicality" or "convenience" are emphasised as values that lead us to participate voluntarily in segmenting life on our own as well. For example, the emergence of car-sharing options such as Drive Now, Car to Go, and so on is a good example for thinking about an intriguing complexity in economic relationships. It accelerates the segmentation of time from car rental per a day or per week to car rental per minute, with an increase in convenience resulting from being able to leave a car anywhere and to grab another that is nearest to you at a later point in time. It's very practical and also inexpensive for short-term use. Some say that it's also ecological as a result of "sharing" a resource. Here, the notion of "common" is integrated into the segmentation of neoliberal capitalism and even transformed into the mind-set of ecology in a tricky way – tricky, because it is now shifted to a capitalistic strategy. Do you see any possibility of segmentation opening up a new model of the "common" in the economy, instead of taking the accumulation of capital away from the individual and shifting it to the system?

HD: Oh, car-sharing is great, but, of course, it doesn't help overcome capitalism. It is indeed capitalism itself. How we might share things in another way that could not be recouped by capitalism is difficult for me to imagine. Maybe we first of all have to share an idea of capitalism, an idea of how the rational and the affective work within its scope, what kind of symbolic formation it provides, and how this symbolic formation interacts with other symbolic formations such as those of politics, technology, media, culture, or art. My fear is that, despite Marx, we are still far from understanding these interactions, and we tend to use the very term capitalism in a quite solutionist way, whereas it might instead be essential to measure its historic scope.

Dialogues between
an Artist and a Scientist

AESTHETICS OF MEASUREMENT

MATT MULLICAN
WHO FEELS THE MOST PAIN?

"My name is Matt Mullican. I live at 370 Mesa Road, Santa Monica, California. I'm 6'2" tall. I weigh 180 pounds. I'm 22 years old and single."

Since the mid-70s, I've been doing a series of lectures titled, "Who feels the most pain?" which consist of stories and fond memories. One of my early memories was giving a lecture to my family in Chickasha, Oklahoma, about what I was doing. I could explain what I was doing without ever mentioning the word "art" or "artist". I was talking about the world and experience. I still believe that one could talk about art and artists in that manner. When I was at the California Institute of the Arts (CalArts) in 1972, I was very interested in light patterns and the quality of the light of colours in a dark room. A great number of my works were a collection of little coloured cards pinned onto the wall to show them under the conditions of changing the lights in the room. For instance, if the light is changed to green, all the colours look different. As my performance, I laid colour cards on the floor in the dark auditorium, then picked up certain colours as best as I could. When the lights were turned back on again, a bunch of cards had naturally missed being picked up. This experience made me recognize that all I saw were light patterns.

If I say "all I see are light patterns," where does life exist in those patterns? When I said "all I see are light patterns" in 1973, what was I saying? I'm saying that there is a huge difference between who I am and what I see. At this very moment, I say that I'm not looking at you, but at the light reflecting off of you. If I say, "all I see is the light reflecting off of you", what does it mean? Does it mean that you're neither living, nor human? Neither man, nor woman, but simply phenomena? People who are sitting in front of me, the floor that is laid out, everything is the same. This is a fairly radical idea, but it was the

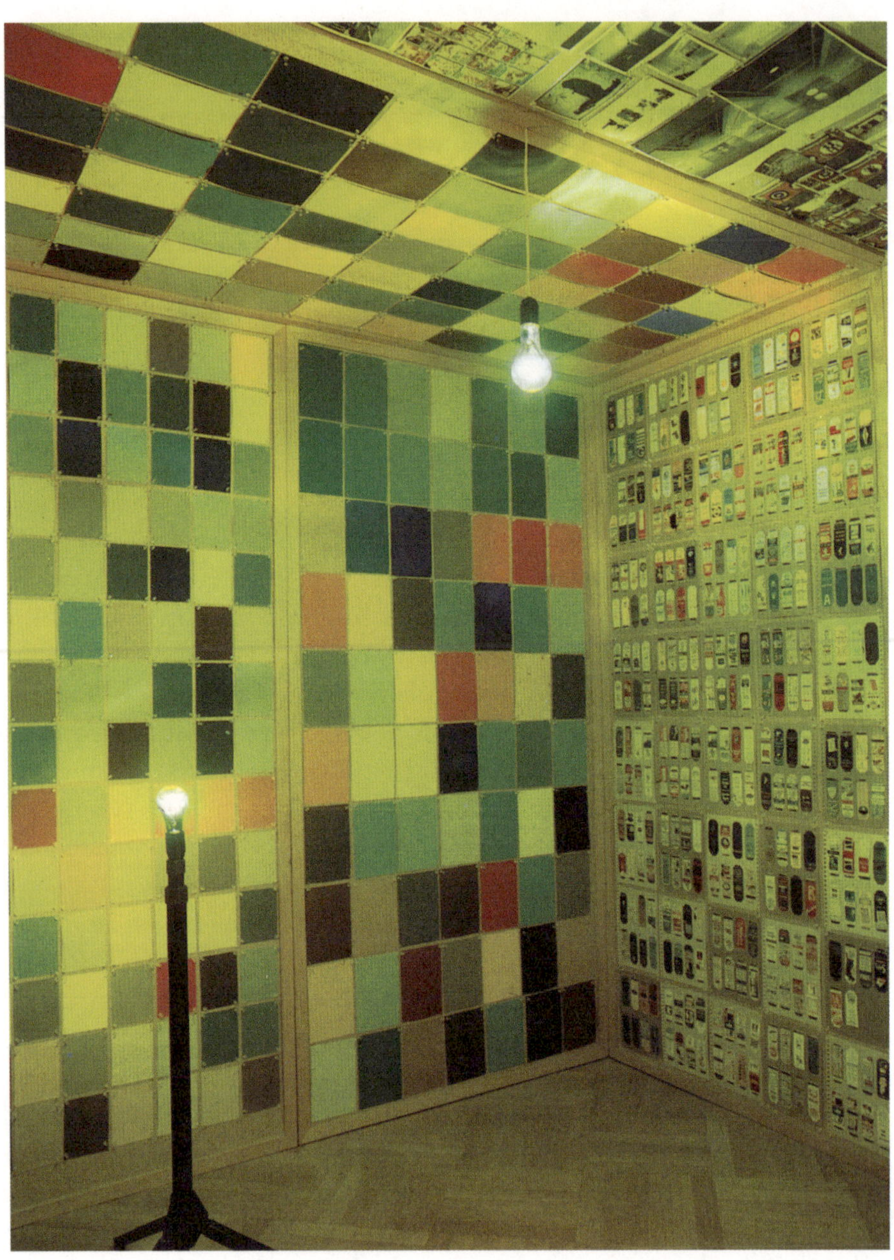

Matt Mullican, *Untitled*, 2000,
mixed media, 250 x 250 x 250 cm,
courtesy Galerie Georg Kargl, Vienna

idea that I was experimenting with. I remember seeing a girlfriend getting out of a car and walking towards me and saying to myself: "I'm not seeing her, I'm just seeing the light reflect off of her." This created a huge distance between me and her, but it also created a huge distance to everybody else. Twenty years later, I was sitting at a bar with my wife on an early date at Magoo's. I'd had my second martini and was telling her that there might be some trouble in our relationship because of these certain attitudes that I have and the way I see things. Later, she confessed that she thought that I was going to confess my sexuality, not being quite straight. But it wasn't about that at all. It was that, as an artist, I look at things in a certain way and always have a distance. There is a distance in my life, which is absolutely still there today. Then, where does life exist in those patterns that I've seen? All my work has been done at this point.

At Easter in 1973, I was on a trip driving back to Santa Monica and had an idea – the idea was about a little line drawing of a detail of a car's tire, that never existed and never would exist. It was a fictional detail. The implication that a detail shows a part of something that exists, but it doesn't exist, it's kind of in-between. Endless questions about this detail occurred in my mind: Who is driving the car? What's the colour of the car? Is it morning, or afternoon? How fast is the car going? What's the make of the car? Is it a Chevy, a Pontiac, a Cadillac, or a Porsche? Is anybody in the back seat? What kind of day is it? What kind of time of day? This idea was the light bulb of my life. When I had the idea after experimenting with optical perception, I decided, "This is my future." It was a hook into something that I could really have fun with for quite a while. I couldn't rationally explain to you why I felt it, but it was instinctive and an exhilarating feeling.

Within months, I was drawing a stick figure named Glen on a drawing page, while taking an undergraduate course in John Baldessari's class called "post-studio art". I didn't have a studio to work in, but I made a fictional studio with Glen in which I did all kinds of experiments. I dealt with his motives, his physicality, his hair, his fear, et cetera. In the end, approximately 500 drawings of Glen inside the place were produced. In the space, there was a clock, a plant, and a calendar that I drew, and he was doing various things. The most important thing he did was to pinch his arm. He pinched his arm and felt pain. I wanted to know where the pain that Glen felt was. "God, I feel it, where is it?" I wanted to identify that pain. I wanted to prove that the stick figure lives life. It may sound ridiculous, but it was the time to experiment with ridiculous plans and statements. As soon as I'd started to invent the form of life, or the living being inside my drawing space, I decided to draw a dead stick figure to contrast with the living one in order to figure out what is really the difference between a living and a dead stick figure. I drew him as a dead man in the corner on the back.

After continuing to work on these works for three months, I went to live in New York City for the first time. I was really getting into the world of comic-book reality, and deeply engaged myself with experiments, cutting up comic books and showing dead comic-book characters. I was interested in seeing a real dead person. I'd become interested in the dead person through this fictional person. This became a quest. I tried to see one, but I was neither allowed to go into the morgue, nor get into the hospital. I couldn't get into any kind of school where they would have them. But one of my friends at Yale University who knew that I wanted to engage with a cadaver called me up and said: "We have a cadaver and we've just uncovered the face." He continued, "The cadaver's face has been covered for the whole first half of the term. Now it's been uncovered. The day after tomorrow, the face will start to be obliterated. We'll go into the eye, then it's going to be different. So please come up here." I immediately got on the train to go up there, because the face is EVERYTHING. When I got there, all the cadavers were on different, beautiful chrome steel tables. I was most interested in the face. We saw one male corpse, the back of whose head was cut to look at the brain. When we turned him over, his left arm fell off on the floor. I picked up the arm and I put it back. There he was. The cadaver looked like it might have been there quite a while, very crusty, smelly and slimy. I looked at the cadaver, and I did what Glen did to himself to the cadaver. Glen had pinched his arm. So I pinched the cadaver's arm, the one that had fallen off. To feel, to understand the pain that could be felt by that action. I put my hand in his mouth, I shouted in his ear, I covered his eyes, I blew the hair on his head to make it move, I touched his intestines, amongst other things. It was a very simple thing to do. But what I was most interested in was pinching the arm. That was really the key. When someone in the movies sees something fantastic, they say to the person next to them: "Pinch me! I want to know if I'm dreaming, or not." I was pinching the cadaver. Clearly, he didn't wake up. The next day my friend and I were talking about "him" and "it", and I said, "He looked sad. He looked like he was a homeless man. He looked like he sold his body for booze. It was crusty, smelly and green, and squished like a sponge." The "him-ness" and the "it-ness" were clearly very obvious. That was a primary insight, that we were flipping back and forth unconsciously about the "him-ness" of the cadaver and the "it-ness".

Every artist deals with form and content. This was absolutely at the core for me, how we define who "we" are, as I had previously defined all humans as phenomena. In parallel, I was taking photographs of my living environment. I took a photograph of my bed, the kitchen, the refrigerator, the stuff in the refrigerator, my shoes, my closet, my books, the bathroom, the tub, the sink, the toilet, the hallway, the light bulbs, et cetera. I took a photograph of everything I was living with. Referring back to the distance I felt, I realised that I was talking about taking my life as I live it. I have a photograph of a person. In parallel, I was cutting up comic books and collecting dead comic-book characters and comic-book men, which were standing in the picture with the trees and the buildings around them. For instance, I put the photograph over here, the comic-book drawing next to it, and next to that Glen, the stick figure in his studio. Next to that, on this side, I put Glen, but simply drew the stick figure by himself, by "itself", without a place. The next object I would put is the sign, the bathroom sign, and to the right of the bathroom sign, a sign broken up, which has a red head, a blue body, two orange legs, and two green arms. It looks like a little body. And I did put the red head above, away from it, the arms up and away from it, so that it's separated and blown up. Together, they become the language that identifies the parts. That's the symbol broken up. That's the man broken up.

As the next step, I have a head and a body in the most minimal way to identify the human form. It was simply about engaging with just the head and the body, which were around me. I have all of those things as photographs or objects, all of which are on the table, and whenever I would give a lecture on my work, I would lay out the photograph, the comic book, the stick figure, the sign, and the whole thing. Then I would get a pin, à-la-voodoo. I would prick the photograph, the cartoon man, with the pin, and would prick the framed stick figure and the one unframed, the sign, the man broken up, and the head and body. Then I would ask the audience: "Who feels the most pain?" The audience always answered: "The person who feels the pain most is somehow between the stick figure that is framed and the one that is unframed." It was sort of where the audience would agree that the most pain was transferred. That was the first time I started working with this idea of "Who feels the most pain?" All my exhibitions in the 70s followed this pattern: laying out my photographs, my drawings, the signs, these stick figures, the signs, the signs broken up, and then going with the head and body, and a piece of wood resting on a pillow, which I call "sleeping child". The whole exhibition was like a chart for trying to understand this. Now, if I was to change the idea and say: "Who feels the most pain? Who can hurt themselves the most that I feel?" I would say: "There is the photograph, in which a person who has a needle is putting it into his/her arm. It is painful to watch. There is a cartoon person putting a needle into his/her arm, the stick figure putting the needle into his arm, the sign of a person putting the needle into its arm", and so forth.

Going in the other direction, we go to a video, which was shot by a Portapak, of myself pricking my finger, called *Bleeding green blood*. I'm jabbing my finger with a pin, trying to get it to bleed. To go beyond it, you can go to technicolour movies and go further beyond, go into a theatrical situation, where the person is on stage pretending to prick his finger. To go further, I will get a volunteer from the audience to come up here and prick their finger, and then you can say: "Who feels the most pain?" It's not the stick figure this time. I would say probably the person from the audience feels the most pain, but it could very well be any of the others as well. I was certainly involved with the idea of what someone or something feels.

Back again in the 70s, I wanted to make a super-theatre that was somewhere in between the volunteer from the audience and the theatrical situation in which the use of hypnosis came into my work. I wanted to hypnotise somebody to believe that they were pricking their finger, to believe their ages as I set up—five years old, or eighty-five years old. I hired three actors and a hypnotist. I found an advertisement in the *Village Voice* for a hypnotist, Jerome Salmon who lived in the Village. It was a weird period around in 1976 in New York. Salmon hypnotised me for the first time. I hired him and he hired these three actors to perform at The Kitchen Center for Performing Arts in SoHo. The three actors acted out details from an imaginary life that I had written in 1973, which would include both big subjects like a birth and little subjects like slamming the door, swimming, shopping, or looking in the mirror and at the audience. One of the statements was: "Looking out of your window". This girl was hypnotised to believe that she was looking out of a window over the audience and screaming at the top of her lungs for her brother to run to give himself up to the police, because they were going to beat him up. She was terrified of her brother not doing it, so that she was screaming for him.

The audience was a bit in shock after the performance and accused me of manipulating these actors into believing that they were living the fiction that I had written. I had an impression that they were very upset.

It was in 1984. I strongly felt the distance that I implied in my self in the 70s, which can be clearly felt in the performance. Accordingly, I decided that I would only perform myself, because I was accused of being a fascist. Afterwards, I performed myself at The Kitchen, being hypnotised to believe that I was five years old. I was even talking about how I felt like I was getting younger and drawing a big picture on the floor in front of an audience. While drawing a picture, I was saying in my head: "This is incredible! Look at yourself." I could even say glancing at my legs: "Your legs are perfect. They are perfectly five years old." It continued like this. When you're in a trance, you may think that you are not aware, but you are hyper-aware. It's funny because you think you can control it, but you can't. He, or I, just performed perfectly. This was the birth of "that person".

In the meantime, over thirty years, "that person" has grown up, and has done lots of things. Once I was talking to a doctor at a cocktail party, but in fact "that person" was the person (who was attending the party). With his eyes closed and his hand put on the table like this, that was "that person". Whenever I talk about my work, "that person" is right there. "That person" is coming out in front of you as I do this. It is a part of who we are. We are not one person but many. At the party, I told the doctor that I was working with hypnosis. She asked me, "Oh, are you a passenger?" I answered: "Yes, absolutely, I was a passenger." I was in my head. I was the little man in my brain, looking at the body and saying: "God, this is bizarre!"

Most of the people who hypnotise me are doctors, and I much prefer working with them than with professional performers. I've had many years of hypnosis. Once I asked the doctor: "Can this effect come back to me later on? What happens with 'that person'? Does he come back to haunt me?" She answered: "No. You can come right back being an artist. It is fine." To a large extent, it's correct, but I admit that there is a backwash. I was in Vietnam on vacation with my family. I was paying a bill to a waiter. It was only less than three or four days after our arrival in Vietnam, so that I didn't know the money so well. My daughter, who is nineteen years old, was filming me with her mobile phone and laughing. At the end of this little action, she showed me on the phone how I was looking in the wallet, reaching down and giving the money when I was paying the bill. It was so evident that it was "that person". I looked like a cartoon. This is "that person" acting. I was completely in shock when I saw it, since I didn't have any idea that I was acting like that. My children invented a term for the face, calling it "rat face".

Here is another anecdote. Once I was walking down the street with my son and feeling perfectly happy. He just looked at me and said: "Rat face. You got a rat face. That's coming out again." The question is, who is "that person"? The person "who feels the most pain?", and this person that I become in a trance state. Who is he? I call him the "icon-brain". I've identified many things about him. He loves Christmas, birthdays, holidays. Christmas Eve is his favorite night. Favorite part of the day is his first cup of coffee in the morning. He loves breakfast, going out to restaurants and the second martini. My theory about the person is the following: Whenever we look at a picture, we somehow project ourselves into that picture. If I could grab that projection that I'm inserting and grab it before it's there, grab it and hold on to it, that is "that person". "That person" is how the person exists. He has a mantra that he repeats, saying, "I LOVE TO WORK FOR TRUTH AND BEAUTY!" I was talking to Lawrence Weiner, a famous conceptual artist. He said, I wouldn't share a beer with "that person" because you can't identify any of those things: What is truth? What is love? What is work? What is beauty? You can only use them for your own game and your own sense of purpose.

On another occasion, I was showing a performance piece in Linz, Austria, and a doctor was in the audience. After my talk and a screening of my film, he came up to me and he grabbed my shirt. He was totally angry with me, and said: "What are you doing? First of all, where did you learn to act like that? You are acting precisely like an autistic person. Why are you doing this?" I had to back up myself to say, "First of all, I was in a trance. Secondly, I saw and heard someone talk about how they think. 'That person' said that they do not think in words, implying that I do. When this other person said that she thinks in pictures, I asked myself: 'Do I think in words?' I answered: 'No, I know I don't think in words. Do I think in pictures? No, I don't think in pictures either.' Then, if I think neither in words nor in pictures, what do I think in? What is it? Who is to say?" I think way too fast and way too many dimensions are involved. It's impossible to identify what it is. It's presumably related to music, context, and memory. When I had the first light bulb about that future, it was such a clear vision, but no clue where it was going. However, I understood everything very quickly. What do you think in when you think? I told this to the doctor. He understood that everything was absolutely okay.

Here is my last anecdote. I have an exhibition up now at the Tamayo Museum in Mexico City. After my lecture about pictures there, someone came up to me and asked: "Why don't you ever use the word 'image'? How come? I'm curious why you don't." I have no idea why I never use the word "image". I was really thinking about the question and started talking about it with friends later at the dinner table. I asked: "Does an image have a thousand words in it?" When I was talking to my class at the University of Fine Arts in Hamburg (Hochschule für bildende Künste Hamburg / HFBK), where I teach, I had this insight that pictures are mental. If all I see are light patterns, then pictures are mental, and the stick figure does exist in that reality. And that reality is a big part of my reality. That pictures are mental, but images, in a way, are the stuff of pictures. They're the language that pictures reside in, but they are not the pictures themselves. A "picture" is something else. A picture holds our relationship to the world and to ourselves.

Transcript of a performance lecture

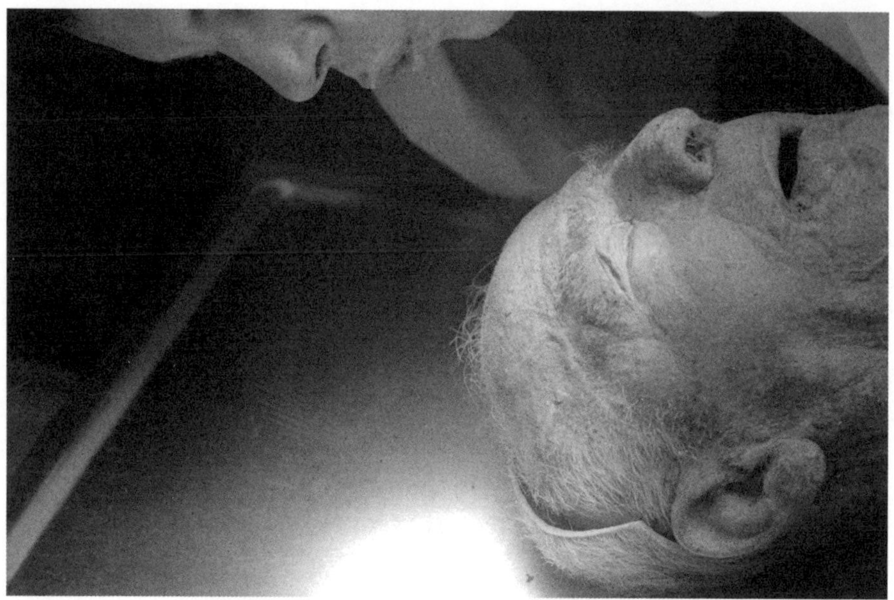

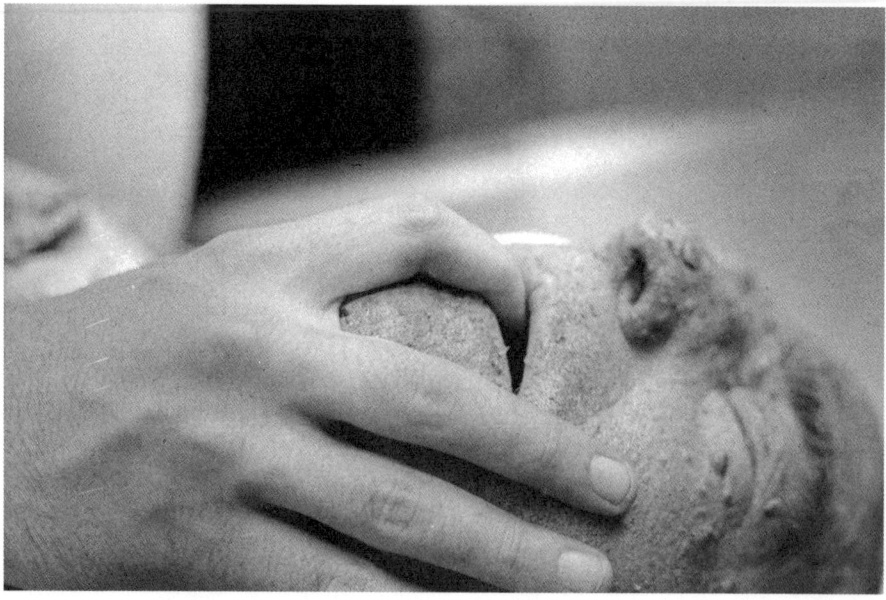

Matt Mullican, *Blowing Hair on the Back of the Dead Man's Head, Watching It Move, Making It Move*, 1973–74, black-and-white photograph, dimensions variable, courtesy Mai 36 Galerie, Zurich

Matt Mullican, *Finger in Mouth*, 1973–74, Black-and-white photograph, dimensions variable, courtesy Mai 36 Galerie, Zurich

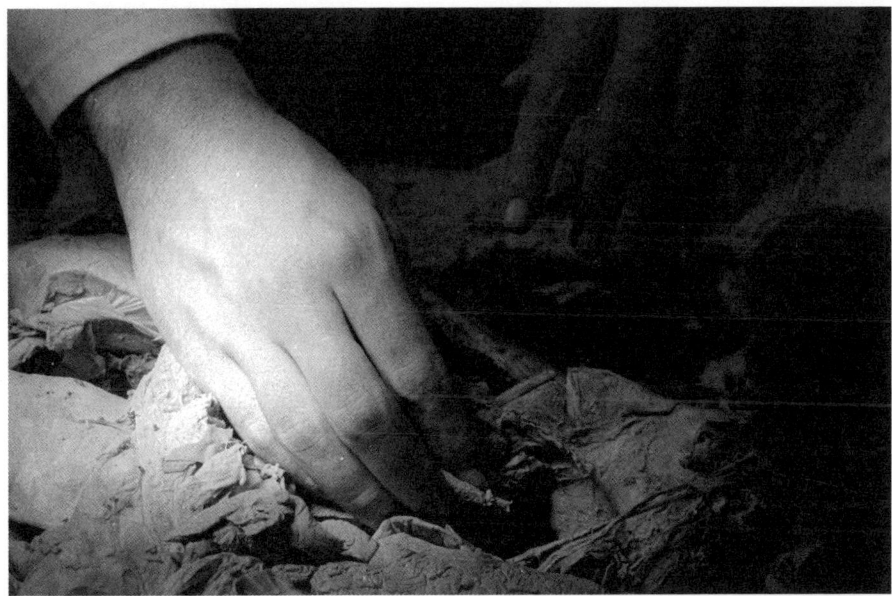

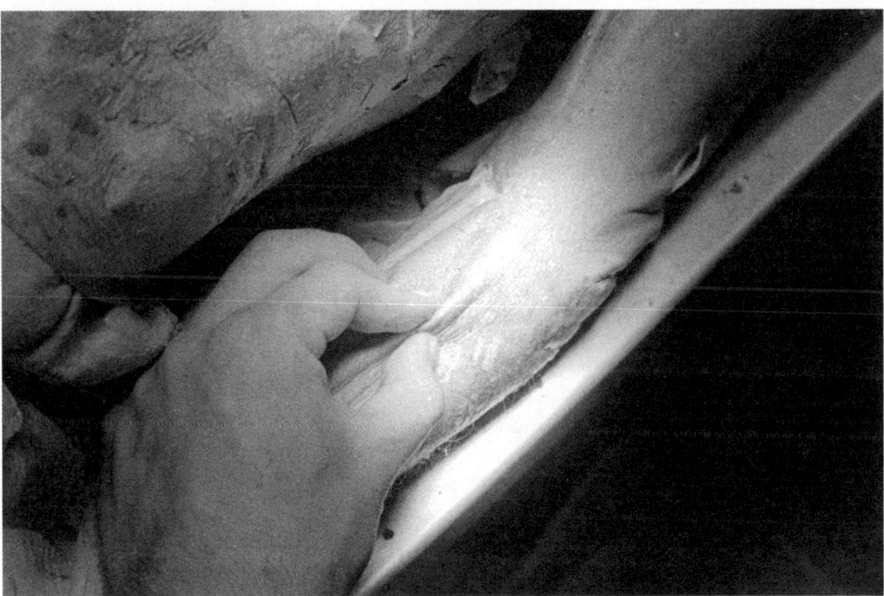

Matt Mullican, *Holding Guts*, 1973–74, black-and-white photograph, dimensions variable, courtesy Mai 36 Galerie, Zurich

Matt Mullican, *Pinching the Dead Man's Arm*, 1973–74, black-and-white photograph, dimensions variable, courtesy Mai 36 Galerie, Zurich

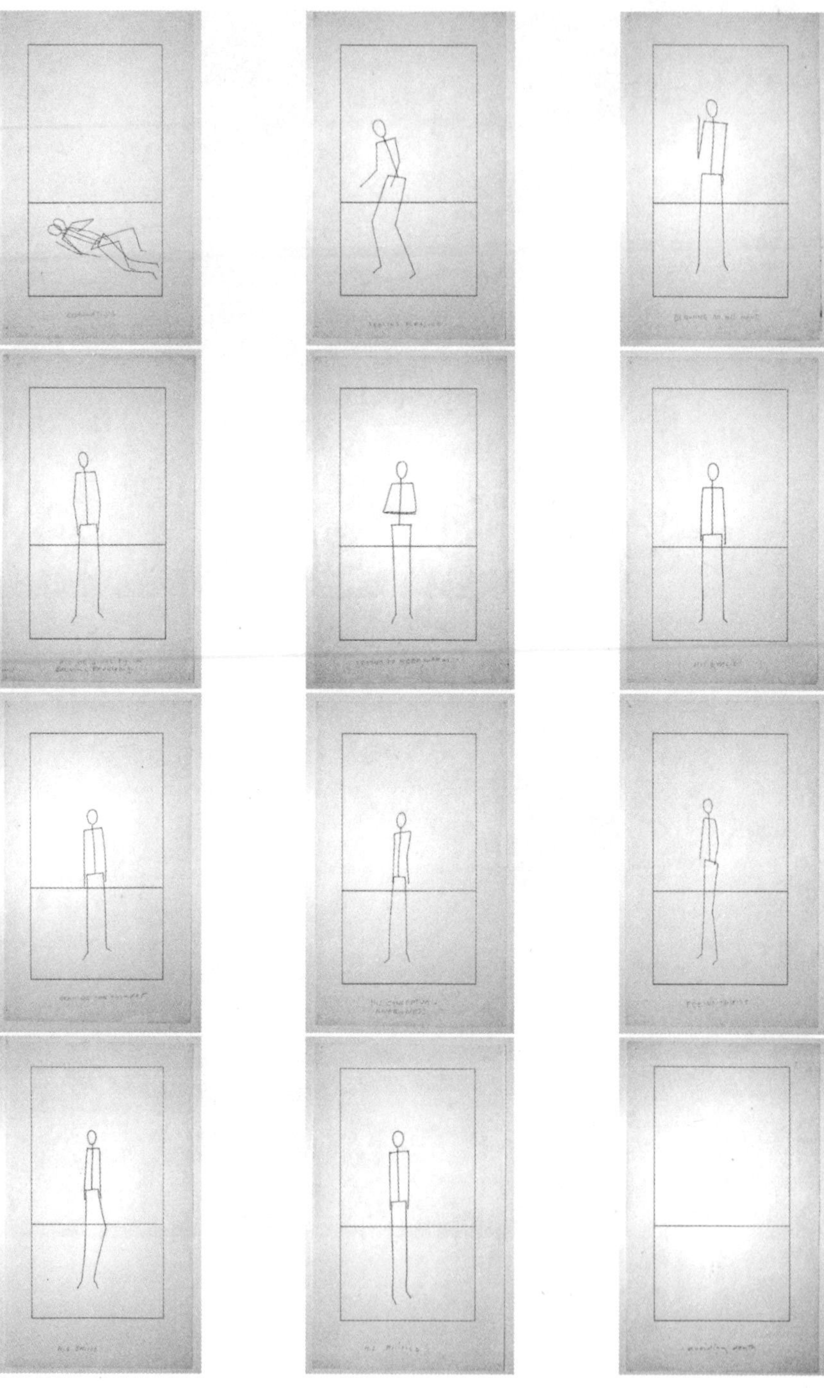

Matt Mullican, all works: *Untitled
(Stick Figure)*, 1974, ink on paper,
35.6 x 21.6 cm, courtesy the artist

Matt Mullican, *Untitled (Stick Figure)*,
1974, ink on paper, 35.6 x 21.6 cm,
courtesy the artist

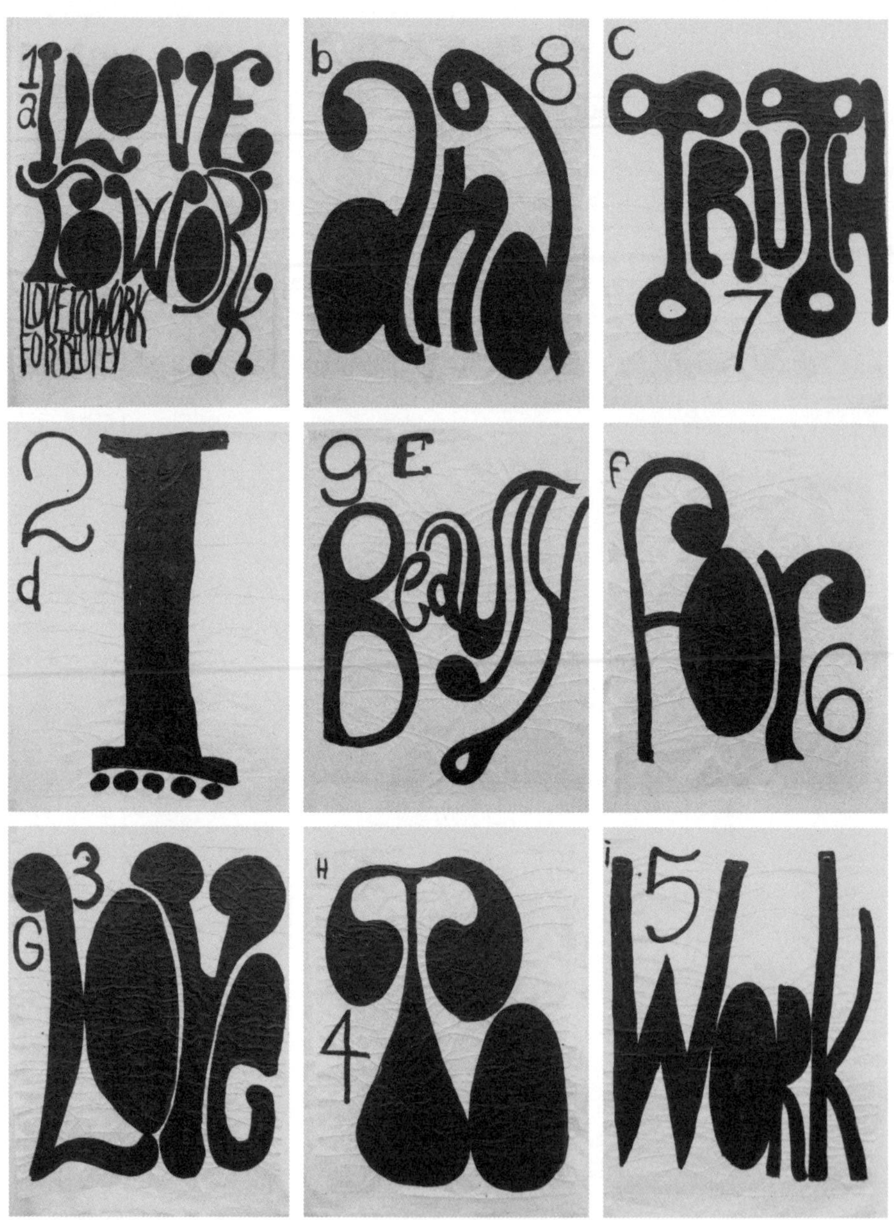

Matt Mullican, *Untitled (Learning from That Person's Work)* (details), 2005, ink and paper collaged on bed sheet, each 243.8 x 187.6 cm, courtesy the artist and Mai 36 Galerie, Zurich

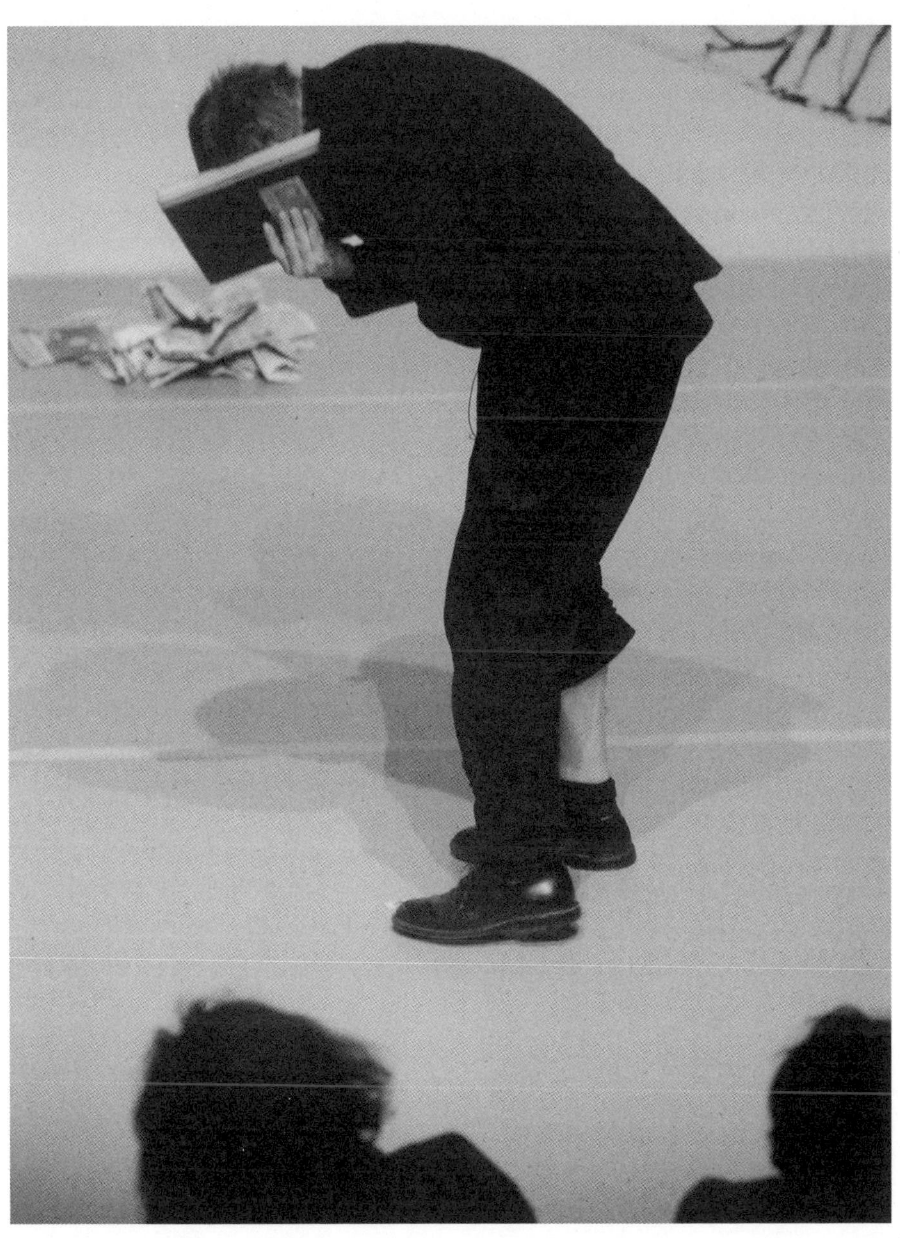

Matt Mullican, *Under Hypnosis*, 2007,
performance view, Tate Modern, London,
photo Sheila Burnett

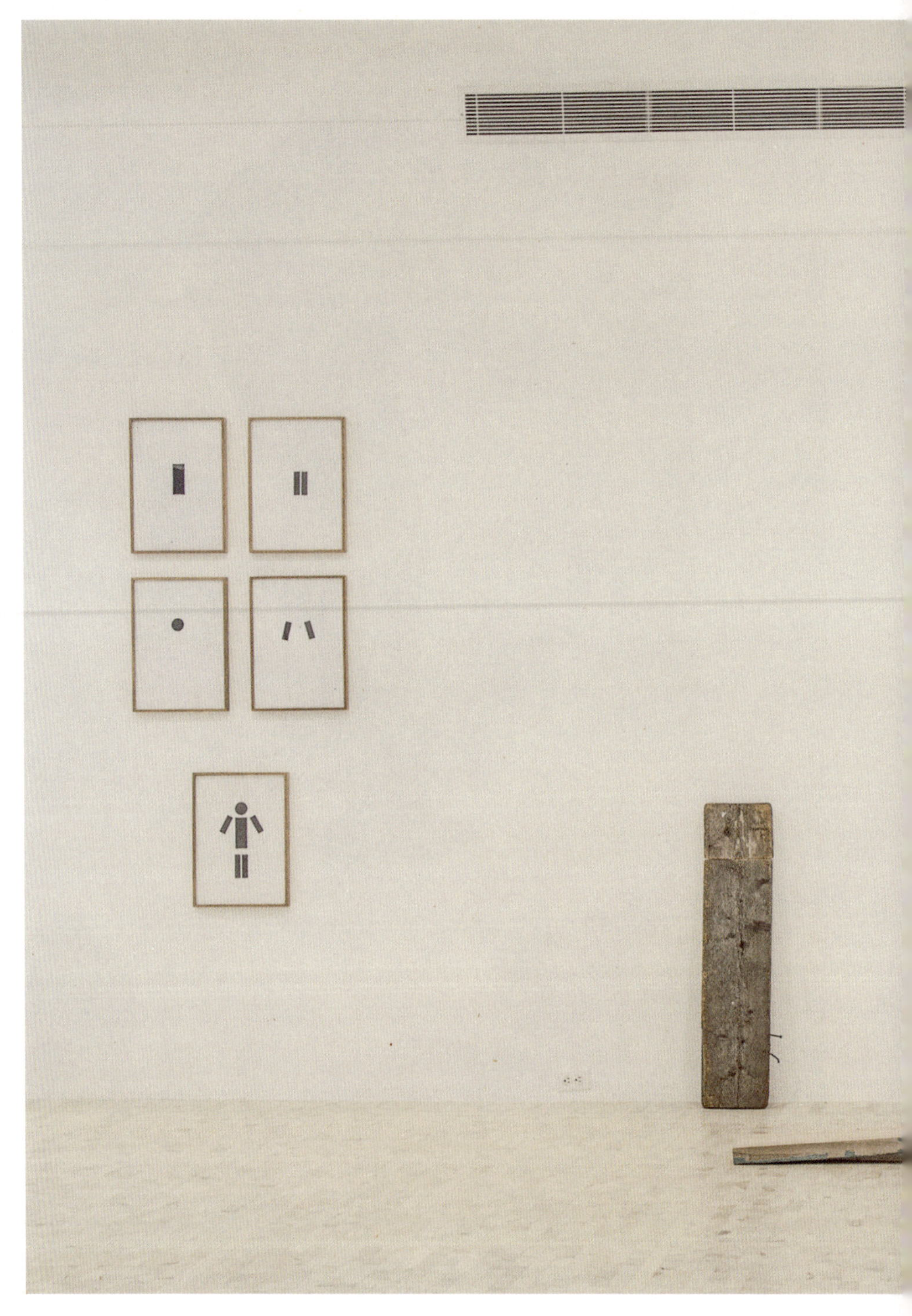

Matt Mullican, *That world/Ese mundo* (installation
view), Museo Tamayo, Mexico, 2013, photo Daniela
Uribe, courtesy Galerie Capitain Petzel, Berlin

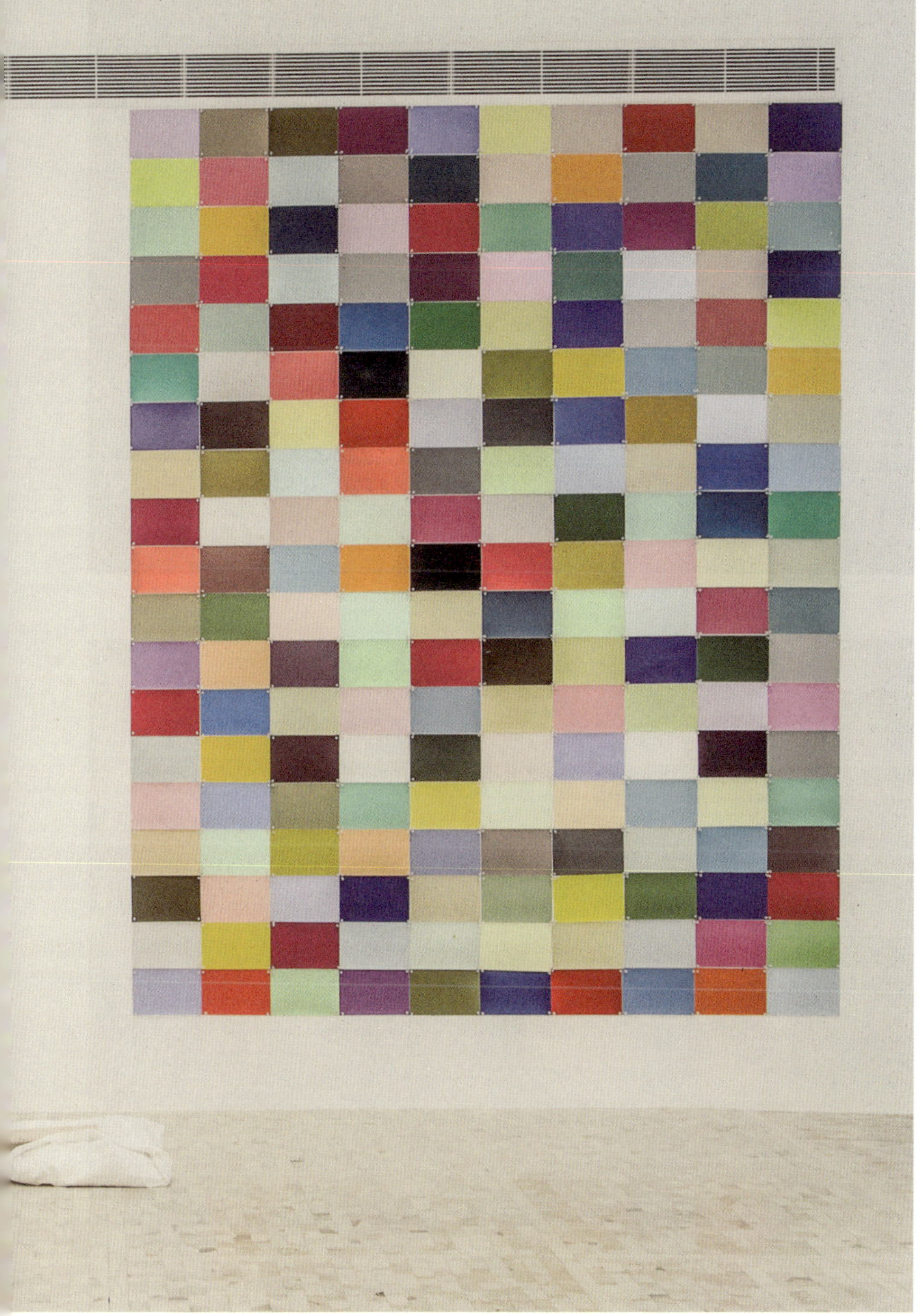

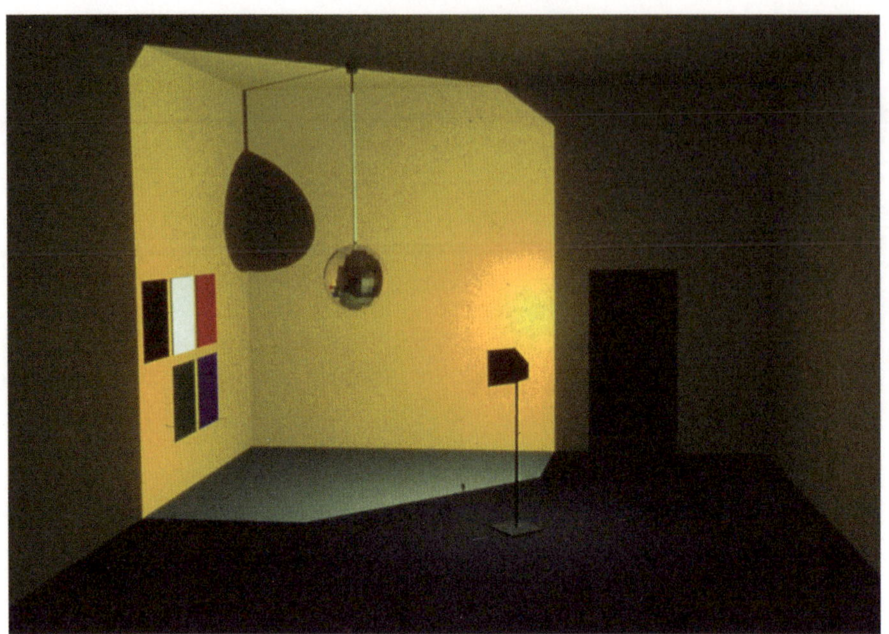

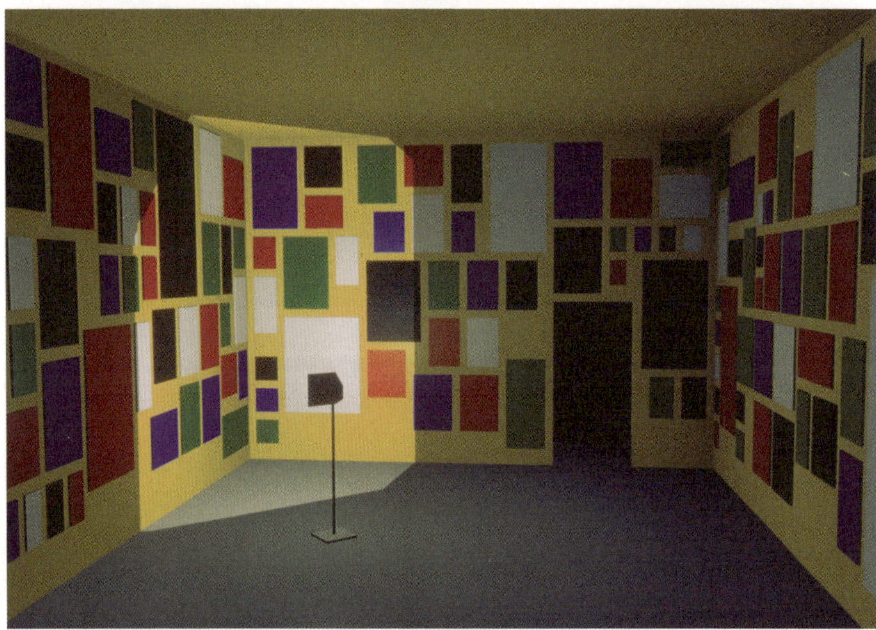

Matt Mullican, all works: *Untitled (Studio Experiment)*, 1995,
computer-generated image, dimensions variable, production by
Martin Dörbaum, Berlin; top left: private collection; bottom
left: courtesy Mai 36 Galerie, Zurich; top right: courtesy the
artist; bottom right: Collection Swiss Re Insurance Company,
Zurich, courtesy Mai 36 Galerie, Zurich

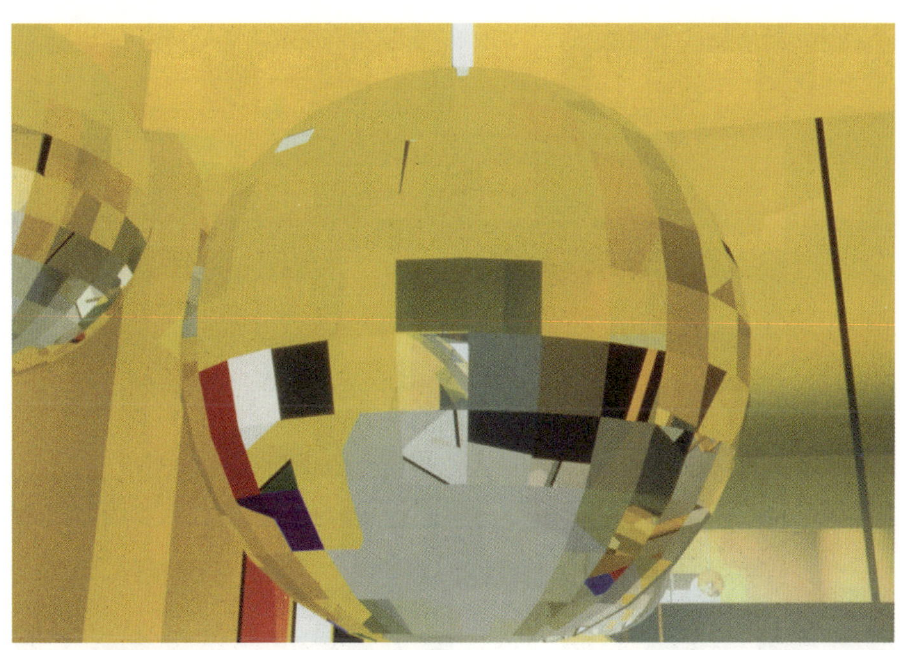

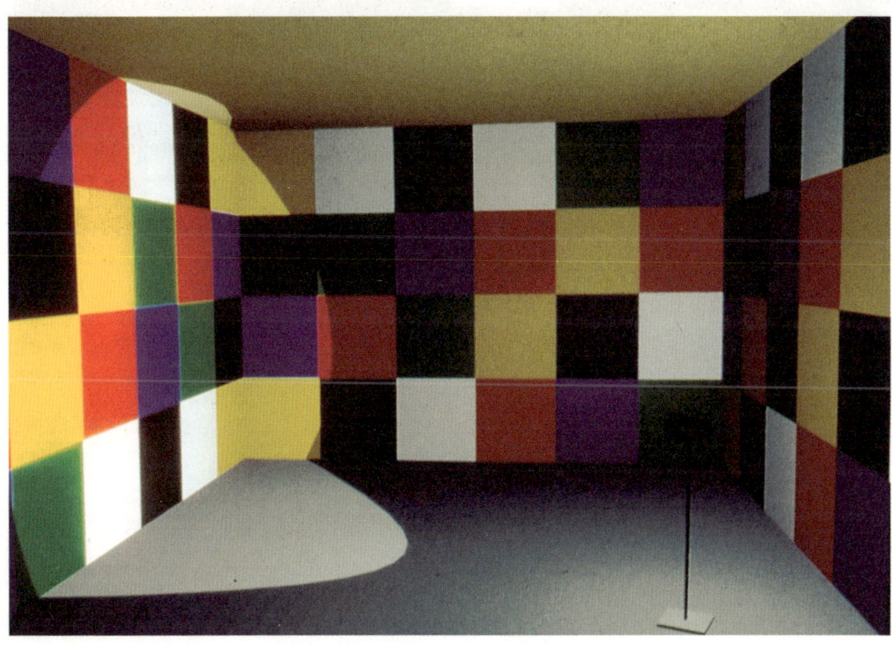

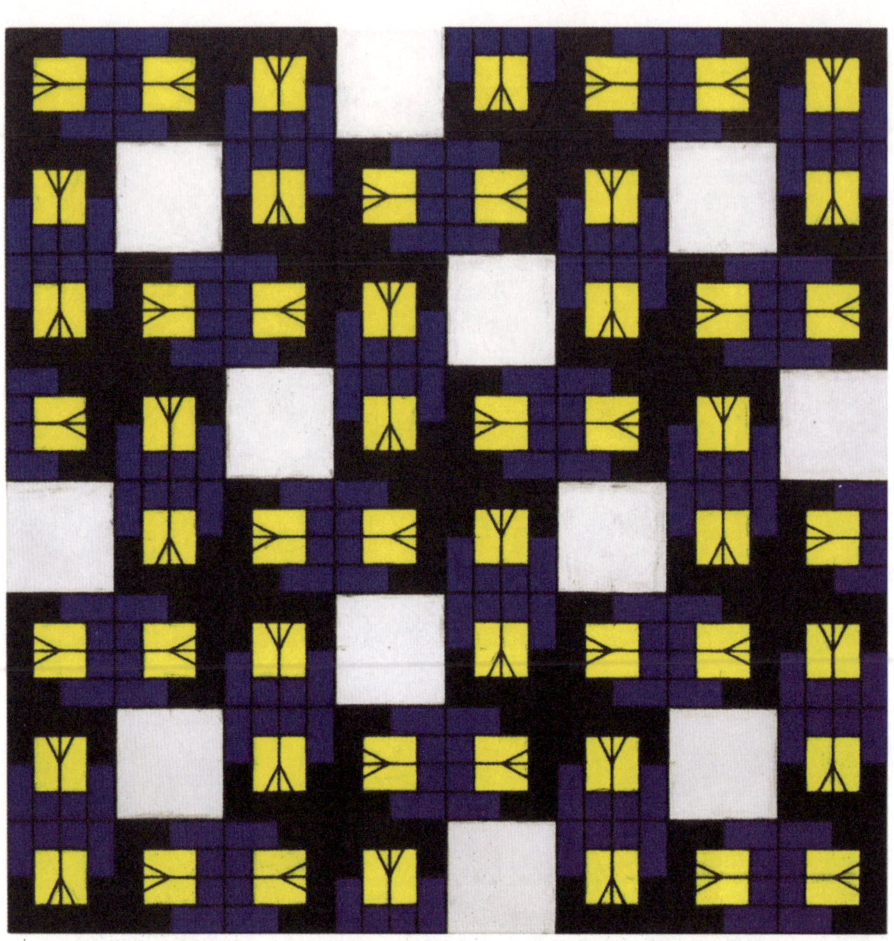

Matt Mullican, *Untitled (Squared colored chart 4)*,
2011, oil, acrylic on canvas, rubbing, 122 x 122 cm
© the artist, courtesy Capitain Petzel, Berlin / Mai
36 Galerie, Zurich

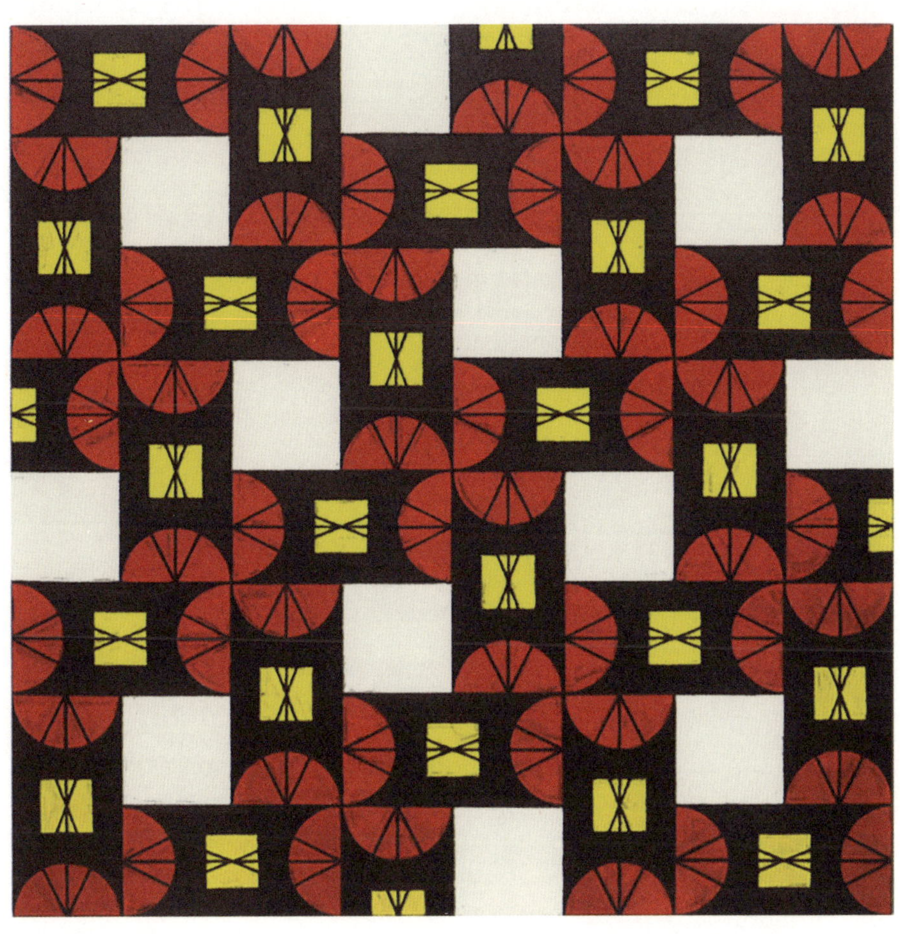

Matt Mullican, *Untitled (World Framed with Subject
on the Outside)*, 2011, oil, acrylic on canvas, rubbing,
122 x 122 cm © the artist, courtesy Capitain Petzel,
Berlin / Mai 36 Galerie, Zurich

PATRICIA TICINETO CLOUGH
THE CALCULATIVE AESTHETIC: OBJECTS AND UNCONSCIOUS DESIRE IN THE AGE OF BIG DATA*

It did not take long before the numbers came easily when asked: seven times six, nine times eight, thirteen times ten, sixteen times fifteen: my father's adding machine and the metronome accompanying my piano playing, counting. 1 2 3 slowly start, 2 1 3 to build a machine. 3 2 1 let the machine. 3 1 2 do it to you. 3 it's easy now. 2 it's easy now. 1 it's easy now. In the operating room the ether drops onto the mask that covers my face. Counting backwards, falling, falling into the white light space of oblivion. Childhood memories, traumatic memories
like the memories of my father
who made a living as an accountant
providing well enough
for my mother, my sister and me.
I can see his fingers.
I can see them at the adding machine.
I can see his fingers, my eyes fixed on them.
Moving quickly and then slowing
Over and across, up and down.
The wedding band, by chance, hits
and there is quick tick of sound
as I go falling falling falling down.

---

* Materials used in this essay can also be found in an expanded form in *The User Unconscious* (University of Minnesota Press, forthcoming March 2018).

The groundless ground of a body being without relation or orientation being in an on-going dissociation as profound anxiety dances free in bodily memory. I have been following the work of Luciana Parisi. She is thinking about numbers. She, like me, is driven to understand numbers and counting at the nonhuman speeds of digitalised algorithmic architectures. Her search has led her to abstract works of mathematicians who make it possible to think that quantity is at the heart of all things,
the dynamism of all things,
all things lively,
all things counting,
all things self-measuring.

For Parisi, algorithimic architectures can no longer be thought of as exclusively aiming to predict or calculate probabilities for an optimal solution. Rather, they are real objects, spatiotemporal data structures, where calculation is "not equivalent to the linear succession of data sets" (2013:9). Instead, "each set of instructions is conditioned by what cannot be calculated: the incomputable in algorithms that discloses the holes, gaps, irregularities, and anomalies within the formal order of the sequence" (9). Algorithmic architectures are, ontologically speaking, real objects, spatiotemporalities where the incomputable is immanent to them and the very condition of their on-going capacity to count. That is to say, like all objects, algorithmic architectures are irreducible to any other reality – either other objects or human subjects.

But be careful. Here, objects are no longer understood to be the objects of our common sense; rather, an object-oriented ontology is proposed in order to initiate a philosophical speculation on a potentiality that is other than human: the potentiality of all things. Object-oriented philosophers like Graham Harman argue that objects are irreducible to any other reality – to any other objects, including subjects. Nonetheless, objects are "multi-mediatic", where the sensual qualities of objects, their colour, smell, shape, weight, are media, yet not mere channels or links in networks of objects (Harman, 2005: 70, 91–92). The qualities are the internal complexity of each object, making each object mediatic in that objects are lured to each other by their sensual qualities. The qualities cause objects to relate to each other and therefore to change each other. Causality is alluring. This is a "vicarious causality", an aesthetic causality. (Harman, 2009: 169–234, 2007).

Or as Timothy Morton puts it: "Causality happens because this dance of non-identity is taking place on the ontological inside of an object" (2012a)
Her red silk gown thrown on the bed
and the white gardenias he gave her browning at the edge.
In my head, there is a sensing without touching, tracing
the flowers of brownish red mahogany on the footboard of their bed.
My fingers move from bead to bead, ten and then one alone, and then ten again: feeling without seeing, tactile before being visible, like a blind person's object or thing, counting and praying, the Rosary. Hail Mary, full of grace. Hail Mary, full of grace.

But Parisi wishes to go further than these philosophers who are so attuned to the sensual, to the object's qualities, to the mediating qualities of smelling, touching, hearing. She is sensing too, but at great speed, and I, like a sister, want to sense with her. I want to sense the great speeds that lead us to consider a calculative aesthetics, an aesthetic causality that is not only about sensual qualities, but quantities as well. Quantity also must be considered since, from the perspective of algorithmic architectures, the quantities involved are not merely a reduction of qualities, sensory or physical; nor are quantities immanent to qualities. Quantities are rather conditioned by their own indeterminacies, since algorithmic architectures are inseparable from incomputable data or incompressible information: that information, that rhythmicity, that liveliness between zeros and ones.

The metronome sat on the piano
just beside the sheets of music in front of me.
It beat out instruction to my fingers as I practiced.
Adagio, andante, allegro, vivace.
Sound and mood shifts all around me
Lento, grave, misterioso.
I felt the piano feeling, feeling for me,
feelings inseparable from the rigours of technicality.
One, two and three.
One, two and three.

Perhaps she and I have shared this – wanting to know why we thought about numbers or the way we thought about the machining of numbers, why we wrote what we wrote about numbers and machines. It seemed my thought was driven to abstraction, to a threshold beyond which nothing would be the same. Not a thinking/writing block that threatens to prevent, but a block ready to implode, the blood still red fresh, at the age of five, the tendon severed in my right hand – the writing hand – by a shard of glass I had picked up to hold and then slipped and went falling into my blood splattering before me, everywhere. Finger tips touching the piano, touching the computer, leaving red stains turning brown, the stains in my brain, the traces of the traumatic turned into numbers calculating at great speed. Brain staining now a matter of computerized axial tomography, the CT scan, the fMIR, and more in the contemporary folds of a neuro-psychiatry.

We who have been forced to insight might perhaps have the foresight to see objects otherwise before we see with only human eyes, seeking an ontograph and discomposing hurt in the objects of a childhood faith.
A rubber doll with washed-out eyes,
a stuffed yellow dog nearly life-sized,
so dirty from being dragged along the street,
outside the window
where no one sits.
And the clock and the metronome –
time machines, mysterious to me,
and the books of fairy tales and poetry

All beloved
the objects more to me
than any of the humans can be.
The objects still
awaiting me
there always
therefore, me.
Attending objects
truly being,
only being, in the bright lights of a dissociation

In linking the programming of algorithmic architectures to object-oriented ontology, it is proposed that we stop thinking of algorithms as simulation or as representing something else. Rather, we can take a conceptual leap and conceive algorithms as being actual entities, what Parisi describes, following Alfred North Whitehead, as "prehensive entities". For Whitehead, all actual entities – organic and inorganic and no matter how small or large – can prehend or feel data from the environment and from other actual entities (1978: 69–72). In other words, prehensions are activities of feeling affective states that register changes in the environment of data. But prehensions are not just physical modes of feeling the way affect is. Prehensions also are conceptual modes of feeling realities that do not actually exist yet. In other words, prehensions also are speculative activities in grasping incomputable data, which allow for the arrival of novelty. Past data is brought into the present through the transformation of that data by the ingress of the incomputable. This means that the arrival of data from the past is not merely an inheritance but a computational transformation, in which experience is infected with abstraction or where incomputable data is a decisive factor in any actual occasion of experience. However, this is not to assume that incomputable data is liberating, but rather that it simply is not exactly controlling or does not control exactly.

Control is no longer intended as the calculation of the future by means of prediction, or the calculation of the unknown through pre-set probabilities. Instead post-probabilistic uncertainties or incomputable data operate in algorithmic architectures that allow parameters to change in real time without preplanned modelling – allowing the arrival of novelty. Novelty is "not something that depends on the subjective impressions of interactive users, but rather involves the parametric prehension of data…" (Parisi, 137). Not preemption but prehension.

He didn't want to be an accountant, he once told me.
It was something else he wanted to be. What was it?
Some thing more frivolous; ah yes, a tugboat captain, he had said, but I wasn't sure he wasn't teasing me and I decided he meant he had wanted to write poetry. I never quite knew whether he was teasing me or ridiculing me.
And I still search for what poetry there might be
in the counting, as the minutes pass,
counting off the time of my sentence.
Sent to stand in the corner,
I will not be set free until I can read the time
on the face of the clock near my parents' bed.
This is how he punished me.

The clock was enclosed in a dome of glass,
a miniature cathedral, an airless space of time,
held still for me a horrid glimpse of eternity.
I had been left there, standing, full of fear
that I would never learn to read the clock's face.
Its hands moving from one Roman numeral to the next, it said nothing to
me. But there was a pendulum hung with delicate wiring between the
golden columns that held up the clock with its indecipherable face. The
pendulum's mechanical movement, turning one way and then
back again, made time flee.
His meanness made a penitent out of me.
My fingers move from bead to bead, ten and then one alone and then ten
again: the Rosary, like a holy abacus for counting mysteries, as I lie there right
near their bed and pray: Hail Mary, full of grace. Hail Mary, full of grace.

What I am suggesting is that criticism of all technical processing (and what
processing now isn't technical?) needs to be done in terms of algorithmic
architectures that are spatiotemporal objects in the calculative ambiance of
incomputable data. "Calculative ambience" is Jordan Crandall's term for
a sociality where "calculation, action and materiality intertwine" such that
"gestures, objects and environments can 'speak', however seductively or
violently, in ways that are not always addressed to humans or known by
them" (2013: 71). Crandell goes further suggesting that through "a
mathematical seeing, patterns come into view that previously could not be
seen by the naked eye, in ways that augment, or occlude, traditional
observational expertise and human intuition" (75).

This, "datalogical turn", the turn to big data and the algorithmic
architectures that parse it brings a new sociality as it challenges sociological
methods of measure, uncovering their entanglement with first and second
order cybernetics of the post-World War II years (Clough et al.). In those
years, sociological methods served to configure the human subject with
statistically measured populations that "made it increasingly plausible that
social practices really were repeatable... a wide range of human practices
could be construed as constant conjunctions of events while ignoring the
historical conditions of possibility of this patterning" (Steinmetz, 2005:
129). If the historical, in all its contingency and uncertainty, was not the
reference for statistical models and replicable experiments, it was because

the historical was displaced by that more powerful concept of "system". In terms of sociality, to maintain a system and its functionality is to reference the capacity for social reproduction in terms of a boundary – that which marks the "outside" of a system. This boundary, combined with a regularity in the interactions or interconnections that constitute the system, allows the system to be modelled so that human behavior becomes predictably expressed as population levels or as statistical probabilities. This is sociology's epistemological unconscious or its unconscious drive to positivism, empiricism, and scientism that, in the post-war years, married phenomenology, or the epistemology of the conscious human knower, to the technical demands of the state, enabling institutions to attach population data to systems of human behavior, on the one hand, and to rationalize the figure of the human subject for state instrumentality, on the other. In the post-war years, sociology's epistemological stance is informed by first-order cybernetics predicated on a homeostatic, equilibrium-seeking model that presumes a certain durability of reactions to observed stimuli, which allows for a probabilistic prediction of future patterns (Hayles, 1999). In first order cybernetics, the researcher stands to some degree *outside* of the system that is being observed and applies technical apparatuses to convert incoming data into repeatable and decipherable patterns.

Gone to war, they say. He's gone to war just days before I am born.
And I wait and wait for that man photographed in his uniform. A loss that becomes a uniformity that we their children would grow up to refuse, thinking we could change the world that got made while he was gone to war. Gone to war, they say. He's gone to war.

Even when in second-order cybernetics and the critical social theories and methodologies that would arise in the 1970s and 1980s, reflexive interventions that were meant to "correct" the dis-identification of the observer with the data of his/her observations were imagined even when the human subject was being figured not only as observing, but as self-observing, even then systems-thinking nonetheless remained intact. There continues to be a presumption of a known relation between the parts and the whole, where the parts continuously constitute the bounded whole through the many interactions between system and environment. Contrary to the presumptions of system-thinking about parts and whole, boundaries and observers, the operation of architectural algorithms that parse big data does not presume parts are reducible to the whole or the system, since parts can be large but quantitatively incompressible and, as such, bigger than the whole. The part may deracinate the whole at any time. Put otherwise, the datalogical turn moves away from representation and its reliance on sociological correlation and correlative datasets, away from systems, and toward the incomputable conditioning of parametric practices in algorithmic architectures.

And there was a moment, I remember,
when we sat, my father and me, on the floor.
There was a tunnel of light
that blocked my peripheral sight
of my mother standing there.
My vision instead was directed straight ahead
to the shelf of books he read to me.
Leather bound with golden letters,
and fancy illustrations
in iridescent colours of purple, blue and red.
But the moment does not hold.
There is a much too intense sense
of a volcanic trembling in my stomach's pit
Blinded by the light,
there in her sight,
I wonder how anyone ever again will sit
with me.

What is crucial in the post-cybernetic logic of big data is that there is no reliable relationship between input and output, but rather that what is valued is the capacity to generate new and interesting sets of relationships. Data fields pass in and out of bodies, feeding on novel and emergent connections within and between bodies. Indeed, the ability of data to smoothly travel away from their original site of collection is highly valued within ecologies of big data. The translation between behaviour and data point or what we have called the individual is often less than clear and subjected to numerous third and fourth party interventions that multiply the networks through which data will travel. These networks move us beyond systems and the observing/self-observing subject. Or, as Bruno Latour and his colleagues put it: Such conceptual pairs as "'specific" and "general", "individual" and "collective", "actor" and "system" are not essential realities but provisional terms…a consequence of the type of technology used for navigating inside datasets'

(2012: 2). These conceptual pairs will not survive the methods of measuring that are parsing big data (2012: 2).

There is not only a crisis of empirical sociology, there is also a further decentring of human cognition, consciousness, and preconsciousness. Mark Hansen proposes that we can no longer "take up embodiment as a site where diffuse data is processed to yield images or experiences…; rather, in the face of technical incursions that render the body directly 'readable' by machines, we must embrace a conception of the body as a society of microsensibilities themselves atomically susceptible to technical capture" (2013). Rethinking the body also involves rethinking thought and consciousness, since consciousness, as Hanson sees it, is after the fact of the presentation of data. Big data and ubiquitous calculation can effectively repress consciousness by operating in technical timeframes to which consciousness has absolutely no direct, experiential, or phenomenological interface; there is no possible *subjectification* of big data or ubiquitous calculation (2013). Consciousness is generated after-the-fact, as an emergence generated through the feeding forward of technically gathered data concerning antecedent microtemporal events. While consciousness continues to experience its own narrow bandwidth reality through sense perception, as Hansen puts it, "this experience is disjoined, both temporally and operationally, by the operational present of technology – where behaviour gets shaped – independently of any conscious access or input" (2013).

The algorithms let poetry arise out of the numbers,
the indeterminacy turning numbers into lines of rhyme, beating out the time,
A numerical poetry hugging the red line
at the margin's edge of the page in a child's copy book.
My name is written on one of the spaces
in the middle of the marbled black and white cover.

It is especially important that we not filter our understanding of the social through representational frames that are understood to supplement reductive quantitative measures, when instead, as a result of complex processes of calculation, computing technologies cannot be thought merely to be reductive: they neither quantify biophysical and cultural capacities, nor are calculation or information understood simply as grounded in such capacities. Digital computing has its own capacity to be adaptable and "creative" in ways that challenge the assumption that the "artificial" nature of computational intelligence is inherently limiting. Rather, big data is revealing digital computation's immanent potential in the operation of incomputable data, thus leaving us with or leading us to a calculative aesthetic.

Adding to the recent conceptualisation of aesthetics offered by philosophers engaged in object-oriented ontology, a calculative aesthetics adapts aesthetics to ubiquitous calculation. What already has been claimed for the aesthetic in contemporary object-oriented ontology is that "the aesthetic dimension is the causal dimension", where causality is a matter of allure. As Steven Shaviro puts it: "It is only aesthetically, beyond understanding and will, that I can appreciate the actus of the thing being what it is, 'the sheer sincerity of existence'" (2010: 7).

But this is no mere return to naïve empiricism or scientistic positivism. Instead, the philosophers presently elaborating an *aesthetic causality* are delivering causality from those forms of causality that for some time have given humans a sense of control over life, over matter, over each other, and have shaped the practices of art and politics. As such, the return to aesthetics is also not a return to the sublime, where there is the experience of the overwhelming disjuncture between imagination and understanding, along with a conscious recognition of this failure of human comprehension. Rather, it is about objects having the capacity to affect and to be affected by each other ... caused to become different things" (2010: 10). It is the aesthetic of the beautiful, where "what is regarded as beautiful is not experienced as a passive thing or as something that merely produces an effect in us but rather as inviting or requiring something from us, a response that may be owed to it..., as if the beautiful thing had an independent life of its own..." (Moran, 2012: 213).

What a calculative aesthetic adds to the sensibility of quality is the poetry of quantity through stipulating indeterminacy as immanent to calculation in these times of big data and ubiquitous computation. It also points to what constitutes the generalised trauma of these times: calculation and incomputable data become the necessary horizon for criticism. All that has stood, and so much has, as qualitative supplement to quantitative measure no longer holds a privileged position. The trauma of the digital, then, is in the displacement of the supplement of meaning and language, subject and self-reflection, from their privileged position in epistemology and ontology. It is in terms of this displacement that our critical practices must be rethought.

Bibliography:

Clough, P. T., Gregory, K., Haber, B. and Scannell, J. (2015). The Datalogical Turn. In Vannini, P. (ed.), *Non-Representational Methodologies: Re-envisioning Research*. New York: Routledge.146–64.

Crandall, J. (2010). The Geospatialization of Calculative Operations: Tracking, Sensing and Megacities. *Theory Culture Society*, 27(6), 68–90.

Hansen, M. (2013, April). Beyond Affect? Technical Sensibility and the Pharmacology of Media. Presented at *Critical Themes in Media Studies*, NYU.

Harman, G. (2005). *Guerrilla Metaphysics: Phenomenology and the Carpentry of Things*. Chicago and LaSalle: Open Court.

Harman, G. (2007). On Vicarious Causation. *Collapse II* , 11.26,187–221.

Harman, G. (2009). *Prince of Networks, Bruno Latour and Metaphysics*. Melbourne: re.press.

Hayles, N. K. (1999). *How We Became Posthuman: Virtual Bodies in Cybernetics, Literature, and Informatics*. Chicago: University of Chicago Press.

Moran, R. (2012). Kant, Proust, and the Appeal of Beauty. *Critical Inquiry*, 38(2), 298–332.

Morton, T. (2012). Objects in the Mirror are Closer Than They Appear. In Sparrow, T. and George, B. (eds.), *Singularum*, Volume 1: *Another Phenomenology: Exploring the Sensuous Earth*, Santa Barbara: Punctum.

Latour, B, Jensen, P., Venturini, T., Grauwin, S., & Boullier, D. (2012). 'The whole is always smaller than its parts'– a digital test of Gabriel Tardes' monads. *The British Journal of Sociology*, 63(4), 591–615.

Parisi, L. (2013). *Contagious architecture: computation, aesthetics, and space*. Cambridge, Mass.: The MIT Press.

Shaviro, S. (2010. April). The Universe of Things. Paper delivered at *Objected Oriented Ontology, A Symposium*, Georgia Technological Institute.

Whitehead, A. N. (1978). *Process and Reality: An Essay in Cosmology*. New York: Free Press.

These lines of poetry come from my "Praying and Playing to the Beat of a Child's Metronome". *Subjectivity* 2010, 3(40):1-17.

These lines of poetry come from my "The Object's Affect: The Rosary", in *Timing of Affect, Epistemologies, Aesthetics, Politics*. Edited by Marie-Luise Angerer, et. al. Zurich: Diaphanes, 2014.

These lines of poetry also are from my "Praying and Playing to the Beat of a Child's Metronome".

These lines of poetry come from my "A Dream of Falling: Philosophy and Family Violence", in *Handbook of Object Matters*. Edited by Eleanor Casella, et al. Abingdon-on-Thames: Routledge, 2013.

These lines of poetry also come from my "Praying and Playing to the Beat of a Child's Metronome" and my "The Object's Affect: The Rosary".

These lines also come from my "A Dream of Falling: Philosophy and Family Violence".

AESTHETICS OF MEASUREMENT

Dialogue between Matt Mullican and Patricia T. Clough
15 January 2014, Kunstraum, Leuphana Universität Lüneburg

1. From Clough to Mullican

PATRICIA T. CLOUGH: Your presentation made me think of a distribution of yourself. There was something that sounded so wonderfully odd, when you said, "I pinched the cadaver because that's what Glen had done," I see Glen as being alive at the moment. You moved actions from one dead thing to another dead thing because none of them are dead. In my philosophical language, they're on the same ontological plane of liveliness through the art. It is a very interesting idea you also suggested: distance as pain. There was this overall sentence that hung over the whole presentation, which is, "Who feels the most pain?" and, "Who gives the most pain?" There is a notion of pain, but we can never feel anyone else's pain. What is the reality of pain?

MATT MULLICAN: The pain was really a matter of how you define reality. If the reality can actually exert pain, it's more real. The possibility about video games is to hurt you when you get into the game. They can do it financially with money by gambling. You lose your money in a video game, but if you wanted to have something super-virtual, pain must be involved. I used this point of reference with the pictures in reality. One of the first things I did in the studio was sex in the studio, where I traced pornographic pictures and put them in the studio. I couldn't show the studio in various places, because it was not only more real, but it also had to do with the fact that they became hot. When you go online, there's so much sex with different views, as well as violence. Both the sex and the violence are very enticing. We do go into those pictures much quicker than we would with normal pictures.

PC: There's a kind of pain in them. Or, it can be pleasure-pain, depending on your sexual aims.

MM: Certainly, it depends on point of view, but sex is generally about pleasure. When my son was playing Grand Theft Auto V, which is an incredible game to watch, I asked him, "Is there a time when we see what the avatar, or your character sees?" He answered, "Yes. All you have to do is to stop. If you're running through a street through a city, or whatever, you simply have to stop running and stand there. If you stand there for a minute, then suddenly you see what the character sees. You see his point of view." That's first person, and then second person is really the character, because that character is you. What I'm becoming very interested in now is first person, second person, in relationship to this sex and this violence, and in terms of a series of pictures that I'm involved with.

For instance, this is my work about a birth-to-death list: her birth, her family, her home, if I turn that all into "my", my birth, my family, my home, et cetera. The whole list I rewrote forty years after I wrote it, and I wrote it in first person and second person. It totally changes the meaning of the list, because what happens is that I'm jumping into the world. Like the Beatles' song *The Fool on the Hill*, I am the fool on the hill. I grew up as I lived in this world. But I am the guy who is still asking these questions, the fool on the hill, because it always is about me and it all comes down to me. But I am a realist. I'm trying to say that we're all like that, in the big part of our life. In other words, I'm trying to depict the true reality. "The true reality" is a way to deal with my subjectivity. The previous generation of artists before me was represented in the super-rational conceptual artists, such as Carl Andre. For example, his representative work, *50 pounds of steel* is simply "fifty pounds of steel". This was the art that I followed. Fifty pounds of steel as I see it is not the same as your fifty pounds.

PC: There's a history in your history, that is, the history of a certain kind of art. It's very interesting how much you're allowed to tell the story of art as the story of your own work, even though it was mediated through all these wonderful other stories. Maybe the particular art to which you are referring requires you to tell the story as the story of your art. Perhaps this is so because the art itself has become a self-performance.

MM: For instance, Lawrence Weiner reduced the artwork down to the statement: "The work doesn't have to be made." Painting died earlier, and now art doesn't have to be made. I come along with my generation and ask what we are supposed to do. How come we can't beat that? It's done. It's perfect, absolutely perfect. There's nothing to be added. When Mel Bochner put this levelling piece up, I put a pillow, instead. Because when we look at things, we personify much more than we do think. That's what we do.

We project our perceptions and create people everywhere. We can't help but do it, because that's the way we're made. For instance, in a body of my works about a cosmology, I used the concept of God, hell, heaven, birth and ghosts and all these super-strange things which are the opposite of rationality. I took a death's cape into my fictional studio and I tore it up into little pieces and put it on the floor like Barry Le Va, or like Richard Serra. So, I took the material of the allegory and inserted it back into reality. I was saying: "There's no possibility."

Reality is not like that. They're creating a fiction in there, but it's a wonderful fiction in the way they are defining the object. When I started, I stated my name and gave myself the gift of being twenty-two. This is a piece of mine, and I was identifying who I was, as a real person. I had a fictional person, same sentence, but only with a person that doesn't exist. The thing about this person is that: There is that distance. I'm here, but I'm not here.

Audience 1: You accounted how you were accused of being a fascist in the performance with the three actors, and later hypnotised yourself. Does it stop you being a fascist?

MM: That's an absurd word to use in that context. I was accused of being a fascist in L.A. because I showed flags. Fascism is not "flags", it's the style. It's an art issue. There was a letter to the newspaper, because this was a review, because I was involved with virtual reality. I had a virtual environment that I had with the cameras going into this landscape that doesn't physically exist, that we were going through, in which I had flags, diagrams, everything else. The reviewer who wrote about my show used the word "fascist" as an aesthetic term. A nasty bunch of letters reacted to say: "You are demeaning the term, you're making the term into something for which it shouldn't be used; the term should not be used in this instance."

When I say that, and it shouldn't have been used in describing my performance either, because it's a lot that's real. That's the style. But it really has to do with the relationship "to" the actors. If I put myself into the hot seat and I start crying, am I a fascist to myself? Am I abusing myself? Once I gave a lecture at the Skowhegan School, and showed a performance of myself in a trance, where I'm acting very weirdly and laughing at myself, and acting like I'm autistic, or schizo, just not acting normal. A woman said, "How can you make fun of the mentally ill? You are making fun. You are representing the mentally ill in an incredibly negative manner. You should be ashamed of yourself for doing this!" I wondered where that came from. I was in a trance state, which means that it's a part of me. It's part of everybody. We are built in this way, we can go there with ourselves. This is a part of life. The woman says, "No, but you were laughing at yourself." I was laughing at myself acting, so making fun of myself was therefore making fun of them. She had broken me into two people and I was doing what a fascist did to myself. In any case, that is an odd word.

Audience 2: Space and spatiality are really prominent in your work, which came out explicitly. I would be interested to see if there's also an issue of time: temporality and temporalities. Could it be described as compartmentalisation, and yet, maybe they "are" different temporalities?

MM: The interesting thing about time is that Glen lives in time. There's a calendar on the wall, there's a clock on the wall, and he does things at different times. Like you would see in any kind of a comic book, there is a comic-book time. What's the difference between Glen and that person? In that person's life, time doesn't exist. Experience exists, but in a true sense, time doesn't exist in that person's life. I cannot identify fully what I'm doing, where I am, how I'm feeling; my sense of time is totally from the inside out, without references. To a large extent, time exists in references. And when I am in that, becoming that person, they don't exist anymore. When I come out, in a trance state, into this, and generally, I'm with the hypnotist in the back room, and I'm led out into the performing area and there might be 200 people and lots of lights, so as soon as I get into that room, I feel the humidity of all the people in there and the bright, hot lights and I don't know what to do, I don't have a specific subject that I'm supposed to do, so what I do is, I start crawling along the wall and feeling the wall, because it's a very sensual experience. And it then just evolves from there, but there is no sense of who I am or what I'm doing. Only experience in time, and even time changes. So, in a way, that is really the expression of time in an experiential sense, whereas Glen, with the clock, that's in a funny sense, another way of defining time, another thing, but I do think that the experience of that person is a truer definition, if I was to define it, because it's not even about space, it's not about time, it's just about feeling, I don't know how to contextualize it. I will discuss it and try to figure it out.

I used to say: "I am an artist, I'm not a doctor." My whole idea about pictures and image could be totally wrong in an academic setting, but it's the way that I'm doing it in art.

MY: To summarize the first session, I would say that the works by Matt are all about measuring the world. The distance you made to yourself, to see everything as light patterns, the invention of Glen, another state of mind such as hypnosis, et cetera, are all an attempt to measure the mental reality, and a collections of pictures in different media function as the ruler for the measurement. The pain – being things that are comfortable, or not – is a measure of where the boundary between life and death is. I would say that these notions – pain, mental reality with the different states of mind, this person, that person, "self" – suggest a new conceptual approach to measurement to us. From such an aesthetic point of view, I would say that the end of measurement hasn't come yet.

2. From Mullican to Clough

MM: I respond back from a different point of view, which is this whole issue of movies and numbers. Movies are defined by numbers now more than they ever were when I was a child. Numbers are somehow more real than the movie itself. What the movie makes is content. It is actually the content of the movie that has been replaced. Movies are not talked about regarding what they say, but regarding the numbers involved. It is reception. My children know all about this. My wife works in a museum. It's the numbers destroying the museum. They have to have numbers. *When attitudes become form* (Kunsthalle Bern in 1969) is considered a landmark exhibition today, however it didn't have the numbers. It didn't matter. It didn't expect such things like numbers. But now they do. Therefore, what the numbers create in terms of the future and expectation is something that gives me an idea of what you said.

PC: My goal is to give a proper place to numbers. We always produce this fear that they're destroying something. However, now, I believe, it's the other stuff, the poetry and the trauma that must sit alongside the numbers. I believe we are certainly looking at a near future where quantity isn't seen as something that's reductive, and that is going to change the relationship between quality and quantity. That's really where I'm going. Of course, there are these other uses, of what you just said of numbers.

MM: Yes, I talked about other uses, other ways of defining them through experience.

PC: We need a richer feeling about these numbers, because they're all over the place, and if we just think of them as reductive, we're going to miss their poetry and what possibilities they bring. Just as other forms both scared us and brought us possibilities. They do have fearful aspects attached to them, but part of bringing my own machines and numbers from my childhood into play is to remember that numbers were probably there before us. They're not just now, right?

MM: I did like the shifting in your presentation. The shifting was really between this place that you're describing with your family and that blood on the piano keys in relationship to calculative aesthetics.

PC: It's my way of situating myself and the work.

MM: Yes, that's understood. It is not only the shifting, but also the timing of the reading, that is, the way that you read it. There are the numbers in your tone of reading.

PC: They are in me.

MY: There are different ontologies of numbers.

WENDY CHUNG: It was really intersting how the two talks came together. It was the struggling with the question of sameness. There is a great phrase, "We're all the same when we're dead." When Matt said that we're all the same by dealing with dead things, but saying as a dead thing, "Who feels the most pain?" This is a struggle with individuality: your singularity within this thing, that is, the saying. Patricia, your way of dealing with numbers is considerably the same. Through the intensity of it, getting to somewhere else. There was a really interesting way in which they came together. However, Matt's was so distant, it was close, and Patricia's was so close that it was in the distance. This was very intriguing, to see those two arts together.

PC: That's the play between us two, as you put it, Wendy. But I would say about us both: everything is lively, especially the undead.

MM: That's a good word, lively.

Audience 2: Is this the thing as an incomputable number and incomputable quantity? What's incomputable about a number? Isn't it equivalent to a failure to compute a number because it's so big? Isn't it just a matter of the fair amount of time, growing a machine, or keeping the machine until it is completed? Is there really something such as incomputable quantity in that sense? Another question is about the idea of the incomputable. It's quite powerful in the relationship to the idea of expanded experience, the idea of encountering the worlds, the idea of the objects, things, and non-direct experience, et cetera. Would you say that the idea of the incomputable offers beyond-ness? Obviously, if the incomputable is in fact computable, if it's sheer quantity, we already know the quantities. Then, how do their units come about? Does it make sense to say there's an incomputable quantity?

PC: I like what you said, if you don't expect me to answer your question. Everything in the piece is drawn from various sources, and this is what I meant about conceptualisations that, in time, might not hold, or might have given us something we wished we hadn't wished, a direction in thought we wished we hadn't taken. What I understand is that algorithms have within them incomputable or incompressible information that can suddenly start to make itself felt in the algorithm, and it's partly what allows the algorithm to change its parameters on its own, without a pre-plan, or without human pre-planning. Without pre-planning of any kind, the algorithm can be grasped as quite lively in the way we're saying, and makes it interesting to think it as temporal-physical object. The media taken as a temporal-physical object, rather than them just being a channel through which things happen, have complexity, have potential. It's a theory: it's a theorising back to where algorithms might be going in the ones that they're developing for parsing big data. That is the incomputable. That is the condition of the possibility of the thing working.

But if we switch our head to something political-ish, because I don't know what politics is anymore, but political-ish, you said an interesting thing: If we're already seeing in mathematics that they can work with the incomputable, the incomputable as any sort of beyond is already lost. You can start thinking of all the capitalists that might find that useful, or how it's used in the derivative economy. It's frightening and fascinating. What matters to me besides that is the demand in that for us to think differently about quality and quantity and supplement. A lot of my thinking comes down to sociological methods that are not thought about enough in the arts. But these methods really affect how we live. These statistical populations and the singular figure made for them or the person – individual and population – is what we live. But that – individual and population – is going to change with big data, and perhaps drastically. There's a lot more to say about big data, too, but the way we conceive of individual and population is not going to survive.

MY: You demanded that we think of quality, quantity and supplement in a different way. Would it make sense to add a notion of "direction" to them? Thinking has a direction. Mathematics has its own direction of thinking. Art has one. Aesthetics of a computation has one, too, no matter how big the data that it deals with is. It may go beyond immeasurability, or initiate changing the relationship with quality, quantity and supplement, but as long as the thinking develops in the same direction, it remains in the same space. It can expand endlessly, but it cannot transform itself to get out of its own space of logics.

PC: You mean the algorithms are directed? Recently, I was at a conference where I had an encounter with a computer scientist. He said that we once knew what the algorithm delivered, but today once the algorithm delivers, they can't go back and find out exactly how they got there. It screws up the notion of direction, and of intention. But it gives a certain quality to quantity. So the phenomenological intentionality that we usually assume to be human-based and consciousness-based is getting screwed up by the quantity. There's work to be done here. We can't just deny it. Somehow, the jinni is out of the bottle. Therefore, an aesthetic approach, and maybe an ethical approach is needed. There might be many new approaches that we have to develop to give in to the capacity of quantity. And, on the other hand, my father really was that father and I really wanted to know about the numbers in his head. When I first read in Luciana Parisi's work about the intimation that all living things are at the base quantity, I thought, I'm done. I found you, daddy, because you're obviously at the base of all things. It's funny, but I really felt a certain joy, so I lean in the direction of trying to rethink what we mean by quantity. I bet all these words might have to be different, because we're used to hearing them a certain way. So, that's why it's important to also make poetry out of our present condition of numbers.

MY: Because we have to pinch our brains.

Audience: My question is whether these instances really work within the discourse of science today. I was rethinking the body – the body as an individual from the 19th century until very recently. Now we get this bacteria-are-us paradigm, which is an epic-genetic line that has a much larger effect on who we are, and we are less the individuals than we though we were. And here it is decisive for the entire time from the 19th century until today what we knew about the bacteria, we knew that bacteria were on us in masses and in vast numbers. But only recently have these numbers seemed to make this kind of sense.

PC: Yes. It has a great deal to do with the speed of digital technology, which now allows us to capture the bacteria by number and then layers of presentational styling to bring that experience to our consciousness, an experience that we could never experience ourselves directly, and never will. And, yet, we will change our understanding of ourselves through art and the like. I think something is happening in science and technology that is giving us non-conscious capacities, that machines are allowing us a realisation of our own non-conscious capacities. The other important thing is, referring to Mark Hansen in my paper, that the body as organism is going to give way. We're so interpenetrated by technology, and the situation is intensifying more and more. It's hard to think that we're in a bounded system, like an organism, so my presentation was my critique of the system.

EPISTEMOLOGY OF MEASUREMENT

LUCY POWELL
NOTES ON THE PRESENTATION EPISTEMOLOGY OF MEASUREMENT

The animal/human divide. The human animal, non-human animal divide. The space between is a space occupied by metaphor, theory, anthropomorphism and, yet, at the same time, it is what John Berger called an "abyss of incomprehension" in his book *Why Look at Animals*. It is an indeterminate zone and also the space we use to define ourselves as humans, to define our human exceptionalism. And what makes it so interesting is that the gaze across this divide can be returned, most famously in the case of Derrida's cat, or blithely ignored – and we have very little influence in the matter. But this divide is also a human construct. Epistemologically speaking, we cannot say we know any more about what other humans are really thinking, feeling, and experiencing than we can with animals. And this gap is being eroded on all fronts. We now know that 99% of our genes are shared with mice – including the genes to make a tail. To summarize Timothy Morton in *The Ecological Thought,* non-human animals have language, imagination, reason, sense of mind (chimps), tool use, improved skills and learning over time, compassion, humour, a sense of beauty and wonder, and choice. Humans are fairly uniquely good at throwing and sweating. He quotes Darwin's *The Descent of Man* when he says that the differences are "of degree and not of kind". And it does not stop at animals, after all, 75% of our genetic make-up is the same as that of a pumpkin. The dragonfly, a predator with a kill ratio of 97%, is so successful because it has selective attention, something only primates were thought to have. Plants have the protein found in the neurons of higher animals, have agency, and use it in their interactions with their environment to secure their survival. The more we know, the more we have to define ourselves without recourse to binaries. Measurability within immeasurability.

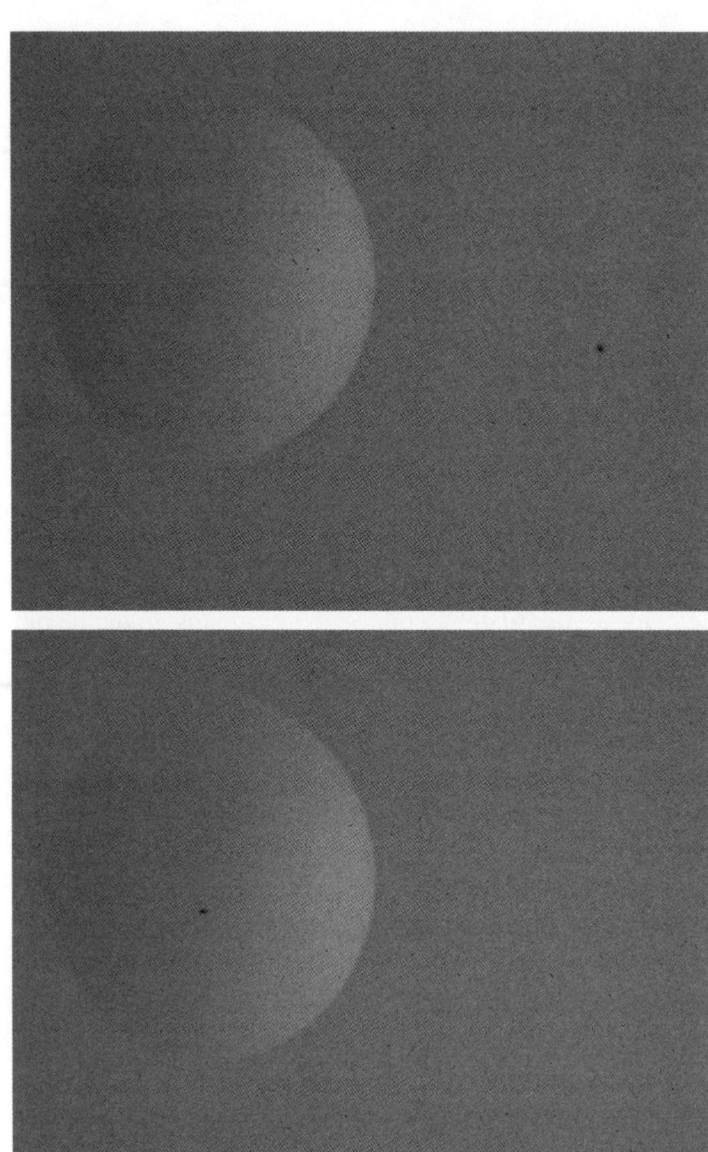

Lucy Powell, *A Place Where Things Are*,
2010, single channel video loop, 5 min.,
video stills, courtesy the artist

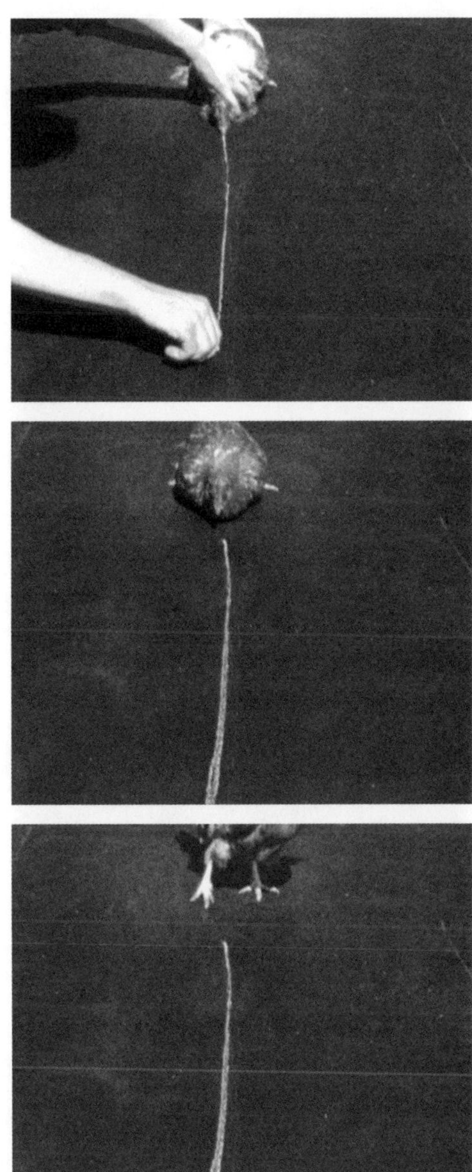

Lucy Powell, *Impossible Line*,
2009, Super 8 (loop), 3 min.,
video stills, courtesy the artist

OXANA TIMOFEEVA
UNCONSCIOUS TENDENCIES IN ANIMAL EPISTEMOLOGY*

What does philosophy have to say about animals? It appears that the general attitude can be inscribed in a traditional pattern of ascending hierarchy. Already in Aristotle the idea can be found that animals are "better" than plants, that humans are "better" than animals, that men are "better" than women, free citizens "better" than slaves, et cetera. Not because whatever is inferior is "bad", but because whoever is superior knows better what is "good". Even those who clearly "side with" animality as opposed to "humanity", and fight for animal rights and animal liberation in order to ultimately achieve equal representation of the animal species in this still all-too-human world, cannot do away with the idea of the domination of mankind over non-human nature, as if the latter needed help, respect, support, recognition.

The fact is that animals, in fact, do not really care that people care about them: we sacrifice them, we put them on transport to the slaughterhouse, we eat them, exploit them, train them, involve them in art processes, give them rights and documents – but they stay indifferent.

The moral attitude of humans towards animals can be easily brought back to its affective root, to the level of desire, which underlines any ethical concern or pragmatic preoccupation. Thus, I think, philosophers are sometimes really jealous of animals' ability to take pleasure in things, which animals, so philosophers think, nevertheless cannot fully experience as they do not have "consciousness" of that.

The philosophy of animality turns to the question of how to think of animal existence – which, supposedly, does not think itself. Here, the question of epistemology and measurement arises. There is a kind of consensus that we cannot deal with animality as such, but only with the human construction of animality.

---

* This essay derives from my article: Oxana Timofeeva (2016) "Living in a Parasite: Marx, Serres, Platonov, and the Animal Kingdom", *Rethinking Marxism*, 28:1, 91–107.

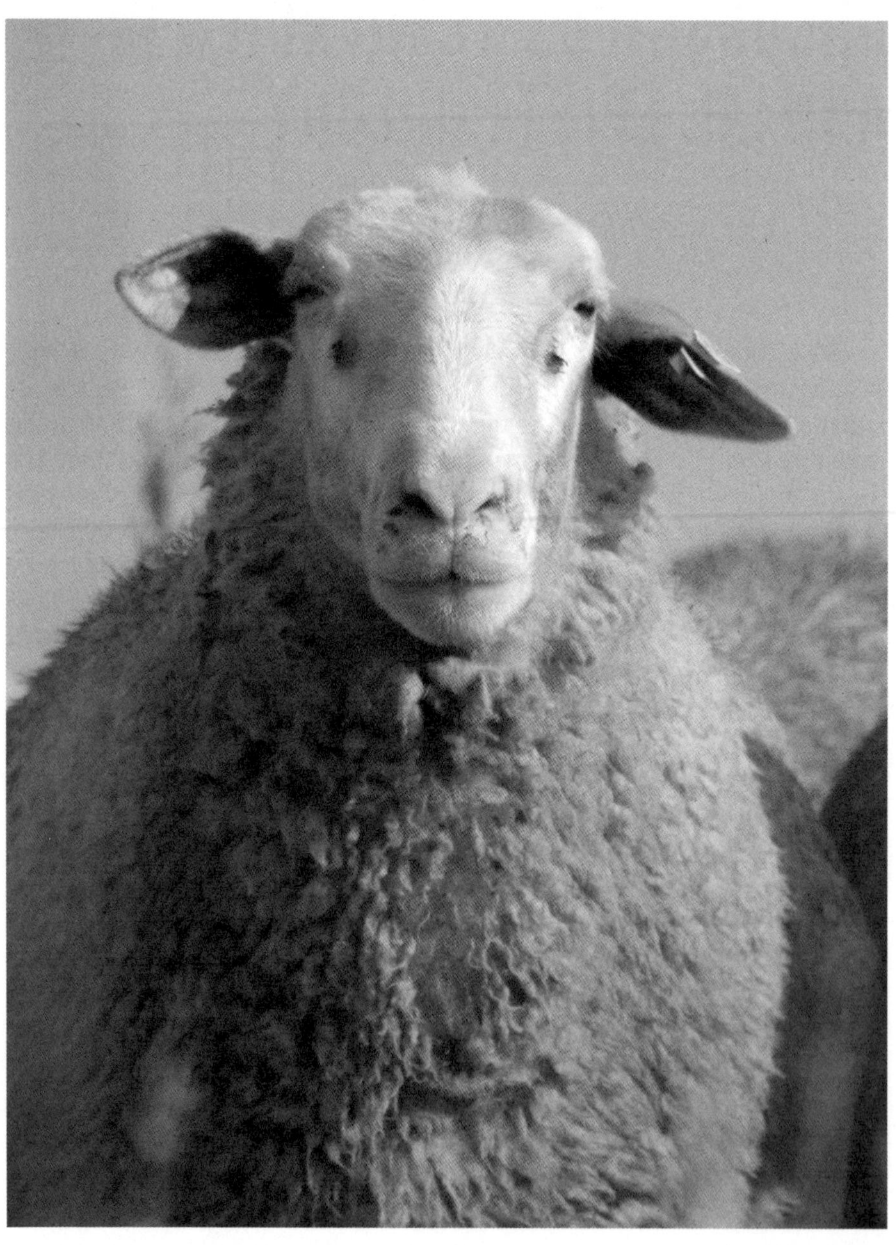

Lucy Powell, *The Memory of Sheep*, 2007,
series of 50 photographs, each 30 x 40 cm,
courtesy the artist

Animals cannot but be represented, which means that they are either a representation or a representative. A representation gives us an "external" idea of what an animal is as an "object" (as in art or popular science or mass culture). An animal as representative comprises a figuration of its "interest" as a "subject" (in the animal rights movement, for instance, as well as in animal studies that critically relate to the human sciences).

However, in bygone cultural traditions animals played a much more "active" role, serving as representatives of something "human" or "divine", as in totemism or in antiquity. There's Incitatus, for example, Caligula's favourite horse, which not only became a citizen of Rome, but a member of the Roman Senate as well. This is a truly ridiculous manifestation of the embodiment of representative power. In classical narratives, animals traditionally represent human weaknesses. To take more recent examples, in psychoanalysis, animals might represent human agents associated with law and order, like the wolf that represents the father in Freud's famous "Wolf Man" case. However, the very inevitability of the representational frame provides viability to the utopia of the "real" animal, which rather than being represented or representing something already given instead "opens" – but always retrospectively – the immediate givenness of the "real" of human beings themselves. The ambiguity of the animal, which is representation par excellence, yet at the same time also unrepresentable, provokes a particular tension between ontology, politics, and psychoanalysis, and it is interesting to track how animality produces itself in a radical way in the unstable field of the "human". Philosophers have always made a distinction between human beings and animals, giving rational thought, language, or consciousness of death as criteria. In a way, one could say that the domain of the human is measured by the animal. The animal measures and mediates an incessant process of the self-alteration of men.

Thus, regarding human madness, Michel Foucault says that animality is the human's internal truth, which shows the limits of the "human". Animality is like an unthinking, unthinkable mirror-twin of subjectivity, which knows itself only insofar as this domain of unknowing exists at the same time. According to Jacques Lacan, looking into the mirror, the human being appropriates its own image as "human" from without. But it is the animal that exists outside the mirror, whereas the human being has to recognise itself and, at the same time, is unable to do so.

The play of inside and outside, of inclusion and exclusion, is a kind of device that Agamben calls an "anthropological machine"; it establishes a kind of boundary between the self and the "animal" other. One can compare, again, this optical devise with the mirror. Human being recognise themselves in the animal and they do in the mirror. This is, to borrow a Lacanian term, a kind of mirror stage, the moment when human beings start to acquire their humanity. Recognising

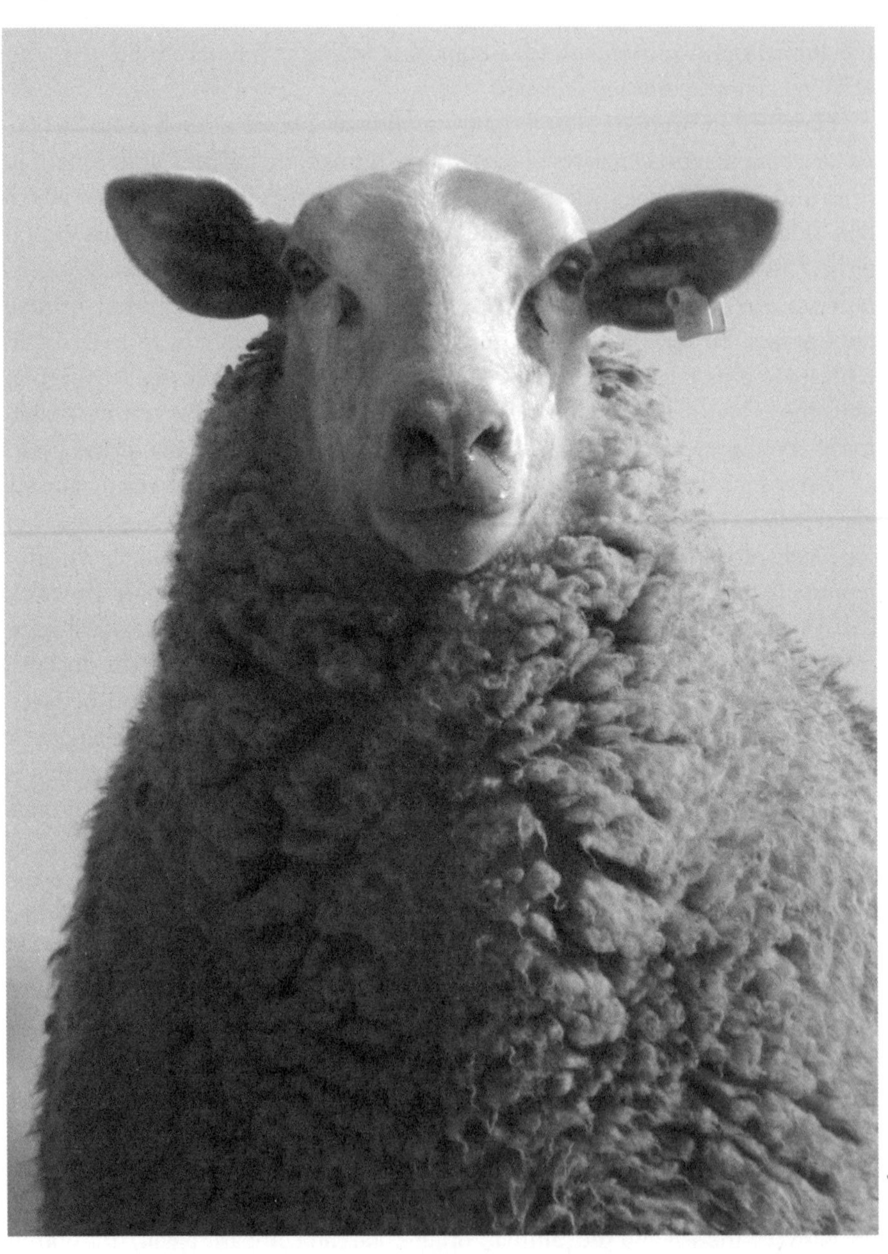

themselves in the animal, they begin to distinguish themselves from it. But in this mirror-machine, recognition goes along with misrecognition. For Agamben, this is not only in a metaphysical sense, but also a political operation, which leads either to humanising the animal, or animalising the human. This machine produces the boundary between human and animal, and at this border, there is a lot of racism, violence, and blood.

Unlike Agamben, I do not pretend to stop the anthropological machine, or the machine of metaphysics, which supposedly devours the living energy of the animal that is hidden inside. I just want to take a certain position from which it will be possible to investigate whether the very same machine can work differently. Whereas in Agamben, who analyses how this boundary between human and unhuman is produced, both animalised humans and humanised humans are objects of violence, manipulation, et cetera, I am rather interested in how this boundary is crossed in this or that direction. What is therefore at stake for me is rather a certain subjectivity, a subjective dimension of animality, which I attempt to interpret in terms of unconscious desire. An argument I've developed in my work is that animal subjectivity can express itself as an unconscious desire, which must be read politically.

To give you an example, let me now make a brief excursus into an animal side of political ontology. In his "Debates on the Law on Thefts of Wood", which was his first immersion in the problem of material interests and economic questions, Marx famously writes:

> The so-called customs of the privileged classes are understood to mean *customs contrary to the law.* Their origin dates to the period in which human history was part of *natural history*, and in which, according to Egyptian legend, all gods concealed themselves in the shape of animals. Mankind appeared to fall into definite species of animals which were connected not by equality, but by inequality, an inequality fixed by laws. The world condition of unfreedom required laws expressing this unfreedom, for whereas human law is the mode of existence of freedom, this animal law is the mode of existence of unfreedom. [...] The animal genus itself is seen only in the hostile behaviour of the different animal species, which assert their particular *distinctive* characteristics one against another. In the *stomach of the beast of prey*, nature has provided the battlefield of union, the crucible of closest fusion, the organ connecting the various animal species.

The natural animal kingdom serves here as both a metaphor and a model for the spiritual one. The natural order contrasts, but also reflects and sets off the

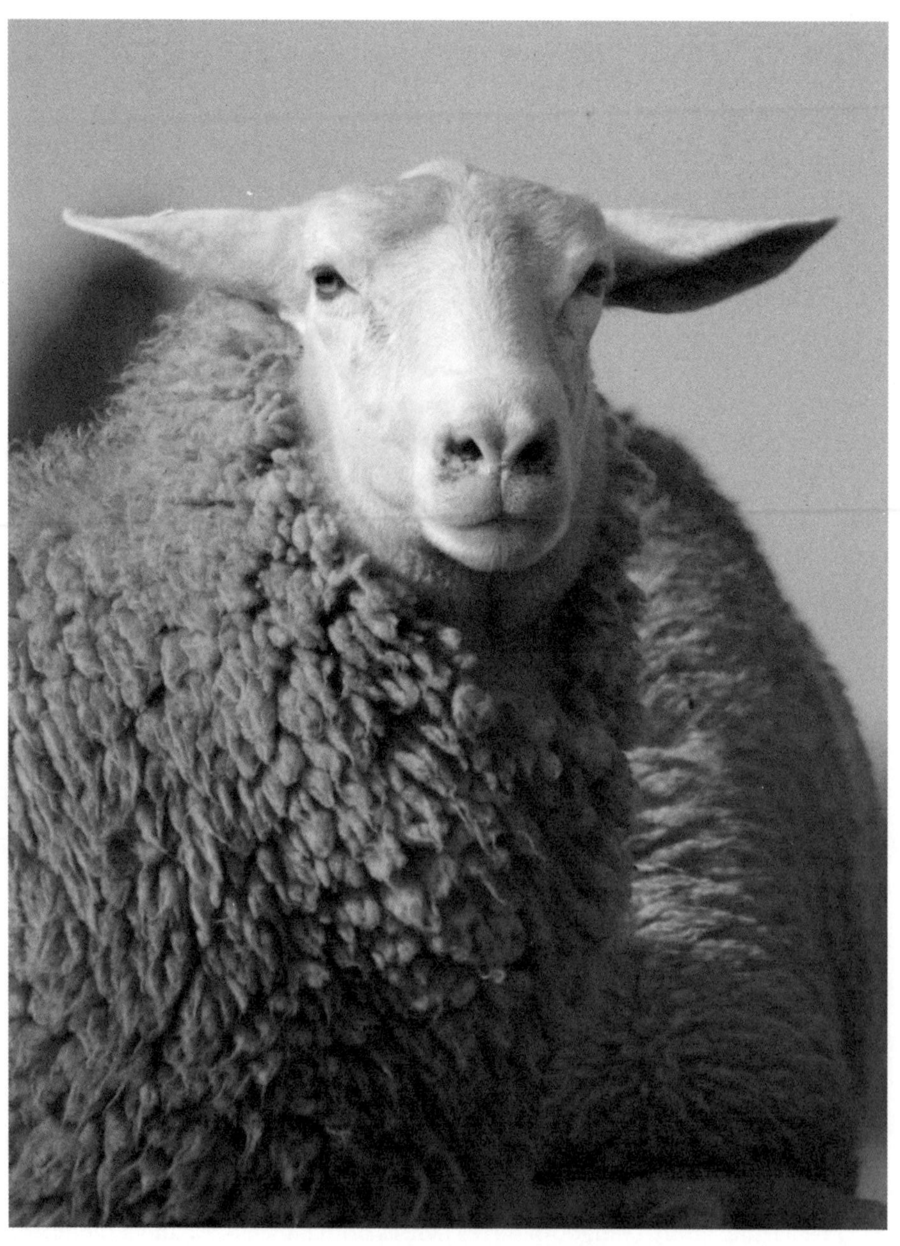

social one. I would like to focus your attention on the first brick in this metaphoric construction, namely, on the natural animal kingdom, in which an unfree society, or the spiritual animal kingdom, finds its reflection.

First of all, the stomach of the beast of prey is of interest. Let us think about this beast. Isn't it a strange figure? The beast of prey with its enormous belly, which is "the battlefield of union, the crucible of closest fusion", and within which the various animal species are connected. What is its story? On the one hand, it is a part of the natural animal kingdom, where hostility reigns; it is among others – other animals, of other species. On the other hand, in a way, it seems to be apart from other animals and other species. Or, better, it had to be apart from them, at a certain point, before pouncing on them, before devouring them. As if it stayed among others for a while, but all of a sudden stepped away, and, from there, attacked and devoured others. Now it is full, has an entire living universe in its belly, which becomes a measure of all bodies. At this state, almost pregnant, it encounters Marx on his way and tells him a sad story of the natural animal kingdom, which Marx then recognises as a story of humanity.

Indeed, Marx was not the only philosopher who used a predator metaphor in a context closely related to the formation of human society. The animal kingdom is a common form of measurement in traditional political thought. It could not be otherwise, since everywhere an oppressive power invariably persists in masquerading as nature. Everywhere, its legal justifications pretend that they are natural law. The most greedy, and malicious human beings don the skin of noble beasts. In the political realm, human beings traditionally wear animal masks.

At the beginning of his seminar *The Beast & The Sovereign,* Jacques Derrida introduces a peculiar series of various cultural representations of wolves, and, within this frame, brings in a very important quotation from Rousseau's *Social Contract* (chapter 2), in which Rousseau critically addresses Grotius and Hobbes, who, in their thinking about the origin of politics, compare human beings to beasts:

> It is doubtful, then, according to Grotius, whether the human race belongs to a hundred or so men, or if that hundred or so men belong to the human race: and throughout his book he seems to lean toward the former opinion: this is also Hobbes's feeling. So, here we have the human race divided into herds of cattle, each one with its chief who keeps it in order to devour it.[1]

---

[1] Jean-Jacques Rousseau, *Du contrat social,* Paris: Classiques Garnier, 1954, 237. Cited by Derrida (quote in

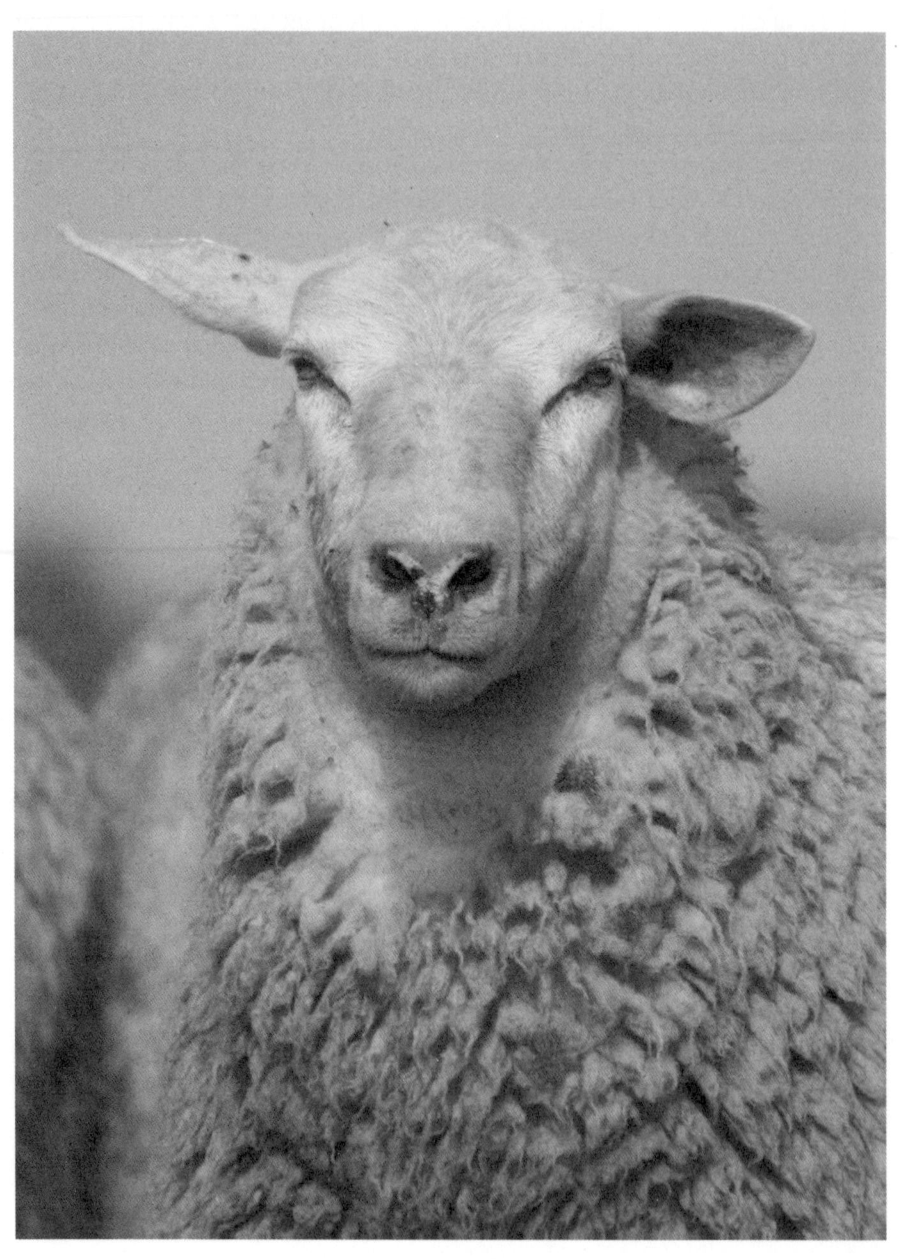

In this figure of the chief of herds of cattle, Derrida discerns "a kind of wolf"[2], and extensively comments on it. He is interested in the becoming-beast of a sovereign, of the strongest, who defines justice by his own reason. The reason of the strongest is what matters here, as a principle of (in)justice, which tends to be a principle of the law, established by a sovereign, who himself stands outside of this law. What is then the rationale of the wolf-chief? It is just that simple – his incredible appetite. Derrida puts a strong emphasis on the "in order to devour it", on the intentional character of the chief keeping the cattle.

But what might this wolf, who keeps the herd of cattle in order to devour it, look like? In the spiritual (i.e. human) animal kingdom, the wolf has to look like others, it has to look like one of the cattle, to be, or to pretend to be, among them, one of us. That's what happens in human societies. The chief of the herd represents himself as a part of the same herd, with the only difference that he occupies a sovereign position. He occupies the same paradoxical position as the Marxian beast of prey – being a part, but also being apart, and, finally, containing all the rest within him. When political philosophies say that the sovereign embodies the society, the state, the nation, or so on, one can read it literally – as an act of devouring.

However, in the actual natural animal kingdom, to put it bluntly, the one who wants to devour the others always looks different; his appearance gives him away. The cattle will immediately recognise the predator as soon as he tries to approach from outside. In order to keep the herd of, say, sheep, with a view to devouring them, a wolf must look like a sheep; he must wear sheep's clothing. At a certain point he will rise up, throw off his sheep's dress, and the flock will see him naked, they will see, but just briefly – and this will be the last scene they see – their naked king – naked, and with a wide-open mouth. Rising up, in animals, must equal showing one's nakedness: that's how humans appeared – by rising up, by exposing their sex, which they immediately covered with animal dress.

In order to devour, the sovereign dons an animal skin. Look, he says, this is a natural law; I am the strongest here, and this is my cattle. But we must raise here one more question: Is he really a wolf? Is he, who is lurking among the cattle, really a beast of prey? There is something dubious about this representation. Isn't it that the strongest wears not only a sheep's clothing (pretending to be a part of this given flock), but also a wolf's mask (pretending to be a part of the hostile, natural animal kingdom as a whole in general)? He is very well covered, but does he really hunt?

Derrida's translation), in Derrida, Jacques, *The Beast and the Sovereign*, Vol. 1, trans. by Geoffrey Bennington (Chicago: University of Chicago Press, 2009), 11–12.

[2] Jacques Derrida, *The Beast and the Sovereign*, Vol. 1, 11.

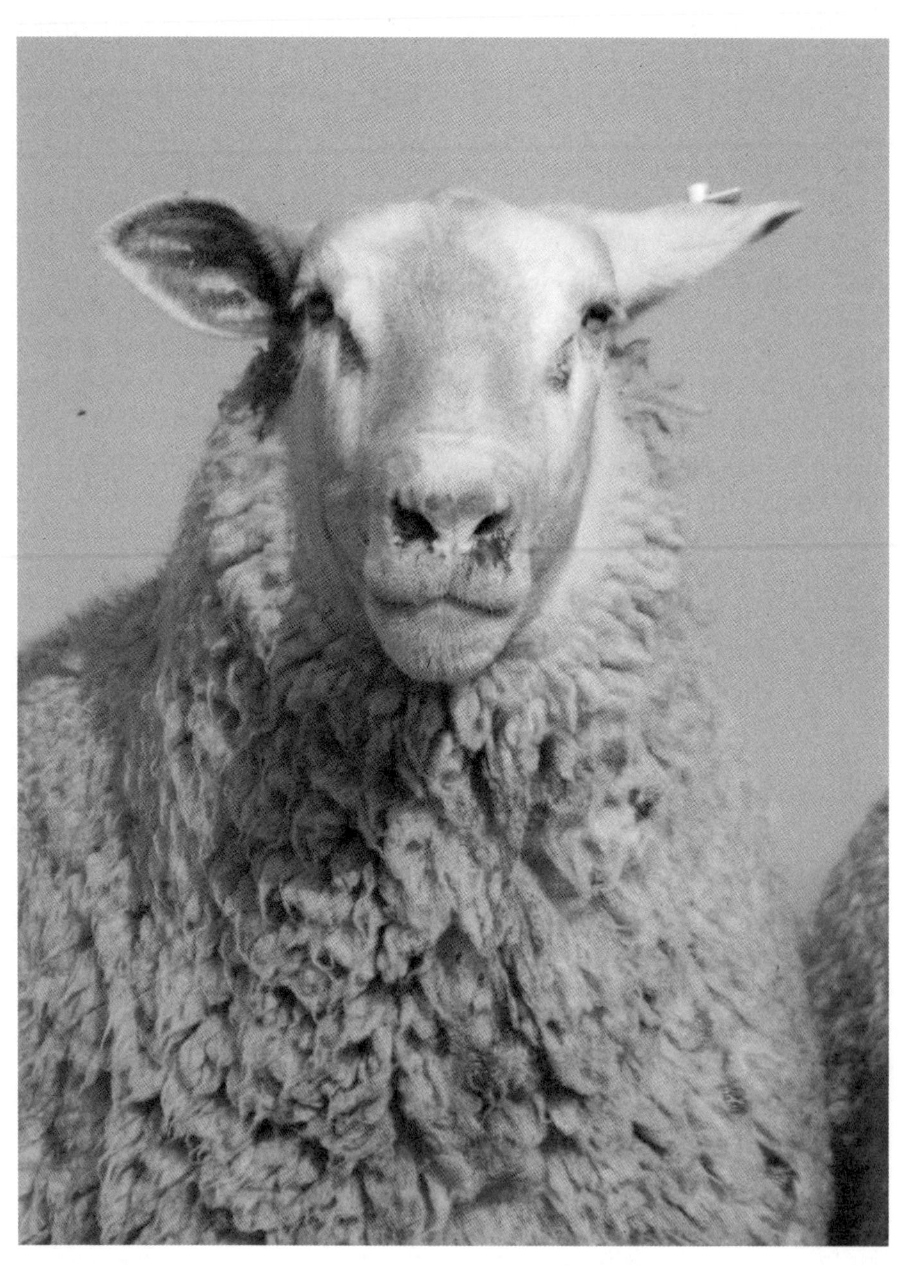

Let us take another step forward, now following Michel Serres, who, in his book *The Parasite*, performs an unexpected turn in the very same traditional direction of representing the social as natural, and reconsiders all relationships in both natural and social economy in slightly different terms. Our relation towards nature and towards each other, according to Serres, is not a predatory, but a parasitic one. What is a parasite? It is the one who lives and benefits at the expense of the other. In parasitology this other is called the host. A parasite attaches to a body of the host, or digs inside it, and eats it. For Serres, the animal clothing is not just a metaphor:

> We adore eating veal, lamb, beef, antelope, pheasant, or grouse, but we don't throw away their "leftovers". We dress in leather and adorn ourselves with feathers. Like the Chinese, we devour duck without wasting a bit; we eat the whole pig, from head to tail; but we get under these animals' skins as well, in their plumage or in their hide. Men in clothes live within the animals they devoured. And the same thing for plants. We eat rice, wheat, apples, the divine eggplant, the tender dandelion; but we also weave silk, linen, cotton; we live within the flora as we live within the fauna. We are parasites; thus we clothe ourselves. Thus we live within tents of skins like the gods within their tabernacles.[3]

From Derrida's predator, who keeps the cattle in order to devour them, we thus moved to Serres' parasite, who lives within the cattle and actually slightly eats it. But, in contrast to a number of small natural parasites, like vermin, insects and so on, he retains his position as chief of the cattle. He not only eats his cattle, but also stays with and within it, he keeps it, as is said, he takes care of it: he is a shepherd. A shepherd is another name for a chief of the cattle, who literally keeps them in order to devour them (and that's why he takes care of them). As a parasite, one might say, he is hosted by the cattle.

No one could better express it, in a fundamentally ontological manner, than Heidegger, who famously said: "The human being is the shepherd of Being."[4] This sentence tends to be understood as a poetic metaphor for being as a flock, a congregation, led by man by way of language. But no one ever re-

---

[3] Ibid.

[4] Martin Heidegger, "Letter on Humanism", in *Pathmarks*, trans. Frank A. Capuzzi (Cambridge: Cambridge University Press, 1998 (1947)), 252.

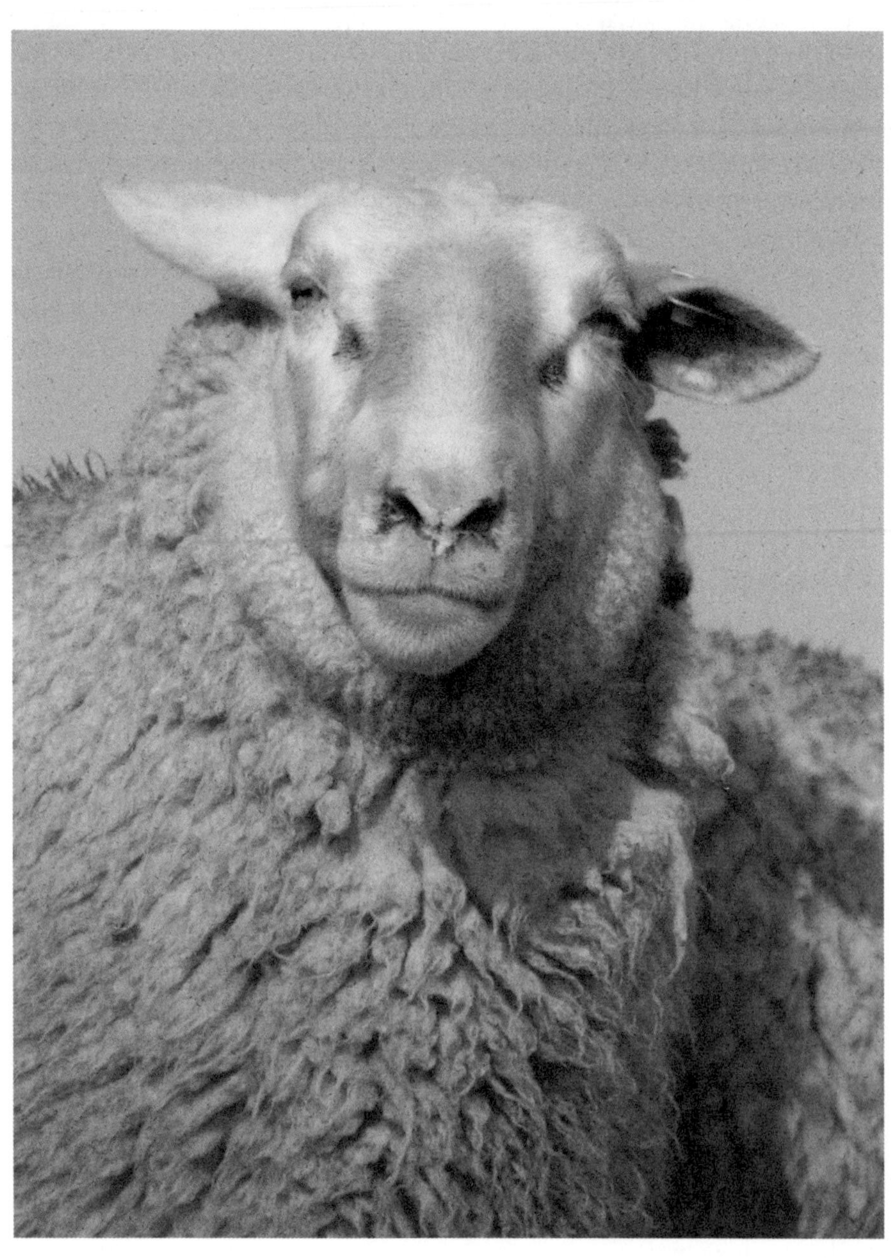

ally took seriously either the literal aspect of man's shepherdship, namely its parasitic intention, or the bestial part of its ontological impact: if the man is a shepherd of being, then being is a herd. The herd of being is man's host, that's where he lives.

In this connection, let's look at another famous quotation from Heidegger: "Language is the house of Being. In its home man dwells."[5] Here, Heidegger's preoccupation with the theme of home, or, to put it in Deleuzian terms, with territorialisation, is very remarkable. A man seeks a proper home, or host.

But how is it possible that these two sentences can be brought together, since, in Heidegger, nothing is more human than language, and since a Heideggerian human being who speaks language is really very far from the animal that just produces a meaningful noise? Here, to move away from Heidegger, I'll make a brief note on the bestiality of language, on its origin in a non-articulated animal voice. Thus, first, according to Agamben, "The articulation of the animal voice gives life to human language and becomes the voice of consciousness"[6], and this articulation passes through the death of the animal. This follows from Agamben's reading of Hegel, and, particularly, from his interpretation of Hegel's assertions that, "every animal finds a voice in its violent death"[7], and that, "the death of the animal is the becoming of consciousness".[8]

Second, bestiality of language finds its perfect expression in the idea of the unconscious. This might sound a bit weird, especially for those who see the problem of the unconscious through a Lacanian lens, since Lacan (almost like Heidegger) posits language precisely at the border between humans, who have language, and animals, which do not. Lacanian unconscious is essentially a language, but this language is not appropriated by any "I"; it is the language of the Other. "It" speaks, Lacan says. But is the gap between the Freudian unconscious, which originates, first of all, in the repression of the organic, in rejection of our own animality, and the Lacanian one, which speaks, really that big? After all, who or what is this "it" that speaks behind our back?

From this perspective, it seems that Heidegger's call of (a deeply forgotten) being comes from this animal multiplicity, from a non-articulated animal voice, which, in psychoanalysis, one would say, always returns as repressed. Meaning and consciousness will come to be articulated when this voice is cut into pieces, as if by someone's teeth, by chewing: "This pure sound is interrupted by mute

---

[5] Ibid., 239.

[6] Giorgio Agamben, *Language and Death: the Place of Negativity*, trans. by P.E. Pinkus and M. Hardt (Minneapolis: University of Minnesota Press, 1991), 45. See also my commentary on this in *History of Animals*, 80–83.

[7] From Hegel's *Jena Lectures*, cit. in Agamben's *Language and Death*, 45.

[8] Ibid.

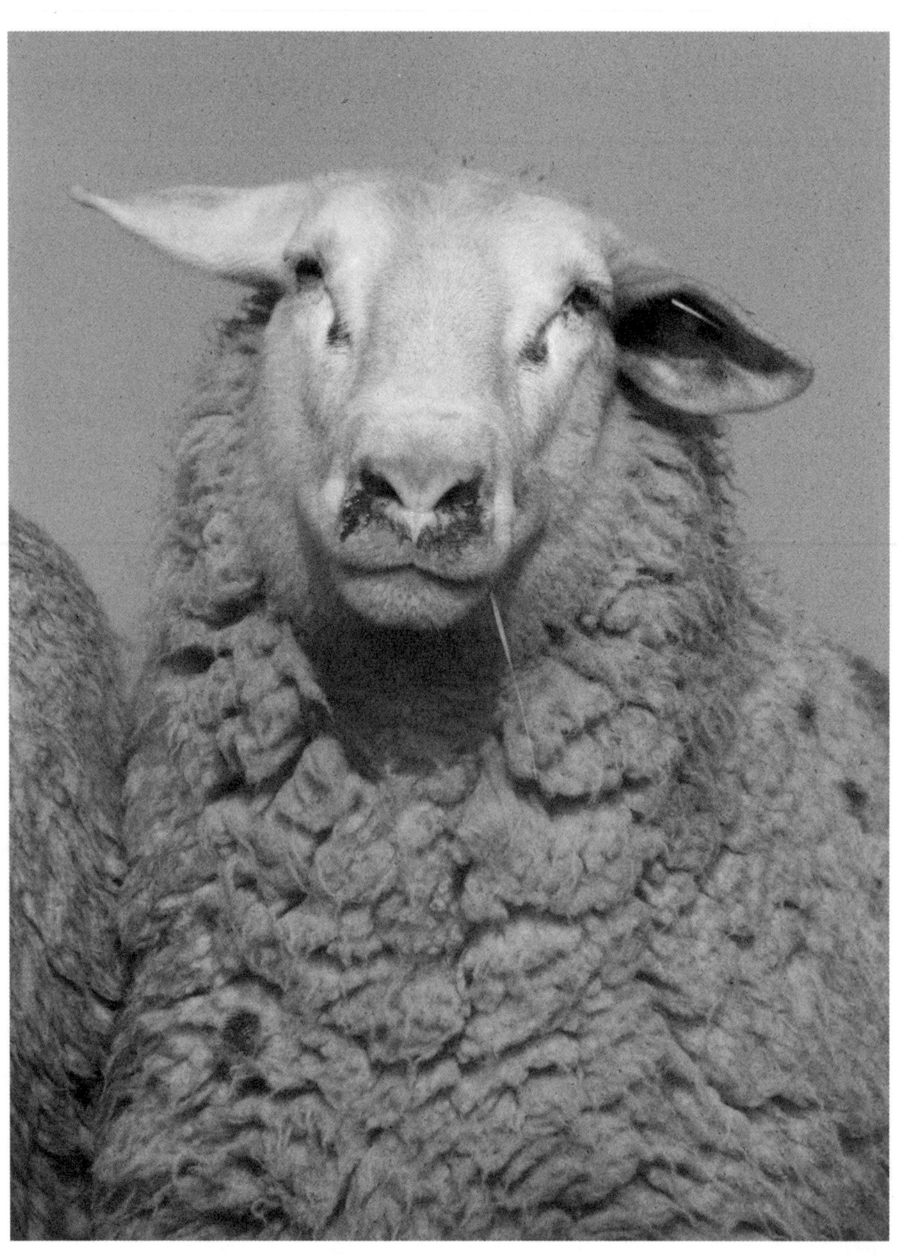

[consonants], the true and proper arrestation of mere resonation."[9] It's not a man, a sovereign – it is cattle that speak this way. A sovereign just opens his mouth, no doubt, in order to devour: articulation as mastication.

Thus, a parasite lives within animals it eats. But there is something else going on here, since, as Serres emphasises, there is a parasitic chain, which knows only one direction. In this chain, one parasite is a host for another one. In a way, sheep, too, are hosted by the shepherd-wolf, as far as he keeps the cattle, but also as far as he devours them (and then keeps them in his stomach). They are hosted in order to be devoured. Cattle are, so to say, basic animals, which are invited to be eaten, but there can be other animals, other parasites, against which the shepherd protects his pasture. As Serres says:

> In the end, there are two kinds of animals: those that are invited and those that are hunted. Guests and quarry. Tame and wild. The wolf and the dog whose neck is irritated by the collar. …There are animals whom we parasite and those who might supplant us and whom we chase away, hunt, and eventually eliminate.[10]

That's how Serres understands repression – as, basically, chasing other potential parasites. The one chases the others in order to purify his habitat, to have all of the cattle for himself:

> This repression is also religious excommunication, political imprisonment, the isolation of the sick, garbage collection, public health, the pasteurisation of milk, and so forth, as much as it is repression in the psychoanalytical sense. But it also has to do with history, the history of science in particular: whoever belongs to the system perceives noises less and represses them more, the more he is a functioning part of the system. He never stops being in the good, the just, the true, the natural, the normal.[11]

It might seem that we have now moved too far away from Marx, but that's not quite true. Do not the goodness, the justice, the truth, as well as naturalness and normality of the one who chases the others bring us back, through the Derridean sovereign, the strongest with his ultimate reason, to Marxian nobles, who tend to raise their customs and privileges to the power of universal law?

---

[9] Hegel, cit. in Agamben's *Language and Death*, 44.

[10] Michel Serres, *The Parasite*, 77–78.

[11] Ibid, 68.

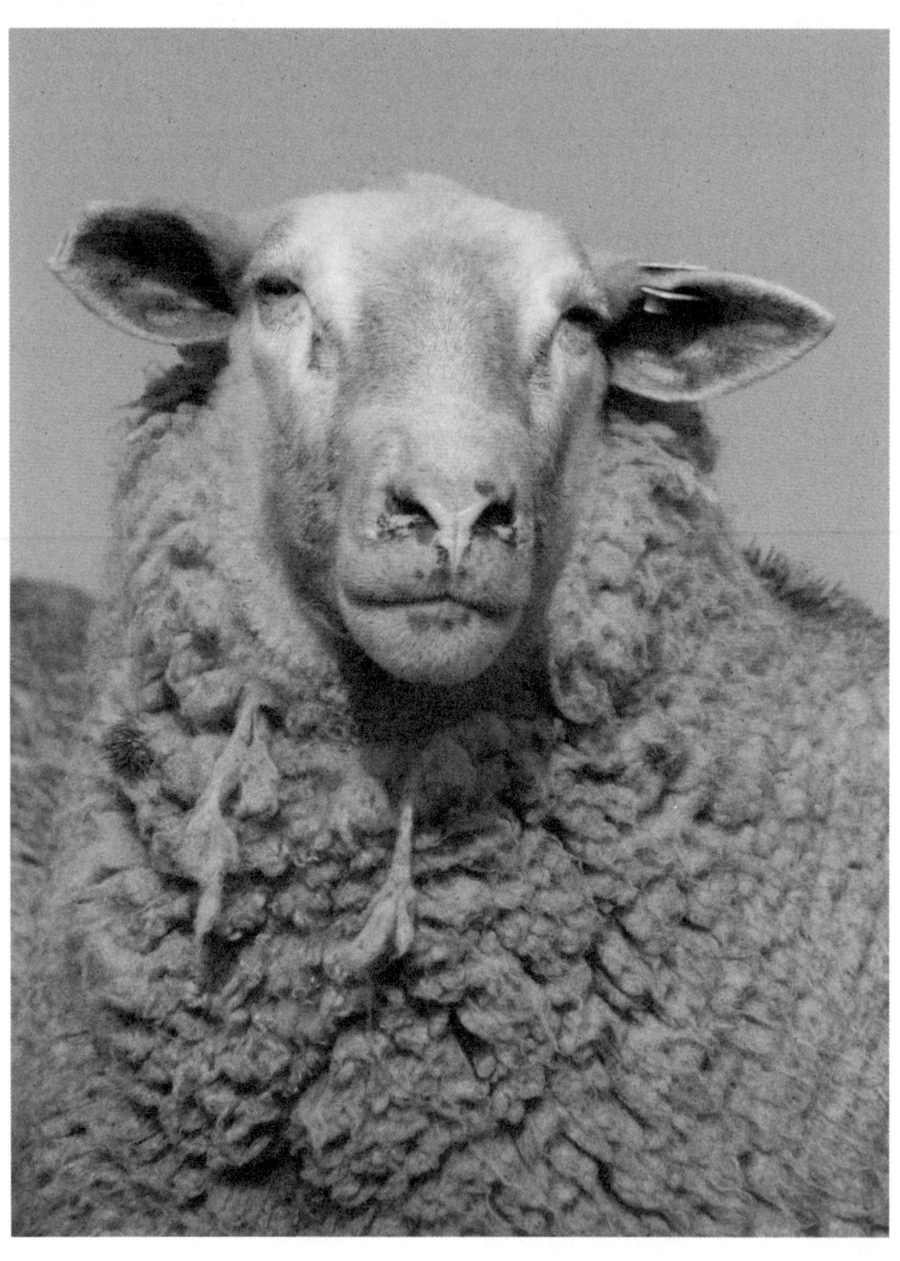

Thus, the motive for bigger parasites chasing smaller ones can be read between the lines of the very same article on the theft of wood. Here, Marx discusses some legislative amendments proposed by the Rhine Province Assembly. To put it briefly, these amendments aim to consider pilfering of fallen wood, gathering of dry wood, and the like, as a crime, which should be punished "as severely as the stealing of live growing timber".[12]

Dry branches fall down from the trees; peasants come and gathering them to fire their furnaces; their children pick up berries for their modest tables… Deadwood, brushwood, berries and other small things, unimportant for the rich, unnoticed by them, still have, according to Marx, an indeterminate property status. These commons[13], as they are called in a current debate, or alms of nature, as Marx himself calls them – are kind of trophies for poor people, like leftovers gleaned from rich men's feasts.

But the strongest extend their property. The owners of the forest with their incredible appetites are not satisfied with only the individual living trees that are at their actual disposal. They feel that the poor are the parasites of their forest – and they try to chase them out, as they chase a hare which nibbles a cabbage in their garden. "They steal", that's what is usually said also about those little birds, sparrows and pigeons, that pick up crumbs of bread on the street. A bigger parasite chases a smaller one, staying always on the side of the good and the natural, using its reason of being the strongest, which he calls the law. In a sense, for Serres, all people are like those hares from the point of view of some bigger and stronger parasite, who doesn't like the fact that someone can pick up fruit that has fallen from his tree: "Our forefathers were excluded from paradise. I left, too; we were all chased out … Never ceasing to chase beings from their paradise and always chased by others from our own."[14]

Paradise is a home where fruits and meals are distributed for free, no one has to pay. An ideal host body. Being expelled means being exposed to an economy: nothing *gratis*. And the chain, as already emphasised, develops in one direction – one parasite parasites another one. Basically, the initial link in the one-way chain of the relations of production (a host body of nature) never benefits, whereas the final one – the sovereign – grabs everything in order to fill his belly. He, a parasite, wearing a prey's cloak and a predator's mask, is the guest in the flock, but, at the same time, he is also another universal host. On the one side of a parasitic chain there is, say, a cattle (an animal multiplicity), but on its other

---

¹² Karl Marx, "Debates on the Law on Thefts of Wood".

[13] See, for example: Peter Linebaugh, in Karl Marx, the "Theft of Wood and Working Class Composition: A Contribution to the Current Debate", in *Crime and Social Justice*, 1976, Vol. 6, 5–16; see also: Peter Linebaugh, *The Magna Carta Manifesto: Liberties and Commons for All*, (Berkeley: University of California Press, 2008), etc.

[14] Michel Serres, *The Parasite*, 89.

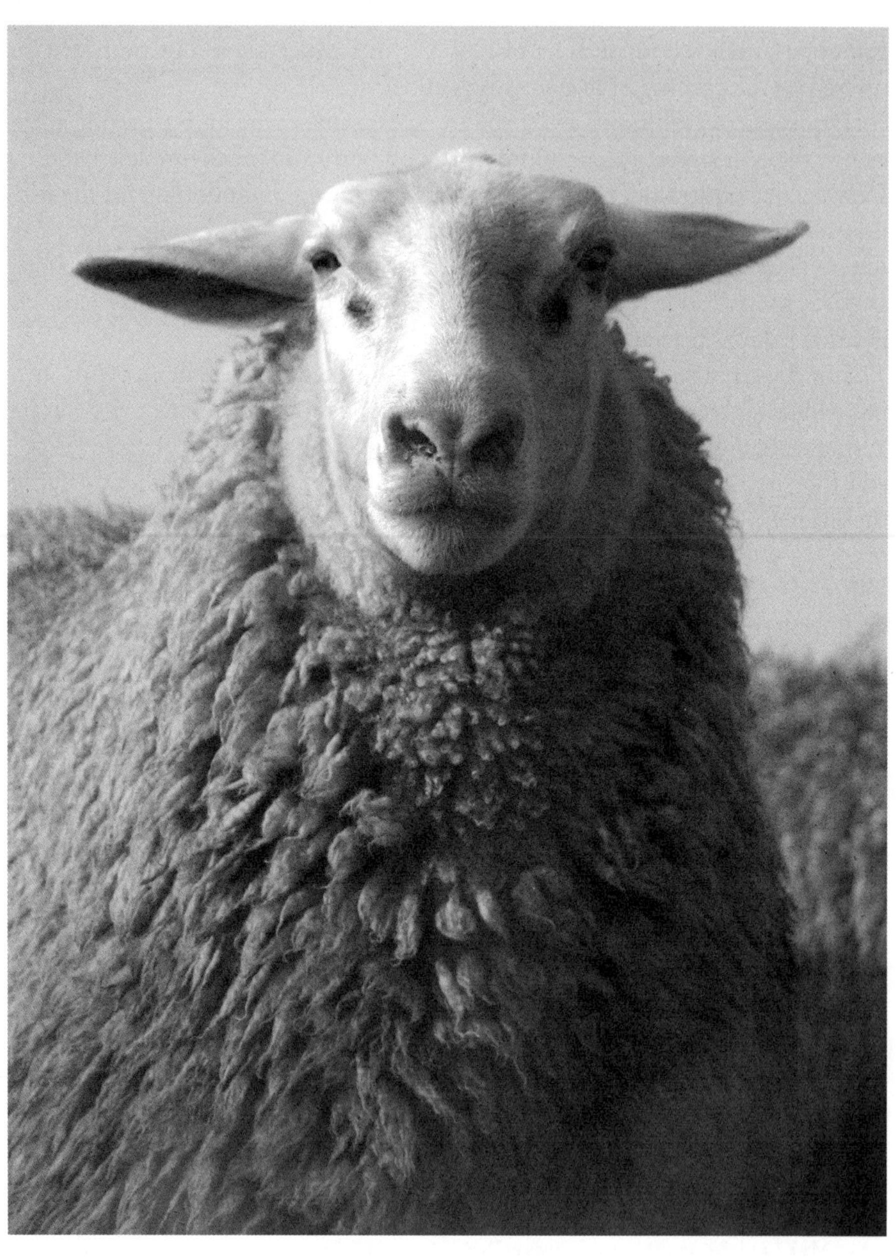

side there is a singular beast, which hosts what is being devoured. From one host to another, the chain closes:

> We parasite each other and live amidst parasites. Which is more or less a way of saying that they constitute our environment. We live in that black box called the collective; we live by it, on it, and in it. It so happens that this collective was given the form of an animal: Leviathan. We are certainly within something bestial; in more distinguished terms, we are speaking of an organic model for the members of a society. Our host? I don't know. But I do know that we are within. And that it is dark in there.[15]

Being within the beast is the other side of our social existence: from the Garden of Paradise we go directly into the belly of a parasite. Think of his stomach, where the natural animal kingdom found its battlefield of union. He still keeps this paradoxical position – being a part, being apart, and containing all the rest within. At the end of the day, all animals are equal in his stomach, as far as his hospitable body presents itself as a universal equivalent. From one Marxian metaphor – the stomach of a beast of prey – we move to another one, introduced in the first edition of the first volume of *Capital*. Here, an indefinite singular beast, running alongside other animals, suddenly incarnates them all:

> It is as if, alongside and external to lions, tigers, rabbits, and all other actual animals, which form when grouped together the various kinds, species, subspecies, families, etc. of the animal kingdom, there existed in addition the animal, the individual incarnation of the entire animal kingdom. Such a particular which contains within itself all really present species of the same entity is a *universal* (like *animal, god,* etc.). Just as linen consequently became an *individual Equivalent* by the fact that *one* other commodity related itself to it as form of appearance of value, that is the way linen becomes – as the form of appearance of value common to all commodities – the *universal Equivalent, universal value-body, universal materialisation of abstract human labour*.[16]

Value: a universal form, or a *uni*form, made of linen or various animal skins, but also a universal body – so paunchy – which wears this uniform. As far as linen takes a value form: 'Its existence as value is manifested in its equality

---

[15] Ibid, 10.

[16] Karl Marx, *Value: Studies*, trans. by Albert Dragstedt (London: New Park, 1976). Quoted from: http://www.marxists.org/archive/marx/works/1867-c1/commodity.htm.

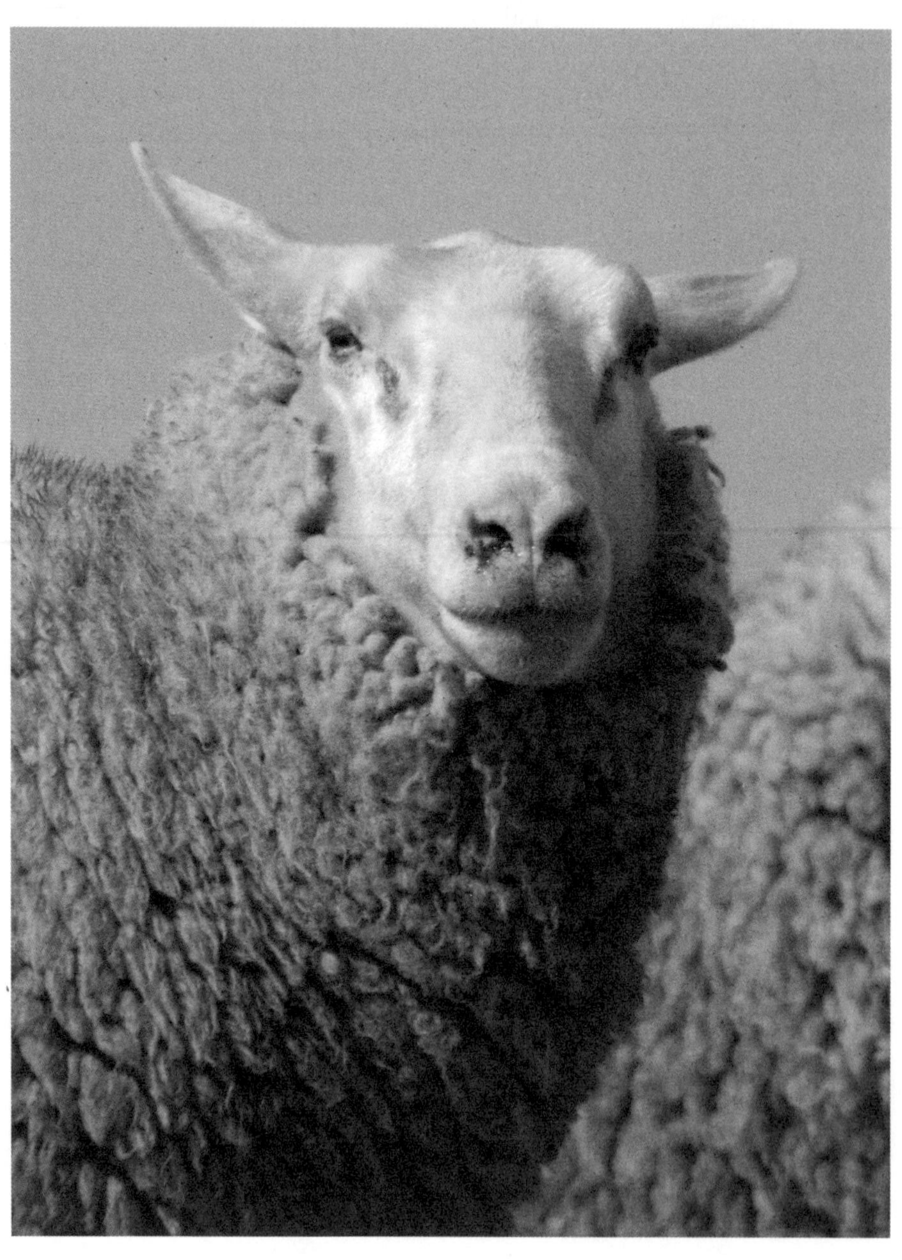

with the coat, just as the sheep-like nature of the Christian is shown in his resemblance to the Lamb of God."[17] The lamb, in its turn, moves from God's
meadows to God's enormous plate. And yes, Marx truly sees a parasitic nature
of capitalist exchange, based on the abstraction of a labour power. A labour power
was not always abstract. It was concrete and living, before being incarnated, or
devoured, by *the* animal. Marx gives a name to this beast – money. The general
equivalent is the measure of a capitalist world, but the multiplicity of animals
apart and inside does its epistemological work, whose aim, after all, must be to
invent a tool that can cut open the belly of the beast, and let other animals go.

---

[17] Karl Marx, *Capital*, Vol. 1, Ch. 1, in PDF Archive of Marx and Engels, 35:
http://www.marxists.org/archive/marx/works/1867-c1/.

EPISTEMOLOGY OF MEASUREMENT

Dialogue between Lucy Powell and Oxana Timofeeva
15 January 2014, Kunstraum, Leuphana Universität Lüneburg

1. From Timofeeva to Powell

OXANA TIMOFEEVA: I was very inspired by your works while I was preparing for this paper. I think you are certainly questioning the divisions, the borders, and the distinctions between the individual and the multiple. For example, *The Memory of Sheep* gives a wonderful illustration of what I would call "the process of individualisation". Just like humans, the non-human animal acquires, step-by-step, certain properties, such as a face, a portrait, a name, a gaze, an individuality, a story, or history. It is as if the yellow ID tags in the sheep's ears actually represented their breeds, names, families or whatever. This process starts from an anonymous multiplicity of the herd of animals – the flock. The division runs between the multiple and the singular, or the multiple and the individual. In this boundary, the question is not, "Do you differentiate between the one and the other?" but rather about the productive possibilities, epistemological potentialities of this division, where the most interesting things happen exactly at this border. When we look at the catalogue, blank papers are occasionally inserted in between the individuals, like a kind of pulsation. Individual sheep are removed from the anonymous flock in order to suddenly appear as singular individuals with their own faces and stories.

The same kind of productive boundary can be observed in another work of yours, *A Place Where Things Are.* However, if in the case of sheep we deal with the process of individualisation, here we find rather the inverse case of deindividualisation. This is something what I call "an anonymous abstraction" of an insect. One can say that the insect is the highest point of animal anonymity. Let me refer to Kafka's *Metamorphosis*, where the protagonist (human individual) suddenly starts turning into an insect. First, he begins losing his individuality – his face, his body, his clothes, his home, his relatives, his name and language. This creature looks at the window and is fascinated by the space. His experience of being an insect is an experience of a very special kind of mimesis. Roger Caillois, a surrealist and a thinker, who wrote about insects, took notice of insects' fascination with space, basically being devoured by space and, related it to mimicry: these insects imitate, and they don't imitate something, but just imitate (mimesis without an object). In the *The Impossible Line,* again, the animal is exposed to the forces of abstraction and anonymity, but at the same time is paradoxically individualised. The line at which the chicken stares, in a way, passes through the chicken itself, a paradoxical internal difference between the chicken and the chicken itself.

The first question is: How do you differentiate between anonymity and individuality? The second question refers to *We Are Here*, which differs from the other three works. It is about the animal and the machine. Where and how do you place yourself between the animal and the machine, the mechanical and the organic? The cat in the video speaks with a mechanical voice, which is how I imagine the voice of the unconscious might sound. And then the articulation comes in.

LUCY POWELL: Thank you for your interesting questions. Your idea of the individual animal versus the mass touches on two discussions. One is the idea of the animal as metaphor, another is the idea of animal as scientific object of study. Epistemology works on a philosophical level and as science, and embraces both. I go in between the two because my interest started with the animal as metaphor and I've moved towards the science, but I'm working with representation. This situated me on an in-between ground, although I've got more and more interested in the science, and that has always influenced my point of view. The idea of the individual is often about point of view. There is an interesting scientific experiment about face recognition in babies. Babies are geared towards face recognition.

The experiment showed the faces of a series of rhesus monkeys to small children, one monkey after the next, in a slideshow. The six-month-old infants were totally fascinated and watched the whole slideshow, while the older children quickly got bored because they thought they were seeing the same monkey time and again. The younger children, whose brains were better attuned to facial recognition, were able to distinguish individual characteristics, which I think is very interesting. It underlines that the idea of mass and individual is a point of view – it depends on your perception. Such things exist on all levels: among different ethnicities, between animals and human beings, among animals themselves, et cetera. Sheep can also distinguish between a certain number of humans. For *The Memory of Sheep*, I chose a particular breed of sheep which was very distinctive looking, at least to my eyes. Other breeds look more similar. I took about 400 pictures and had to isolate fifty different individuals. Honestly speaking, I had problems distinguishing between them, and sometimes I differentiated them just by the tag in their ears. Perceiving them as individuals was an interesting process, yet when I was photographing them, they were behaving as a herd. If I called out something or stood up, then they'd all run off, and, so, in my mind I was thinking: "Why am I taking pictures of you as individuals and you're behaving like a herd?"

OT: We just recognise individuals in the multiplicity or in the crowd when we are part of it. If we see some other multiplicity, we tend to see it as the crowd rather than as a gathering of individuals. It looks more anonymous, and all parts of this other crowd tend to appear to have similar faces.

LP: What you just mentioned relates to selective attention. The dragonfly, for example, has excellent selective attention – something only primates were thought to have. This focus makes it an incredibly effective predator, much better than lions or tigers, for example. I have moved my interests away from the idea of the animal in general to very specific details, because science keeps revealing new animal abilities and the "boundaries" between animals and humans are continually dissolving.

MY: You use an artistic speculation between metaphor and science, or language and visual images. Can we say that it is "your" epistemological methodology to elaborate that we're usually caught up in either one or the other of them?

LP: Very different approaches are taken in the four works. This is my way of working and dealing with stuff that I'm reading and finding out. It's evolving as I read and as science throws up new evidence. I would say that it's my own research path. Regarding the second question; the voice was not mechanical, but my voice imitating a mechanical one. I got a computer voice to read the text over and over, and I internalised it. When I spoke it for the video, I had embodied the rhythm. I was playing with an idea of the machine and animal with the human voice in between; I was interested in seeing what happens when you throw them all together as a "we".

2. From Powell to Timofeeva

LP: I would like to come back to metaphor. Do you consider the notion of the animal in other terms other than as metaphor? I met an historian of science, Etienne Benson, who said: "Sometimes with all the metaphors surrounding them, the animals themselves get lost." The metaphor keeps you in the human realm, in the realm of projection, and the animal actually disappears.

OT: It's a naïve scientific reciprocity. You get lost in metaphors, because the animal is nothing but metaphor and metaphoric constructs. Natural science also deals with metaphors. Look at the terminology in quantum physics, or in other sciences: particles, strings, flavour, topness, bottomness, beauty, or whatever metaphors are applied to nature. Science is full of metaphoric constructs, so I don't mind working with metaphors rather than with the real animals, because the real is also a kind of metaphoric construct. Metaphors can be productive when applied to a social reality. Marx, for example, uses metaphors when he talks about humans, animals, and society. A naïve reading of classical texts is an important element my work, because it gives us an alternative view. When you pick such a seemingly marginal figure as an animal, and from this animal perspective try to read what Hegel says about the system of knowledge, you can get an alternative view on history. My position is rather close to surrealist thinkers such as Roger Caillois or Georges Bataille, who worked at the boundary between art, science and theory, between philosophy and literature, between concept and metaphor.

MY: You pay particular attention to the way the metaphor of the animal is used in philosophy, and perceive a philosopher as an individual – a person situated in a specific time, location and condition – rather than a singular of philosopher. Your new perception reveals the order embedded in the cultural context in order to reinterpret the philosophical thinking in the text. Is this a sort of methodological experiment to de-/reconstruct a traditional line of philosophy so as to create another point of view?

OT: Yes, it's rather a methodological key to a certain door, to a certain system, or to a certain history of the development of philosophical thought in a strong connection with literature, arts and psychoanalysis. Every philosopher has another hidden, unconscious philosopher inside. Sometimes this inner philosopher says something completely opposite to what was said by the "official" one.

MY: I realise that interesting crossings between epistemology and ontology are taking place in this dialogue as well as in your book, *History of Animals*. In the first chapter, you say:

> For Aristotelian creatures, it does not require any particular effort to participate in this pause. They are just expected to do what they do naturally and at their specific place and in their specific manner. So the order they all maintain was not established by human beings, but humans measure it. We mind not that everyone in his own way already conforms to some general law and prohibition which seems all too human.

Measurement is a way to define ontological relationships. It is an act to create an order, so that measurement is synonymous with ordering. In your text, how do you distinguish these words, order and measure?

You previously referred to the notion of "a principle of life" by Gilbert Simondon. It all actually sounds like animism without using the term. The notion proposed reconsidering the boundary between machines, animal and human beings from the perspective of function. It denies a hierarchical structure in life, which shifts a view from epistemology – how we "see" the world – to ontology – how we should exist in the world within the network of nature. By taking a position of being in-between, you combine both views here. This seems to be close to an idea of animism without any specific cultural connotation.

OT: This chapter of my book is partly dedicated to Aristotle and Aristotelian animals, and, in general, to the Greek cosmos. I refer to Simondon, who was also inspired by animals and wrote about them. He emphasised that in Aristotelian thought there is a principle of life as a common measure, as something shared by plants, animals, humans, gods, stars, all kind of creatures. The ancient Greek universe in general is still inspired by animist belief in metempsychosis, the idea of a living soul passing from one body to another. In connection with Aristotle, I give one amazing example. In one chapter of his book *History of Animals*, Aristotle describes animal characters and tells the following story about a horse:

> It is said that the king of the Scythians had a high quality mare, all of whose colts were good; the king wishing to breed from the best out of the mother, brought it to her to mate; but after she had been concealed under a wrap, it mounted her in ignorance; and when the mare's face was uncovered after the mating at the sight of her the horse ran away and threw itself down the cliffs.

Imagine the horse that mates with its mother and commits suicide! Here the question of measurement and order comes in. The prohibition against incest is not only characteristic of ancient Greek culture, but also seen as universal, so that it is easily projected onto animals. If we have the prohibition, why don't horses? The horse in this story could be called Oedipus-the-Horse. The problem here is not the anthropocentric view, but the order of things, the maintenance of the cosmos. In order to maintain a cosmic order, there must be a certain measurement. There must be the law, and someone who knows the law, who has the power, who has the capacity to interpret the law, or who says what is the law, what is good, et cetera. There must be also those who obey the law. If someone cannot manage to do that, the whole construction of the universe can collapse. If one element of the cosmic structure fails, everything can fail. Everything and everyone in this universe try to be good. But what is being good according to Aristotle? To be good is to keep the way of behaving as it is, or to follow those who know better, to do what they say I should do. Thus, the great cosmos functions, and everything works there in harmony. But this horse does something that makes this cosmic order collapsed, namely, it violates the law and the prohibition. The same happens with Oedipus. Measurement appears here as a way of knowing, interpreting, and observing the law.

That's what they mean when they say that human beings measure this universe – they consider these laws to be universal.

MY: In other words, the horse is outside of the Aristotelian system of measurement, and immeasurable. This dialogue shows two different methods for creating a space for alternative thinking – using metaphor and practicing art. The common key word that emerges from the methods is "in-betweenness"; situating the self in between the existing disciplines and taking a position in-between ontology and epistemology. This suggests that crossing and shifting conceptual boundaries by means of metaphor and art may create an alternative space for new imaginaries regarding the concept of measurement. Thank you very much for your great contributions.

POLITICS OF MEASUREMENT

CHIHIRO MINATO
MEASURING THE MEASURER

My presentation is about the measurement project that we – artists, scientists, and engineers – began after the March 11th catastrophe in Fukushima. The project started with us asking ourselves what kind of crazy aftermath would hit us after that date. We feared a reality in which everything would be based on radiation measurements that would take control over our lives. This is a map showing the extent of the explosion at the Fukushima Daiichi nuclear plant located 250 kilometres north of Tokyo. Soon after the incident, the Japanese government announced that residents living within a circumference of thirty kilometers should stay in their houses for an unspecified number of days. On 25 March, however, that announcement was changed and turned into a warning to evacuate the area. The nuclear plant and the centre of the evacuation area were called Ground Zero, just like the centre of a nuclear bomb detonation. The decision to evacuate was based on a chain of rather simple lines established for measuring the radiation according to the distance from the explosion's centre.

In 2011, Japanese mass media distributed many diagrams. Here we see a map of Fukushima. Fukushima city, where high levels of radioactivity were measured, is located seventy kilometres from the Fukushima Daiichi nuclear power plant. In May 2011, it was revealed that the distance on the map did not allow for conclusive statements regarding the spread of radiation and the area of contamination. Sometimes very high radiation would be measured at a point far from the centre, sometimes hardly any radiation at a distance of no more than five kilometres from the centre. The U.S. government's evacuation warning, issued on 16 March, was related to an eighty-kilometre circumference. It was not easy to understand the contradicting information that the two maps presented. Surprisingly, it was snow particles that absorbed the radiation and kept it on the ground. The movement of the particles followed the wind and water streams, rain, and snowfall. This raised the question: What do maps actually tell us?

The measuring project compares the information distributed by authorities and media after 11 March to our own field research. Walking around in the vicinity of the coast of Japan, we measured the radiation close to the Fukushima

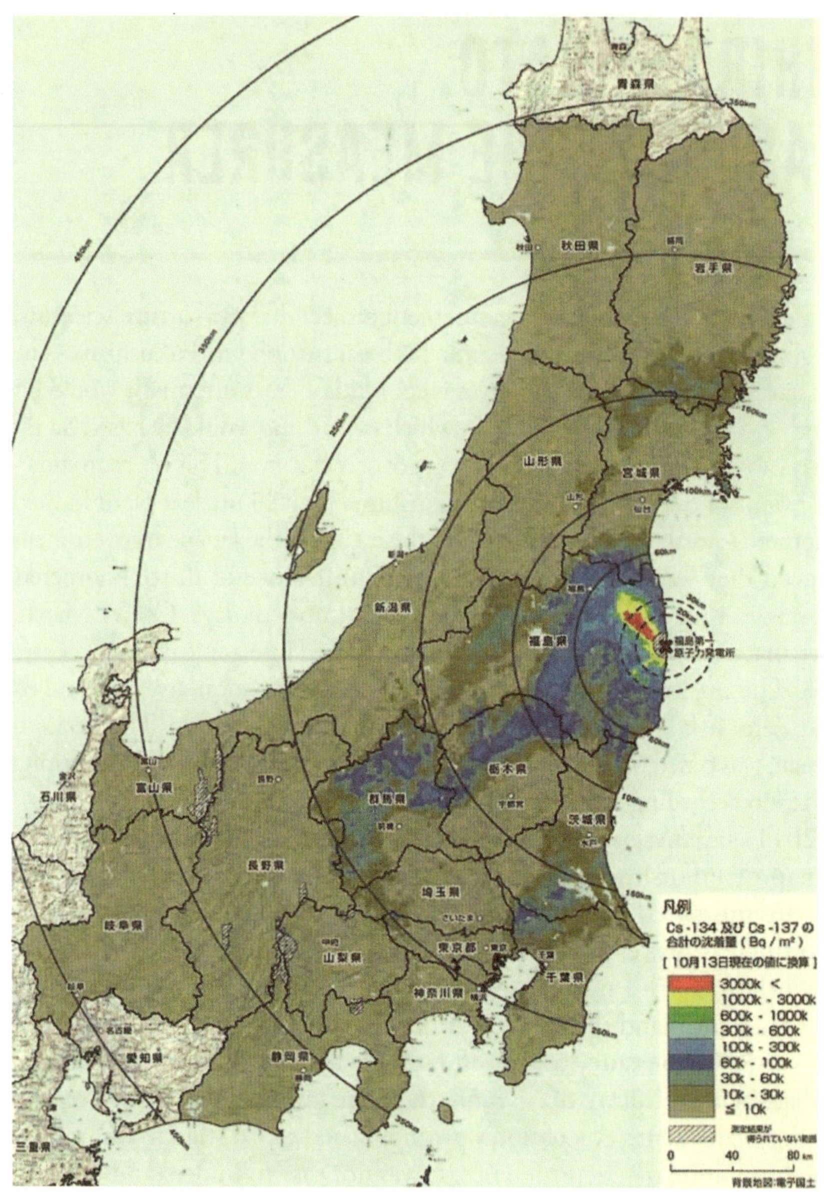

Measurement of the total amount of deposition flux
of Caesium 134, 135 based on aircraft monitoring
data, issued on 11 November 2011 by the Ministry of
Education, Culture, Sports, Science and Technology,
Japan, measuring date: 13 October 2011

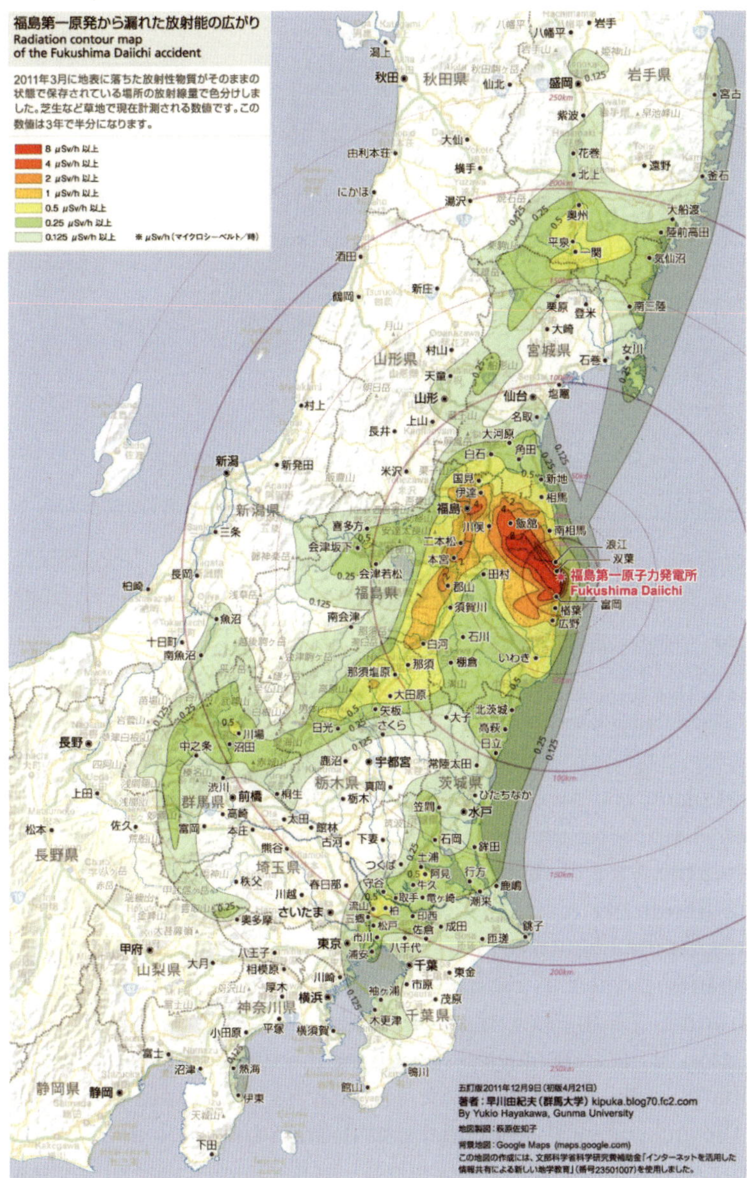

Radiation Contour Map of the Fukushima Daiichi accident, produced by Yukio Hayakawa, volcano geologist, Prof. Gunma University (8th revised edition, 1 February 2013 / 1st edition, 21 April 2011)

This map shows the level of deposition flux of radioactive materials since March 2011. It is based on the data from September 2011, which was measured on the lawn or one metre above the ground (μSv/h). The measurement level tends to be lower on the ground or on the asphalt, as radioactive materials are easily swept away by winds and rains, while the spots where radioactive materials accumulate, such as a drain spouts, under the eaves, by the roadside, etc. could be many times higher than what the map shows.

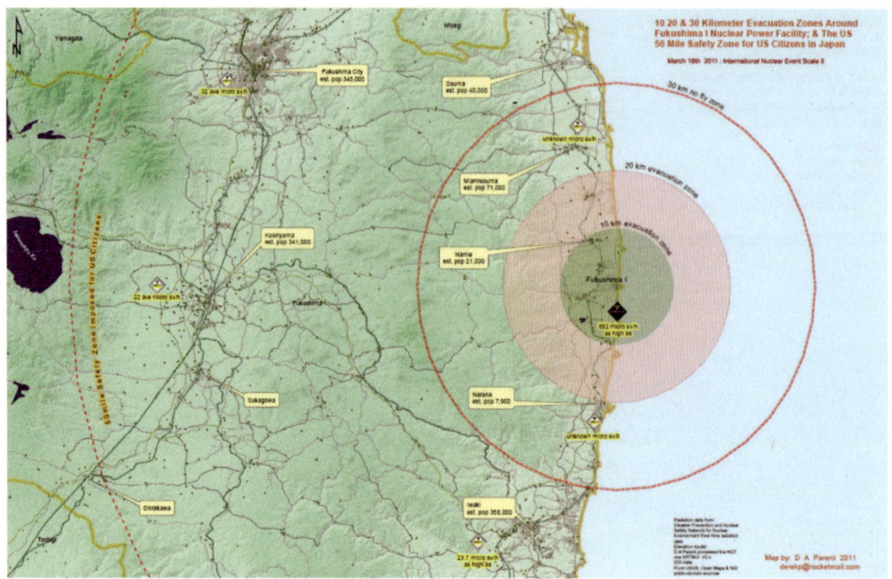

10, 20 & 30 Kilometre Evacuation Zones Around
Fukushima I Nuclear Power Facility; & The US
50 Mile Safety Zone for US Citizens in Japan, 18
March 2011: International Nuclear Event Scale 5

Daiichi nuclear plant, and we compared it to the line of radiation mapped by the authorities. A year after the incident, I invited my colleagues in Japan to take a walk with me. One of them was Yukihiko Mori, an archaeologist specialised in the Jomon era (ca. 3500 years ago) as it is documented in the Fukushima area. At the Fukushima Museum he presented tiny balls of thread coated with Japanese lacquer. These balls were found at the Jomon archaeological site in Mishima-cho in Aizu, traditionally known for its arts and crafts. Mori told me most of the archeological sites on the Fukushima coast were intact after the tsunami. The same was true for Miyagi and Iwate (north of Fukushima), the archeological residential sites dating from the Jomon period overlap with the zone left intact by the tsunami – as if this ancient people knew the boundary where a tsunami would stop. These facts made me imagine that the balls of thread must have been laid out around the boundaries of the intact zone in order to measure something. Before all the houses were demolished within ten to thirty kilometres away from Fukushima Daiichi, I decided to take measurements of the tsunami's traces, traces indicating the maximum height of the waves, and to mark these traces with a thread on the walls. I called the resulting lines Duchamp lines, as I adopted the concept of line dropping by used by Marcel Duchamp in his famous work *3 Standard Stoppage* of 1913.

282

The second person to accompany me on a visit of the region was Masao Okabe, an artist. He imagined that our measured line of radiation indicates the seasonal wind in the region. If the earthquake had come later in summer, the winds would have been directed towards Tokyo and the waves of radiation would have hit the city directly. Okabe and I recently started the project "Touching Contaminated Trees" in Fukushima. This project aims at documenting traces of the radiated trees by frottage and measuring the radiation at the site where the trees stand. The third person involved was Ryoko Sekiguchi, a Japanese poet living in Paris. Walking along with our strings, we measured the distance from the shore and the height of the wave, we referred to the stone tablets scattered along the northern coast in Miyagi, Iwate, through Aomori, which again commemorate tsunamis and earthquakes that happened long ago. The stone tablets in Aneyoshi, Iwate Prefecture, came to be known due to the fact that they indicate the boundary of the intact zone, which possibly translates as "Do not build homes below this level!" Because it followed this recommendation, the village was not destroyed by the tsunami. The Namiwake Temple is a similar example: it was also built on the Fukushima coast – right on the spot where the big waves stopped in 1611.

During the walks we found many strange phenomena created by the last tsunami. One of them was a massive concrete wave breaker pushed away by the wave. A number of these blocks can be found deep inland, which clearly demonstrates that they were useless in stopping the destructive force of a tsunami. Since the tsunami, the Japanese government has kept ordering the same concrete blocks, but now continues to position great numbers of them where the tsunami hit, based on the belief that quantity will solve the problem. After running simulations of future tsunamis, the government is now placing hundreds more blocks per metre to protect the inland region. This is a kind of measurement where the underlying pretext is furnished by national politics and economy. Building one of these concrete block costs approx. 10,000 Euros. The government plans to lay them out on at least 400 kilometres of the Japanese coast. This requires a tremendous amount of money, and eats up construction budgets needed for rebuilding the affected areas.

In 2013, our first research result from the measuring project was presented in an old rice warehouse in Kitakata city, Fukushima, during the Aizu Lacquer Art Festival. The region is traditionally well known for rice and sake production, as the land is rich in water. While conducting the measurement project, we met the owner of the oldest sake brewery, who turned out to share our interest in measurement and immediately understood the purpose of our project. This is why the warehouse came into play. For more than a hundred years, farmers and sake makers have measured wind, water, and snowfall. They measure not

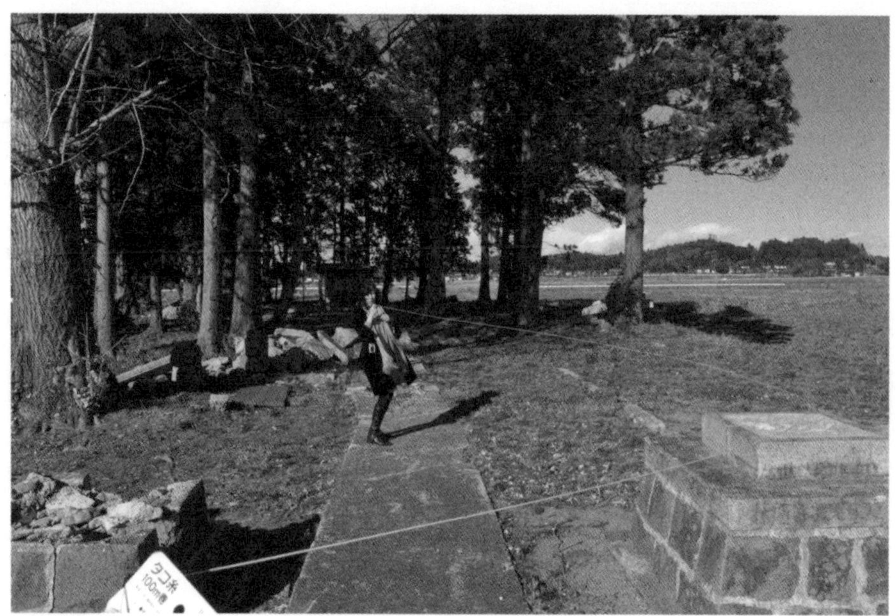

Measuring Project, documentation photo,
2013 © Chihiro Minato

only using technical devices but also their own senses, e.g. sight. The direction
of the wind, the shapes of snowflakes, the movement of water is the basis of
their decision when to plant rice. When winter is too long, they might postpone
it for a week, or sometimes even for a month. Measurement based on unaided
human perception has succeeded in maintaining the land for a thousand years.
Accounts of this can also be found in local literature, poetry, dance and theatre.
Art has served to document and preserve these methods of measurement. That's
why the brewery owner kindly gave us this space next to his sake production.

Japanese politics continues to follow its own logic – like measuring on false
premises and constructing enormous amounts of concrete blocks. For Japanese
citizens, it is quite impossible to compete with this powerful flow of data and
actions. However, we should not stop our walks and continue measuring landscapes with our threads. The Jomon thread balls direct our attention to invisible
landscapes dating back thousands of years ago. Taking recourse to the ancient
uses of thread measurement, the measurement project situates acts of measuring
as part of the continuity of time and space in nature, and does not limit itself
to measuring by means of technological devices alone – such as Geiger counters
– but also employs human perceptions. This may lead us to a more fundamental
understanding of the irregularly scattered radiation than those data collected
only by locals, who experienced the limitations of disaster technologies.

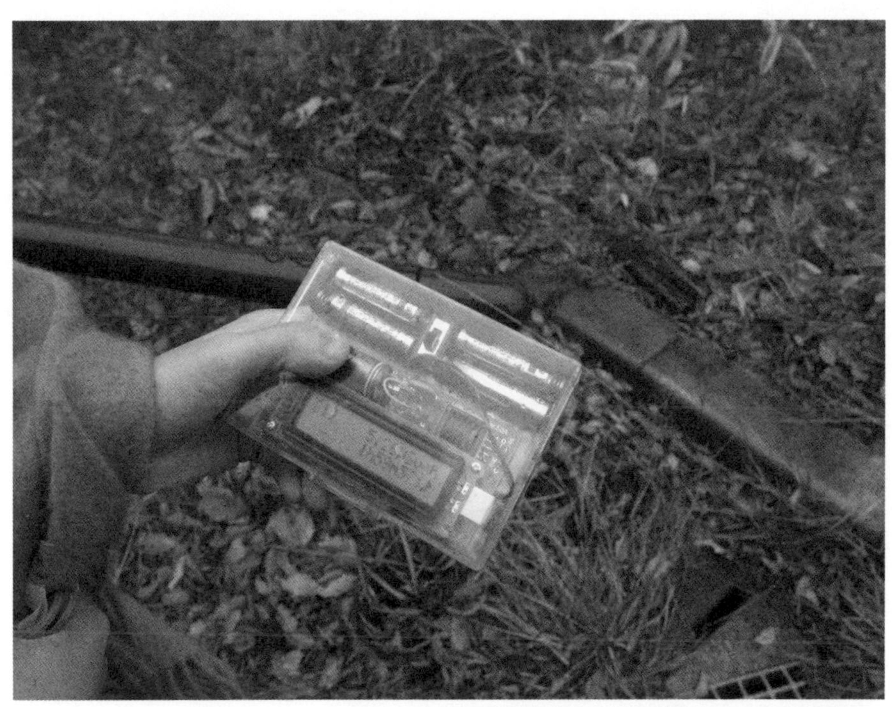

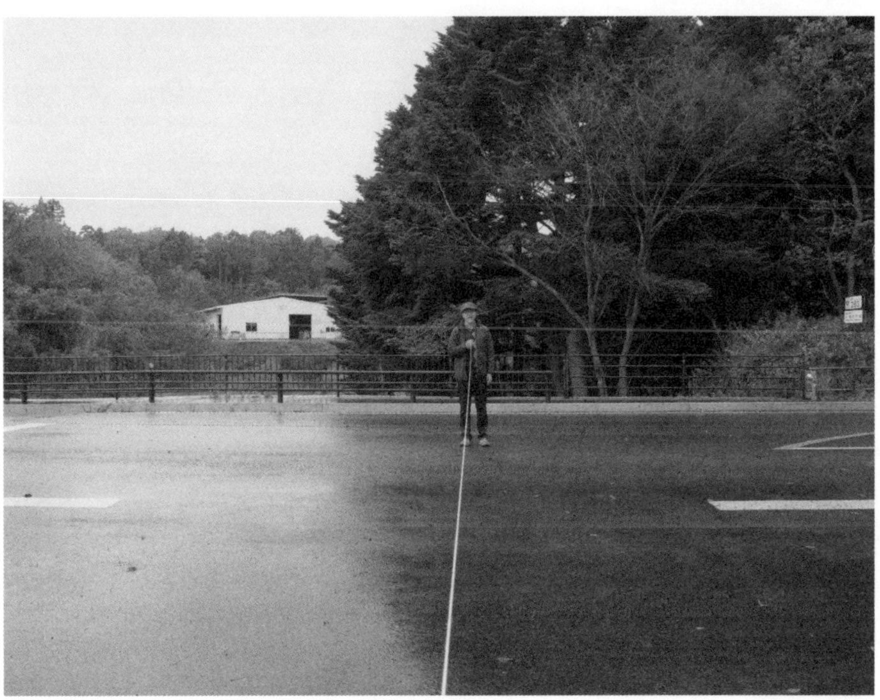

Measuring Project, documentation photo,
2013 © Chihiro Minato   285

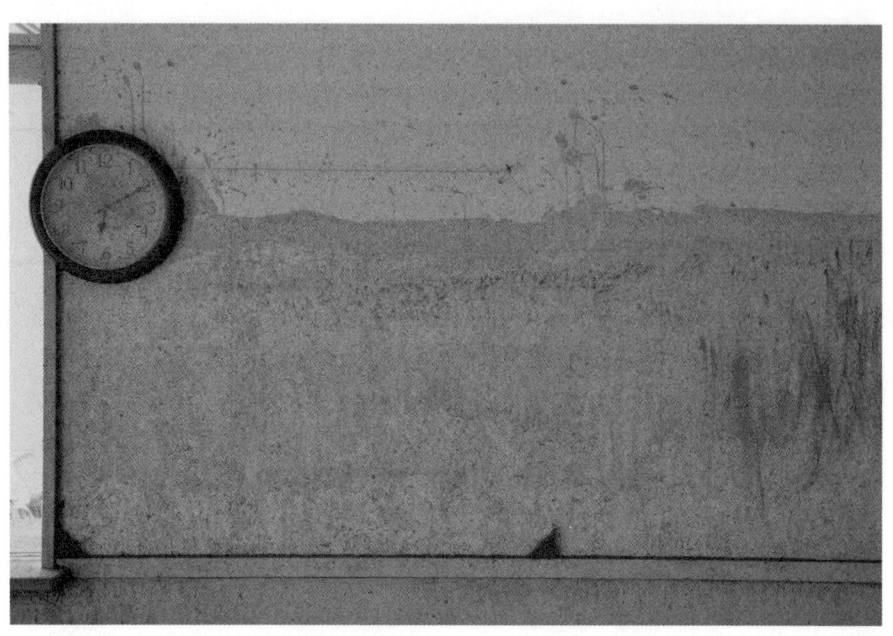

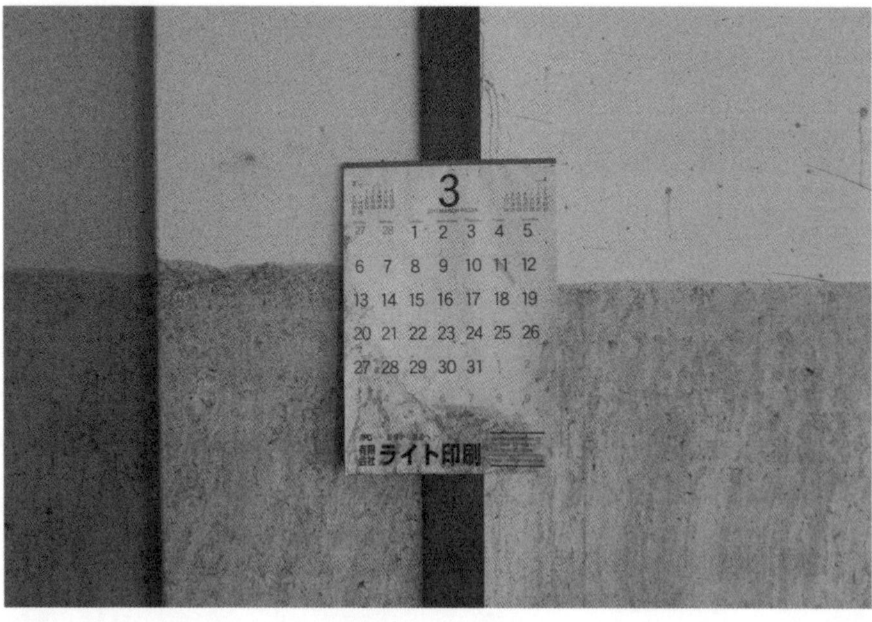

Chihiro Minato, *Untitled*, 2012,
photographs, courtesy the artist.

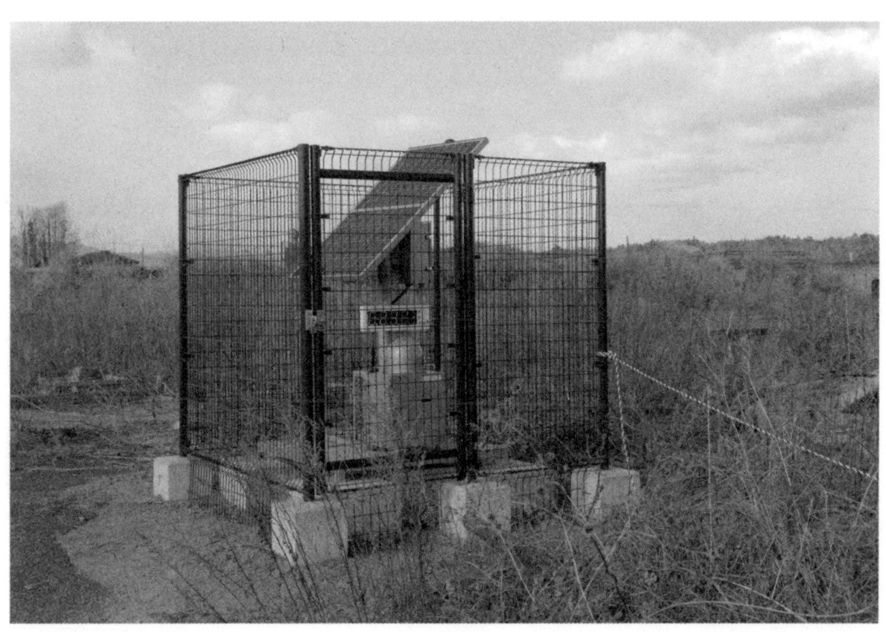

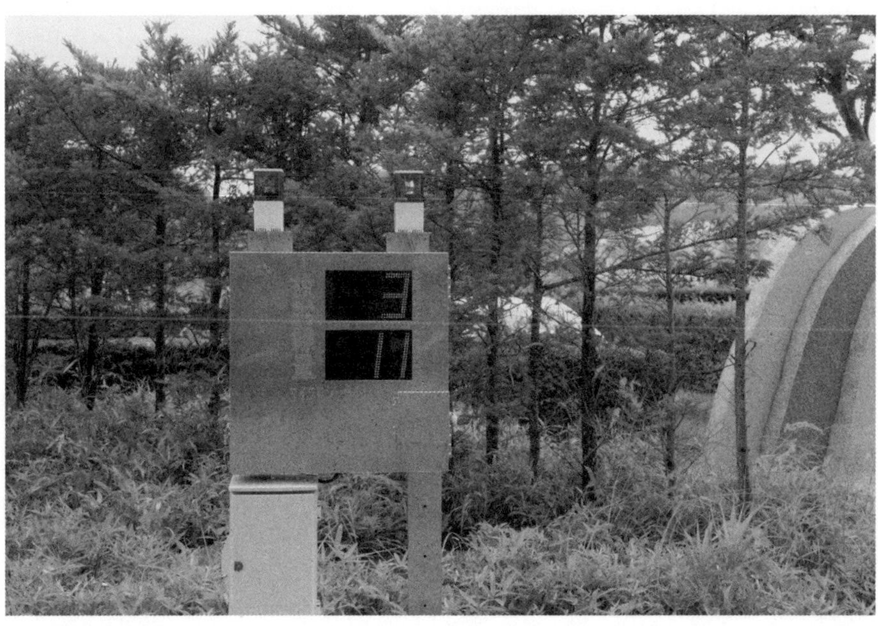

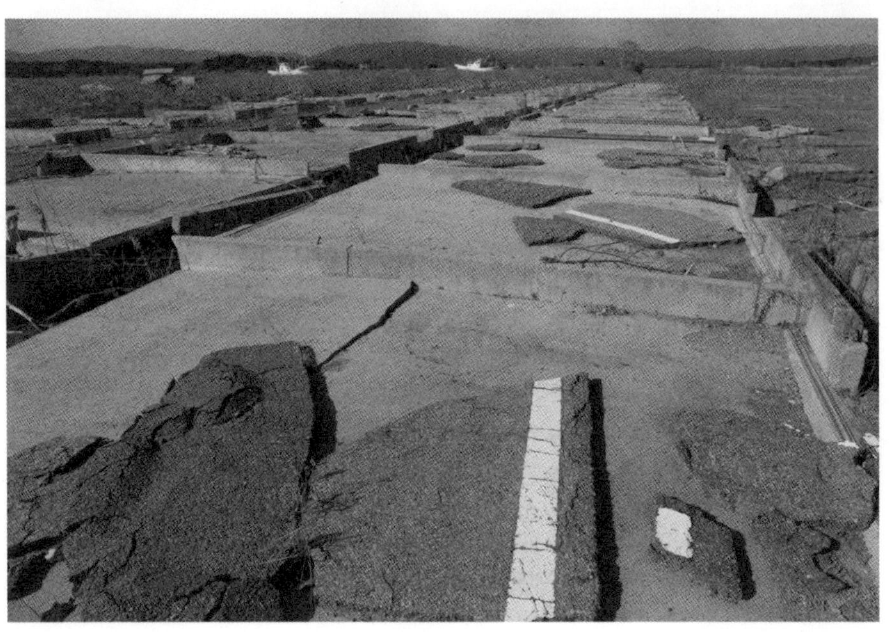

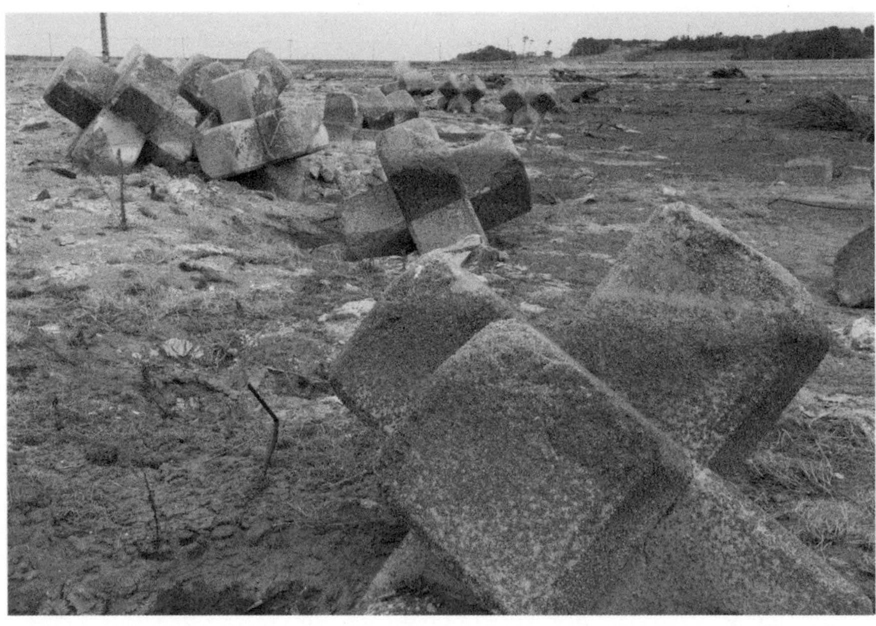

Chihiro Minato, *Untitled*, 2012,
photographs, courtesy the artist.

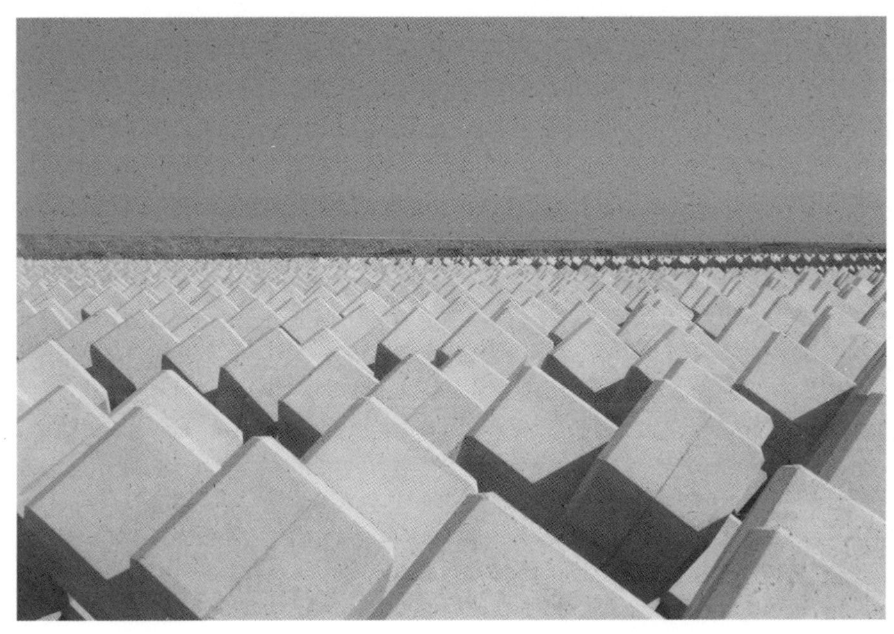

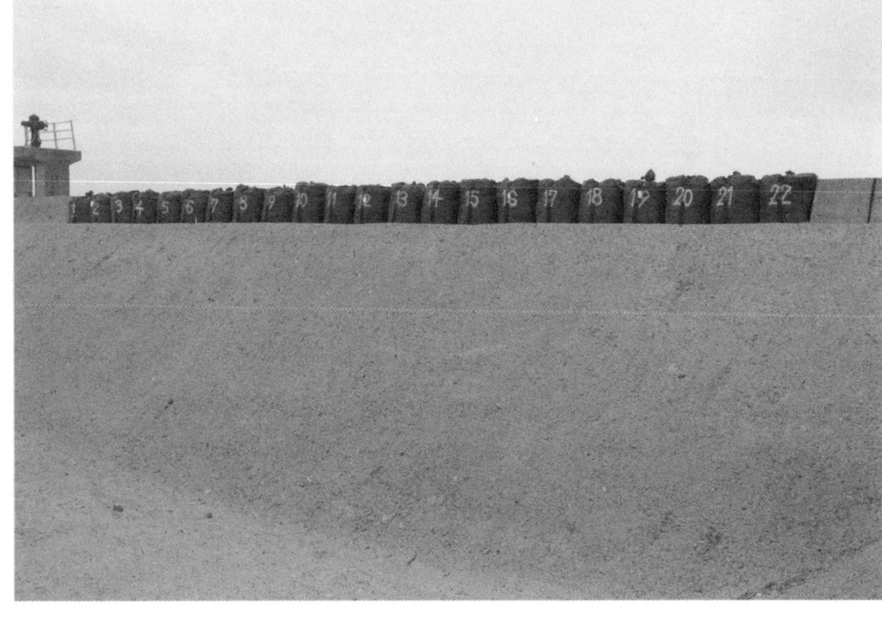

SOPHIE HOUDART
WHAT IS IN THE AIR? OR HOW WE GET TO KNOW WHAT WE KNOW ABOUT INVISIBLE THINGS

The Tōhoku earthquake and the subsequent nuclear explosion that happened on 11 March 2011, constituted a disruptive experience for many people in Japan and elsewhere. Since the Tōhoku disaster, a lot of questions have been raised in writing and thought, attempting to grasp what happened that day and what the event's social, environmental and political implications might be. There have been dozens of symposiums, regularly held seminars, many books published and movies made, all attempting to make sense of and deal with the natural disaster and/or the nuclear accident. These varied responses and mediums address the human consequences or political inconsequence at hand, and often the intertwining of the two. Four years after the disaster, however, it is clear that what happened was not a single disruption that left behind traces, but is rather a continuous disruptive experience that is saturated with measurements and experiments of diverse kinds of effects, and has resulted, as we shall see, in a form of "calibrated sensitivity" (Dettelbach 1999: 503): a sense of feeling and knowing strongly connected to the peculiarities of radionuclides (those entities that one can't see or touch or hear) as well as to the peculiarities of the land, time and place where radionuclides express themselves.

Being an anthropologist of science, I started a project on the measurement of air following the disaster, aimed at scrutinising how people learn about their new environmental situation as a consequence of what happened when the earthquake, the tsunami, and then the nuclear explosion occurred. To discuss this particular aspect, I met with groups of governmental experts, citizen association members as well as farmers who have been working on producing reliable numbers – and beyond, reliable knowledge – on the basis of where to undertake actions in their lives.

Because the event and its impact is still happening, and continuously since March 2011, people in the Fukushima area have had to learn *to live with* a new state of their surroundings.

In order to comprehend what happened, I felt the need to move myself away from what was addressed in the most direct manner by the disaster. Contrary to a feeling of urgency and irrevocability that often goes with analysing disasters, I decided instead to follow the invitation of the philosophers Philippe Pignarre and Isabelle Stengers or the sociologist Bruno Latour and to *slow down* the speed of thought: "This is precisely because it is urgent – or critical or dramatic – that we should take our time and think slowly." In what follows, I will therefore try *to think with* (instead of thinking *about*) what happened, through analysing the measurements occurring in the Tōhoku environment as well as various historical moments when the measurements of air acquired significant and explicit political dimensions.

Life with Measures

What environment have people lived *in* since March 2011? At first glance, it is obvious that life after the Tōhoku disaster is overwhelmed with measurements and numbers of all sorts: reports and balance, graduations, mapping, monitoring… These are all very diverse kinds of measuring and numbering operations that fix thresholds, establish scales and standards in order to evaluate the danger of a given situation (Houdart et al. 2015). Each of them comes with its own genealogy, its own history, in which ways to act or react are inscribed. Right after the disaster, maps produced by governmental offices organised a set of perimeters around the Fukushima Daiichi nuclear power plant consisting of round circles of twenty kilometres (a "No-go Zone", a "Difficult Return Zone", a "Preparation for Return Zone"…) that was based on maps designed after the Second World War bombing of Hiroshima and Nagasaki. Only days later, new maps that showed the dissemination of radionuclides as leopard skin motifs were published. Evacuations went on, one village but not the neighbouring one, or just one part of a village and not the other, according to the amount of contamination. Strict distance from the nuclear plant ceased to be relevant.

Minami-sôma, Ôdaka district, less than two kilometres from the forbidden zone, and in the so-called "Preparation for Return Zone": here people are allowed to come for the day to take care of their belongings (their house, their garden, their fields, their animals) but can not stay at night. The zoning therefore designates what mathematicians would call a *discrete* life, organised along discontinuous states, which are not connected with each other. From the point of view of any observer, this form of only day-time visitation or residence doesn't really populate the environment anymore. The village looks like a ghost town: shops closed, roads deserted. Most of the fields and rice paddies are not cultivated anymore. Mister Nemoto, a farmer, and his wife, come almost every day from faraway temporary accommodations to look after their fields and their belongings. But their presence is not enough to get a sense of how life before was, despite all their efforts; the house without heating system is cold, humid, and use is now restricted to the main room.

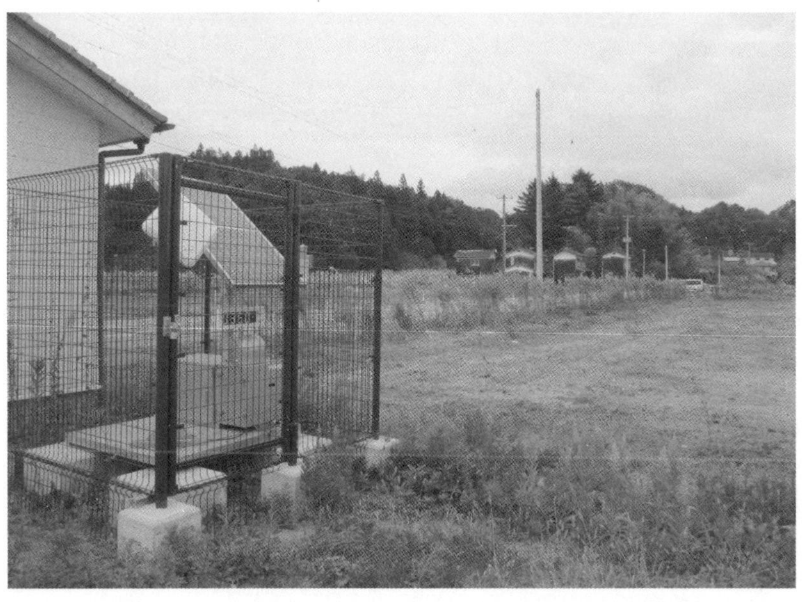

Minami-sôma, Ôdaka district (photograph by the author, Autumn 2012)

Here and there, at street corners, the government has installed measurement devices that ostensibly show the amount of radioactivity in the air. The obvious bulkiness and stationary nature of the device contrasts with the lightness and portable nature of the measuring device used by most of the inhabitants of the Fukushima area, a simple pocket Geiger counter:

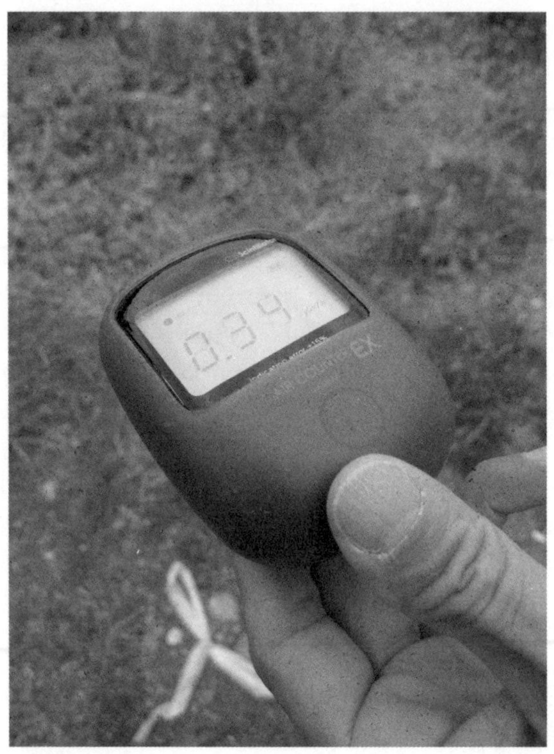

Minami-sôma, Ôdaka district (photograph by the author, Autumn 2012)

Fundamental discrepancies exist within an operation that basically consists of *knowing by measuring*, as exemplified by the two devices mentioned. As in other pollution cases, these discrepancies can be summarised in two general models. The first model, related to the first picture, gives priority to few but reliable devices. This is the basic position of the expert. It can be formulated this way:

Low Frequency / High Fidelity => the Expert

On the contrary, the second model gives priority to more devices – the most that people acting as a collective can get – even though these devices are said to be less reliable. The formula would then be:

High Frequency / Low Fidelity => Citizens

In the first model, the expert speaks with the authority inherent in his/her position, and this authority is reinforced by the *device of precision* (Wise 1994), which he/she can afford and is the only one to know how it works. As Isabelle Stengers abundantly argues, according to the model of the expert, measurement is faithful to reality, it sticks to reality, it *is* the reality itself. It enacts a truth about reality. As such, it is supposed to be disengaged from politics. Pinpointing the *measure for all things* every day, as published in local newspaper, for instance, serves to attest to a specific state of reality: that day, measures obtained through long-term studies of food products by the Prefectural Agricultural Center of Fukushima give the amount of cesium 134 and cesium 137 for fish; the day after, for vegetables or for meats or wild plants. Moreover, a long list of places and their related amount of radioactivity allow everyone to appreciate the specific *texture* of the day.

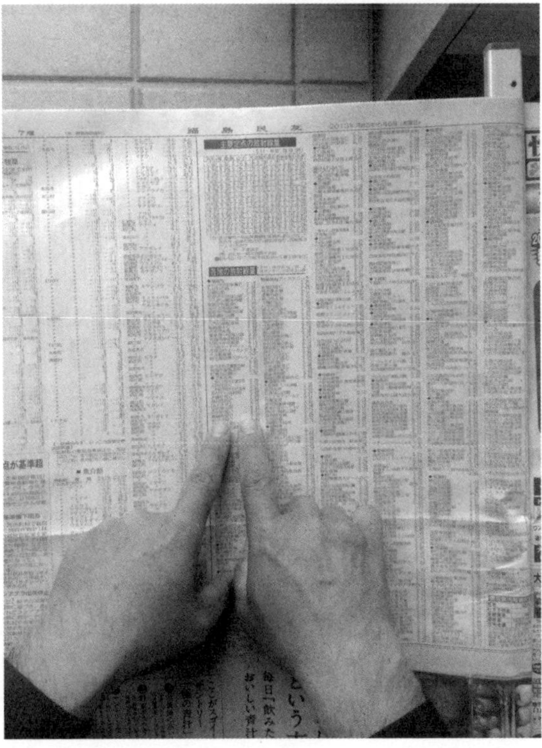

The measure of all things as a daily routine (photograph by the author, Spring 2013)

In the second model, citizens are constructed with – emerge from – the very act of nurturing a collective review of reality (Morita & Co. 2013). In the model enacted by citizens, there is no such thing as one reality: reality is as diverse as localities, and diverse over time. It requires volunteers to go into the field as often as they can to organise monitoring of water in rivers, of trees in forests, of wild plants, of airs, in order to circumscribe the movement or settling of radionuclides.

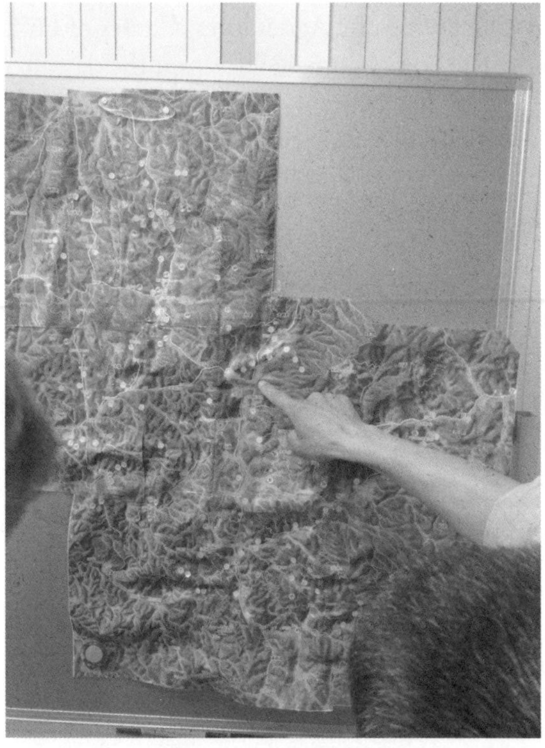

Realities along points of measure (photograph by the author, Spring 2013)

Within the schematic distinction between the experts' model and the citizens' one, which are accompanied by differences in the measuring processes, the people I met have to find their way around the sea of numbers. When I met representatives from the Citizens' Radioactivity Measuring Station (CRMS) at Fukushima City, a year after the disaster, they explain that the first months were devoted to producing alternative numbers with the explicit aim of convincing local people to move away from their homes.

It was not long before they realised, however, that the final decision could only be their own, that numbers have no coercive force and are closely intertwined with ways of life, visions of the world, and political positions. In this configuration, measurement therefore involved a political position: it is a question of *information* ("we have the right to know by ourselves as a collective force and to produce alternative numbers"), and it is a question of *choice* ("we give ourselves numbers, then each of us can *decide* for him/herself what to do").

One of the most striking features of all these operations, however, is the difficulty of obtaining knowledge – a sort of stable knowledge – through them. It is as if no knowledge about what was really going on could ever be stabilised: as if, due to this most dramatic state, there was a resistance or *recalcitrance* of numbers to give an unequivocal statement about the situation. This is especially true when considering measurements of the radioactivity, which easily contradict each other, are versatile, fluctuate, and change over time along significant scales. The simple experience that consists of walking with a Geiger counter, looking at numbers going up and down at almost every move becomes a real challenge for logic and understanding. If measurements are meant to help us objectify the reality outside, they seem inadequate to fully grasp such a sentient entity as radioactivity. And while every number is given as obvious and evident, they are basically critical and intimate numbers, intrinsically tied to the people, time and space, but also to the institutions that organise their collection. Perhaps in this field more than any other, numbers and measurements barely speak for and by themselves – they need spokespersons, translators, and morality or trustfulness of those who soon appear to be decisive (Gooday 2004). They request each person to delineate for her/himself the position she/he needs to adopt. The *values* of numbers, here, take on a specific meaning as they relate to the various ways people *charge* measurements with personal histories, political beliefs, and representations of reality and of the world.

Let us, however, briefly move away from what is at stake in the disaster and take measurements differently by looking at the tools designed throughout history to grasp something that is *in the air*, to grasp something ungraspable. What is in the air? This history shows that knowledge goes from the sky as populated by objects (such as clouds) to the sky as something that gradually takes on the properties of a flux rather than an object.

Back to the 18th Century

How did people measure the sky? The air? How did they comprehend what surrounded them, the atmosphere they were living in? And is this history of some help in understanding the situation that arose after the Tōhoku disaster?

Derived from the British experimental philosophy that developed starting in the mid-17th century and especially the work of Robert Boyle and his air pump, devices aimed at remedying the "infirmities" of the human senses with instruments and at seeing things that were previously invisible – such as air, sky, atmospheric phenomena – flourished here and there around the mid-18th century. As science historian Simon Schaffer explains: "Resources drawn from the early work included [...] a faith in the accumulation of *quantitative* meteorological data; and a strict attention to what seemed to be obviously mephitic sites, such as marshes, sewers and graveyards" (Schaffer 1990: 293). Until the 1770s, air purity was tested by means of the barometer, by measuring the survival time of animals enclosed in glass vessels. In 1772, the English theologian and natural philosopher, Joseph Priestley designed a test called the "nitrous air test", which could be used to measure the "goodness" and "respirability" of a sample of ordinary air. Later on, the test was transformed by Marsilio Landriani into an instrument named the eudiometer (after *Eudios*, a Greek word meaning "goodness of the air").

The purpose of the instrument was to stabilise a technology for measuring the *virtue of air*, to thus provide a quantitative basis for the management of the medical environment. According to physicists as well as social reformers of all kinds, pneumatic chemistry was able to provide "a new practice of policy recommendations for the better management of the social economy and the human body" (ibid.: 283). As Priestley puts it in the language of his time: "If it be of importance and of use to us to know the principles of the element we breathe, surely it's not of much less importance nor of much less use to comprehend the principles, and endeavour at the improvement of those laws, by which alone we breathe it in security." By means of instruments that could quantify and qualify the air people breathed, the idea naturally emerged that, "there must be processes which *restored* vitiated air and rendered it virtuous and respirable" (ibid.: 288). The best example of such a concept of air as a social controller is the well-known Panopticon, first promoted in the 1780s by the jurist Jeremy Bentham as an architectural model to administrate prisons, but also schools, factories or hospitals.

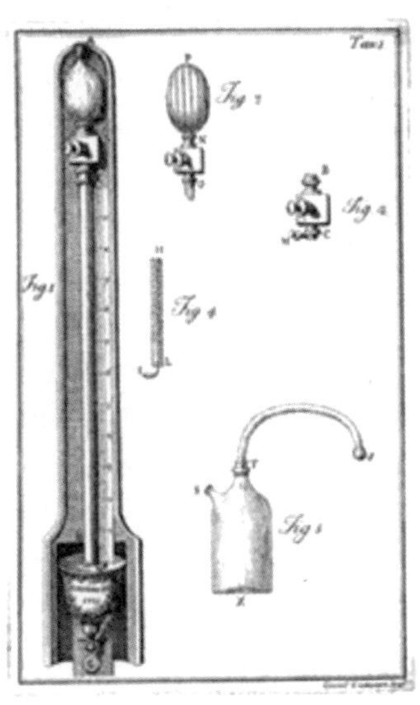

Marsilio Landriani's eudiometer
(©Museo Galileo – Institute and Museum of
the History of Science)

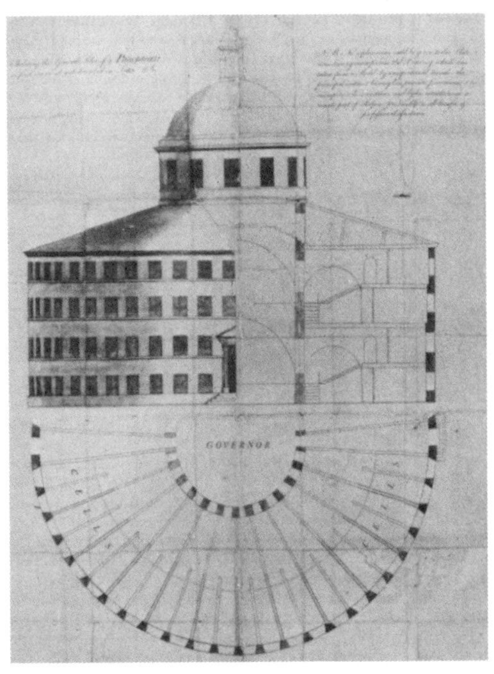

Jeremy Bentham's Panopticon

As one of the first attempts to *condition* air, the Panopticon was based on the idea that the air one breathes very much influenced the way one acts and that manipulating the first could benefit the second. Knowledge about air then organised itself along a line that linked air with management, management with security, security with social development, and eventually social development with civilisation.

A few years later, Alexander von Humboldt gave a tremendous extension to the programme set up by Priestley and Landriani, which consisted of mapping and collecting airs. In 1799, Humboldt left for South America for five years, bringing with him a whole set of precise instruments, among them the eudiometer. His aim was to review, through measurements, all that could exist on earth, from botany to geology, from zoology to meteorology: his volume, *Cosmos* (first published in 1845) was conceived as the sum of all that could be knowable – that is, measurable – on the planet. Not limiting himself to prisons and local places, he aimed at establishing and coordinating the monitoring of the variations of the atmosphere all around the globe – a "global atmospheric chemistry" (Dettelbach 1999: 480).

Although this kind of monitoring occupied much of the extant diaries with which Humboldt came back from America, it was silently removed from the public expedition results. The main reason for this withdrawal of what he observed on site with the eudiometer was that the instrument required reliable conditions – conditions that look like laboratory ones – and failed to provide the expected precision he was looking for in the density of the Amazonian jungle. "Producing a large quantity of reliable numbers over vast territories" (ibid.) would have required transforming the jungle into a lab (Latour 1995), but Humboldt had to *do with* the jungle – its peculiarities, its own atmosphere, from which he couldn't detach his own body, his own relationship to the field: he got sick, was attacked by mosquitoes, suffered from humidity and heat, which also affected his instruments. The sensitivity of the instruments and the sensitivity of the philosopher, of the observer, were both linked to the environment.

Radioactive Beings

During the course of 2011, the Fukushima Departmental Golf Clubs associated with the Sunfield Nihonmatsu Golf Club initiated a legal case against TEPCO, the operator of the nuclear plants. They asked for the decontamination of a field located forty-five kilometres from the nuclear plant and tried to get compensation for the stoppage of their activities. TEPCO's answer specified in return that, "radioactive substances dispersed by Fukushima Daiichi don't belong to TEPCO but to private owners". In this case, radioactive substances are regarded as mere objects that can subsequently be owned by people: whatever its nature, what was deposited on the surface of their field is now considered their property. Beyond the obvious limit of such an argument, it is true that private owners as well as farmers in the Fukushima area have to consider radionuclides as a certain kind of presence they have to learn to deal with. To talk about radionuclides as presence – at least *things* – rather than as objects: we get closer to the actual configuration. One would suppose that objects can be removed at will; but one has to cohabitate with a presence, to find for it a place, to learn about its behaviour, the ways it moves, and the ways it remains still. It is about considering radionuclides as "vibrant matter", animated by a "thing-power" of their own; it is about "encountering" radionuclides as complex entities rather than as conglomerates or homogeneous objects that could be numbered (Bennett 2010).

Beyond measuring the amount of radioactivity in the air here and there, several experimental approaches have been set up over time by farmers in collaboration with agronomists, which aim at understanding how radioactivity *behaves*, how it expresses itself ("detekuru" in Japanese) – always in relationship with a specific environment. In these experiments, rice paddies, fields, forests are transformed into observing platforms from which to capture *fluxes,* but also *frictions,* and to reveal the always specific, always complex relationships between small beings such as radioactive particles and an environment.

One of these experiments consists of putting a camera into rice paddies, protected by a box: measuring *while* standing in an environment, the device makes it possible to follow not only the flow of the water coming in and coming out of the rice paddy, but also the flow of radionuclides.

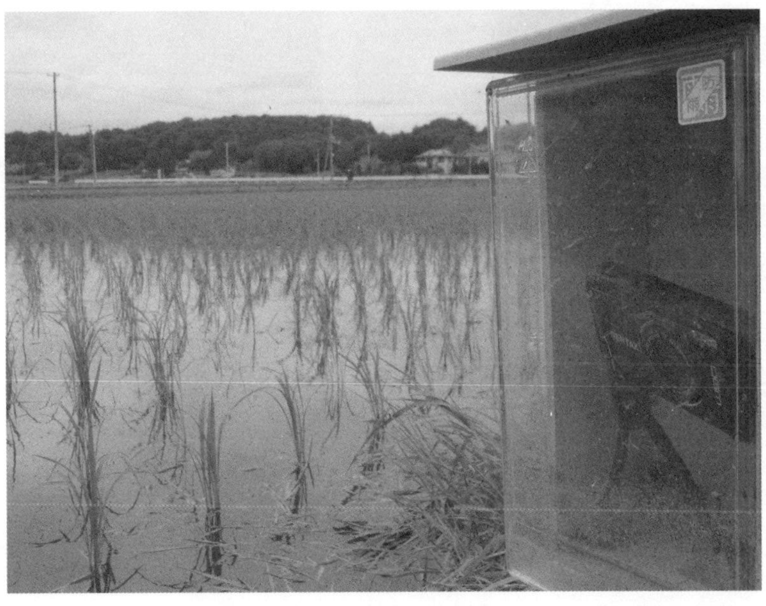

Capturing fluxes of water (photograph by the author, Spring 2013)

At the same time, these data on fluxes wouldn't mean much, from the point of view of the farmers, if they weren't connected with the kind of "calibrated sensitivity" previously mentioned (Dettelbach 1999: 503), the "appropriate sensibility" in confronting radionuclides, acquired on the spot, after years and years of commitment to the natural surroundings.

Transforming a rice paddy into a rational surface – a grid – capturing images of the movement (of water), measuring radioactivity at the borders of the rice paddy using Geiger counters: all of these operations become significant as long as farmers can mobilise their knowledge of the paddies, fields or forests surrounding their own piece of land; and also mobilise their knowledge of seasonal cycles or of the specific texture of rains in the area.

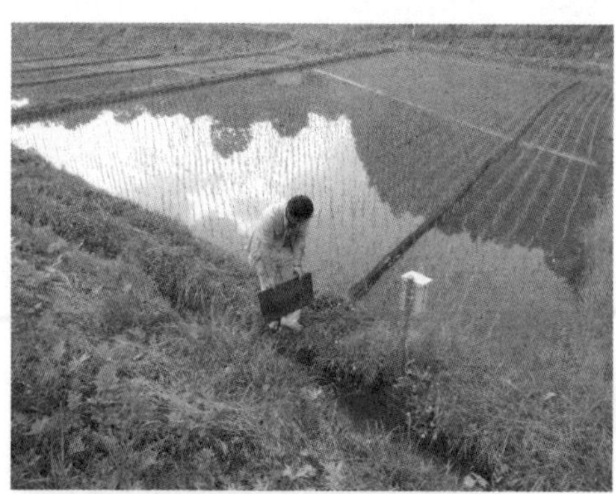

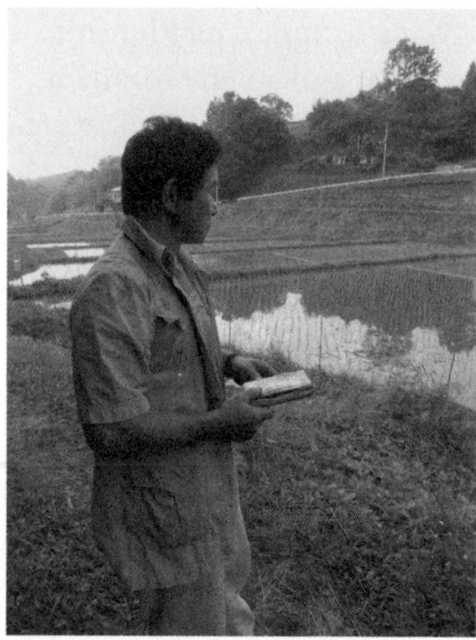

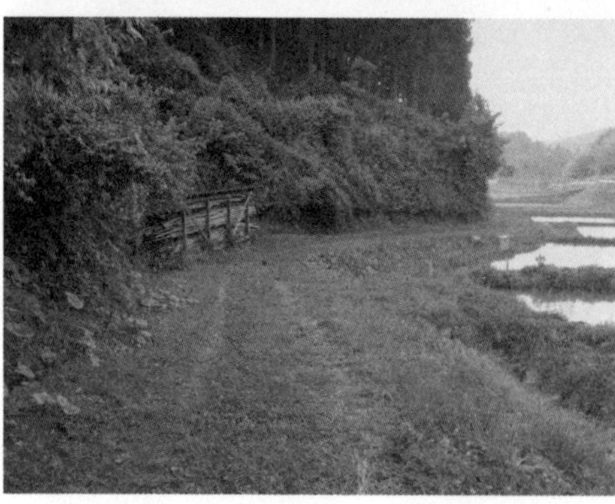

Radioactivity, the farmer, his rice paddies and the environment (photograph by the author, Spring 2013)

Far from an object, radioactivity, in such constellations, is considered within a set of relations – the relation between humans and their land being one of them.

Concluding Remarks

It is significant that relationships to measurements change over time. In 2014, three years after the disaster, people I used to see walking around with Geiger counters have put them aside in the glove box of their car, and pass by the monitoring stations without a glance. Something that has more to do with understanding the mysterious and unstable entities with which people have to share their land and their daily life is going on. To borrow Jane Bennett's expression, they could have said: "If we think we already know what is out there, we will almost surely miss much of it" (Bennett 2010: xv).

This last decade, in the same vein as Bennett, several authors have come to argue for an ecological approach that would take into account non-humans and their agencies as much as human ones. The *de-objectification* of the world shouldn't be regarded merely as a philosophical gesture aimed at expanding our scope and our imagination or at saving the world from slow but pervasive destruction: although not contradictory with such aims, such an approach instead concerns changes in the world itself that somehow remind us of its existence (Hache 2014). Tim Ingold's theory of *dwelling*, for instance, provides clues for comprehending what one calls the environment as an intertwining space filled with non-human as well as human entities that are mutually permeable and intrinsically bound: "It is not through being furnished with objects that the open sphere of sky and earth is turned into a habitable environment. [...] To understand how people can inhabit this world means attending to the dynamic processes of world-formation in which both perceivers and the phenomena they perceive are necessarily immersed" (Ingold 2007: 28). Confronted with what has happened since March 2011, people inhabiting the Fukushima area are experiencing the long-lasting intimacy of their lives with radionuclides. In the words of Timothy Morton, they are "glued to [their] phenomenological situation" (Morton 2013: 36), it becomes "ambient" (op.cit.: 30). When one extends the frame of such an analysis, an irreducible relationship to a familiar landscape (in other words, an *intimacy*) that complicates the work of measurement and makes it denser suddenly appears in the network of measurements. This intimacy is worth taking into account as it makes it possible to revisit what it means to measure as well as what it means to do politics.

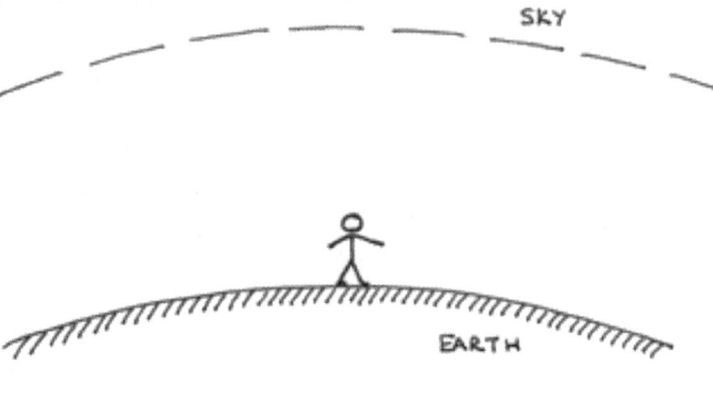

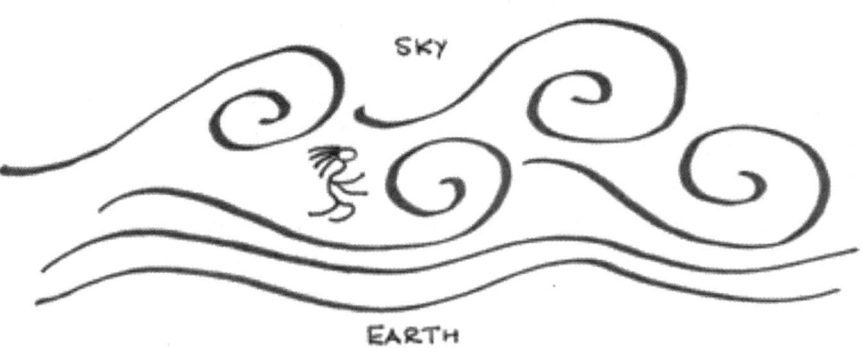

A: The exhabitant of the earth.
B: The inhabitant of the weather-world
(in Ingold 2007).

Bibliography:

Bennett, J. (2010). *Vibrant Matter. A political ecology of things*. Durham: Duke University Press.

Dettelbach, M. (1999). The Face of Nature: Precise Measurement, Mapping, and Sensibility in the Work of Alexander von Humboldt. *Studies in History and Philosophy of Biological and Biomedical Sciences* 30(4), 473–504.

Gibson, J. J. (1979). *The ecological approach to visual perception*. Hillsdale: Lawrence Erlbaum Associates.

Hache, Emile (ed.) (2014). *De l'univers clos au monde infini*. Bellevaux: Editions Dehors.

Houdart, S., Manceron, V. & Revet, S. (2015). La mesure du danger. *Ethnologie Française* 1. Janvier (1).

Ingold, T. (2007). Earth, Sky, Wind and Weather. *Journal of the Royal Anthropological Institute* 13(1), 19–38.

Latour, B. (1995). The 'Topofil' of Boa Vista-A Photo-Philosophical Montage. *Common Knowledge* 4(1), 144–87.

Latour, B. (2012). *Enquête sur les modes d'existence. Une anthropologie des Modernes*. Paris: La Découverte.

Morita, A., Blok, A. and Kimura, S. (2013). Environmental Infrastructures of Emergency: The Formation of a Civic Radiation Monitoring Map during the Fukushima Disaster. In Hindmarsh, R. (ed.), *Nuclear Disaster at Fukushima Daiichi. Social, Political and Environmental Issues*. New York: Routledge. 78–96.

Timothy, M. (2013). *Hyperobjects. Philosophy and Ecology after the End of the World*. Minneapolis and London: University of Minnesota Press.

Pignarre, P. and Stengers, I. (2005). *La sorcellerie capitaliste. Pratiques de désenvoûtement*. Paris: La Découverte.

Schaffer, S. (1990). Measuring Virtue: Eudiometry, Enlightenment, and Pneumatic Medicine. In Cunningham, A. and French, R. (eds.), *The Medical Enlightenment of the Eighteenth Century*. 281–318. Cambridge and New York: Cambridge University Press.

Stengers, I. (2009). *Au temps des catastrophes. Résister à la barbarie qui vient*. Paris: Les Empêcheurs de Penser en Rond. Paris: La Découverte.

Stengers, I. (2014). Penser à partir du ravage écologique. In Hache, E.(ed.), *De l'univers clos au monde infini*. Paris: Editions Dehors.

Wise, M. N. (1995). *The Values of Precision*. Princeton: Princeton University Press.

POLITICS OF MEASUREMENT

Dialogue between Chihiro Minato and Sophie Houdart
11 December 2013, Kunstraum, Leuphana University, Lüneburg

1. From Houdart to Minato

SOPHIE HOUDART: I have a few comments and questions. One of the maps depicting the danger of radioactivity, which illustrates how Chernobyl is now a standard of measurement, was interesting: One disaster becomes a normative entry-point for measuring another. There are a lot of links between Chernobyl and Fukushima, and some of the measurement tools used at Fukushima actually originated at Chernobyl, which is also linked to Hiroshima regarding the radioactivity. It is important to understand how these maps are made, not only from data in Japan but everywhere. My presentation goes back in the history of science and representation in order to grasp what hides in these schematic lines of drawings. Although this series of lines looks very informational, one should ask the questions: How can a line become a container? Is there any idea of a frontier in these maps, in the drawings you showed? There is the map, and then you talked about the blocks, the concrete wave breakers. Before the beginning of the workshop, you told me that in some parts of Japan people are about to get their view of the landscape blocked. They won't be able to see or hear the sea anymore. It's a frontier, and Japan is then no longer an island open to the sea. The country will be like an enclosed room. What will it look like?

CHIHIRO MINATO: The most spectacular news is that a big earthquake will hit the Tokyo Metropolitan Area directly in four years, with a probability between 40 and 70%. This means you should not buy any real estate the next four years. This is the kind of news you find both in electronic mass media and in the newspapers, and this ultimately supports construction of the massive concrete blocks. The danger of an imminent earthquake does not only cover the east coast of Tokyo, but all the southwest of Japan. I went to the south of Kyoto, and what we found in the coast was something that the authorities make in small bays: the construction of a wall, 5.9 metres in height. It is the end of the perception there. You do not see, and you do not hear anymore. You even don't know if there is a sea behind the wall or not. In such an environment, how do you know where to go when a big wave comes? If this is the result of the classical perspective, a kind of mathematical rationalisation of space, it cuts a space into two worlds. One is the world calculated and schematised, the other is the world of your perception. It is hard to live in both worlds at the same time.

Responding to your second question, the line in the map is created through such a mathematical schema. What we do not know, and what we really want to know, is not how serious the accident is or the level of it. The only thing Hiroshima left us in that sense was data on low radiation. But what happened in Hiroshima? We still do not know. We cannot say whether the low level of radiation was harmful for the population or not. But nonetheless the population at the other side of the hill, outside the "dangerous" zone, is still suffering severely from post-radiation diseases. At Fukushima the same schematics of radiation were used. I propose paying attention to the model of entanglement by British archeologist Ian Hodder, together with the Duchamp line. In his book, *Entangled: An Archeology of the Relationship between Human and Things*, Hodder discusses the co-constitution of humans and things by exploring the notion of entanglement. He embraces its asymmetrical relationship, or what he calls "a darker side to the entanglements" of human existence between social life and material things, in order to add a perspective of particularity on existing thing theories (Hodder, 2012). For Duchamp one metre is not always the same length. Thus a metre could be understood as something like an entanglement. A measuring project aims at seeking a counter concept of measurement, in which entanglement could be an interesting subject.

SH: That's very interesting, because it is also related not only to aesthetic theories, but also to most physical theories, like the plural-universe or multi-universe theories. It reminds me of the Japanese novelist Haruki Murakami and his recent book, *1Q84*, where the two protagonists cross a line and enter another world – a world with two moons – parallel to this one. You cannot be in both worlds at the same time; either you see one moon or you see two moons. Your comment reminds me of this story. I have another question: You explained how farmers, for example sake producers, use perceptive tools to measure and to organise their world. I heard that right after a tsunami, if you want to have a solid prediction of an impending disaster, you should just follow the monks, because they have this sensibility to what vibrations are in the air and which are in the earth. Are these two anecdotes, in your view, linked to animism – the traditional religion in Japan? In animism you can attribute energies to objects such as trees or rocks, but also to phenomena, such as winds, air and so forth. Would it be related, or is this too culturalistic?

CM: We can brand this kind of belief and sensibility passed on through centuries as part of animism. The ancient poetry on the stone stairs was marking an event on site. Sometimes the words say: "Don't build any house on specific days." The village is very small, and there were no casualties during the last tsunami. But how was it before the writings, more than 3,000 years ago? This is too far back for any material to preserve the poetry; just the way of living and the way of believing remains. I was very excited to learn about the lacquer-coated thread from the archeologist. From ancient times, lacquer has been used for preservation. That is, they wanted to keep the thread for a long time, even protect it from water. Why? Presumably, this thread is more than just a thread. Today we only have the term animism for this kind of long-term memory or sensitivity.

A1: I am interested in this archaeology. Does this mean the ancient Japanese in the Jomon era knew where to escape to?

CM: Obviously, we can only base our assessment on what is left today, as earthquakes or tsunamis have shifted and washed much away over thousands of years. One thing is clear and proven: the Shinto shrines dating after the 15th/16th century were constructed on top of the Jomon archaeological site.

The architects of the shrines built according to the outline of the archaeological site we see today. When we trace the shrines and the Jomon site in Fukushima, we find the original coastline before the 19th century, where so many boats were found after March 11, 2011. This indicates that the land was not land before the 19th century. In animistic thinking, you could say, that the boats carry on the memory of the seascape and the exact coastline of the past. Sometimes the original coast is ten kilometres inland, and close to this old coastline one or two shrines are always to be found.

MY: It's quite interesting to interpret the disaster through the eyes of archaeology. It makes the invisible visible and opens up alternative views on what we see in the contemporary landscape. A stunning part of the current scenery is that everybody carries a Geiger counter to constantly measure. Such emotional scenes present the helpless conditions of dysfunctional measurement. At one level, the act of measuring transforms itself into an act of mediation, like repeating a mantra, just to follow the rule and the habitual. At another level, this represents an extension of bureaucracy – a further intrusion into everyday life. Therefore, the hype of measuring produces complicated bio-politics. Under such complicated circumstances, how do you see the role of images? Many photos and videos were produced, but two critical issues have been raised – the impossibility of representation and the consumption of the images. It has been claimed that they cannot represent any of the situations fully and even lack the power to spark our imagination.

CM: Radioactivity is clearly invisible. That's why it is important to take photos on site, with the Geiger counter in them. For at least six months it was like a daily ritual. When we met friends in Fukushima, we asked, "have you measured?" instead of, "how are you?" The art of photography changed a lot after March 11th in the Fukushima region. Many of the images that I have presented are landscapes which you cannot visit anymore. This summer, the scenery inside the 10-km zone is turning especially beautiful, as no humans live there anymore. The humans returned the area to the original inhabitants, the animals – wild horses, monkeys and deer.

SH: Peter Galison, an American historian of science, is working on a project about dark tourism in wild nature – precisely in areas abandoned due to nuclear tests. People go and look for real nature in places where, basically, the air is really contaminated. It is a very strange modernist experience.

2. From Minato to Houdart

CM: You already published a book on the comportment of Japanese scientists in the laboratory studying fruit flies, and you recently studied lab research on the super collider of CERN (The European Organisation for Nuclear Research). Based on the comportment of the group of humans you have observed, how do they conceive or conceptualise nature through their activities? What kind of special knowledge have the farmers working their rice fields produced since 11 March?

SH: In order to answer your questions, I need to explain my previous research and contextualise it first. I did extensive fieldwork during my PhD in a Japanese laboratory of genetics. Scientists were working on the *Drosophila*, small fruit flies traditionally used in genetics. This project was about how people do science in Japan, where the conception of nature is traditionally different from the one in Europe. This is not the same story that I presented today. Actually one big missing part of the story is about air, atmosphere, and wind instruments in Japan. My doctoral research was really focused on how they produce knowledge in Japan and then present it in an international context. The other project is more recent fieldwork at the Large Hadron Collider (LHC) in Switzerland, which is the biggest experimental device used in particle physics, to learn more about the cosmos and the Big Bang. My aim in this fieldwork is not to follow physicists and their theory of particles, but to observe the daily work of the hundreds of people who take care of this huge machine, most significantly the link between the machine and the ground. I followed the process of recording all the slight movements of the machine in order to observe a physical signal. At one point, I also began following people working at the environment department for CERN. And this is where I was when the Fukushima disaster happened. As that kind of particle-physics device can produce radioactivity, it is monitored. As we walked from one monitoring station to another, the technician on duty told me that we were able to observe the radiation from Fukushima from there. This gives us an understanding of the disaster. It doesn't concern only Japan, but in Geneva, all the recording and monitoring machines used actually recorded the heightened radioactivity in the air. The technician quoted Antoine Lavoisier, the 18th century chemist, and kept telling me, "Nothing gets lost in the air, everything transforms itself."

In these two projects, my work was to understand how people get to know about things and how people attain knowledge about very small, invisible components.

One of the main differences between the scientists and the organic farmers is that the farmers don't possess abstract knowledge: They enter into radioactivity and all kinds of radioactive stuff very pragmatically. They have learned more and more about it, but have neither a scientific nor a engineering background. This gives them a kind of freedom to produce alternative knowledge about what radioactivity is. Furthermore, I'm very struck by the fact that they attain very subtle knowledge about what radioactivity is and how it behaves.

CM: Another question is about Alexander von Humboldt, a geographer and a great explorer of knowledge at the beginning of the 19th century. Humbolt and Amié Bonpland, a French botanist and his companion on the entire expedition, intensively travelled in South and Central America from 1799, and arrived in Ecuador in 1802. About twenty years ago, I did a project around the equator, where I visited one of the first antique seismometers, which is still in working condition at the Quito Astronomical Observatory in Ecuador. Humboldt was a scientist who believed in such scientific measurements and instruments, but, simultaneously, he was a good artist who fully used his perception during his long journey. Do you still find such a mix between artistic and scientific point of views in contemporary laboratory research?

SH: Yes, very much in seismology. Some seismologists employ the Aristotelian view of the world, in which the cosmos is something chaotic that resists numbers, predictions, et cetera. They portray themselves as having a really small existence compared to the scale of the universe, and they are very humbled by the knowledge they carry. They use their sensitivity to a great extent. The notion of the laboratory where scientists only work with numbers and rational methods immediately dissolves when you enter any laboratory. This is very different to the experts, who are the ones in charge of translating what happens in laboratories. In the lab, a lot of things happen, but the technicians might not understand them fully, like in the case of the particle-physics device. They watch the particles and say, "... they crashed", "we don't know", "maybe it's not a good day for the particles ..."

It doesn't sound like science to most of us. It's the experts who transform the observations into knowledge. This is very different, but I assume that, in every laboratory, this is what is fascinating about science in practice.

A1: Yes, I was very interested in the fact that there was a link between the eudiometer and Jeremy Bentham's panopticon. I understand it as: if you control the air, whether the air is clean enough or not, you can control the social mechanism of the inmates. How does the eudiometer work – is it mechanical?

SH: I don't know the exact workings of the eudiometer. It was used by Bentham, but I don't know to what extent the eudiometer was used in prisons. I think there were experiments at one point, where they organised collections of air and went to different spots – very natural and very critical ones like cemeteries, prisons and so forth. They tried to compare and purify the air. This was the basic philosophy of the device, even for Priestley. It's not the translation of Bentham, who used the device in his own way. His idea was that air has virtue and that by altering the air we can influence virtue.

As Humboldt went from site to site collecting air samples he realised that a single life wouldn't suffice to make all the recordings. He believed that citizens should be personally equipped to make their own recording of the places they go on a daily basis. And that's why in the 1770s you would find the eudiometer in regular shops in London and people were encouraged to use it, because they believed it worked. The eudiometer got a lot of public attention because of the extensive air pollution in the city. People were really eager to learn how to deal with their environment.

A2: Around 1850, the canalisation and the water closet, or flush toilet, were introduced throughout London. That removed the stench, but not cholera, which people originally thought was carried by air. Three decades later, Robert Koch discovered that it came from bacteria, which are also an invisible, but biological organism carried by water and food.

SH: The eudiometer had a very short life because the scientific argument behind it claimed the existence of a gas called phlogiston. Around the 1780s, it was shown that the phlogiston didn't exist and oxygen was discovered.

All the ideas had to be changed. Despite its short life, the history of recording air and the related devices continued into the beginning of the 19th century, and there are plenty of books concerning the polluted fog of London, though these books mostly deal with the devices and filters used on chimneys. It's about the air you breathe, hygiene and health, and not so much about virtue any more.

CM: The drawing by Tim Ingold might be a reference to the Chinese character for wind, and many different variations of this sign were used in ancient China. The idea is that something is partially in the air, and that the air contains virtue and you can have a dialogue with air. In Japan, this notion is understood as animism. Animism is not a belief in what we see, but the timeless knowledge of establishing a relationship between things and humans.

MY: Sophie's presentation pointed out the gap between the notion of what mechanical objectivity is and what precise accuracy and judgment is. In their book *Objectivity*, Daston, Lorraine, and Galison state that a process of constructing objectivity reflects a certain desirability and a distinct will of the subject/researcher, meaning that objectivity and subjectivity are mutually defined and shaped in tandem. I wonder if you find any differences in the role of scientific objectivity, especially when the scale of measurement is very tiny and invisible or, conversely, very big but still invisible. The second question is: Why are you interested in art in your research activities? What kind of accuracy can art provide in comparison with mechanical objectivity?

SH: I think that objectivity is challenged somehow when applied to objects or situations that one can't see, because one can't commensurate them with human scales, since they are either too small or too big. It is as if invisible objects, precisely because of this problem of scale, make room for, or even require imagination in order to be grasped. Therefore, my interest in art lies in its power of imagination.

MY: One could say that scientific objectivity coincides with subjectivity, and there are different understandings of accuracy and preciseness. The relationship between objectivity, accuracy and preciseness is not fixed, but negotiable. It therefore needs to be investigated in detail every time to rearticulate a space of imaginaries, since "nothing is lost and all is in the invisible".

Artist and
Author Biographies

Patricia T. Clough: Professor of Sociology and Women's Studies at the Graduate Center and Queens College of the City University of New York. Her publications include *Autoaffection: Unconscious Thought in the Age of Teletechnology* and, as editor, *The Affective Turn: Theorizing the Social,* and *Beyond Biopolitics.* Forthcoming is *The User Unconscious; Affect, Media and Measure* (University of Minnesota Press, forthcoming March 2018). Clough's work draws on theoretical traditions concerned with technology, affect, unconscious processes, political economy and experimental methods of research and presentation. She also is a practicing psychoanalyst in NYC.

Helmut Draxler: Art historian, cultural theorist, and curator. Based in Berlin, he currently holds a position as Professor for Art Theory at the University of Applied Arts in Vienna. He has published extensively on the theory and practice of contemporary art. From 1992 to 1995, he was Director of the Kunstverein in Munich. His recent research projects include a "Theory of Splitting" and a "Philosophy of Flemish Painting". His current publications are: *Abdrift des Wollens. Eine Theorie der Vermittlung,* Vienna (Turia + Kant) 2016, *Exhibition as Social Intervention. 'Culture in Action' 1993,* London (Afterall Books Exhibition Histories), 2014, (with Joshua Decter), *Theorien der Passivität,* Munich (Fink) 2013 (with Kathrin Busch), *Ein kritischer Modus? Die Form der Theorie und der Inhalt der Kunst,* Vienna (Schlebrügge) 2013 (with Tanja Widmann).

Sophie Houdart: Research Director at the French Center for Scientific Research (CNRS) and member of the Laboratory of Ethnology and Comparative Sociology. Trained in social anthropology, her focus is on various practices within the field of innovation studies, in the realm of science as well as art, especially in Japan.

She is the author of several books, including *Kuma Kengo. An Unconventional Monograph* (ed. Donner Lieu, 2009), dedicated to the studio practice of the famous Japanese architect; and *Humains, non humains. Comment repeupler les sciences sociales* (with O. Thiery, La Découverte, 2011) or *Les Incommensurables* (Zones Sensibles 2015), which portraits the Large Hadron Collider at CERN.

Chihiro Minato: Artist, writer, founding member of the Institute for Art Anthropology, currently head of the Information Design Department at Tama Art University. He was an artistic director for the Aichi Triennale 2016 and has curated various international exhibitions, including the Japanese Pavilion at the Venice Biennale 2007. His latest works since 2011 include *Distance/Continuity* (Nantes, France) *Gourd Museum* (12th Taipei Biennale) *Peace meets Art* (Hiroshima Prefectural Museum), *Shiori project* (Heidelberg), *Thinking Landscapes* (Ulaan Bator, Mongolia).

Matt Mullican: Artist and Professor of Visual Art, Art Academy Hamburg (HFBK). Mullican deals with questions of perception of reality, fiction and the imaginary, and the possibilities of its representation. Mullican's work has been widely exhibited both internationally and nationally since the early 1970s, at venues including Haus der Kunst, Munich, Stedelijk Museum Amsterdam, Museum of Contemporary Art, Los Angeles, Museum of Modern Art, New York, and many others.

Lucy Powell: Artist based in Berlin. Her interest lies in navigating the wonders and horrors of living through the Capitalocene and the Sixth Extinction, while the body of evidence of consciousness and intelligence in all life forms amasses. In 2011, she co-founded the Satellite Salon, a forum for facilitating art-science conversations and collaborations.

She studied Fine Art at Wimbledon School of Art and Liverpool John Moores University. Her recent exhibitions include: *On the Edge*, Tieranatomisches Museum, Berlin; *Screening Nature*, Whitechapel Gallery, London, *The Animal Gaze Returned,* SIA, Sheffield / John Cass Gallery, Metropolitan University, London; *The Worldly House*, Documenta 13, Kassel; *Shooting Nature*, Oberhausen Kurzfilmtage, and others.

Oxana Timofeeva: Senior lecturer on contemporary philosophy at the European University in St. Petersburg, a senior research fellow at the Institute of Philosophy at the Russian Academy of Science (Moscow), a member of the artistic collective Chto Delat? (What is to be done?), a deputy editor of the journal *Stasis*, and the author of the books *History of Animals: An Essay on Negativity, Immanence, and Freedom* (Maastricht, 2012), and *Introduction to the Erotic Philosophy of Georges Bataille* (in Russian, Moscow, 2009).

Miya Yoshida: Researcher and curator based in Berlin, who engages internationally with different forms of art projects based on her artistic research. She obtained her PhD from Malmö Art Academy, Lund University in 2007 and worked as a postdoctoral researcher at Leuphana University, Lüneburg (2012–14) Her recent curatorial projects are *World in Your Hand* (Kunsthaus Dresden, 2010), *Labour of Love, Revisited* (Arko Art Museum, Seoul, 2011), *Amateurism!* (Heidelberger Kunstverein, 2012), *Sharing as Caring* (Heidelberger Kunstverein, 2012–16, 2018–).

*Towards (Im)Measurability
of Art and Life*

Editor / Herausgeberin
Miya Yoshida

Design / Gestaltung
Chiara Figone

Translation of the introduction /
Übersetzung Vorwort
Clemens Krümmel

Copy Editing / Lektorat
Brigitte N. Grice, Amy J. Klement

Proofreading / Endkorrektur
Amy J. Klement

Printed at / Druckerei
Bianca & Volta, Milan

Published by / Verlag
Archive Books, Berlin
www.archivebooks.org

©2017
Archive Books, Miya Yoshida,
the artists and authors.

ISBN 978-3-943620-64-1

Thanks / Dank

Hikaru Funaki, Sion Production Ltd., Tokyo
Genevieve Fong, EAMES OFFICE, LLC, Los Angeles
Rashell George, John Baldessari Studio, Los Angeles
Stephan Hepworth, Reversible Destiny Foundation,
New York
Reiko Ishiguro, 21st Century Museum of
Contemporary Art, Kanazawa
Nadja Klier, Studio Karin Sander, Berlin
Lisa Kluckert, Naturkundemuseum Berlin
Katrin Mayer, Mai 36 Gallerie, Zurich
Manuel Miseur, Esther Schipper Galerie, Berlin
Johnen Galerie, Berlin
Albrecht Pischel, Studio of Matt Mullican, Berlin
Claudia Rümmele and Claudia Bergmann, Stiftung
Kunstfonds zur Förderung der zeitgenössischen
bildenden Kunst, Bonn
Takashi Suzuki, Yumiko Chiba Associates, Tokyo
Fosca Ugoletti, Biblioteca Collezione Maramotti,
Reggio Emilia

Towards (Im)Measurability of Art and Life
was supported by / wurde unterstützt von:
Stiftung Kunstfonds zur Förderung der
zeitgenössischen bildenden Kunst, Bonn, Germany
and / und Stephan Oehmen, Stiftung für moderne
und zeitgenössische Kunst, Hilden, Germany

STIFTUNGKUNSTFONDS